ORGANIZATIONAL LEARNING
IN THE GLOBAL CONTEXT

Organizational Learning in the Global Context

Edited by

M. LEANN BROWN
University of Florida, USA

MICHAEL KENNEY
Pennsylvania State University, Capital College, USA

MICHAEL ZARKIN
Westminster College, USA

Routledge
Taylor & Francis Group

LONDON AND NEW YORK

First published 2006 by Ashgate Publishing

2 Park Square, Milton Park, Abingdon, Oxon OX14 4RN
711 Third Avenue, New York, NY 10017, USA

First issued in paperback 2017

Routledge is an imprint of the Taylor & Francis Group, an informa business

British Library Cataloguing in Publication Data
Organizational learning in the global context
 1. Organizational learning 2. Organizational learning - Case
 studies
 I. Brown, M. Leann II. Kenney, Michael III. Zarkin, Michael J.
 658.4'03

Library of Congress Cataloging-in-Publication Data
Organizational learning in the global context / edited by M. Leann Brown, Michael Kenney, and Michael Zarkin.
      p. cm.
 Includes bibliographical references and index.
 ISBN 0-7546-4842-7
 1. Organizational learning. I. Brown, M. Leann. II. Kenney, Michael,
1967- III. Zarkin, Michael J.

 HD58.82.O7429 2006
 302.3'5--dc22

                                                          2006003154
ISBN 978-0-7546-4842-0 (hbk)
ISBN 978-1-138-26266-9 (pbk)

Contents

List of Figures

List of Tables

List of Contributors

M. Leann Brown is an Associate Professor of Political Science/International Political Economy at the University of Florida. Previously, she was a Fulbright European Union Research Fellow, and spent a semester in Brussels affiliated with the Environmental Committee of the European Parliament. She was also Program Coordinator for the International Studies Association. Her current research focuses on how scientific uncertainty and organizational learning affect environmental policymaking in the European Union.

William J. Campbell currently works for Heart of Florida United Way. He is a graduate of the International Development and Public Administration Program at the University of Florida, and was employed for some time in the Government Affairs division of a Washington, DC-based law firm. A lifelong Roman Catholic, he is interested in how dogma deters the Church's and other principle-driven organizations' ability to "learn" and address constituents' needs.

Lynn Eden is Associate Director for Research and Senior Research Scholar at Stanford University's Center for International Security and Cooperation. The Cold War and nuclear history, organizational approaches to security, the American state and security policy, and science and technology studies are among her primary research interests. Her most recent book, *Whole World on Fire*, received the American Sociology Association's 2004 Robert K. Merton Award for best book in science, knowledge and technology.

David C. Ellis is a Visiting Assistant Professor of International Relations at New College of Florida. He holds a master's degree in International Development Studies and International Marketing from The George Washington University, and a PhD from the University of Florida. He studied briefly in Canada, Costa Rica and Syria, and interned with UNICEF in the Dominican Republic. His research interests focus on the relationship between the corporate interests of the United Nations and the concept of the "international community," UN peacekeeping, international development, ethnic conflict, and organizational learning theory.

Karen Guttieri teaches in the National Security Affairs Department of the Naval Postgraduate School (Monterey, California). Previously, she taught at the University of British Columbia and Simon Fraser University. Her primary research focus is military operations in civilian environments, including the effectiveness of civil-military operations, military organizational learning from peace operations, and civil-military relations issues in peace implementation.

Goran Hyden is Distinguished Professor of Political Science at the University of Florida. He is the author of *Making Sense of Governance, Governance and Politics in Africa, No Shortcuts to Progress: African Development Management in Perspective,* and *Beyond Ujamaa in Tanzania: Underdevelopment and an Uncaptured Peasantry.* He is also past President of the African Studies Association.

Brian A. Jackson is an Associate Physical Scientist at RAND. Previously, he was a Policy Studies Fellow in the Center for International Science and Technology Policy in the George Washington University's Elliott School of International Affairs. His research interests include the technological aspects of national security and counter-terrorism, technology adoption by individuals and organizations, and national science and technology policy. He is the author of more than 20 technical and policy articles and reports in a range of areas, the most recent of which focus on the protective technology needs of emergency responders and the use of technology by law enforcement organizations.

Michael Kenney is Assistant Professor of Public Policy and Political Science in the School of Public Affairs at the Pennsylvania State University, Capital College. He has held research fellowships with the Center for International Security and Cooperation at Stanford University and the Center for International Studies at the University of Southern California, and is the author of *From Pablo to Osama: Trafficking and Terrorist Networks, Government Bureaucracies, and Competitive Adaptation* (forthcoming 2007).

Eric A. Morgan is Assistant Public Defender of the Eighteenth Judicial Circuit of Florida (Brevard and Seminole Counties). He served a full tour as a US Peace Corps volunteer in Uzbekistan, and is a graduate of the Florida International University Law School.

Michael J. Oliver is currently Professor of Economics at the *École Supérieure de Commerce de Rennes*, France and the University of Plymouth Colleges, Jersey in the Channel Isles. His research interests include monetary policy, policy learning and behavioral finance. He has written numerous articles and books on monetary economics and economic history. *The Liquidity Theory of Asset Prices*, his latest book with Gordon T. Pepper, was published by John Wiley in 2006.

Paolo Spadoni is a Visiting Assistant Professor in the Department of Political Science at Rollins College. He received his Master in Latin American Studies from the Center for Latin American Studies at the University of Florida in 2002, and his PhD in Political Science (International Relations) from the University of Florida in 2005. He is a frequent editorial contributor on US-Cuban relations to periodicals, including the *Christian Science Monitor*, the *Orlando Sentinel*, the *South Florida Sun-Sentinel*, and *The Washington Times*.

Michael J. Zarkin is Associate Professor of Political Science at Westminster College in Salt Lake City, UT. While currently focused on issues relating to U.S. telecommunications policy, Professor Zarkin's research interests more broadly include the role of political institutions and social learning in policy processes. He is the author of *Social Learning and the History of U.S. Telecommunications Policy, 1900-1996*, and coauthor of *The FCC: Frontline in the Culture and Regulations Wars* (with Kimberly A. Zarkin). Zarkin has also published articles in *Telecommunications Policy, Policy and Politics, Polity*, and other journals.

List of Abbreviations

AARs	after action reviews
ALF	Animal Liberation Front
AT & T	American Telephone and Telegraph Company
BSE	bovine spongiform encephalopathy
BST	bovine somatotropin
CA	Civil Affairs
CALL	Army Center for Lessons Learned
CELAM	*Consejo Episcopal Latinoamericano*
CENTCOM	Central Command
CJD	Creutzfeldt-Jakob Disease
CM	Council of Ministers
CMEA	Council for Mutual Economic Assistance
CMO	Civil Military Operations
DAC	Development Assistance Committee
DEA	Drug Enforcement Administration
DGVI	Directorate General for Agriculture
DGXI	Directorate General for the Environment
DGXXIV	Directorate General for Health and Consumer Protection
EDs	endocrine disruptors
EFSA	European Food Safety Agency
EP	European Parliament
ERM	Exchange Rate Mechanism
EU	European Union
FARC	Revolutionary Armed Forces of Colombia
FCC	Federal Communication Commission
GAO	General Accounting Office
GDP	Gross Domestic Product
GOELRO	State Plan for the Electrification of Russia
IEA	International Energy Agency
IMF	International Monetary Fund
JULLS	Joint Universal Lessons Learned System
MCI	Microwave Communications, Inc.
MIT	Massachusetts Institute of Technology
MOFERT	Chinese Ministry of Foreign Economic Relations and Trade
NATO	North Atlantic Treaty Organization
NSPD	National Security Presidential Directive
NTC	National Training Center
OECD	Organization for Economic Cooperation and Development

OIE	*Office International des Epizootes* [World Organization for Animal Health]
OJ	*Official Journal of the European Communities*
ORHA	Office of Reconstruction and Humanitarian Assistance
PhD	Doctor of Philosophy
PIRA	Provisional Irish Republican Army
rBST	recombinant bovine somatotropin
SCF	Scientific Committee for Food
SCVPH	Scientific Committee on Veterinary Measures relating to Public Health
SF	Special Forces
Sida	Swedish International Development Cooperation Agency
SOF	Special Operations Forces
StCF	Standing Committee for Foodstuffs
SVC	Scientific Veterinary Committee
UES	Unified Energy Systems
UK	United Kingdom
UNICEF	United Nations International Children's Emergency Fund
UNPROFOR	United Nations Protection Force
US	United States
USAID	United States Agency for International Development
USITC	United States International Trade Commission
USSR	Union of Soviet Socialist Republics
WHO	World Health Organization
WMD	weapons of mass destruction
WTO	World Trade Organization

Chapter 1

Organizational Learning: Theoretical and Methodological Considerations

M. Leann Brown and Michael Kenney

The social sciences assign fundamental importance to learning. For example, cognitive psychologists and educators investigate how human beings acquire, organize and store information, ideas and knowledge. Anthropologists and sociologists examine how cultural values, norms and group identities are transmitted across collectives and generations. And, economists and the business community study the development of new technologies and how firms survive and become more effective over time.[1]

No less than their cross-disciplinary kin, political scientists have exhibited considerable interest in learning. Dating back to Herbert Simon's seminal formulation in 1947,[2] a significant body of scholarship focusing on "organizational learning," "political learning," "government learning," "policy learning," and "social learning" has emerged. Taking theoretical cues particularly from psychology, organizational sociology and economics, scholars of public policy and administration, and international and comparative politics have sought to understand how individual decision-makers, government bureaucracies, states and societies draw upon experience, information and knowledge to change their understanding of the world, their policies and their behaviors.

In spite of the breadth of this work—or perhaps because of it—learning scholars employ divergent concepts, assumptions, units of analysis and methodologies, creating discourses that speak past rather than to each other. Among these islands of learning, consensus has yet to emerge around a number of basic questions, including: a) What are organizational and social learning? Is learning best understood as a process or an outcome? What are the most appropriate units of analysis, indicators

---

1   Dan Reiter, *Crucibles of Beliefs: Learning, Alliances, and World Wars* (Ithaca, NY: Cornell University Press, 1996). Mark Dodgson, "Organizational Learning: A Review of the Literatures," in *Organizational Studies* vol. 14 (1993), pp. 375-394. C. Lanier Benkard, "Learning and Forgetting: The Dynamics of Aircraft Production," *Research Paper No. 1560* (Stanford, CA: Graduate School of Business, Stanford University, 1999).

2   Herbert A. Simon, *Administrative Behavior: A Study of Decision-Making Processes in Administrative Organizations* (New York: Macmillan, 1947).

and measures of learning? b) Which internal and external factors tend to facilitate or deter organizational learning? What conditions are necessary and sufficient for learning to take place? c) How do politics and power affect learning? d) What are the implications for learning when those that learn are engaged in socially undesirable or illegal activities? These persisting theoretical uncertainties hamper empirical research in organizational and social learning, and this volume will address them within the context of several empirical studies.

Table 1.1 Summary of Case Studies

Chapter/ Contributor	Theoretical Contribution	Issue Area	Unit of Analysis
2 – Brown	orders of learning	food policy	European Union
3 – Spadoni	leadership and learning	the Cuban embargo	US Congress
4 – Morgan	competing epistemic communities	energy	the Russian energy sector
5 – Zarkin	social learning; paradigmatic change	telecommunications	the US government
6 – Oliver	social learning; orders of learning	macroeconomic policy	UK government
7 – Ellis	learning "ecologies"	humanitarian intervention	US government
8 – Kenney	competitive learning; crisis and learning	illicit drugs	drug cartels, the state
9 – Jackson	illicit learners; technology	terrorism	terrorist groups
10 – Campbell	middle managers and learning; dogmatic organizations	liberation theology	the Catholic Church
11 – Eden	"framing" and learning	the physical world	corporations, various
12 – Guttieri	compartmentalization and learning	stability operations	US military
13 – Hyden	drawing the "wrong" lessons	direct foreign assistance	aid agencies

The case studies in this volume are organized to consider, firstly, several aspects of learning processes including levels or orders of learning, leaders and learning, and the role epistemic communities play in learning. We then devote a segment to social and policy learning that draws particularly on the social learning literature in comparative politics and constructivism. The third segment, Chapters 8 and 9, considers learning by illicit organizations, drugs cartels and terrorist groups, under crisis conditions. The final four chapters acknowledge the potential challenges and pitfalls involved in organizational learning under the heading "Deterrents to Learning." Table 1.1 on page 2 summarizes the theoretical contributions of each empirical chapter. We next turn our attention to the divergent conceptualizations of organizational learning found in the literature.

Defining Organizational Learning

As was noted, organizational and social learning scholars define "learning" in disparate ways, and consequently focus their attention on different units of analysis, indicators and measures of learning. A partial accounting of this definitional and conceptual diversity includes:

- the acquisition of information, knowledge or skills,[3]
- the detection and correction of errors by organizational personnel,[4]
- changes in leaders' beliefs or worldviews,[5]
- the "...process by which consensual knowledge is used to specify causal relations in new ways so that the results affect the content of public policy...",[6]
- a change in cognitive structure; increased cognitive complexity,[7]

---

3   See Ernst B. Haas, *When Knowledge is Power: Three Models of Change in International Organizations* (Berkeley, CA: University of California Press, 1990), Jack S. Levy, "Learning and Foreign Policy: Sweeping a Conceptual Minefield," *International Organization* vol. 48 (1994), p. 288, and Reiter, *Crucibles of Beliefs.*

4   Chris Argyris, *On Organizational Learning,* 2nd ed. (Oxford: Blackwell Publishers Ltd., 1999), p. 83.

5   See Levy, "Learning and Foreign Policy," p. 283, and Philip E. Tetlock, "Learning in U.S. and Soviet Foreign Policy: In Search of an Elusive Concept," in George W. Breslauer and Philip E. Tetlock, eds., *Learning in U.S. and Soviet Foreign Policy* (Boulder, CO: Westview Press, 1991), p. 22.

6   In *When Knowledge is Power,* p. xxii, Haas writes that "governments learn to apply new patterns of reasoning to the formulation of environmental policy, which reflect a more sophisticated understanding of the complex array of causal interconnections between human environmental and economic activities."

7   Lloyd S. Etheredge, *Government Learning* (Cambridge, MA: Center for International Studies, Massachusetts Institute of Technology, 1979), pp. 76-79. When discussing increased sophistication, Etheredge differentiates between cognitive complexity (connoting a variety of different underlying sets of beliefs) and valuative complexity (which refers to the level of

- changes in organizational routines and practices as a result of experience,[8]
- governments' embracing new epistemologies or policy paradigms as a consequence of experience and social interaction,[9]
- the ability of the political system to meet new conditions,[10] and,
- increased effectiveness of behavior.[11]

Some contend that organizational learning is a metaphor or heuristic device for understanding collectives of individuals engaged in learning. For example, Mark Dodgson writes that "organizational learning…[is a] metaphor for individual learning, and the contextual and internal stimuli to learning in people…"[12] Similarly, Daniel Kim asserts that organizational learning is a metaphor derived from our understanding of individual learning, and that organizations ultimately learn via their individual members.[13] Bo Hedberg argues, however, that

> Although organizational learning occurs through individuals, it would be a mistake to conclude that organizational learning is nothing more than the cumulative results of their members' learning. Organizations do not have brains, but they have cognitive systems

---

inconsistency among values held and the manner in which inconsistencies and value trade-offs of different arguments are dealt with within the larger valuative framework). See also Haas, *When Knowledge is Power*, p. xxii; Tetlock, "Learning in U.S. and Soviet Foreign Policy," pp. 22, 32-35; and Levy, "Learning and Foreign Policy," p. 299.

  8   See Barbara Levitt and James G. March, "Organizational Learning," *Annual Review of Sociology* vol. 14 (1988), pp. 319-340.

  9   In *When Knowledge is Power*, p. 60, Haas writes: "The most sophisticated learning could be seen as a type of transcendental learning, quite uncommon among governments, consisting of a recognition of historical rupture and the development of an awareness of historical differences between eras, from which states would adopt new fundamental objectives." See also Peter A. Hall, "Policy Paradigms, Social Learning, and the State, the Case of Economic Policymaking in Britain," *Comparative Politics* vol. 25 (1993), pp. 275-296, and Lawrence C. Dodd, "Political Learning and Political Change: Understanding Development across Time," in Lawrence C. Dodd and Calvin Jillson, eds. *The Dynamics of American Politics: Approaches and Interpretations* (Boulder, CO: Westview Press), pp. 331-364.

  10 Karl W. Deutsch, *The Nerves of Government: Models of Political Communication and Control* (New York: The Free Press), p. 163.

  11 Chris Argyris and Donald A. Schon, *Organizational Learning: A Theory of Action Perspective* (Reading, MA: Addison-Wesley, 1978). In the 1996 2nd edition, Argyris and Schon decide that learning need not increase effectiveness, and recommended differentiation between productive and nonproductive learning. See also Etheredge *Government Learning*, p. 4; *Can Governments Learn?* (New York: Pergamon, 1981 and 1985), p. 66; Tetlock, "Learning in U.S. and Soviet Foreign Policy," p. 22.

  12 Dodgson, "Organizational Learning," p. 378.

  13 Daniel H. Kim, "The Link between Individual and Organizational Learning," *Sloan Management* vol. 35 (1993), p. 37.

and memories.... Members come and go, and leadership changes, but organizations' memories preserve certain behaviours, mental maps, norms and values over time.[14]

James N. Rosenau concurs:

Collectivities are conceived as having institutionalized ways of storing information and memories of historical turning points, of transmitting goals and values, and of maintaining procedures for adapting to new challenges.[15]

However, given the conceptual and the methodological challenges associated with assigning causality to cognitive factors and changes in foreign policy, Jack Levy recommends that analysts content themselves with focusing on changes in beliefs and worldviews of individual organizational leaders.[16] Paolo Spadoni's (Chapter 3) and, to some extent, Michael Oliver's (Chapter 6) contributions embrace this approach and examine changes in leaders' beliefs as a potential source of policy change. In contrast, several chapters embrace Levitt and March's definition of organizational learning as changes in routines and practices in response to experience, including Leann Brown, Michael Kenney and Brian Jackson in Chapters 2, 8 and 9.

Social learning analysts such as Hugh Heclo, Peter Hall, and Larry Dodd are concerned that simply examining changes in leaders' beliefs and world views and changes in organizational routines and practices is overly parsimonious.[17] They define government and policy learning as paradigmatic or epistemological change deriving from the social interactions of multiple state actors and the wider society. The Michael Zarkin, Michael Oliver and David Ellis contributions (Chapters 5-7) explore the interactions of state and societal actors that foster policy learning.

Orders of Organizational Learning

Most scholars concur that organizational and social learning varies in complexity and sophistication. Some classify small changes in organizational routines, procedures and policies in response to new information and experience as *adaptation* rather than "learning." Haas describes adaptation as:

---

14 Bo Hedberg, "How Organizations Learn and Unlearn," in Paul C. Nystrom and William H. Starbuck, *Handbook of Organizational Design* vol. 1 (Oxford: Oxford University Press, 1981), p. 3.

15 James N. Rosenau, *Turbulence in World Politics, A Theory of Change and Continuity* (Princeton, NJ: Princeton University Press, 1990), p. 139.

16 Levy, "Learning and Foreign Policy."

17 Hugh Heclo, *Modern Social Politics in Britain and Sweden: From Relief to Income Maintenance* (New Haven, CT: Yale University Press, 1974); Hall, "Policy Paradigms, Social Learning, and the State;" and, Dodd, "Political Learning and Political Change."

the ability to change one's behavior so as to meet challenges in the form of new demands without having to evaluate one's entire program and the reasoning on which that program depends for its legitimacy.[18]

Argyris and Schon, however, label adaptation as *single loop learning*, the most simple level of learning:

> Organizational learning involves the detection and correction of error. When the error detected and corrected permits the organization to carry on its present policies or achieve its present objectives, then that error-detection-and-correction process is single-loop learning.[19]

This most simple level of learning is also referred to as evolutionary, cybernetic, tactical, operational or instrumental learning.[20] Argyris and Schon add two additional levels of complexity, *double-loop* and *deutero-learning*:

> Double-loop learning occurs when error is detected and corrected in ways that involve the modification of an organization's underlying norms, policies and objectives.

They regard deutero-learning or "learning how to learn" as the most sophisticated level of learning:

> When an organization engages in deutero-learning its members learn about the previous context for learning. They reflect on and inquire into previous episodes of organizational learning, or failure to learn. They discover what they did that facilitated or inhibited learning, they invent new strategies for learning, they produce these strategies, and they evaluate and generalize what they have produced.[21]

Hall discusses "orders" of learning rather than embracing Argyris and Schon's "loop"-related discourse. His conceptualization of first order learning (adjusting policy techniques and settings while holding policies constant) coincides with single loop learning, however, he provides two further distinctions within the double-loop category. Second order learning occurs if policy goals and instruments are altered as a consequence of social learning. Third order learning is present if the organization's paradigm or worldview and overarching goals are changed. In Chapters 2, 5 and 6, we attempt to differentiate among these distinct levels of learning.[22]

---

18 Haas, *When Knowledge is Power*, pp. 33-34.
19 Argyris and Schon, *Organizational Learning*, p. 3.
20 See Deutsch, *The Nerves of Government;* Hedberg, "How Organizations Learn and Unlearn;" C. Marlene Fiol and Marjorie A. Lyles, "Organizational Learning," *Academy of Management Review* vol. 10 (1985), pp. 803-813; and Haas, *When Knowledge is Power.*
21 Argyris and Schon, *Organizational Learning*, pp. 3-4.
22 Other scholars discuss the various levels of complexity and sophistication in learning in terms of lower and higher learning (Fiol and Lyles, "Organizational Learning"), adaptive and generative learning (Peter M. Senge, *The Fifth Discipline: the Art and Practice of the*

Endogenous Conditions that Affect Organizational Learning

A parsimonious model of organizational learning may portray organizations as monolithic entities with clearly defined goals, rationally promulgating policies designed to achieve those goals, soliciting information and feedback, assessing policy effectiveness, and adjusting and changing organizational routines, policies and even paradigms, i.e. learning in simple and complex ways, as a consequence of these latter activities. However, Levitt and March point out a host of cognitive and practical difficulties may arise at each stage of this model. Organizational goals may be many, ambiguous and/or contradictory, and/or different groups within the organization may have different goals, understand or prioritize the goals differently, and/or evaluate the outcomes differently. Goals may change over time, levels of aspiration with regard to organizational goals may change, and/or indicators of policy success may change. Decision-makers may consciously or subconsciously reinterpret goals and objectives or interpret policy feedback in ways that make them appear successful even when failure is rather obvious.

While assessing outcomes as successes or failures is essential for productive organizational learning, organizational personnel are susceptible to a number of reasoning errors when "drawing lessons" from experience. In particular, decision-makers tend to overestimate causal relationships between discrete organizational decisions and behaviors and policy outcomes due to their "recentness or saliency." Decision-makers are frequently insensitive to sample size, and tend to assign too much weight to intentional actions of decision-makers and organizational policies at the expense of other factors, like chance. Personnel may assign success or failure to a decision or policy on the basis of how satisfying the decision-making process itself was rather than less-temporally-proximate outcomes.

"Competency traps," or drawing the wrong lessons from success, may occur if the organization improves its performance or achieves its goals while employing a sub-optimal procedure, policy or technology. Organizations may be particularly susceptible to competency traps when external pressure or crises force them to choose rapidly among alternative procedures and policies.[23]

Most analysts agree that organizations are more likely to learn as a consequence of failure than of success. However, as will be discussed below, profound failure and crises may have particularly negative consequences for productive learning. Several cases in this volume explore how organizations solicit and evaluate feedback and learn productively or unproductively from policy feedback. In Chapter 3, Spadoni provides evidence that members of the US Congress have learned that economic embargoes fail to achieve their stated goals of regime change in Cuba. In Chapter 12, Karen Guttieri describes the United States military as actively soliciting and

---

Learning Organization (New York: Doubleday, 1990) and tactical and strategic learning (Dodgson, "Organizational Learning").

23 See Levitt and March, "Organizational Learning," p. 322 and James G. March and Johan P. Olsen, *Rediscovering Institutions: The Organizational Basis of Politics* (New York: Free Press, 1989), p. 63.

evaluating feedback by routinely undertaking formal studies of what worked and failed to work in stability operations. And, in Chapter 13, Goran Hyden contends that international aid agencies fail to learn productively due to the poor quality of feedback data, among other difficulties.

Organizations not only learn from their own successes and failures but also may learn from the experience of others through active research, policy imitation, and the diffusion and transfer of ideas and technologies. A robust literature confirms that organizations may consciously undertake primary and secondary research to create information, knowledge, technologies, and policies as a part of problem-solving and policy-making. March writes that an organization draws from a pool of alternative routines and policies, adopting better ones when they are discovered. The rate of discovery is a function of the richness of the pool and the intensity and direction of search.[24] The policies and experiences of similar organizations are an obvious source of new information, knowledge and skills, and analyses of "lesson drawing," "policy imitation or transfer" and "contagion" are abundant across literatures.[25] In Chapter 6, Oliver discusses these bodies of literature.

Experts acting as leaders, bureaucratic personnel, consultants, and/or as members of epistemic communities are an additional potent source of information and understanding. Aristotle used "episteme" to refer to a conception of knowledge about the order and nature of the cosmos.[26] More contemporarily, John G. Ruggie derived his notion of "epistemic community" from Michel Foucault's broader concept of "epistemes," which refer to:

> broader visions of reality...through which political relationships are visualized...a dominant way of looking at social reality, a set of shared symbols and inferences, mutual expectations and a mutual predictability of intention. Epistemic communities may be said to consist of interrelated roles which grow up around an episteme, they delimit, for their members the proper construction of social reality.[27]

Peter Haas expands upon this definition: Epistemic communities are "networks of knowledge-based experts....with recognized expertise and competence in a particular domain and an authoritative claim to policy-relevant knowledge within that domain or issue-area." Community members may be scientists or researchers; governmental

---

24 James G. March, *The Pursuit of Organizational Intelligence* (Malden, MA: Blackwell Publishers Ltd, 1999), p. 77.

25 Richard Rose, *Lesson-Drawing in Public Policy: A Guide to Learning across Time and Space* (Chatham, NJ: Chatham House Publishers, Inc., 1993); Paul A. Sabatier, "Knowledge, Policy-Oriented Learning, and Policy Change," *Knowledge: Creation, Diffusion, Utilization* vol. 8 (1987), pp. 649-692; Heclo, *Modern Social Politics in Britain and Sweden.*

26 Mark Neufeld, "Reflexivity and International Relations Theory," in Claire Turenne Sjolander and Wayne S. Cox, eds., *Beyond Positivism, Critical Reflections on International Relations* (Boulder, CO: Lynne Rienner Publishers, 1994), p. 17.

27 John G. Ruggie, "International Responses to Technology," *International Organization* vol. 29 (1975), pp. 557-583.

staff persons; planning, evaluation and budget officials, academics; interest group analysts, and so on. They have:

1. a shared set of normative or principled beliefs, which provide a value-based rationale for the social action of community members;
2. shared causal beliefs which are derived from their analysis of practices leading or contributing to a central set of problems in their domain and which then serve as the basis for elucidating the multiple linkages between possible policy actions and desired outcomes;
3. shared notions of validity – that is intersubjective, internally defined criteria for weighting and validating knowledge in the domain of their expertise; and
4. a common policy enterprise – that is, a set of common practices associated with a set of problems to which their professional competence is directed...[28]

Members of an epistemic community interact with each other; ideas and policy alternatives circulate among them. They test their ideas on their colleagues by disseminating papers, publishing articles, holding conferences, consulting, drafting and promoting legislative proposals. They know each others' ideas, proposals, and research; they may know each other personally.[29]

External actors who bring knowledge into organizations include what social psychology literature calls "boundary spanners" and the innovation literature refers to as "technological gatekeepers." Haas writes that epistemic communities may facilitate learning through teaching, persuasion and claims of superior knowledge and understanding. Epistemic communities may compete with political and bureaucratic actors to shape decisions and policies, and/or they may "capture" organizational divisions responsible for decision-making via persuasion or personnel change. With regard to the United Nations plan to enhance environmental protection and economic development of the Mediterranean, Haas contends that very little learning occurred as a consequence of persuasion. Instead, learning occurs as the epistemic community appropriates the policy debate and achieves bureaucratic control over decision-making and implementation. Even if an epistemic community fails to capture an organizational bureaucracy or persuade other political actors of the validity of its paradigm and policy recommendations, its discourse forces other actors to reexamine and negotiate their ideas, paradigms and policy positions to address and accommodate the experts' alternative perspectives. In Chapter 2, Brown discusses the role experts play in European Union policy processes dealing with BSE and bovine hormones. In Chapter 4, Eric Morgan examines the cooperative and competitive interaction of domestic and global epistemic communities in the Russian energy sector. And, in Chapter 5, Zarkin discusses how an epistemic community

---

28 Peter M. Haas, "Introduction: Epistemic Communities and International Policy Coordination," *International Organization* vol. 26 (1992), p. 3.

29 John W. Kingdon, *Agendas, Alternatives, and Public Policies* (Boston: Little, Brown and Company, 1984), pp. 122-124.

helped foster an epistemological (or paradigmatic) shift in US telecommunication policy between 1980-96.

Several organizational process and structural attributes may facilitate or deter effective learning, including such factors as the quality of information storage systems and communication, available social capital including levels of trust and cooperation among personnel, and hierarchical versus horizontal patterns of authority and communication. Organizational personnel draw upon information storage systems or organizational memories when interpreting experience and making decisions. To the extent that these systems record knowledge in a manner that is relevant, understandable and accessible, they likely shape how members interpret new information and experience. While well-maintained information storage systems may be orderly, they of necessity simplify descriptions and explanations of reality, and may also contain inconsistencies and ambiguities. These problems may derive from different experiences among personnel, conflicting interpretations of experience, errors in recording experience, and the ongoing challenge of drawing consistent inferences from shifting realities.[30] Even when organizational memories provide clear information and interpretation is relatively unambiguous, the inferences' implications for policy-making and actual behavior may be unclear to decision-makers.[31]

The challenges of information and knowledge acquisition, storage and interpretation are exacerbated when organizational personnel fail to communicate and share information. Rapid, frequent, regular and substantive information flows among the various divisions of the organizations are essential to provide decision-makers the best available information and understanding. Organizational norms such as openness, fairness, trust, affirmation, dialogue, cooperation and empowerment are important to creating an administrative culture that facilitates productive learning. Argyris contrasts competitive management models with more cooperative ones. The former "will create conditions of undiscussability, self-fulfilling prophecies, self-sealing processes, and escalating error. These conditions act to reinforce vagueness, lack of clarity, inconsistency, and incongruity" which makes personnel strive for unilateral control and to minimize losing and maximize winning. "[T]hese conditions tend to create win-lose groups and intergroup dynamics with competitiveness dominating over cooperation, mistrust overcoming trust, and unquestioned obedience replacing informed dissent." Argyris asserts that cooperation is a necessary condition for productive learning.[32]

In an administrative culture that facilitates productive learning, goal achievement and excellence of performance are emphasized over norms like obedience to superiors, "loyalty," or congeniality. Conflict within the organization is adjusted by interaction with peers, rather than adjudicated from the top. And, prestige and

---

30 Levitt and March, "Organizational Learning," pp. 327-328.

31 David Garvin, *Learning in Action: A Guide to Putting the Learning Organization to Work* (Boston: Harvard Business School Press, 2000), p. 26.

32 Argyris, *On Organizational Learning*, pp. 84-87.

rewards within the organization are conferred on the basis of task achievement, performance excellence, professional ability and reputation rather than office and rank.[33]

While inefficient information storage systems and uncooperative administrative cultures may contribute to weak information flows, many complex organizations, such as transnational corporations, intentionally compartmentalize knowledge to protect proprietary information from outsiders. Maintaining secrecy may be necessary to prevent competitors from obtaining access to production methods and innovations, however, it can also limit organizations' ability to benefit from in-house knowledge and learn productively from their own and others' experience. If one organizational division lacks access to other's knowledge, including its trial-and-error experience, it may make similar mistakes. Similarly, secrecy among organizations limits vicarious learning.[34]

The issue of knowledge sharing among subunits underscores the fact that organizations are not monolithic learning entities. Instead, subunits within complex organizations interpret information and experience and learn in different ways. Each individual personnel member and subgroup has its own information, knowledge, culture and learning capacity. Further, subunits may learn at different paces; for example, one would expect research and development units to learn rapidly. Organizations may or may not benefit from diversity and heterogeneity of learning among subunits. The organizational structure defines how these processes interact to affect productive learning.

Both size (the number of personnel) and the number of managerial levels may influence the quality of organizational learning. In general, organizations with four or fewer levels of management are characterized as nonhierarchical, horizontal or flat decision-making structures. Size and the number of management levels influence learning as a consequence of their effect on the collection and analysis of information. The greater the number of organizational personnel (leaders, middle managers, consultants, lower-level personnel), the greater the likelihood information will be misunderstood, distorted or manipulated. Fewer information handlers increases the speed with which information can be processed and decisions may be taken. Also, changes in organizational routines may be selected and discarded more rapidly if policy feedback and routines and policy changes travel through fewer personnel.

Levels of management influence learning indirectly through their impact on information and decision flows. The more hierarchical the organization, the more management layers through which information and decisions must flow. Each management level represents a distinct channel of information processing. As with

---

33 Nicholas Henry, *Public Administration and Public Affairs* (Englewood Cliffs, NJ: Prentice Hall, 1989), p. 58.

34 Scott D. Sagan, *The Limits of Safety: Organizations, Accidents, and Nuclear Weapons* (Princeton: Princeton University Press, 1993), p. 43; George P. Huber, "Organizational Learning: The Contributing Processes and the Literatures," *Organizational Science: A Journal of the Institute of Management Sciences* vol. 2 (1991), p. 95.

number of personnel, the greater the number of information processing levels, the more likely information will be unconsciously or intentionally misunderstood, distorted or manipulated. More horizontal or flat management structures represent fewer channels through which information and decisions must flow, and fewer opportunities for processing errors and machinations. More horizontal structures also decrease the speed of information processing and decision-making.[35] Beyond the effects of hierarchical structures on information flows, more hierarchical structures commonly are characterized by unity of command, win-lose competitive dynamics, specialization of tasks, and a focus on rationality of ideas to the exclusion of rationality of feelings, all of which detract from a productive learning culture.[36]

Relatively horizontal organizational structures allow all levels of personnel – leaders, middle managers and those in the lowest echelon – to interact, share information and ideas, and contribute to goal articulation, planning and decision-making. There is frequent and regular interaction between leadership and lower-level personnel, allowing lower-level personnel to provide input into goal articulation and planning processes. Emphasis within the organization is placed on ends rather than means, conferring upon lower-level personnel the discretion to decide how goals are to be achieved. In Chapters 8 and 9, Kenney and Jackson compare the learning advantages of the horizontal, cell-like structures of Colombian drug cartels and terrorist groups to hierarchical state structures. In Chapter 10, Bill Campbell discusses the role of middle managers, in this case Latin American bishops, as communicators and transformers of information between the leadership of the Catholic Church, the papacy, and lower-level personnel including the parish priests and laity.

Several analysts and contributors to this volume point out leaders' essential role in fostering productive organizational learning. Levy contends that leaders' acquiring new information, ideas, understanding, values, beliefs and paradigms is the most methodologically satisfactory definition for organizational learning.[37] Argyris points out the practical imperative of leadership to productive organizational learning when he writes that if leaders don't implement new learning systems and behaviors, it is doubtful that personnel below will possess the ability to do so. Leadership and learning directs again our attention to the level of analysis difficulties associated with organizational and social learning.[38] Kim asks if elites or leaders are agents of organizational learning, then how is learning transferred from the individual to the organization? How does individual learning become embedded in the organization's structures, procedures and memories? The most facile response to this dilemma is that a leader occupies a role within the organizational structures; there is no leader without the organization.[39] Marcus Jacktenfuchs discusses a model of leader as teacher within an organization: Some individuals are particularly productive learners

35 Argyris and Schon, *Organizational Learning II*, p. 187.
36 Argyris, *On Organizational Learning*, p. 83.
37 Levy, "Learning and Foreign Policy."
38 Argyris, *On Organizational Learning*, p. 85.
39 Kim, "The Link between Individual and Organizational Learning," p. 37.

because of their intelligence, unique past experiences, and/or privileged access to information due to their prominent role in the organization. They may be able to teach others and transform organizational routines, procedures and policies as a consequence of the usefulness and persuasiveness of their ideas, personal charisma, communicative abilities, and/or abilities to foster a cooperative and learning culture.[40] At this juncture, it is clear that causal influences become very intertwined. Does the leader facilitate productive learning within the organization as a consequence of her intelligence, superior repertoire of information and experience, ability to argue and persuade or as a consequence of the power conferred by her leadership role? The answer, of course, is both. Several contributions to this volume attempt to get at these nuances. In Chapter 7, David Ellis portrays the US President and government agencies as teachers and students in an ecology of learning concerning the humanitarian crisis in Somalia. And, as was previously noted, Campbell, in Chapter 10, further distinguishes between the role of papal leadership and middle level managers in the Catholic Church.

Even when an organization manages to acquire and circulate useful information and knowledge, and its information processing systems provide unambiguous interpretations with clear behavior prescriptions for decision-makers, this knowledge may fail to influence organizational behavior in useful ways. Structural rigidities and inertia may prevent the organization from adopting new routines, procedures and policies that could improve goal achievement. Organizations have significant "sunk costs" in existing procedures, policies, technologies and personnel, and as Garvin observes, change usually has no constituency.[41] Established procedures and policies reflect the interests of and are the product of, and, thus, are supported by powerful actors and coalitions. If organizational leaders perceive their interests threatened by new procedures and policies, they are less likely to be embraced.[42] When this occurs, some personnel and sub-divisions may acquire new information and understanding, but procedural, policy and paradigmatic change will not occur on the organizational level.[43]

Recent organizational learning literature has also exhibited the constructivist trends across the social sciences in emphasizing the importance of discourse in creating, utilizing and disseminating knowledge. Constructivists reject the dichotomies and distinctions implied in structure-agent, individual-collective, and other mainstream modes of analysis that disaggregate thought, choice and action. They instead point out the importance of discourse (narrative forms of knowledge,

---

40 Marcus Jachtenfuchs, *International Policy-Making as a Learning Process? The European Union and the Greenhouse Effect* (Aldershot, UK: Ashgate, 1996), p. 38.

41 Michael T. Hannan and John Freeman, "The Population Ecology of Organizations," *American Journal of Sociology* vol. 82 (1977), p. 931; Garvin, *Learning in Action*, p. 33.

42 Hannan and Freeman, "The Population Ecology of Organizations," p. 931.

43 Argyris and Schon, *Organizational Learning II*, p. 17; James G. March and Johan P. Olsen, "The Uncertainty of the Past: Organizational Learning under Ambiguity," in James G. March, ed., *Decisions and Organizations* (New York: Basil Blackwell, 1988), p. 347.

the role of storytelling and informal conversations) and tacit understanding in creating and storing knowledge. Ralph Stacey explains:

> Knowledge creation is…an active process of communication between humans. It follows that knowledge is not stored, but perpetually constructed. Knowledge is not shared as mental contents but perpetually arises in action. Knowledge is not transmitted from one mind to another but is the process of relating.

And, he reiterates:

> [K]nowledge arises in complex responsive processes of relating between human bodies…. [K]nowledge itself is continuously reproduced and potentially transformed. Knowledge is not a 'thing,' or a system, but an ephemeral, active process of relating.[44]

Communication is a function of both explicit and implicit or tacit knowledge. Explicit knowledge is formal, systematic knowledge easily transformed into verbal, mathematical and numerical language. Tacit knowledge is a more subjective phenomenon of mental models involving insight, intuition and hunches and may be below the level of consciousness. Tacit knowledge is more difficult to formalize and communicate in that it is rooted in action and exhibits itself as skills or "know how."

Those that assign importance to "learning by doing" or "learning by discourse" stress the importance of working and learning in groups or "ecologies." How group members relate to each other, how they converse and the language they employ are important. Once tacit knowledge has been made explicit, others must internalize it so that it becomes part of their paradigms. Further, explicit knowledge may be embodied in cultural artifacts in formal and informal norms, rules, routines and procedures. As this knowledge is disseminated throughout the organization it will be tested and transformed via dialogue and disagreement.[45] In Chapter 7, Ellis provides the most straightforward example of constructivist analysis. The seemingly tortuous deliberative processes ("pure" research, input from epistemic communities, investigative reports by Member-State and EU bodies, and policy negotiations), by which the European Union comes to understand and act on policy issues described in Chapter 2 also provide some inkling of how learning via discourse or "learning by doing" occurs. In Chapter 9, Jackson discusses distinctions between tacit and explicit knowledge in terrorist organizations.

Exogenous Influences on Organizational Learning

The quality of incoming information including feedback from previous policy experience influences the productivity of organizational learning. As was previously

---

44 Ralph D. Stacey, *Complex Responsive Processes in Organizations, Learning and Knowledge Creation* (London: Routledge, 2001), pp. 4, 6.

45 Stacey, *Complex Responsive Processes in Organizations*, pp. 17-18.

noted, incoming information may be more or less accurate, relevant, comprehensive and clear. Ambiguous information and policy feedback may be a two-edged sword that deters or facilitates productive learning. Some contend that ambiguity and uncertainty make decision-making and productive learning difficult if not impossible. For example, individual personnel and organizations operating under conditions of incomplete, unclear and/or contradictory information may resort to heuristic devices such as ideological models and other shortcuts to help them make sense of the poor data. These cognitive schema, however, may bias interpretation in subtle or profound ways. Again, March and others' work demonstrates that because of the ambiguities associated with any single incident, interpretations and policy changes tend to be adopted more as a result of their temporal proximity, cognitive availability, or political expedience than by virtue of their valid understanding. However, high levels of uncertainty may enhance the importance of knowledge, ideas and beliefs relative to more overtly political dynamics, and make decision-makers more willing to undertake research or solicit advice from outside experts or epistemic communities. In Chapter 2, Brown portrays a European Union actively engaging in "pure" research and embracing the recommendations of epistemic communities in response to the high levels of scientific uncertainty associated with food security issues. And, in Chapter 13, Hyden investigates how aid agencies, faced with poor-quality policy feedback, undergo successive paradigmatic changes as a consequence of endogenous ideological trends.

Organizations do not learn independently of the context in which they operate. As more or less "open systems," they interact with and depend upon the external environment for information, ideas, resources, and personnel.[46] Other organizations constitute the external environment from which understandings may be drawn via the transfer of knowledge, technologies, rules, standard operating procedures, and other routines. Knowledge diffuses throughout the environment as organizations learn from each other by cooperative or competitive means. Successful organizations with superior technologies, procedures and success rates are the most common sources of information and knowledge. Knowledge diffusion may occur via various means including joint ventures, personnel transfer, professional publications, consultants, professional networks, and, in the case of the corporate and illicit world, espionage. In Chapter 6, Oliver provides an in-depth discussion of the policy transfer literature while investigating the British government's embracing of neoliberal economic policies during the 1980s.

Knowledge diffusion and the interaction within ecologies of learners represent relatively benign external sources of learning, however, occasionally the external environment may pose a profound and/or sudden threat to organization's basic goals and existence. Within organizations, attention, time and effort are scarce resources and are often forthcoming only in times of crisis, which means that information acquisition and interpretation may be profoundly affected by crisis conditions

---

46 Richard W. Scott, *Organizations: Rational, Natural and Open Systems*, 4th ed. (Upper Saddle River, NJ: Prentice Hall, 1998).

defined as an unanticipated threat to the organization's primary values and goals under conditions of limited time and duress. Under these conditions, organizations may be forced to learn to survive; indeed paradigmatic learning may be most likely to occur within these extreme conditions. However, the time constraints and stress under which learning occurs may make these processes susceptible to a host of "learning disabilities," including blind spots, filtering, flawed interpretation, and secrecy. Blind spots occur when organizational search is narrow or misguided, which causes decision-makers to miss important feedback signals, misunderstand them or understand them very slowly. Filtering occurs when critical information is ignored or downplayed because it is inconsistent with decision-makers' prior beliefs and/or powerful interests within the organization.[47] For example, organizational leaders may be receptive to information that assigns success to their own behavior and failure to the actions of others or to exogenous sources.[48] As Sagan points out, problems "are not simply internal data points to be used to improve organizational performance. They are also political events for which credit and blame must be assigned." Interpretation may be politicized, with a possible consequence that "the messenger is killed" (and information suppressed or distorted) rather than responsibility for failure being assigned to individuals or powerful coalitions within the organization.[49]

Several of our contributors provide empirical examples of organizational learning in conditions of crisis. In Chapter 6, global economic crisis, stagflation, fostered a new political movement under British Prime Minister Margaret Thatcher, whose government initiated paradigmatic change in economic-political thought from Keynesianism to neoliberalism. And, in Chapters 8 and 9, Kenney and Jackson describe the continuous and profound threat from the external environment under which illicit actors operate that destroys unproductive learners and results in constant and complex productive learning networks.

Consideration of anti-social actors as potential productive learning organizations is an important contribution of this volume to the learning literature. Chapters 8 and 9 consider the implications for learning when those that learn are engaged in socially harmful or illegal activities. Ecologies of learners are customarily described as more or less cooperative and competitive, however illegal organizations act in environments that are overtly hostile to their existence. Organizations that err in such environments may face extinction at the hands of their competitors.[50] The survival imperative must take precedence over other factors that affect productive learning.[51]

---

47 Garvin, *Learning in Action*, pp. 28-29.
48 See Levitt and March, "Organizational Learning," p. 324.
49 Sagan, *The Limits of Safety*, p. 208; Huber, "Organizational Learning," p. 95.
50 Hedberg, "How Organizations Learn and Unlearn," p. 14.
51 Andrew Farkas, *State Learning and International Change* (Ann Arbor: University of Michigan Press, 1979), p. 8.

Alternative Explanations for Organizational Change

This volume's focus on organizational learning is not meant to imply that "learning dynamics" are the only or even the most likely sources of change in organizations. Indeed, we have encouraged our contributors to acknowledge and explore alternative explanations for the changes including power-related dynamics. Levitt and March discuss several alternative theories of analysis and choice including theories that emphasize intention and calculation; theories of bargaining and conflict that emphasize exchange, strategic action and power; and theories of variation and selection.[52] We pointed out earlier that political power may allow leaders to impose new paradigms and understandings as well as to persuasively teach and lead organizations to embrace new ideas. Powerful coalitions and other factors within institutions may also deter new understandings from disseminating throughout organization and affecting routines, procedures and policies. Policy change may emerge as a consequence of negotiations, bargaining, and other overtly political dynamics.

Rational choice theories provide an additional cognitively-oriented explanation for organizational learning. The rational choice model assumes that actors engaged in repeated iterations of an activity will achieve some level of optimal behavior as a consequence of trial and error. The assumption is that subjective probabilities converge to objective frequencies as additional information becomes available through iteration. Rational choice theorists assume that the quality and speed of learning are affected by the salience of the issues, the availability of information, and the frequency of decision-making. In general, rational choice explanations postulate the same outcomes as learning theories but employ stronger assumptions. The cases of this volume reveal that organizational learning theories have much to offer investigations of complex political-economic-social phenomena relative to the ahistorical, deterministic and parsimonious assumptions of rational choice perspectives. The next three chapters will explore several processes associated with organizational learning.

---

52 See Levitt and March, "Organizational Learning," p. 319.

PART 1
Learning Processes

Chapter 2

Learning and Food Security in the European Union

M. Leann Brown

The European Union (EU) has been confronted recently with a series of food-related crises that potentially endanger citizens' health and peace of mind, threaten the political survival of Member State governments, undermine the legitimacy of the organization and its free trade objectives, and embroil the EU in disputes with its trading partners.[1] The case may be made that food issues are always potentially highly controversial because they pertain to every citizen's basic needs. However, the novelty and scientific uncertainty of recent concerns, including the use of hormones to enhance beef and dairy production[2] and the BSE epidemic,[3] have fostered unusually high levels of public controversy. By what means have EU policymakers sought to address these crises?

Political scientists commonly assign causal or intervening significance to such factors as national interests, political power, bargaining dynamics, institutional factors, individual leadership, cultural and/or ideational factors such as ideology. However, when faced with food security and human and veterinary health crises fraught with high levels of scientific uncertainty, policymakers may also learn from their own and others' policy experience and/or rely on their own research or other

---

1　In Britain, the bovine spongiform encephalopathy (BSE) or "mad cow" crisis helped seal the fate of John Major's government, and revelations about dioxins in poultry and dairy products two-weeks before the general election contributed to the defeat of the Jean-Luc Dehaene government in Belgium in June 1999. Stephen Bates, "Belgium Removes Pork from Sale as New Dioxin Scare Hits Country," *The Guardian* (July 24, 1999).

2　Hormones may be administered to enhance production in both beef and dairy cattle. Dairy cows naturally produce a protein hormone called bovine somatotropin (BST) that affects distribution of feed to bodily functions like growth and lactation. In the early 1980s, the gene governing the synthesis of BST in cows was isolated and cloned by the United States (US) corporation Genentech, and since 1982, large quantities of BST have been produced through genetically-engineered bacteria. The hormone harvested from the bacteria is called recombinant bovine somatotropin (rBST). Administering rBST to lactating cows results in an approximately 10% increase in milk.

3　See Table 2.1 on page 23 for specific information on the increasing numbers of BSE cases reported in EU Member States between 1995 and 2004.

scientific experts to delineate causal aspects of the problem, to design and prescribe policy solutions, and to define and evaluate policy effectiveness.

An important area of theoretical inquiry focuses on the role of organizational learning in the formulation of policy. In the strictest empirical sense, individuals perceive, cogitate and learn. However, a growing literature on organizations also employs language associated with "learning" to describe and explain certain policy processes and outcomes.[4] The methodological difficulties of testing organizational learning theories are numerous; however, the tautological consequences of operationalizing "learning" as both process and outcome is likely the most common. Barbara Levitt and James March point out that learning does not always lead to more effective policies or intelligent behavior.[5] The same processes that foster productive experiential learning may also yield superstitious learning, competency traps and erroneous inferences, a result of some combination of inadequacies of human cognition, organizational attributes and aspects of the experience itself. Thus, this investigation conceptualizes learning as the organization's acquiring new information, causal understandings and paradigms as a result of experience, research and expert input into the policy process as evidenced by their incorporation into organizational procedures, policies, and behaviors.

Within the context of organizational learning theory, this study looks comparatively at EU policymaking to deal with the issues of bovine hormones and BSE as "most similar," "best cases" to ascertain if and how organizational learning figured in the policymaking.[6] These cases reveal that while learning is not the exclusive source of policy change, there is little doubt that at least three orders of organizational learning are discernible over time in EU decision making to address these food security issues.

---

4   See Chapter 1, pp. 3-4 for various definitions of organizational learning.

5   See Barbara Levitt and James G. March, "Organizational Learning," *Annual Review of Sociology* vol. 14 (1988), p. 335; also see Jack S. Levy, "Learning and Foreign Policy: Sweeping a Conceptual Minefield," *International Organization* vol. 48 (1994), pp. 279-312.

6   Adam Przeworksi and Henry Teune, *The Logic of Comparative Social Inquiry* (New York: Wiley-Interscience, 1970), pp. 31-46.

Table 2.1 Reported Cases of BSE in Affected EU Member States, 1995-2004

	1995	1996	1997	1998	1999	2000	2001	2002	2003	2004	2005
Austria	0	0	0	0	0	0	1	0	0	0	2
Belgium	0	0	1	6	3	9	46	38	15	11	2
Denmark	0	0	0	0	0	1	6	3	2	1	1
Finland	0	0	0	0	0	0	1	0	0	0	0
France	3	12	6	18	31	161	274	239	137	54	31
Germany	0	0	2	0	0	7	125	106	54	65	32
Greece	0	0	0	0	0	0	1	0	0	0	0
Ireland	16	73	80	83	91	149	246	333	183	126	69
Italy	0	0	0	0	0	0	48	38	29	7	8
Luxembourg	0	0	1	0	0	0	0	1	0	0	1
Netherlands	0	0	2	2	2	2	20	24	19	6	3
Portugal	15	31	30	127	159	149	110	86	133	92	46
Spain	0	0	0	0	0	2	82	127	167	137	98
UK	14562	8149	4393	3235	2301	1443	1202	1144	611	343	225

Source: Office International des Epizooties; for the UK: <http://www.oie.int/eng/info/en_esbru.htm>; for remaining EU Member States: <http://www.oie.int/eng/info/en_esbmonde.htm>, last accessed June 24, 2006.

Organizational Learning Theory

Human beings alter their ideas, beliefs and cognitive frames of reference as a result of acquiring new information ("know what") and causal understandings ("know how" and "know why") from personal experience, research or perceived authoritative sources. "Learning" is also a heuristically useful way to conceptualize these phenomena in organizations. As noted in Chapter 1, Mark Dodgson writes that "organizational learning...[is a] metaphor for individual learning, and the contextual and internal stimuli to learning in people...."[7] Bo Hedberg argues, however, that although organizational learning occurs via individuals, such learning is more than the cumulative results of personnel's learning. Leadership and other personnel come and go, but organizations preserve certain paradigms, norms and routines over time within information systems and memories.[8]

Chris Argyris and Donald Schon distinguish organizational learning into what they label single-loop, double-loop, and deutero-learning. Single-loop learning involves the detection and correction of error via relatively small adjustments in policies that allow the organization to better carry out its present policies and/or achieve its current objectives. However, if the organization responds to error by changing its underlying objectives, policies, norms or paradigm, then double-loop learning has occurred. Single-loop learning tends to derive from discrete quantities of information, to be incremental in pace, and to result in small-scale change. Single-loop learning may enhance an organization's ability to function in its current environment, but is no substitute for double-loop learning. Argyris and Schon further contend that organizations may also move beyond single- and double-loop learning and develop the capacity to "learn how to learn," i.e. engage in deutero-learning:

> When an organization engages in deutero-learning its members learn about the previous context for learning. They reflect on and inquire into previous episodes of organizational learning, or failure to learn. They discover what they did that facilitated or inhibited learning, they invent new strategies for learning, they produce these strategies, and they evaluate and generalize what they have produced.[9]

Peter Hall concurs with Argyris and Schon's conceptualization of single loop learning as simple changes in policy instruments and techniques (first order learning); however, he asserts that double loop learning should be further disaggregated into changes in policies and instruments (second order learning) and changes in overall

---

7   Mark Dodgson, "Organizational Learning: A Review of Some Literatures," *Organizational Studies* vol. 14 (1993), p. 378.

8   Bo Hedberg, "How Organizations Learn and Unlearn," in P. Nystrom and W. Starbuck, eds. *Handbook of Organizational Design* vol. 1 (Oxford: Oxford University Press, 1981), p. 3.

9   Chris Argyris and Donald A. Schon, *Organizational Learning* (Reading, MA: Addison-Wesley, 1978), pp. 3-4.

organizational paradigms, goals and norms (third order learning).[10] While he does not elaborate, Hall also acknowledges that a fourth order of learning is possible, "learning how to learn," which is similar to Argyris and Schon's notion of deutero-learning. The disparity of language employed to describe similar phenomena has been a problem in the organizational learning literature. This chapter embraces the labels first-, second-, third- and fourth-order learning to connote graduated levels of learning sophistication rather than the process dynamics implied in the use of "loops."

Following this characterization, this investigation finds that although over time the EU acquired new information and causal understandings in the bovine hormones and BSE cases, it initially exhibited little first-order learning in the BSE case. There is, however, evidence crises deriving from this lack of first order learning necessitated higher levels of learning. Second- (embracing new objectives and policies), third- (embracing new issue framing and norms) and fourth-order-learning (consciously reflecting upon its learning experience and enhancing its ability to learn) occur in both cases. Indicators that learning is occurring or has occurred include modifications in personnel, programs, policies and the modification or creation of new legal and organizational structures that incorporate new information (including policy feedback) and causal understandings. Programmatic, personnel, legal and organization structural changes may include the incorporation of new actors and organizational structures into deliberative processes such as scientific working groups, consultants, and epistemic communities.

Most analysts agree that organizational learning is facilitated by certain prior conditions, including a culture congenial to learning; an existing knowledge base; specific competencies and processes of acquiring, articulating and enhancing knowledge; and decentralized, flexible organizational structures and procedures that encourage self-examination and openness to negative feedback and innovation. The next segment explores how the EU acquired information and understanding about bovine hormones and BSE from its own and other's experience, input from scientific experts, and "learning by doing."

The Impact of Issue Novelty, Scientific Uncertainty, and Politics on First Order Learning

Theory suggests that an organization may achieve first order learning via its own policy experience, in-house expertise, and tapping into exogenous sources of information and knowledge including the global scientific community and others' policy experiences. As the organization exerts itself to understand the substantive nature of the issue and various actors compete to frame the issue, present their

---

10 Peter A. Hall, "Policy Paradigms, Social Learning, and the State: The Case of Economic Policymaking in Britain," Comparative Politics vol. 25 (1993), pp. 275-296. Also, see Michael Zarkin's and Michael Oliver's discussion of paradigmatic change in Chapters 5 and 6.

preferred policy alternatives, and achieve policy consensus, the organization may also effectively "learn by doing." After policies are promulgated, feedback as to their effectiveness (which emerges over time via such indicators as the extent to which problems are ameliorated or policies are regarded as legitimate by the public and/or suffer legal challenge) may allow the organization to further achieve first order learning.

Because of the novelty of the issues, scientific uncertainty, and time pressure generated by their potential threat to public health, learning from scientific research and immediate policy feedback was not initially available to EU policymakers. Indeed, the learning curves for BSE and bovine hormones have been steep for all West Europeans – scientists, policymakers and the public alike. In 1979, a British Royal Commission headed by Lord Zuckerman, set up to examine potential pathogenic transmissions in meat rendering processes, first warned against feeding animal remains to ruminants.[11] A veterinarian in Surrey brought BSE to the attention of authorities in 1985, but five years transpired before scientists discovered that the disease had transmitted across species to cats and pigs.[12] In March 1996, a joint memo from the health and agriculture ministers to Prime Minister John Major confirmed that scientists were prepared to assume a link between BSE in cattle and Creutzfeldt-Jakob Disease (CJD) in humans.

The gene governing the synthesis of BST in cows was isolated and cloned by the Genentech corporation in the early 1980s. Rather than policy learning, the EU's initial policy response to the new technology appears a consequence of some combination of economic motivations deriving from an already burgeoning supply of agricultural goods generated by the Common Agricultural Policy, a desire to limit agricultural imports, and cultural aversion[13] for the genetically modified injections. Almost immediately, in 1981 and 1985, the EU promulgated directives prohibiting the use of hormones for fattening cattle effective until 1 January 1988.[14] In 1989, Directive 96/22/EC broadened the scope of legislation to prohibit domestic producers' administering to farm animals by any means substances having a thyrostatic, oestrogenic or gestagenic effect to promote growth, and prohibited imports of meat from animals treated with growth hormones from third countries.

In 1993, the US Food and Drug Administration approved use of a milk production enhancing BST, which was introduced into US markets by the Monsanto

---

11 European Parliament, *EP BSE Inquiry Report* (February 7, 1997), A4-0020/97/A, p. 6, <http://www.mad-cow.org/final_EU.html>, last accessed December 5, 2005.

12 Robin Oakley, "Analysis: Hope and Blame in Britain," (October 26, 2000), <http://europe.cnn.com/2000/WORLD/europe/10/26/bse.oakley/index.html>, last accessed December 5, 2005.

13 It is commonly asserted that West Europeans are less trusting of scientific innovation and technology than are North Americans. During the 20th century, scientific experimentation undertaken by the Nazi regime and the thalidomide disaster provided tragic evidence that science and scientists can be malevolent.

14 See the *Official Journal of the European Communities*, hereafter *OJ,* L 222, 07.8.1981, *OJ* L 352, 31.12.1985.

Corporation as Posilac in February 1994. Immediately, two applications for marketing authorization for these products came before the EU Commission.[15] The Commission turned for advice to its expert advisory Committee for Veterinary Medicinal Products which recommended that trial herds be allowed to investigate health and welfare effects on the targeted animals (particularly with regard to mastitis) in two-year, post-marketing studies.[16] At the end of 1994, EU Council Decision 94/936/EC instead extended the moratorium on marketing and use of BST until 1998 and called for preparation of a report on its use by independent scientists. Thus, a veterinary advisory committee provided input into EU decision-making regarding BST, but its advice was not the determining factor in shaping the legislation; i.e. EU policy was not a consequence of first order learning via policy transfer (from the US) or scientific input.

These cases bring into strong relief the question: what roles do scientists, scientific committees, and scientific uncertainty play in organizational learning? Policymakers may turn to scientific experts for clear statements of the nature, scope and immediacy of risks, and for identification and cost-benefit assessments of alternative policy solutions. However, often these needs are not well met by slow, deliberative scientific methodologies. As the cases of this study demonstrate, policymakers may need, desire or assume higher certainty levels than science can provide. A lack of scientific consensus may provide policymakers greater scope to choose among the range of credible sources of advice, allowing them to select the risk assessment and policy prescriptions that coincide with their political purposes.[17]

Richard Topf explains that the degree to which scientific advice and ultimately the governmental policy are regarded as legitimate may rest on the legitimacy of the processes. Governments need to be seen taking expert advice, but how, why and from whom they accept advice are important. Political culture and constitutional factors determine the legitimate ways to receive information and advice.[18] Micheal Saward concurs:

---

15 The European Commission provides executive functions for the EU. It is responsible for drafting legislation for consideration by the Council of Ministers and the European Parliament, and subsequently drafting, administering and monitoring regulatory compliance of EU legislation.

16 Commission of the European Communities (hereafter Commission), *Final Scientific Report of the Committee for Veterinary Medicinal Products*, Documents No. III/3006-7/93 FINAL (January 23, 1993).

17 Michael Saward, "Advice, Legitimacy and Nuclear Safety in Britain," in Anthony Barker and B. Guy Peters, eds., *The Politics of Expert Advice* (Pittsburgh, PA: University of Pittsburgh Press, 1993), p. 74.

18 Richard Topf, "Conclusion, Advice to Governments – Some Theoretical and Practical Issues," in B. Guy Peters and Anthony Barker, eds., *Advising West European Governments; Inquiries, Expertise and Public Policy* (Pittsburgh, PA: University of Pittsburgh Press, 1993), p. 190.

...On issues which are both technically complex and politically or morally contentious, where little grasp of (or even interest in) the strictly technical questions involved can be presumed in the general public, governments need first and foremost credible expert testimony. This is a necessary, though mostly not a sufficient, condition for public credibility.[19]

The BSE case provides striking evidence of political and economic interests (and issue framing) taking precedence over scientific evidence and public health concerns even within the context of scientific advisory committees. The Scientific Committee for Food (SCF) was set up by a Commission Decision in April 1974 and revised in July 1995.[20] Although most of its expert members come from within the Union, occasionally some particularly qualified non-EU expert will be invited to contribute information. The primary task of the SCF is to interpret and translate data into criteria that can be used by EU legislators. The Committee gives its opinion at the request of the Commission, but also may draw the attention of the Commission to any food safety problem on its own initiative.[21]

As might be anticipated, debate centers on the extent to which SCF is the source of objective scientific information or serves the political interests of the Commission. The Commission is not required to solicit input from the SCF, and may decline to do so in cases where it anticipates a ruling incongruent with its preferences. The Commission organizes the sessions, sets the agenda and controls the flow of information to SCF committee members. The Commission's using SCF findings as an instrument to further economic harmonization is heavily criticized. The Commission uses its agenda setting powers to introduce multiple topics for consideration in a single SCF session which may facilitate "package deals" but also places high demands on the technical expertise of Member State delegations which they are not always able to meet. The EU Commission has also been known to impose such a tight schedule that Member State delegations have insufficient time to consult with domestic constituents, formulate their positions and respond to Commission proposals. Despite these concerns, the SCF was the EU body most directly responsible for scientific assessment with regard to food safety. By 1998, the SCF has provided the Commission assessments of thousands of substances and only in one case, the safety of gelatin derived from bovine bones, did the Commission propose use of a substance that had received an unfavorable SCF assessment.

The gelatin embargo also provides good evidence of inappropriate scientific studies being used for political purposes. In early April 1996, a proposal to lift the

---

19 Saward, "Advice, Legitimacy and Nuclear Safety in Britain, p. 74.

20 Commission, *Commission decision of 16 April 1974 relating to the institution of a Scientific Committee for Food, OJ* L 136, May 20, 1974 (Luxembourg: EU Publications Office); and *Commission decision 95/273/EC of 6 July 1995 relating to the institution of a Scientific Committee for Food, OJ* L 167, July 18, 1995 (Luxembourg: EU Publications Office), p. 22.

21 Paul Gray, "The Scientific Committee for Food," in M.P.C.M. Van Schendelen, ed., *EU Committees as Influential Policymakers* (Aldershot, UK: Ashgate, 1998), pp. 69-72.

embargo on gelatin imposed by the EU to stem the BSE epidemic was presented to the Scientific Veterinary Committee (SVC) by the Director of Directorate General for Agriculture (DG VI), but was blocked by opposition from a majority of the committee delegations.   Between April 11-15, 1996, the Scientific Committee on Cosmetology, the Scientific Committee for Food, and the European Medicine Evaluation Agency all opposed ending the embargo on gelatin. Disregarding these recommendations, the Commission, citing the provisional 1994 Inveresk report which had been commissioned by the Association of Gelatin Manufacturers of Europe, persuaded the SVC that gelatin derived via certain procedures are low-risk, and obtained an SVC report favoring lifting the embargo. No one had expressed confidence in the Inveresk Report – the experiments cited related to scrapie, a sheep disease, rather than BSE; the veterinary services of DG VI were aware of the provisional and incomplete nature of the report; and, a representative of the gelatin manufacturers' association said of the Inveresk report: "the results are not clear enough and we had to extend the study."[22] The EP's 1997 Report charges that the Agriculture Commissioner or the Director of DG VI decided to lift the embargo before the several scientific committees delivered their opinions, two weeks before the Inveresk Report was submitted to the SVC. Thus, again, policy change was not a consequence of scientific input. Further, this demonstrates that policymakers may cite incomplete or inapplicable scientific evidence to persuade or justify policy preferences. The lack of consensus among the international scientific community regarding the potential risks associated with BST and BSE has allowed political decision-makers to respond to political and economic interests rather than act predominantly on scientific information and advice.

In the hormones case, Commission inquiries in the late 1990s drew upon information from in-house and Member-State scientific communities as well as Canadian, United States, World Health Organization and transnational corporate research. Divergence in EU values, goals, and framing resulted in EU scientific advisors' interpreting the emerging global pool of knowledge, admittedly characterized by high levels of uncertainty, in different ways. The high level of scientific uncertainty allowed politicians to privilege other objectives and advice such as that focusing on the dangers of genetically modified products and concern about the welfare of farm animals. The 1999 *Report of the Scientific Committee on Animal Health and Animal Welfare* encapsulates the cluster of issues that framed EU policymakers and scientists' thinking about the use of BST in dairy cattle: ethical views of and moral obligations to animals, animal welfare, the political debate, and the quality and changing nature of scientific evidence.[23]

---

22 European Parliament, *EP BSE Inquiry Report*, p. 31.

23 A sample of the discourse from the Scientific Committee on Animal Health and Animal Welfare's 1999 *Report on Animal Welfare Aspects of the Use of Bovine Somatotrophin*: "There is widespread belief that people have moral obligations to the animals with which they interact, such that poor welfare should be minimized and very poor welfare avoided. This has led to animal welfare being on the political agenda of European countries. In addition to the

Once a policy record was established, the BST case provides a robust example of negative policy feedback also failing to elicit first order learning in the form of policy change. The 1989 decision prohibiting imports of meat from animals treated with growth hormones from non-EU countries generated negative feedback in terms of its running afoul of EU trading partners and multilateral trade obligations.[24] The 1995 World Trade Organization (WTO) Agreement of Sanitary and Phytosanitary Measures allows signatories to impose sanitary protection standards that limit imports only on the basis of scientific risk assessment. Canada and the United States charged that the EU's banning use of six beef hormones[25] contravened those provisions. The WTO found in favor of the plaintiffs, and the Appellate Body found that the EU had provided:

> general studies which do indeed show the existence of a general risk of cancer; but they do
> not focus on and do not address the particular kind of risk here at stake – the carcinogenic

---

political debate, the amount of information based on the scientific study of animal welfare has increased. Scientists have added to knowledge of the physiological and behavioural responses of animals and philosophers have developed ethical views on animal welfare. All agree that decision about animal welfare should be based on good scientific evidence...." Scientific Committee on Animal Health and Animal Welfare, *Report on Animal Welfare Aspects of the Use of Bovine Somatotrophin* (March 10, 1999), p. 6.

See Chapter 1, pp. 8-9 for a discussion of experts as sources of learning. It should be emphasized that scientific advisory bodies not the same as epistemic communities. Advisory bodies at all levels are inherently political, created to inform intra- and intergovernmental negotiations and represent some combination of intergovernmental relations and scientific transnationalism. Advisory bodies funnel existing research from Member States and around the world to EU political decisionmakers, providing evaluation, meta-level assessment and analysis rather than the generation of new facts. These "switchboard operations" are constructed by science and policy needs and processes. And, as was demonstrated in the case of the SVC, advisory bodies commonly have closure mechanisms in place to end the debate and finalize their conclusions and recommendations. Jan-Stefan Fritz, "Knowledge and Policymaking for the Environment: A Critique of the Epistemic Communities Approach," Paper presented at the Annual Convention of the International Studies Association, Washington, DC, (February 16-21, 1999), pp. 17, 20.

24 While negative feedback was conspicuous in the form of Canadian, US and World Trade Organization condemnation of the EU ban on imports, it appears that more diffuse and ambiguous positive feedback may have been forthcoming in the form of public opinion. In 1996, Bijman informed that although no international comparative studies exist on how EU consumers might react to BST-derived dairy products, in 1991 and 1993, EUROBAROMETER studies of public attitudes towards biotechnology included questions about knowledge and risk perception regarding biotechnology and genetic engineering. The public is more likely to accept genetic engineering in micro-organisms and plants than animals. The combining of biotechnology and animals in BST may raise concern in the average consumer. Jos Bijman, "Recombinant Bovine Somatotropin in Europe and the USA," *Biotechnology and Development Monitor* vol. 27 (1996), pp. 2-5.

25 Estradiol-17*B*, progesterone, testoterone, zeranol, trenbolone acetate and melengestrol acetate.

or genotoxic potential of the residues of those hormones found in meat derived from cattle to which the hormones had been administered for growth promotion purposes...those general studies are in other words relevant but do not appear to be sufficiently specific to the case at hand.[26]

In February 1998, the WTO's Dispute Settlement Body adopted the reports of the Appellate Body and Investigatory Panel as modified by the Appellate Body Report regarding EU meat and meat products hormones. In response to these negative findings, and in an effort to respond specifically to the WTO's finding that general studies are an inadequate basis for the import bans, the Commission commissioned 17 new studies,[27] and requested the Scientific Committee on Veterinary Measures relating to Public Health (SCVPH) to conduct hormone- and residue-specific risk assessment for the six hormones in question on the basis of existing data and to review EU legislation by April 1999. The Commission stated that in addition to scientific data, SCVPH risk assessment should take into account the difficulties of control, inspection and enforcement of the requirements of good veterinary practice, and three particular EU interests: a) maintaining a high level of protection for consumers' health; b) establishing objective, transparent and reliable procedures for the evaluation of risk (which alludes to EU desires to promote process and organizational legitimacy), and c) avoiding WTO members' erecting reciprocal barriers against EU exports.[28]

The report of the Commission's SCVPH Committee pointed out the incongruities in EU framing of the issue relative to that of the global community, raised questions concerning the scientific methodologies of existing hormonal research, and pointed out multiple areas of scientific uncertainty surrounding the issue. In the end, the committee found that only:

> In the case of 17B [is] there is a substantial body of recent evidence suggesting that it be considered as a complete carcinogen, as it exerts both tumour initiating and tumour promoting effects. The data available does [do] not allow a quantitative estimate of the risk.[29]

---

26 Commission, *Communication from the Commission to the Council and the European Parliament, WTO Decisions Regarding the EC Hormones Ban* COM (1999) 31 final. Brussels (February 10, 1999), p. 1.

27 While the commissioning of research provides evidence of the Commission's desire to enhance information about the issue, making the causal connection between basic research and first-order learning is difficult due to the fact that research outcomes are uncertain and diffuse and long time horizons are involved. See James G. March, "Exploration and Exploitation in Organizational Learning," *Organization Science* vol. 2 (1991), reprinted in James G. March, *The Pursuit of Organizational Intelligence* (Malden, MA: Blackwell Publishers Inc., 1999), p. 117.

28 Commission, *Communication from the Commission to the Council and the European Parliament, WTO Decisions Regarding the EC Hormones Ban*, pp. 2-3.

29 Commission, *Opinion of the Scientific Committee on Veterinary Measures relating to Public Health, Assessment of Potential Risks to Human Health from Hormone Residues in*

Operating on the basis of the precautionary principle, the EU elected to continue its ban, despite these scientific findings and its contravention of WTO agreements. Again, the EU failed to adjust policy in response to scientific input and negative policy feedback.

BSE's highly emotive and politicized nature clearly affected EU willingness to learn, and evidence suggests that the EU actually engaged in denial and avoidance behaviors during the early years of the crisis. For example, when due to problems with animal identification and inspections, the Assistant Director-General for Agriculture presented a proposal drawn up by its veterinary services permitting exports of British beef only in deboned form to an extraordinary meeting of the EU Council, June 6-7, 1990, he later reported that: "The reaction has been quite rough and we have not got any longer the possibility of discussing it because we had been excluded from the meeting room." Although participants at the extraordinary meeting noted that slaughterhouse inspections would be undertaken in the UK, EU veterinary inspectors were not invited to publish their findings or present them to the EU Council or Scientific Veterinary Committee.[30] Except for regulation on embryos, legislative activities to address BSE were suspended between 1990 and 1994. The EP's 1997 Report reproved the Council for not actively seeking to know about the problem and for hiding behind scientific committees: "There was also an attitude of 'benign neglect' of the issue (a willingness to let a British problem be dealt with by the British) on the part of the Commission and, through the veterinary committees, by the other Member States."[31] The EP opined that EU BSE legislation was adopted without benefit of the available data and scientific knowledge of the disease. It may therefore be generalized that within certain contexts, policymakers may very well seek to avoid learning, perpetuate scientific uncertainty, and may not expend all efforts to ensure that legislate is based on current scientific understanding. In Chapter 1 (pp. 10-22) it is noted that rapid, frequent, regular and substantive information flows among the various divisions of an organization are essential to provide decision-makers the best available information and understanding. Further, organizational norms such as openness, trust, dialogue and cooperation are important to creating an administrative culture that facilitates productive learning. However, it is also pointed out that crises may or may not facilitate productive learning. This case suggests that rather than fostering first order learning, the BSE crisis overwhelmed EU decision-makers.

While the evidence suggests that the EU did not achieve first order learning as a consequence of scientific input and negative policy feedback, policy change was clearly affected by decision-making processes among the various EU bodies, i.e.

Bovine Meat and Meat Products XXIV/B3/SC4 (April 30, 1999).

30 European Parliament, *EP BSE Inquiry Report*, pp. 19-20.

31 European Parliament, *EP BSE Inquiry Report*, p. 8. As the Parliamentary inquiry proceeded, the Commission admitted that it had been pressured by the British government to exclude BSE checks in the general slaughterhouse inspections carried out between June 1990 and May 1994.

first order learning occurred as a consequence of "learning by doing" and/or learning by discourse. March and Lounamaa argue that simultaneous learning on multiple levels within an organizational hierarchy may reduce overall learning effectiveness due to specialization.[32] However, although most policy drafting occurred within the Commission, other EU bodies also grappled with the hormone issues as participants in the legislative processes, and a dialogue ensued among the various units. The agenda was also expanded to include endocrine-disrupting chemicals in general, which suggests that organization's understanding of the issues was becoming broader and more sophisticated. In October 1998, the EU Parliament passed a resolution on endocrine disrupting chemicals.

The Commission customarily seeks to educate other EU bodies regarding salient issues by means of "communications," and, in December 1999 in response to the Parliament's resolution, the Commission issued *Public Health: Effects of Endocrine Disrupters on Human and Animal Health.*[33] The Parliament's Committee on Industry, External Trade, Research and Energy mulled over these matters. On April 18, 2000, the Committee on the Environment, Public Health and Consumer Policy (hereafter the Environment Committee) held public hearings and received submissions from interested parties on the matter, and in July 2000 the Environment Committee issued its own response to the Commission *Communication.*[34]

Commission- and European Parliament-orchestrated conferences also provide a forum for consultation with experts beyond the EU. For example, the June 24-25, 1996 BSE inquiry convened by the European Parliament heard testimony and took evidence from several external experts including the General Director of the World Organization for Animal Health (*Office International des Epizootes*, OIE), the Director of the World Health Organization's (WHO) Division of Emerging and other Communicable Disease Surveillance and Control, and a member of the technical committee of the European Renderers Association in Rotterdam.[35]

---

32 James G. March with Pertti H. Lounamaa, "Adaptive Coordination of a Learning Team," reprinted in James G. March, *The Pursuit of Organizational Intelligence* (Malden, MA: Blackwell Publishers Inc, 1999), p. 158.

33 COM (1999) 706- C5-0107/2000-2000/2071 (COS).

34 European Parliament, Committee on the Environment, Public Health and Consumer Policy, *Report on the Commission Communication to the Council and the European Parliament on a Community Strategy for Endocrine Disrupters – a Range of Substances Suspected of Interfering with the Hormone Systems of Humans and Wildlife* COM (1999) 706-C5-0107/2000 – 2000/2071 (COS), Final A5-1097/2000.

35 The General Director noted that the OIE, with 143 member countries and headquartered in Paris, is the only world organization devoted to animal health. OIE assets include a permanent staff of 30, an estimated 100 expert volunteers, and 104 reference laboratories. The organization's objectives include global surveillance of 104 animal diseases (including BSE), and the harmonization of regulations relating to trade in animals and animal products through the OIE International Health Code. The EU and World Health Organization participate in the OIE's fact-finding meetings.

Most EU analysts agree that public hearings and conferences serve some combination of learning and more overtly political purposes. With regard to conferences devoted to water legislation, Jeremy Richardson writes: "[T]he conference forces the disparate members of the issue network/constellation to be more aware of each other's positions. Second, it helped the Commission define what the political and technical issues were." The conference yielded lists of issues to be resolved rather than agreed-upon solutions; it was "a complex process of mutual learning" as well as political persuasion. The Commission operates under the assumption that "if all relevant voices have been heard and if proposals can indeed attract a broad coalition of support, then dealing with the CM [Council of Ministers]...ought to be somewhat less troublesome."[36]

While the beef hormone case provides little evidence of learning strictly derived from scientific information and the input of scientific committees, feedback in the form of negative feedback from the WTO provided a strong impetus for the organization to commission new research and revisit the scientific data and its policies. Intraorganizational efforts to grapple with the issue and dialogue among the various EU units, suggest that "learning by doing" was the strongest source of first order learning with regard to hormone issues. March and his colleagues argue that "Learning [is] embedded richly in the taking of action, rather than simply in considering its ultimate consequences."[37] Lessons derived from the policy experience itself are proximate in terms of time and those involved. Decision-making involves such activities as soliciting information about the problem; grappling with the complexities of its causal relationships; framing the policy issue; identifying the various interests involved; calculating the costs and benefits; and negotiating, devising and articulating policy solutions. Organizations discover values, aspirations and identities while making decisions, and are more likely learn from the process than actual policy outcomes and feedback.

One might hypothesize that the emotive content of food quality issues and the crisis associated with the threat to public health associated with BSE would create an environment wherein attention is mobilized and learning would occur across a broad

---

The WHO initiated regular monitoring of BSE's potential risk to human health in 1986. It convened four expert meetings in 1991, 1993, 1994 (with the OIE) and 1995. Following the report of ten cases of the new variant of CJD in the UK in March 1996, the WHO convened two consultations to review the public health issues related to BSE and the new variant of CJD. European Parliament, Committee on the Environment, Public Health and Consumer Protection and Committee on Agriculture and Rural Development of the European Parliament, *Bovine Spongiform Encephalopathy (BSE) - (Creutzfeldt-Jakob Disease) CJD: Our Health at Risk?* Info Memo: Hearing No. 17 (June 24-25, 1996), Brussels, pp. 2-4, 8-9.

36 Jeremy Richardson, "EU Water Policy" in Hans Bressers, Laurence O'Toole, Jr. and Jeremy Richardson, eds., *Networks for Water Policy, A Comparative Perspective* (London: Frank Cass, 1995), pp. 146, 152-156.

37 James G. March with Lee S. Sproull and Michal Tamuz, "Learning from Samples of One or Fewer," *Organization Science* vol. 2 (1991), reprinted in James G. March, *The Pursuit of Organizational Intelligence* (Malden, MA: Blackwell Publishers Inc, 1999), pp. 139, 141.

spectrum of actors.[38] Although it is difficult to tease out their independent impact, the BSE case demonstrates that when confronted with high levels of scientific uncertainty, potentially devastating consequences and public agitation generated by potential threats to public health, policymakers may instead refuse to learn. They may exhibit denial and avoidance behaviors such as refusing to adequately fund research and investigations into the problem with the intended or unintended consequence of perpetuating scientific uncertainty. Also, instead of scientific committees serving as sources of learning, officials may transfer the issue to scientific committees to delay decisions or shift responsibility for dealing with the problem to actors and venues less susceptible to public scrutiny.

Second and Third Order Learning: Changes in Issue Framing, Policy Goals, Norms and Paradigms

By definition, second and third order learning entail more profound and sophisticated forms of learning, including changes in the organization's norms and paradigm, how the specific issue is framed (its structures of meaning), and transformation of objectives and policies. Although a complete revamping of the organization's paradigm would be a rare event, the BST and BSE cases provide evidence of second order learning in the form of a gradual transformation and expansion of the way the issues were framed and policy change. Beginning in the 1980s, the EU deliberated and initiated legislation forbidding use of growth-enhancing hormones, and, as the technology evolved, in 1994, moved to deter use of milk-production enhancing BST. By 1999 the Commission and the EU Parliament were discussing investigating the effects of more than 560 suspected endocrine disrupting substances identified by Commission consultants.[39]

Over an even shorter time period, the BSE case evolved from being framed as an economic and agricultural issue to be dealt with by the British to one of an EU-wide human health crisis and crisis of organizational legitimacy. Levitt and March contend that transformation of the framing of historical events, including the redefinition of events, concepts and alternatives through consciousness raising and culture building, is more important to what is learned than the actual events themselves.[40]

With regard to use of hormones in cattle, the EU began discussing the need for framework legislation to integrate what the organization has learning from previous

---

38 March with Sproull and Tamuz, "Learning from Samples of One or Fewer," p. 149.

39 In 1999, EU experts had surveyed the available literature on only 116 of these approximately 560 substances, most of which were high production volume chemicals and some metals. European Parliament, *Opinion of the Committee on Industry, External Trade, Research and Energy for the Committee on the Environment, Public Health and Consumer Policy on Public Health: Effects of Endocrine Disrupters on Human and Animal Health (Communication)*, COM (1999) 706- C5-0107/2000-2000/2071 (COS), p. 15.

40 Levitt and March, "Organizational Learning," p. 324.

legislative experiences, render congruent the various existing regulations to correct inconsistencies, to adjust the legislation to recent scientific understanding, and to ameliorate implementation difficulties. And the 1997 Commission *Green Paper on General Principles of European Foodstuff Legislation* proposed a framework directive on foodstuffs legislation, and revision and consolidation of the directive on food labeling, among other things.[41] It cannot be said that the EU underwent paradigmatic change as a consequence of these admittedly traumatic experiences. While change was obvious in issue framing and policy content, the paradigm of the body remained devoted predominantly to enhancing economic integration and growth.

Fourth-Order Learning: Reflexivity and Learning How to Learn

Evidence that an organization not only responds to short-term policy feedback and information and undergoes significant policy change, but is also capable of reflecting upon the factors and activities that facilitate and deter learning constitutes fourth-order learning. Activities such as putting into place organizational structures, programs and processes to draw upon internal and external sources of expertise and undertake "pure" research into food-related areas and generalizing from food-related learning to other issue areas are examples of an organization's increasing its capacity to learn and engaging in more sophisticated levels of learning. Within the context of these EU cases, this fourth order learning is discernible in organizational investigation and discussion documents, the restructuring of existing and creation of new research bodies, and the funding of long-term research. To a significant extent, the inquiries, communications, reports and multi-year planning instruments emanating from the various EU bodies are vehicles whereby their authors and audiences reflect upon the nature of the issues, evolving knowledge and policy experience, their successes and failures, and their aspirations for the future. The 1997 European Parliament *BSE Inquiry Report* and the Commission's 1997 *Foodstuffs. Green Paper: The General Principles of Food Law in the European Union* and 2000 *White Paper on Food Safety*[42] are robust examples of this category of reflective instruments.

To illustrate, the 1997 green paper reflected upon the EU's previous experience, articulated general principles to guide subsequent legislation, and stimulated public consultation and dialogue on the future of EU food legislation. It sets out major policy objectives and six regulatory goals, as well as posing six clusters of questions.

---

41 Commission, *Foodstuffs* (2001), <http://europa.eu.int/scadplus/leg/en/lvb/l21060. htm>, last accessed June 20, 2005.

42 European Parliament, *EP BSE Inquiry Report*; Commission, *Foodstuffs. Green Paper: The General Principles of Food Law in the European Union*, 1997. Commission, *White Paper on Food Safety*. COM (1999) 719 final, Brussels (January 12, 2000). The 2000 *White Paper on Food Safety* announced a comprehensive package of 84 measures, the cornerstone of which was the Regulation on General Food Law and the establishment of the European Food Safety Agency.

One of the latter well articulates the multiple competing and potentially contradictory policy goals: "How can we reconcile legislative simplification, subsidiarity, a high level of protection, and the smooth operation of the internal market and the common agricultural policy?"[43]

In addition to presenting general principles for foodstuff legislation, the green paper lays down three broad guidelines on control and inspection: introduction of risk assessment procedures so as to establish monitoring priorities, reorganization of monitoring operations to encompass the entire food chain, and introduction of procedures for auditing the Member States' monitoring systems. Two of seven points that emerge pertain to activities designed to enhance input from scientists and the wider society: "adequate consultation of the socio-economic partners when drafting legislation is the foundation of transparency;" and, "it must be possible to adapt legislation to scientific and technical progress quickly by means of simplified procedures…"[44]

Most analysts would contend that rearranging organizational structures may be an important indicator of second-order learning. The EU's reorganization of its scientific committee system indicates that they were identified as a source of policy failure, but this change also aimed at increasing the organization's future capacity to learn. In November 1997, after its traumatic experience with the BSE crisis, the Commission completely restructured its scientific advisory system to include eight new scientific committees and a Scientific Steering Committee. In May 1999, it was reported that these new scientific committees had generated approximately 150 scientific opinions. Although the committees were assigned only an advisory role, many of their opinions served as a basis for Commission legislative proposals. The scientific committees were consulted whenever a legal act required it, and were increasingly consulted on a voluntary basis. They also acted as a "whistleblower," directing the Commission's attention to new risks for consumer health.[45]

The Standing Committee for Foodstuffs (StCF) was established by the Council of Ministers to institutionalize intraorganizational cooperation with regard to implementation of food legislation. As part of the restructuring, the Commissioner for Consumer Affairs appoints StCF members. By 1998, more than 30 directives and regulation had been referred to the StCF and the committee had taken on more than 117 different categories of mostly regulatory tasks. Scientific standards and consumer protection are the normative principles around which committee discourse and decisions occur. Legislation outlining its role notes the necessity for consulting the most recently available scientific evidence and its mandate focuses exclusively on the regulatory need to meet safety requirements on a case-by-case basis. Despite

---

43 Commission, *Foodstuffs.*

44 Commission, *Product Safety, Consumer Health and Food Safety,* and *Foodstuffs. Green Paper: The General Principles of Food Law in the European Union.*

45 Directorate General for Health and Consumer Protection (DGXXIV) of the European Commission, *Midterm Review of the Commission's Scientific Advisory System,* Brussels (May 21, 1999), p. 1.

some evidence of Commission efforts to control the work of the StCF, votes in the StCF are unanimous less than 50% of the time. Of 25 votes analyzed by Neyer, 24% were disputed but resulted in positive votes and 8% of Commission proposals were rejected.[46] In 1999, DGXXIV (Health and Consumer Protection) undertook a "Midterm Review of the Commission's Scientific Advisory System," to monitor the effectiveness of the new system.

Creation of the new European Food Safety Agency (EFSA) via Regulation 178/2002 in January 2002 also enhances EU capacity for future analysis and learning. The EFSA is now responsible for scientific assessment of food safety issues previously undertaken by the Commission. Its mandate covers all stages of food production and supply, from production to the safety of animal feed to the supply of food to the consumers. It will gather data and remain abreast of scientific developments around the world. The European Commission, Parliament and Member States can refer cases to the EFSA, but it may also act independently. The 164 members of the EFSA's Scientific Committee and eight panels[47] are appointed for three-year, renewable terms. In addition to the panels, the EFSA will have its own scientific staff and the support of the Member States' food safety organizations. In June 2003, the EFSA had 35 full-time staff persons, but personnel resources were expected to eventually rise to between 200-300.[48]

It was noted previously that funding long-term research does little to facilitate short-term first and second order learning because basic research yields more diffuse and less certain outcomes over longer time horizons. However, research programs represent capacity for future learning. With regard to bovine hormones, the Fourth European Framework Programme for Research, Technology and Development provided funding for research mostly on environmental aspects of endocrine disrupters (EDs) and began to investigate links between EDs and human health. One project addressed the possibility that exposure to EDs may lower human sperm counts and increase testicular cancer. Another developed a bioassay to detect EDs in the environment. Progress made under the Fourth European Framework Programme was outlined in the report *Indocrine Disrupters, How to Address the Challenge?* issued as the proceedings of a Joint Conference of the European Commission, DG XI, and the Austrian Presidency in Vienna, November 18-19, 1998. Under the Fifth

---

46 Jurgen Neyer, "The Standing Committee for Foodstuffs: Arguing and Bargaining in Comitology," in M.P.C.M Van Schendelen, ed., *EU Committees as Influential Policymakers* (Aldershot, UK: Ashgate, 1998), p. 150.

47 The EFSA panels are as follows: food additives, and processing aids and materials in contact with food; substances used in animal food; plant health and protection products; genetically-modified organisms; dietetic products, nutrition and allergies; biological hazards; contaminants in the food chain; and animal health and welfare. European Information Service, "Food Safety: European Authority Up and Running," *European Report* (June 4, 2003), Section No. 2781, pp. 1-2.

48 European Information Service, "Food Safety;" Section 2781 and "Food Safety" Section 2787. The EFSA was allocated a budget of E8.2 million in 2003. "Euro 8m Budget 'Insufficient' Warns Food Authority Chief," *European Voice* vol. 8 (December 19, 2002).

European Framework Programme, a new project funded under the auspices of the "Environment and Health" portion of the Quality of Life Programme attempted to identify the dietary and environmental factors responsible for male urogenital malformations and low sperm counts. Additional research was funded between 1999-2001 in both the Quality of Life and the environment programs.[49]

Conclusion

Learning does not provide the exclusive explanation for policy outcomes, but there is little doubt that three orders of learning are discernible in EU decision-making over time with regard to these cases. Although the literature commonly asserts that first order learning is most commonly experienced by an organization and that more sophisticated levels of learning are rare,[50] these EU cases also provide strong evidence of second- and fourth-order learning. This is likely due to the fact that for years, the EU failed to respond to scientific input and negative feedback with significant first-order learning, thus, necessitating more profound levels of learning over the long-term.

Although the novelty and scientific uncertainty associated with these issues deprived the organization of robust immediate previous policy experience and definitive scientific advice, the EU exhibited a mixed record with regard to proximate policy feedback. For example, it did not tend to respond to such feedback as was available, as in the BST case, scientific advice from the Committee for Veterinary Medicinal Products to allow herd trials and negative feedback from the WTO judgment. Instead the legislation that emerged incrementally over the roughly two decades involved appears more a consequence of economic motivations and cultural preferences. EU scientific advisers availed themselves of information from the transnational scientific community and corporations, but when they interpreted this data within dissimilar frames of reference, they drew diametrically opposition conclusions from the data. The BSE case demonstrated that some combination of economic interests, power of the agricultural lobby, scientific uncertainty and fear of public panic actually led to the organization's avoiding soliciting information and policy feedback. The BSE case also provided policymakers ample negative feedback in terms of the public health concerns, the cost of destroying herds,[51]

---

49 European Parliament, *Opinion of the Committee on Industry, External Trade, Research and Energy for the Committee on the Environment, Public Health and Consumer Policy on Public Health*, p. 14; European Parliament, *Report on the Commission Communication to the Council and the European Parliament on a Community Strategy for Endocrine Disrupters – a Range of Substances Suspected of Interfering with the Hormone Systems of Humans and Wildlife*, pp. 7, 9.

50 See, for example, Ernst B. Haas, *When Knowledge Is Power: Three Models of Change in International Organizations* (Berkeley, CA: University of California Press, 1990).

51 By October 2000, the new variant Creutzfeldt-Jakob had claimed the lives of 80 persons in Britain and infected at least five more in Britain and France. The crisis was

lost trade opportunities, and in-fighting among the Member States had called into question the legitimacy of the organization's free-trade mission. High levels of negative feedback may result in policy paralysis and denial rather than productive learning. Thus, most first order learning derived from "learning by doing" rather than from policy feedback and scientific advice. However, the BSE crisis eventually facilitated second and fourth order learning. March explains that it is difficult to match the powerful effects of crises for learning; the drama mobilizes attention and learning across a broad spectrum of actors.[52] The Chernobyl accident provides a further excellent example of this phenomenon; the EU established the European Environment Agency at least in part as a consequence of this event.

An explanation for the occurrence of the unusual degree of second- and fourth-order learning may be found in the nature of the issues. Because these novel issues represented an immediate threat to human health, and were characterized by high levels of scientific uncertainty, the organization was simply forced to alter the framing, norms, objectives and policies surrounding the issue. The consequences in the BSE case were so devastating, the organization was forced to subject itself to inquiries, to adjust institutional structures to address perceived institutional weaknesses, and to enhance its long-term capacity to learn. Among the several interesting conclusions that may be drawn from these cases are that organizations facing novel, highly controversial issues, fraught with high levels of scientific uncertainty may actively seek to avoid first order learning. While organizations may avoid some sources of first order learning (for example, responding to policy feedback and scientific feedback), it is difficult to avoid "learning by doing." However, insufficient or unproductive first order learning increases the likelihood that the organization will be forced to engage in higher order learning in response to crisis conditions.

---

estimated to have cost the British government £4 billion. In February 2001, the European Union announced several new anti-BSE measures at a cost of £971 million.

52 March with Sproull and Tamuz, "Learning from Samples of One or Fewer," p. 149.

Chapter 3

The US Congress and the Cuban Embargo: Analysis of a Learning Process

Paolo Spadoni

It is widely acknowledged that the United States (US) embargo against Cuba, first established in the early 1960s and tightened repeatedly since, has failed to promote fundamental political and economic reforms in the Caribbean island. In addition, it has failed to hasten the demise of Fidel Castro's government while reinforcing Cuban authorities' arguments that the United States promotes economic deprivation in Cuba and seeks to constrain its sovereignty.

In the last few years, economic sanctions against Cuba have been under fire in the US Congress. An increasing number of lawmakers have pushed for *rapprochement* with the Castro government and lifting of some of the restrictions on trade. In October 2000, Congress passed a resolution that allows direct commercial exports of food and medicines to Cuba for the first time in almost four decades. It should be noted that a clause in the final version of the bill prohibits US companies and financial institutions from providing credit for such transactions, thus obligating Cuban authorities to complete their purchases with cash or through third-country financing. Enraged by that restriction, Cuba initially said it would not buy food until the embargo was completely lifted. However, after hurricane Michelle caused widespread damage to the island in November 2001, the Castro government decided to take advantage of the law and buy American products. Since shipments to Havana began in December 2001, total US food sales to the island have been valued at approximately $800 million,[1] making Cuba an increasingly attractive export market for US agricultural firms.

This is a case study on how organizational leaders learn. While drawing insights from several scholars, its hypotheses mostly derive from Jack Levy's work on individual learning[2] and his view of experience-induced changes of beliefs among national policymakers as the most appropriate indicator of learning. To what extent is Congressional leaders' learning the source of changes in US policy toward Cuba, and how does this learning occur? Is there empirical evidence that US Congressmen have changed their beliefs about the role and usefulness of economic sanctions as a

---

1   The figure refers to sales between December 2001 and January 2005. Statistics on US food exports to Cuba are available at < http://www.fas.usda.gov>.

2   Jack S. Levy, "Learning and Foreign Policy: Sweeping a Conceptual Minefield," *International Organization* vol. 48 (1994), pp. 279-312.

tool of foreign policy? And finally, did changes of beliefs lead to changes in policy and new patterns of behavior? Providing answers to these questions is important for two main reasons. First, it serves the general debate on the use of economic sanctions by showing how legislators of a sanctioning country evaluate the results of their policy toward a target state. Second, it allows us to identify a potential learning process and test some theoretical assumptions on political learning among policymakers.

Most studies in political science conclude that economic sanctions do not work, at least in the sense of bringing about a desired change in the policy of the target countries. Sanctions often entail tremendous economic costs to the latter (and to a certain extent to the sanctioning country), but fail to change the political behavior of their leaders. Scholars such as Hufbauer and his co-authors, with a generally optimistic view, contend that sanctions succeed in about one-third of cases.[3] On the other hand, Robert Pape's pessimistic view of sanctions holds that they succeed in at most five percent of cases.[4] Organizational learning scholars agree that learning is a process linked to the accumulation of knowledge and the observation and interpretation of experience, especially experience deriving from previous failures. To some degree, they also concur that there are different levels or complexity of learning, mostly ranging from simple adjustments of existing tactical beliefs, strategies and policies to more fundamental changes associated with transformations in the policy norms, goals or paradigms.[5]

Two main hypotheses are tested and supported by this study: First, a significant number of US legislators have indeed "learned" from experience that economic sanctions against Cuba do not serve the interests of the United States. Mostly as a result of the failure of the embargo to achieve its main objectives while seriously affecting US domestic economic interests, several Senators and Representatives have pressed for increasing trade with the island and the removal of the travel ban for US citizens. In fact, the policy of denying hard currency earnings to the Cuban government limits a powerful source of American influence because it cuts off a free flow of people, activities, and ideas between the two countries. In addition, whereas US farmers and producers face restrictions in selling their commodities to Cuba, many other countries are developing commercial and business ties with Havana and taking advantage of the lack of US competition. Second, the evidence suggests that all learning has not been translated into policy change. Although the 2000 bill on food and medicine sales represents an important change of the instruments of

---

3   Gary Clyde Hufbauer, Jeffrey J. Schott and Kimberly Ann Elliot, *Economic Sanctions Reconsidered: History and Current Policy* (Washington, DC: Institute for International Economics, 1990).

4   Robert A. Pape, "Why Economic Sanctions Do Not Work," *International Security* vol. 22 (1997), p. 93.

5   Barbara Levitt and James G. March, "Organizational Learning," *Annual Review of Sociology* vol. 14 (1988), pp. 319-340; Peter A. Hall, "Policy Paradigms, Social Learning, and the State: The Case of Economic Policymaking in Britain," *Comparative Politics* vol. 25 (1993), pp. 275-296; Levy, "Learning and Foreign Policy," pp. 279-312.

US policy toward Cuba, political factors have limited the extent of that change and prevented the legislators from implementing some of the lessons learned.

Learning Theories and Government Policymaking

Since the 1980s, theories of learning have been increasingly applied to government policymaking in the comparative politics and foreign policy literature. As a result, three major branches of political learning have evolved: psychological theories of cognitive change within decisionmakers, organizational theories of bureaucratic or corporate behavioral change, and social learning theories of policy change.[6]

What is the most appropriate unit of analysis or indicator of learning and is there more than one level or complexity of learning? The most prevalent definition of learning in the foreign policy literature involves changes in beliefs and perceptions. Levy, for example, focuses on individual decision-makers and defines learning as a change of beliefs (or the degree of confidence in one's beliefs) or the development of new beliefs, skills, or procedures as a result of the observation and interpretation of experience. He acknowledges that "learning" may occur at different levels of sophistication. "Simple learning" occurs when new information leads to a change in means but not in ends. "Complex learning" takes place when recognition of conflicts among values leads to a modification of both goals and means.[7] Tetlock has elaborated on this distinction and identifies low, intermediate, and high levels of learning in foreign policy beliefs systems. He argues that most learning takes place at the lowest level, when decision-makers reconsider their basic tactical beliefs and assumptions. Intermediate levels of learning occur when policymakers change their strategic policy beliefs and preferences, while highest levels of learning occur when policymakers change their fundamental assumptions and policy objectives after repeated strategic failures.[8]

By defining learning as any experience-induced belief change, and by stating that belief change is not always accurate and knowledge does not always translate into skills, Levy excludes criteria based on accuracy, efficiency and effectiveness. Besides a belief change, the accuracy criterion of learning requires that actors make the correct inferences from experience and acquire an improved understanding of how the world works. The more demanding effectiveness criterion assumes that actors learn only if belief change and greater accuracy also increase their ability to match means and ends. By definition, Levy contends that a change in the content of one's belief as a result of experience is both necessary and sufficient for learning

---

6   Jennifer L. McCoy, *Political Learning and Redemocratization in Latin America: Do Politicians Learn from Political Crises?* (Miami: North-South Center Press at the University of Miami, 2000), p. 2.

7   Levy, "Learning and Foreign Policy," p. 286.

8   Philip Tetlock, "Learning in U.S. and Soviet Foreign Policy: In Search of An Elusive Concept," in George W. Breslauer and Philip Tetlock, eds., *Learning in U.S. and Soviet Foreign Policy* (Boulder: Westview Press, 1991), pp. 27-31.

to take place (simple learning). However, this is not sufficient for achieving greater accuracy about the world (learning *that*); the latter, in turn, is necessary but not sufficient for facilitating the ability to achieve one's goals (learning *how*).[9]

Several scholars criticize reducing learning to an individual cognitive phenomenon requiring psychological analysis. Jennifer McCoy, for instance, argues that learning must be manifested in at least an attempt to implement lessons learned, that is, it must affect behavior by either reinforcing it or changing it.[10] Jarosz and Nye associate learning with the acquisition of knowledge or information that leads to a change in behavior. According to them, learning that does not affect behavior is not useful for developing a more general theory of foreign policy.[11] Likewise, Hall contends that learning is a deliberate attempt to adjust the goals or techniques of policy in response to past experience and new information. He also identifies three levels of learning that are the result of three different processes related to policy changes. These processes range from simple changes (adjustments) of the existing techniques or policy instruments to other kinds of changes associated with potentially more complex and radical transformations in the basic instruments of policy or its encompassing goals.[12]

Identifying levels of learning from policy changes as suggested by Hall may be misleading, given that adjustments of existing techniques or deeper transformations in the basic instruments of a policy may be determined by factors other than learning. Rather than equating learning with policy change, it is more useful to conceptualize a political learning model in terms of cognitive changes among organizational leaders that can involve either the adoption of different strategies for pursuing their original goals or the redefinition of their goals. The learning process among US Congressmen on the Cuban embargo, as demonstrated by their changes of beliefs, can be considered an "intermediate" or "strategic" level of learning as defined by Tetlock. Some US policymakers no longer believe that a policy toward Cuba based on economic sanctions would undermine the Castro government and foster democratic changes on the island. While these fundamental objectives remain virtually unaltered, they can better be achieved through engagement with Cuba that would enhance the influence of American ideas and values (change of strategic policy beliefs). In addition, policymakers' new goal to help US farmers by relaxing restrictions on food sales to Cuba suggests that the learning process is not just "simple learning" (changes in means but not in ends) as defined by Levy.

What are the factors that enhance learning among national policymakers? Is learning a consequence of policy failures, travel experience, and new information

---

9 Levy, "Learning and Foreign Policy," p. 292.

10 McCoy, *Political Learning and Redemocratization in Latin America*, p. 10.

11 William W. Jarosz and Joseph S. Nye, "The Shadow of the Past: Learning from History in National Security Decision Making," in Philip Tetlock, Jo L. Husbands, Robert Jervis Robert, Paul C. Stern and Charles Tilly, *Behavior, Society, and International Conflict* (New York: Oxford University Press, 1993).

12 Hall, "Policy Paradigms, Social Learning, and the State," p. 278.

made available by experts in the field? Levy argues that failures are more likely to lead to learning than successes, especially those failures that were either unexpected at the time or unpredictable in retrospect. Considering that success and failure are often influenced by expectation and aspiration levels rather than measured in objective terms, we can fairly expect that predictable outcomes generate fewer incentives for a change in beliefs and policy, as compared to those outcomes that fall short of one's goals.[13] A similar argument is made by March in his analysis of the myopia of learning. March contends that organizational leaders' confidence in control over outcomes leads to learning from expectations of consequences before the consequences are observed, and it leads to reinterpretation of results to make them more favorable. In these ways, learning could be misleading given that risks of failures are underestimated and confidence finds confirmation in its own imagination. In short, since organizations promote successful people to position of power and authority (rather than unsuccessful ones), it is the biases of success that are particularly relevant to decision making.[14] A clear implication of March's argument is that political leaders' confidence decreases and exploration of new strategies is triggered when failures of a policy are so evident to make a reinterpretation of its results in favorable terms difficult to justify.

By the end of the Cold War, US political leaders could fairly argue that their hard-line policy on Cuba had met with some success. Although Fidel Castro kept ruling Cuba, he was no longer able to support revolutionary movements in Latin America and Africa, and the collapse of the Soviet Union in late 1989 had put an end to its preferential relationship with Havana. In addition, the disappearance of the economic and financial system (Council for Mutual Economic Assistance, or CMEA) in which the island had been inserted for almost twenty years raised the United States' confidence on economic sanctions as an effective policy instrument. While Cuba's deep economic recession in the early 1990s can hardly be attributed to the impact of the embargo, there were reasonable expectations among US policymakers that further sanctions would undermine Cuba's attempts to reinsert itself in the international market, hasten the demise of the Castro government, and foster fundamental democratic changes in the island. However, since 1993 the Cuban economy has begun to recover, and the inability of US policy to reach its main objectives has become increasingly evident. Given that Castro remains firmly in power and very few democratic changes have been introduced in Cuba's political and economic system, several US policymakers have changed their beliefs on the embargo and pressed for a normalization of relations with Havana. This is indeed a learning process that has been triggered mostly by the failure of US policy to produce outcomes that are consistent with political leaders' expectations.

The issue of learning as a result of travel experience is not specifically addressed by Levy. Nevertheless, he argues that organizational leaders learn more from their own

---

13 Levy, "Learning and Foreign Policy," p. 305.

14 James G. March, *The Pursuit of Organizational Intelligence* (Malden MA: Blackwell Publishers Inc., 1999), p. 203.

experience than they do from the experience of others. Moreover, organizations learn only through individuals who serve in those organizations, by encoding individually learned inferences from experience into organizational routines.[15] Regarding Cuba, US Congressional leaders (especially Senators of both parties) who traveled to the island in recent years had the opportunity to observe and evaluate first-hand the results of the embargo, and that particular experience might have triggered a change of their beliefs on the role and usefulness of economic sanctions against Cuba.

The acquisition of knowledge as a result of new information available from experts is also central to the concept of learning. The literature on epistemic communities emphasizes the crucial role of new information, ideas and policy proposals provided by the scientific community that is transferred to the policy community and form the basis for "consensual knowledge." Adler notes that networks of knowledge-based experts may be able to facilitate governmental learning by providing new information and a new interpretation of reality, and by becoming actors in the process of political selection of their own ideas.[16] Similarly, Haas argues that control over knowledge and information is an important dimension of power. The diffusion of new ideas and information can lead to new patterns of behavior and prove to be an important determinant of international policy coordination.[17]

In order to be effective and highly influential, experts must have access to top policymakers. In the end, a change in behavior or action (new objectives and strategies) results not only from the circulation of new information, new ideas, and increased knowledge promoted by members of epistemic communities, but also from their interaction and negotiation with policymakers and other groups characterized by the interplay between power and knowledge.[18] Building upon Haas' argument on power competition, other scholars conclude that learning by public organizations must originate outside politics, since political competition among rival decision-makers determines changes in policy, rather than a learning process leading to improved evaluation of situations. As noted by McCoy, politicians rely for new ideas and information on scientists who work in institutional settings different from those of competitive politics.[19]

This study does not analyze the role of epistemic communities in learning processes related to US economic sanctions against Cuba. Nevertheless, it offers some evidence that new information about the impact of the embargo on US-Cuba bilateral trade has been provided in recent years by independent agencies and foundations, scholars, and specialists in various economic fields. It also points

---

15 Levy, "Learning and Foreign Policy," p. 287.

16 Emanuel Adler, "The Emergence of Cooperation: National Epistemic Communities and the International Evolution of the Idea of Nuclear Arms Control," in Peter Haas, ed., *Knowledge, Power, and International Policy Coordination* (Columbia, SC: University of South Carolina Press, 1997), p. 106.

17 Peter Haas, *Knowledge, Power, and International Policy Coordination* (Columbia, SC: University of South Carolina Press, 1997), pp. 2-3. See also Chapter 1, pp. 17-19.

18 Haas, *Knowledge, Power and International Policy Coordination*, p. 370.

19 McCoy, *Political Learning and Redemocratization in Latin America*, p. 3.

out to specific links between such experts and US Congressional leaders in order to highlight the potential impact of new information on policymakers' beliefs and actions.

Is all learning translated into policy change? What are the factors that may prevent national policymakers from implementing some lessons they have learned? Levy states that learning is neither necessary nor sufficient for policy change because not all learning is translated into changes of policy. States might alter their foreign policies not only as a result of learning, but also because of changes in the external environment, a change in political leadership, or a realignment of coalitions at the bureaucratic or societal levels.[20] More specifically, Levy contends that political struggles within and between groups will determine whose learning counts and that political or bureaucratic constraints may prevent the implementation of some lessons learned. According to him, policy entrepreneurship, which involves political maneuvering and persuasion, plays a key link between learning and policy change.[21] Similarly, Hermann recognizes that learning is not the only source of policy change; the latter is also the result of struggles for political power, changes of the attitudes of the dominant domestic constituents, and a realignment of those essential constituents.[22] In the case of Cuba, attempts to promote a wider opening toward Havana have been thwarted by anti-Castro groups in the Cuban American community and House Republican leaders. The interaction of power and knowledge factors is an essential dynamic of the learning process on the Cuban embargo and its translation into policy change. The 2000 bill on food and medicine sales to Cuba highlights the importance of coalition groups, leadership positions, maneuvers and specific interests of some policymakers (especially Cuban-Americans), and loyalties among Congressional members.

This brief review has presented some of the most common interpretations of political learning and policy changes. The remaining part of the study analyzes the recent debate in the US Congress about the role and usefulness of economic sanctions against Cuba in order to identify specific changes that may confirm or call into question these interpretations as well as provide evidence for the hypothesized learning process. However, considering that the latter has mostly been triggered by the failure of previous policies, it is useful to first recall the key events in US-Cuba relations with a particular attention to the economic sanctions promoted in the 1990s and their overarching goals.

US Economic Sanctions with Respect to Cuba

On January 7, 1959, the United States recognized the new Cuban government led by Fidel Castro, but relations quickly deteriorated. The US policy toward Cuba

---

20 Levy, "Learning and Foreign Policy," p. 290.

21 Levy, "Learning and Foreign Policy," p. 300.

22 Charles F. Hermann, "Changing Course: When Governments Choose to Redirect Foreign Policy," *International Studies Quarterly* vol. 34 (1990), pp. 7-10.

was initially a reaction to Cuba's confiscation of American properties without compensation, its alliance with the Soviet Union, and its declared intention to spread the revolution to other Latin American countries.[23]   While economic sanctions were established to punish Cuba for the expropriations, increase the cost of Cuban adventurism in Latin America (and later in Africa), and raise the cost to the Soviet Union of maintaining its new relationship with the Castro regime, the United State's ultimate goal was the economic and political isolation of Cuba.[24]

On February 7, 1962, the Kennedy administration announced a total embargo of all US trade with Cuba. On May 5, 1966, the US Congress further expanded the embargo by passing the Food for Peace Act. The act outlawed food shipments to any country that sold or shipped strategic or non-strategic goods to Cuba, except for certain circumstances in which the President could allow shipments of medical supplies and non-strategic goods. Since that time, and in spite of some efforts toward normalization with Havana during the presidency of Jimmy Carter in the late 1970s, economic sanctions against the communist island have been repeatedly intensified. On April 19, 1982, the Reagan administration reestablished the travel ban, dropped by Carter in 1977, prohibiting US citizens from spending money in Cuba, despite the fact that US courts had upheld the constitutional right to travel. That same year, it warned US subsidiaries in third countries not to exceed the limits allowed by the Treasury Department. Finally, on August 22, 1986, the US Treasury announced new measures tightening the embargo. These measures prohibited US businesses from dealing with a list of foreign firms operating in the United States, Jamaica and Panama, considered "Cuban fronts intended to break the U.S. embargo."[25]   They also included lower limits on cash and gifts Cuban Americans could send to relatives in the island as well as tighter regulations on companies that shipped food and care packages to Cuba from Cuban-Americans.

After the fall of the Soviet Union in late 1989 and the end of its special relationship with Havana, the massive amount of aid that had allowed Cuba to weather the US embargo began to dry up. Without Soviet subsidies and external markets for its main products,[26] the Cuban economy went into a deep recession. Cuban authorities were forced to develop a strategy of reinsertion into the international market by promoting

---

23 Daniel W. Fisk, "Cuba: The End of an Era," *The Washington Quarterly* vol. 24 (2001), p. 93.

24 Philip Peters, *A Policy toward Cuba that Serves U.S. Interests* (Washington, DC: The Cato Institute, 2000), p. 5.

25 Adolfa Leyva De Varona, *Propaganda and Reality: A Look at the U.S. Embargo against Castro's Cuba* (Miami: The Endowment for Cuban American Studies, 1994), p. 9.

26 At end of the 1980s, some 81% of Cuba's external commercial relations were with Soviet countries. It is also reported that Soviet subsidies and aid to Cuba averaged $4.3bn a year for the period 1986-1990. Ernesto Hernández-Cata, "The Fall and Recovery of the Cuban Economy in the 1990s: Mirage or Reality?" *International Monetary Fund Working Paper* (2001), p. 4.

timid free-market economic reforms and opening the island to foreign investment.[27] One might expect that the normalization of US international relations following the demise of the Soviet Union would favor new commercial exchanges with countries, including Cuba, previously ostracized by the superpowers' confrontation.[28] Instead, the United States tried to capitalize on Cuba's precarious economic situation. Seeing an opportunity to finally get the most out of economic sanctions that had failed for thirty years to overthrow the government of Fidel Castro, hard-liners within the US Congress and an increasingly powerful Cuban American community stepped up efforts to reinforce the embargo. Jorge Dominguez notes:

> The Cold War had turned colder in the Caribbean. Cuba was the only country governed by a communist party whose domestic political regime the United States was still committed by law and policy to replace, albeit by peaceful means.[29]

The influence exerted by domestic politics, especially the electoral context linked to the partisan bidding for Cuban American votes in the pivotal state of Florida, played a key role in promoting tougher economic measures against the Castro government. In September 1992, in the heat of the presidential campaign, a Democrat-controlled Congress approved the Cuban Democracy Act (better known as the Torricelli law).[30] The law, initially criticized but then signed by the first President George Bush a few weeks before the election, was conceived as an instrument for exerting pressure on the Cuban economy while offering positive inducements for democratic reforms in Cuba.[31] On the one hand, it permitted humanitarian donations including medical supplies after onsite verification. On the other hand, it prohibited foreign subsidiaries of US corporations from engaging in any transaction with Cuba, and any vessel from entering a US port for a period of 180 days if that vessel had handled freight in a Cuban port.

Washington enacted an even harsher package of measures against Cuba in 1996. The story of the Cuban Liberty and Democratic Solidarity Act (better known as

---

27 Cuba's response to the deteriorating economic situation was the implementation in September 1990 of an economic austerity program called "special period in time of peace." The program consisted of a series of measures aimed to conserve energy and raw materials, stimulate food production, expand markets for export and imports, attract foreign investment, and introduce some management and selective structural reforms. Foreign exchange needed to acquire imported inputs was provided on a priority base only to industries that generated foreign exchange.

28 Joaquin Roy, *Cuba, the United States, and the Helms-Burton Doctrine, International Reactions* (Gainesville, FL: University Press of Florida, 2000), p. 18.

29 Jorge I. Dominguez, "U.S.-Cuban Relations: From the Cold War to the Colder War," *Journal of Interamerican Studies and World Affairs* vol. 39 (1997), pp. 49-75.

30 Robert Torricelli, the proponent of the law, is a Senator from New Jersey (D-NJ).

31 Todd Piczak, "The Helms-Burton Act: U.S. Foreign Policy toward Cuba, the National Security Exception to the GATT and the Political Question Doctrine," *University of Pittsburgh Law Review* vol. 61 (1999), pp. 4-5.

the Helms-Burton law)[32] is very similar to that of the Torricelli law. Approval of the bill coincided with the 1996 Republican presidential primary elections in Florida and preceded just a few months the general presidential election of November of the same year. Furthermore, the conservative faction of the Cuban American community lobbied aggressively for passage of the legislation. The only real difference was Jesse Helms' new role within the US Congress.[33] The conservative Senator from North Carolina was installed as chairman of the Senate Foreign Relations Committee after the Republican electoral victory in the Congressional elections of November 1994. The Congress, mainly out of fear that Castro would seek to cure his capital crunch by selling properties expropriated from US nationals to foreign companies,[34] was successful in capitalizing on the outrage of a tragic event that occurred in early 1996. On February 24, 1996, the Helms-Burton law was rapidly approved by an overwhelming majority in both chambers after Cuban forces shot down two small planes operated by Cuban exiles over the Straits of Florida.[35] President William J. Clinton, despite concern about possible retaliations from major trade allies such as Canada, the European Union, and Mexico, signed the legislation on March 12, 1996.

Besides codifying the existing restrictions that collectively formed the US economic embargo against Cuba, Helms-Burton aimed to halt the flow of foreign investment into Cuba by creating a riskier and more uncertain business environment as well as to complicate Havana's access to external financing. The rationale was that this plan would ultimately lead to the collapse of the Cuban government or at least seriously undermine the slow but constant economic recovery witnessed by the island since its lowest point in 1993. The attempt to undermine Cuba's opening to foreign investment is linked to the possibility of lawsuits and the imposition of travel restrictions against foreign companies or other entities that "traffic" in US properties expropriated during the early days of the Revolution. The right to sue foreign companies is also granted to Cubans who became US citizens after the expropriation occurred, in an attempt to further increase the potential impact of the legislation.[36]

As reported in the next section, the strengthening of the US embargo during the 1990s has mostly failed to achieve the goals of its supporters. While acknowledging that policymakers may have incentives to conceal or distort what they have learned

---

32 The Cuban Liberty and Democratic Solidarity Act is widely referred to as the Helms-Burton law after its sponsors, Senator Jesse Helms (R-North Carolina) and Representative Dan Burton (R-Indiana).

33 Dominguez, "U.S. Cuban Relations."

34 Cuba's opening to foreign investment, initially centered in the tourist sector, was extended after 1993 to other sectors such as basic or heavy industry (mostly oil, mining and energy), light industry (manufacturing), food processing, construction, agriculture, telecommunications, real estate, and services.

35 Antroy A. Arreola, "Who's Isolating Whom? Title III of the Helms-Burton Act and Compliance with International Law," *Houston Journal of International Law* vol. 20 (1998), pp. 353-378.

36 Mark A. Groombridge, *Missing the Target, The Failure of the Helms-Burton Act* (Washington, DC: The Cato Institute, 2001), p. 3.

from experience, Levy contends that policy failures tend to trigger changes of beliefs among them by affecting the plausibility of the "lessons of history,"[37] This appears to be the case within the US Congress where, in the last few years, several legislators have reevaluated some of their beliefs and policy preferences with respect to Cuba.[38]

Sources of Learning

There is no doubt that economic sanctions with respect to Cuba enacted during the 1990s have failed to achieve their main objectives. First, while certainly having an impact on Cuba's overall economic performance, they have ultimately failed to hasten the collapse of the Castro regime. Thanks to economic adjustments introduced between 1993 and 1994 and the opening to foreign investment, the Cuban economy slowly began to recover around the mid-1990s.[39] Second, sanctions have been unable to curtail the flow of foreign capital delivered to the island,[40] promote a democratic change in the behavior of the target government, and undermine Castro's hold over the political apparatus. Third, they have galvanized the international community against the embargo. Prior to the passage of the Torricelli law, Cuba had never been able to obtain a resolution condemning US sanctions in the United Nations General Assembly. In November 1992, as a consequence of a widespread concern regarding the extraterritorial character of the US legislation, the General Assembly condemned the embargo by a vote of 59 to 3 (with 71 countries abstaining). Since then, the vote has been more lopsided with every passing year. By 1998, the governments siding with Cuba were 158. Instead of gaining international support for its policy toward the island, the United States could not be more isolated. Roy observes, "Washington had lost a public relations war."[41]

In October 2000, the US Congress passed the "Agriculture, Rural Development, Food and Drug Administration, and Related Agencies Appropriations Act of 2001." Title IX of the bill, signed into law by President Clinton a few weeks later, includes provisions that allow direct sales of US food products and medicines to Cuba for the first time since the embargo was put in place in the early 1960's. The first hypothesis of this study is that several US Congressmen have learned from the aforementioned failures and changed their beliefs regarding the role and usefulness of economic sanctions as an instrument of foreign policy. The second hypothesis is that this

---

37 Levy, "Learning and Foreign Policy," p. 305.

38 Wayne Smith, "Our Dysfunctional Cuban Embargo," *Orbis* vol. 42 (1998), pp. 533-544.

39 While decreasing at an average annual rate of 10% between 1990 and 1993, Cuba's real Gross Domestic Product averaged almost 3.3% per year for the rest of the decade and around 3.7% per year since the enactment of the Helms-Burton legislation in 1996.

40 Paolo Spadoni, "The Impact of the Helms-Burton Legislation on Foreign Investment in Cuba," *Cuba in Transition* vol. 11 (Washington, DC: Association for the Study of the Cuban Economy, 2001), p. 36.

41 Roy, *Cuba, the United States, and the Helms-Burton Doctrine*, pp. 102-103.

process had a causal impact on US policy toward Cuba, although not all learning has been translated into policy change.

According to Levy, studies of learning must incorporate research designs that allow analysts to differentiate between genuine learning and the instrumental use of history, and to avoid spurious inferences of causality between historical learning and policy preferences and decisions.[42] Considering the difficulty of this task and the number of elements that should be considered in order to carry out such a rigorous analysis of learning, this study does not claim to produce definitive results. Nevertheless, it aims to advance our understanding of the role of learning in US foreign policy toward Cuba by monitoring the behavior of Senators and Representatives over time and their votes in Congress on the use of economic sanctions. In order to assess the impact of policy failures on learning, and possibly avoid spurious relations between the latter and individual preferences, the study also presents specific cases of Congressmen whose beliefs on the embargo have recently changed. This is mostly done by comparing their public declarations before and after the enactment of the Helms-Burton legislation.

Finally, in order to support the claim that current policy changes do not reflect entirely the learning process, this study shows how proponents of a wider opening toward Cuba succumbed to the lobbying efforts of the Cuban American Community and hard-liners in Congress. The final version of the 2000 bill prohibits US financing of any sales to Cuba and establishes that potential changes of the US travel ban, previously under the jurisdiction of the executive branch, have now to be made by Congress.[43] Certainly, Senators and Representatives committed to a relaxation of US restrictions respond to particular interests, especially those of the business community. However, it seems conceivable that they have at least learned that previous policies did little to undermine the Castro government while hurting US producers prevented from exporting their products to Cuba.

Unlike Levy, I am not convinced that variations in beliefs correlated with economic interests do not constitute learning. While economic interests may trigger changes of beliefs among policymakers in relation to a specific policy, they still learn if those changes are also the result of new information made available to them. Epistemic communities can enhance learning by providing new information on a specific issue.[44] On March 15, 2000, the Committee on Ways and Means of the House of Representatives requested the US International Trade Commission (USITC) to examine and report on the economic impact of sanctions on US-Cuba bilateral trade. The Commission is an independent, nonpartisan, federal agency whose responsibility is to monitor trends in international trade matters. Economists and industry analysts of the USITC collected data from both US and Cuban sources. They also used testimonies provided by US scholars and specialists in various

---

42 Levy, "Learning and Foreign Policy," pp. 307-308.

43 Mark P. Sullivan, "Cuba: U.S. Restrictions on Travel and Legislative Initiatives in the 106th Congress," *U.S. Congressional Research Service*, October 13, 2000.

44 Haas, *Knowledge, Power, and International Policy Coordination*, p. 385.

economic fields before the USITC on September 12, 2000. The report estimates that US exports to Cuba in the absence of sanctions, based on average 1996-98 trade data, would have been approximately $658 million to $1 billion annually.[45] Another study, completed in January 2001 by the Texas A&M University for the pro-trade Cuba Policy Foundation, concludes that continuing financing restrictions on US trade with Cuba cost farmers $1.24 billion a year in lost business. Even more striking, a July 2002 study produced by the University of Colorado at Boulder predicts that the normalization of commercial relations with Cuba could represent for the United States a gain of $545.6 million in trade and the creation of 3,797 jobs in the short term as well as $1.9 billion in trade and 22,000 new jobs in the next five years.[46]

Although it is difficult to establish the impact of these findings on changes of beliefs among US policymakers, we cannot exclude such a possibility. Some legislators who had previously supported economic sanctions now argue that they are damaging US producers. For instance, Senator Pat Roberts (R-KS), who voted in favor of the Helms-Burton law in 1996 (when he was still a Representative), has become a leading advocate for the removal of trade and travel restrictions on Cuba. In early April 2002, commenting on the Bush administration's decisions on steel tariffs and the refusal to grant visas to some Cuban officials needing to travel to the United States to purchase US grain, Roberts noted:

> American agriculture could be hit hard with retaliation over the administration's decision to put tariffs on steel imports. Cuba, which was opened just a year ago for exports of U.S. farm products, was a bright spot in an otherwise grim world trade picture. Since November of last year, Cuba signed contracts to buy nearly $73 million in U.S. agriculture products. Recent studies indicate that will quickly grow to $1.2 billion, making Cuba one of our most important trade partners.

He then concluded: "the United States is exploring agricultural trade relations with other nations that pose a much greater security [risk] than does Cuba. With Cuba, we have an opportunity to help US farmers, feed hungry people and spread the seeds of democracy."[47]

The case of Senator Byron Dorgan (D-ND), who had voted for both the Torricelli and the Helms-Burton law, underlines the importance of trade with Cuba for US producers and, perhaps, of new information on the impact of the embargo on American products. In early October 1995, commenting on the Helms-Burton law on the Senate floor, Dorgan stated:

---

45 Jonathan R. Coleman, "The Economic Impact of U.S. Sanctions with Respect to Cuba," *Cuba in Transition* (Washington, DC: Association for the Study of the Cuban Economy, 2001), p. 87.

46 For further information on US trade potential with Cuba, see < www.ciponline.org/cuba/trade>.

47 Senate Press Release, "Senator Roberts: Administration's Cuba Policy Undermines Trade Promotion Authority Bill," Washington D.C. (April 11, 2002). http://www.lawg.org/roberts.htm.

Frankly, Fidel Castro and Cuba are not the most important things in the lives of people I represent... I was in North Dakota all last week because the Senate had no votes last week. I did not hear one North Dakotan talk to me about Cuba. It does not mean Cuba is not interesting or important; it is that they are interested in the issues that affect their daily lives such as farm programs, Medicare, and so on.[48]

In 2001, after successfully leading the effort in Congress to lift the ban on US sales of food to Cuba, Dorgan declared: "The best strategy is to open up Cuba to U.S. trade and travel. It's potentially a $1 billion market for food products that Canadians and Europeans and others are able to serve and we're not. That doesn't make much sense to me."[49] In addition, a declaration by Dorgan in August 2002 highlights a new scenario for North Dakotan producers hardly foreseeable in 1995. Announcing Cuba's interest in buying dry peas from his state, the Senator said: "Once again we have evidence of how important this new market can be for North Dakota family farmers. There is clearly a desire to buy and a recognition that what we have to sell is of highest quality."[50]

Overall, Roberts and Dorgan's declarations suggest that new information made available by experts might have had an impact on Congressional leaders' beliefs. With many countries taking advantage of the lack of US competition, the negative effects of the embargo on US producers (as reported by experts in the field) have become increasingly evident. For example, in late March 2003 the US Senate announced the creation of a bipartisan Cuba Working Group, which plans to focus its efforts on trade and travel restrictions. Both Roberts and Dorgan are members.[51] In the letter announcing the launch of the initiative, the US Senators stated:

> The sanction policy of the United States has been ineffective since it was adopted in 1962. Other nations trade with Cuba, and their producers benefit from that trade. The U.S. policy places our farmers, workers, and companies at an international competitive disadvantage. By some estimates, the United States loses out on an export market of nearly $1 billion per year.[52]

---

48 Senate Record, S14998-15000. "Cuban Liberty and Democratic Solidarity [Libertad] Act of 1995." U.S. Senate (October 11, 1995).

49 "Interview with Byron Dorgan," *Newsweek* (September 7, 2001), <http://www.ibike. org/cuba/ofac/010817-dorgan.htm>.

50 Senate Press Release, "Dorgan Says Cuba Interested in Buying Additional Peas from North Dakota," (August 7, 2002), <http://dorgan.senate.gov/newsroom/record. cfm?id=186307>.

51 The ten members of the Senate Working Group on Cuba are: Max Baucus (D-MT); Byron Dorgan (D-ND); Maria Cantwell (D-WA); Blanche Lincoln (D-AR); Jeff Bingaman (D-NM), Michael Enzi (R-WY); Chuck Hagel (R-NE); Norm Coleman (R-MN); Jim Talent (R-MO); Pat Roberts (R-KS). The House of Representatives also formed a Cuba Working Group in 2002. By mid-2003 the group had 50 members, equally divided between Democrats and Republicans.

52 Center for International Policy. "U.S. Senate Announces Cuba Working Group" (March 23, 2003).

Table 3.1 Votes of Select US Legislators on Economic Sanctions against Cuba

Legislator	Torricelli Law 1992	Helms-Burton Law, 1996	Food/Medicine Sales to Cuba, 2000
Senator			
Ashcroft, John (R-MO)	-	Yes	Yes
Akaka, Daniel (D-HI)	Yes	No	Yes
Baucus, Max (D-MT)	No	Yes	Yes
Burns, Conrad (R-MT)	Yes	Yes	Yes
Conrad, Kent (D-ND)	Yes	Yes	Yes
Daschle, Tom (D-SD)	Yes	Yes	Yes
Dorgan, Byron (D-ND)	Yes	Yes	Yes
Durbin, Dick (D-IL)	No	Yes	Yes
Leahy, Patrick (D-VT)	Yes	No	Yes
Roberts, Pat (R-KS)	-	Yes	Yes
Specter, Arlen (R-PA)	Yes	Yes	Yes
Representative			
Barcia, James A. (D-MI)	-	Yes	Yes
Bishop, Sanford Jr. (D-GA)	-	Yes	Yes
Brown, Corrine (D-FL)	-	Yes	Yes
Brown, Sherrod (D-OH)	-	Yes	Yes
Clement, Bob (D-TN)	Yes	Yes	Yes
Costello, Jerry F. (D-IL)	No	Yes	Yes
Ganske, Greg (R-IA)	-	Yes	Yes
Gonzales, Charles A. (D-TX)	No	Yes	Yes
Hilliard, Earl F. (D-AL)	-	Yes	Yes
Jackson, Lee Sheila (D-TX)	-	Yes	Yes
Jefferson, William J. (D-LA)	No	Yes	Yes
LaHood, Ray (R-IL)	-	Yes	Yes
Leach, Jim (R-IA)	Yes	Yes	Yes
Levin, Sander (D-MI)	Yes	Yes	Yes
Manzullo, Donald (R-IL)	-	Yes	Yes
McNulty, Michael (D-NY)	Yes	Yes	Yes
Nethercutt, George (R-WA)	-	Yes	Yes
Ramstad, Jim (R-MN)	No	Yes	Yes
Rivers, Lynn N. (D-MI)	-	Yes	Yes
Roemer, Tim (D-IN)	Yes	Yes	Yes
Stenholm, Charlie (D-TX)	No	Yes	Yes
Walsh, James T. (R-NY)	Yes	Yes	Yes

Source: US Congress (Roll Call Votes – Sessions of 1992, 1996, and 2000).

In short, the role of epistemic communities in the learning process toward Cuba provides an alternative hypothesis and a potential area for further research, perhaps to be developed through a series of interviews with those Congressmen who argue that the embargo is damaging US food producers.

Legislators' Learning Processes

Table 3.1 presents data on the vote of select US legislators on economic sanctions with respect to Cuba.

Several who voted in favor of both the Torricelli and the Helms-Burton laws also supported the bill allowing direct food sales to Cuba. Given that the exemption on trade sanctions and US exports (Title IX) is one section of a general appropriations bill for agriculture, rural development, and the Food and Drug Administration, the list includes only those legislators who, in addition to their vote, supported easing economic restrictions on US-Cuba trade.

For example, in August 1999, the full Senate voted 70-28 in favor of an amendment by Senator John Ashcroft to remove agriculture trade sanctions against countries such as Cuba, Libya, Sudan, and North Korea. Supporters included all Senators reported in Table 3.1. According to transcripts of the Foreign Relations Committee hearing in which the amendment was discussed, they argued: "Unilateral food and medicine sanctions do not work and hurt American farmers." In stressing the potential benefits for US food producers, they also claimed: "United States' wheat farmers are currently shut out of ten percent of the world's wheat market due to unilateral sanctions...that also cost American soybean growers up to $147 million annually in lost income."[53] Curiously, the Ashcroft amendment, later rejected by a House-Senate conference committee, was attached to the 2000 farm spending bill with the acquiescence of Senate Foreign Relations Chairman Jesse Helms. In a dramatic departure from his well known resistance to closer economic relations with Cuba, Helms said: "The impetus for this reform comes from our farm community, which is hurting today, and which is asking us in Congress to look at ways in which we can expand markets for American farm products." He emphasized that he agreed with that goal as long as "moral and national security interests of the United States" were protected.[54]

As argued before, US policymakers might have changed their beliefs on the usefulness of the Cuban embargo as a result of travel experience. In July 2000, Senators Max Baucus and Daniel Akaka traveled to Cuba, where they met with Fidel Castro, several Cuban ministers and dissidents, a number of foreign ambassadors, and the head of the largest nongovernmental organization on the island. On July 25, 2000, Akaka, who had voted in favor of the Torricelli law, declared:

---

53 *Senate Record*, Vote No. 251. "Agriculture Appropriations," US Senate (August 3, 1999).

54 *Congress Daily*, "Helms, in Dramatic Departure, Backs Easing of Cuban Embargo," (March 24, 2000).

I returned from Cuba convinced that lifting the trade embargo and restrictions on travel, especially for educational exchanges, are extremely important steps in an effort to foster economic and political liberalization in Cuba. While this was denied by the Foreign Minister, I came away convinced that the (Cuban) government does not want the American embargo on Cuba lifted because the lack of economic ties allows the government to blame the United States for its own economic failures. If the embargo was lifted, Cuba's leaders might find another excuse for their failed policies, but it might make it harder for them to find widely acceptable excuses.[55]

The following day, Baucus (who had voted in favor of the 1996 Helms-Burton law) echoed Akaka's remarks: "The U.S. embargo actually helps Castro by providing him a scapegoat for Cuba's misery and by preventing Cubans to come into contact with U.S. tourists, business people, students, and scholars." He continued:

My reason for opposing unilateral sanctions is entirely pragmatic. They don't work. They never worked in the past and they will not work in the future. Whenever we stop our farmers and business people from exporting, our Japanese, European, and Canadian competitors rush in to fill the gap. Unilateral sanctions are a hopelessly ineffective tool.[56]

Among US Representatives, Jim Leach, who had previously voted in favor of tougher restrictions against Cuba, called in June 1997 for an end to the embargo on food and medicine sales. He stated: "In maintaining appropriate pressure on Cuba's communist regime, it is imperative that compassion for the suffering people of the island not be lost and humanitarian exceptions to the U.S. embargo be allowed to go forward."[57] In 1999, he also noted:

Cuba represents one of the thorniest issues in American foreign policy. While there is a case for isolation of an irrationally dictatorial leader, there is also a case for opening up to the Cuban people. The provision of food and medicine and allowance of easier communication between families may represent a credible first step toward a people-to-people, as contrasted with a governmental, rapprochement.[58]

More recently, Leach has continued to oppose sanctions against Cuba and financing restrictions on trade. In December 2002, he said he favored lifting the embargo before the current Cuban government is gone because "nothing would be more revolutionary or destabilizing to the Castro regime than opening up trade."[59]

---

55 *Senate Record*, S7537, "Flexible Trade Policy Toward Cuba," US Senate (July 25, 2000), <http://thomas.loc.gov/cgi-bin/query/D?r106:16:./temp/~r1061bX9ky>.

56 *Senate Record* S7629, "Embargo on Cuba," U.S. Senate (July 26, 2000), < http://thomas.loc.gov/cgi-bin/query/D?r106:7:./temp/~r106RmLQ1G>.

57 *Congress Daily*, "Twelve Members Seek Easing of Cuba Embargo," (June 18, 1997).

58 *Senate Record*, "Statement of First District Rep. Jim Leach Regarding the Cuban Food and Medicine Security Act of 1999," US Senate (April 29, 1999).

59 Jerry Perkins, "Embargo hurts U.S., Cuban tells Iowa," *The Des Moines Register* (December 11, 2002).

Finally, George Nethercutt, who had voted for the Helms-Burton law, declared in Spring 2000 that food and medicine restrictions were "an abhorrent foreign policy tool that heaps suffering on the innocent people while doing little to alter the behavior of dictatorial regimes that rule the sanctioned countries." He also cited a US Agriculture Department estimate that American rural communities are loosing $1.2 billion a year in foregone sales to sanctioned countries. He concluded by saying that "sanctions are not fair to U.S. farmers or to the humanitarian interests of the United States."[60] In June 2000, Nethercutt wrote a piece in the *New York Times* that found parallels between US relations with China and those with Cuba. According to him, "if a normal trading relationship with China is a home run for America, then lifting sanctions against Cuba is the equivalent of a grand slam."[61]

The cases presented so far highlight significant changes in the behavior of several legislators on US economic sanctions against Cuba. However, we still do not know what they really believed when they voted in favor of tougher restrictions against the Castro regime. Given that the failures of recent policies (and eventually the loss of opportunities for US producers) are hypothesized to be the sources of learning and current policy preferences, we should provide evidence that legislators changed their minds by analyzing both their current beliefs and the ones they held prior to the enactment of the Torricelli or the Helms-Burton law. Important examples are Arlen Specter, Byron Dorgan, and Charlie Stenholm.

In June 1995, during a session of the Subcommittee on Western Hemisphere and Peace Corps Affairs,[62] Senator Specter commended the authors of the Helms-Burton law noting:

> I think it is very important to put the maximum pressure on Fidel Castro, the dictator of Cuba, to try to achieve his ouster at the earliest possible time in the interests of the people of Cuba and the interests of the Western Hemisphere and the world. Although they (the Cubans) are not quite the security menace which they once posed when the Soviet Union was keeping them buoyed up with money…they still represent a government which ought to be delegitimized, and to the extent that the United States can act to accomplish that result, it is very, very important.[63]

More recent remarks of Specter on Cuba represent an astonishing change. In June 1999, after his first trip to Cuba, he said he saw "hope for improving people-to-people relations" and that he would work to increase ties between the United States and the island in the areas of public health and drug interdiction. At that

---

60 David Hess, "Farmers Win Cuba Vote as Panel OKs Spending Bill," *National Journal* (May 10, 2000).

61 Bill Ghent and David Hess, "Seeking an End to Sanctions," *National Journal* (June 24, 2000).

62 The Subcommittee is part of the Committee on Foreign Relations of the United States Senate.

63 *Senate Record*, S. HRG. 104-212, "Cuban Liberty and Democratic Solidarity Act," US Senate (June 14, 1995).

time he called the US embargo against Cuba "a complex matter," without saying whether he supported or opposed the sanctions. However, it seems that the failure of economic sanctions to hasten the demise of the Castro government had an impact on his beliefs. Noting that "Castro is still robust, hale and hearty at age 73" and that "he is going to be on the scene for many more years," Specter made clear that he believed the United States should not wait for a change of power in Cuba to cultivate exchanges that can benefit both countries.[64] In October 2001, Specter cosponsored a bill aimed to remove financing restrictions on food and medicine sales to the Castro regime, ease travel restrictions to Cuba, and provide scholarships for certain Cuban nationals. A few months later, after a second trip to Havana, he observed that some changes in US policy toward Cuba had taken place. Referring to the bill introduced in the Senate, but later dropped in the House of Representatives, Specter concluded that it was "a very small step which ought to be uncontested."[65]

Byron Dorgan is another Senator who appears to have changed his beliefs on the Cuban embargo. In 1992, then-Representative Dorgan was one of the co-sponsors of the Torricelli bill. Therefore, we can assume that he believed in the effectiveness of a policy toward Cuba based on tougher sanctions. Since 1998, Dorgan has become a leading advocate in the US Congress for an easing of the Cuban embargo. In an interview with *Newsweek* in September 2001, he stated:

> We are really shooting ourselves in the foot with a continued embargo that does not work and, in a bizarre way, actually helps Fidel Castro keep his hold on power... It's a completely inconsistent policy. With other countries like China, Vietnam, North Korea (all communist countries), our policies have been to engage them, and through that engagement, move them toward more constructive approaches to human rights and other issues... But with Cuba, we do just the opposite. Our policy is to prevent travel to Cuba, to prevent trade with Cuba and we even deny them food and medicine. Using food and medicine as a weapon is, in my view, entirely immoral. That's not good policy, that's not accomplishing anything, and frankly, that doesn't hurt Fidel Castro, it helps him.[66]

Finally, Representative Charlie Stenholm has changed his beliefs on economic sanctions in the last few years. In June 2000, commenting on the possibility of removing existing restrictions against Cuba, he admitted: "In the past 18 months, I've changed my position 180 degrees. With the collapse of the Soviet Union, this is no longer a question of fighting communism. It is a question of how to best bring about change in Cuba. It could also be of help to Texas farmers." One month later, Stenholm joined a strong majority of his colleagues in supporting two amendments aimed to lift sanctions on US food, medicine, and tourists traveling to Cuba. In discussing his vote before the House of Representatives, he declared:

> In no way do I support the communist government created by Fidel Castro. He has infringed upon human rights, impeded religious freedoms, ignored economic contracts and blocked

---

64 "U.S. Senator Urges Cuban Ties," Associated Press, (June 3, 1999).

65 *Senate Record*, S1241, "Trip to Latin America," (February 27, 2002).

66 "Interview with Byron Dorgan," *Newsweek*.

the advancement of democracy. But past American policies toward Cuba clearly have failed. My strong belief is that face-to-face diplomacy and economic engagement are the best ways to expose the Cuban people to the benefits of democracy and capitalism.

Stenholm concluded then:

> When you try a policy like unilateral sanctions for 40 years and it brings you no success, it's time to rethink your strategy. We have done virtually nothing to change the behavior of Cuba's government and, in fact, our refusal to sell them food and drugs has given Castro an easy target to blame for some of their failures. It's time for us to try engagement instead, not only for democracy, but also for the benefit of our producers here at home.[67]

From the evidence presented in this section, it is clear that the failure of the embargo to reach its main objectives is the major source of learning. Changes of beliefs among US policymakers can reasonably be considered an "intermediate" or "strategic" level of learning as defined by Tetlock. Several political leaders no longer believe that incremental sanctions against Cuba will bring sufficient pressure on the Castro regime to bring about economic and political liberalization. They believe, instead, that the removal of sanctions would undermine the government of the island by exposing Cubans to the influence of American values and ideas and by preventing Castro from using the embargo as a scapegoat for its economic failures. In short, while the fundamental objectives of US policy toward Cuba remain in place, beliefs on how to accomplish them have drastically changed.

Several legislators who voted for and publicly supported the Torricelli and the Helms-Burton laws now advocate a policy of engagement with Cuba. It is important to recall that Title II of Helms-Burton lays down a series of conditions demanded by the United States for re-engagement with some future Cuban government. The central one is that neither Fidel nor Raul Castro be part of it. Therefore, US policymakers' attempts to foster democracy in Cuba through a normalization of relations with its current government represent a fundamental change of strategic policy beliefs and preferences toward Cuba. In addition, their attempts to relax existing restrictions on trade for US citizens and companies reflect not only a change in means but also the pursuit of a new goal: to help American farmers develop agricultural trade relations with Cuba and to generally benefit from exports to the island. Thus, we can argue that the learning process among US legislators goes beyond Levy's definition of "simple learning," which states that the observation and interpretation of experience lead to a change in means but not in ends.

The Interaction of Power and Knowledge

The second hypothesis of this study is that not all learning is translated into policy change. There has been a dramatic change in US political dynamics lately, with

---

67 *House Record*, "Stenholm Votes for Increased Exports, Democracy," US House of Representatives (July 31, 2000).

legislators from both parties demonstrating their willingness to loosen trade and travel restrictions on Cuba. They mainly argue that an opening toward Havana would increase US agricultural exports while providing visiting Americans an opportunity to promote democratic values among ordinary Cubans. However, an analysis of the links between learning and policy change with respect to Cuba requires an understanding of the interaction of power and knowledge factors. Policy change is determined not only by increased knowledge as a result of the observation and interpretation of experience, but also by factors such as political struggles among various groups, leaders' policy positions and maneuvers, the highly-focused interests of some policymakers such as Cuban-Americans, and party loyalties.

Although many US legislators learned that economic sanctions against Cuba do not serve US interests, anti-Castro groups in the Cuban American Community and House Republican leaders have halted or limited attempts to weaken the embargo in recent years. The initial version of the 2000 bill on food and medicine sales to Cuba, as introduced by Representative George Nethercutt in the early summer of that year, and supported by all legislators listed in Table 3.1, did not include restrictions on financing. Having assembled a sizeable partisan coalition of farm state members and human rights advocates, Nethercutt was confident he had more than 280 votes for the measure.[68] However, the leverage over the House leadership he had envisioned failed to materialize. In fact, while being sympathetic to Nethercutt's bill, members of the Republican Party were also increasingly uneasy about voting against their leadership. Moreover, Democratic Caucus Vice Chairman Robert Menendez, a Cuban American, rounded up a number of anti-Castro Democrats prepared to defeat the measure. Likewise, Cuban American Representatives such as Diaz-Balart and Ros-Lehtinen built a coalition in both houses of Congress to render the passage of the bill more difficult. In the end, Nethercutt was forced to work out a compromise with the House Republican leaders and submit a revised version of the bill that allows Cuba to pay cash for food and medicine but denies credit guarantees to the island.[69] It also establishes that only the Congress can lift restrictions on travel to Cuba, a prerogative that fell previously under Executive jurisdiction. Several Congressmen called the compromise a step backward and said it was so restrictive it would hardly lead to significant food sales. Representative Jose Serrano, echoing the thoughts of most of his colleagues, stated: "Nethercutt gave in too quickly in his negotiations with the House leadership and Cuban American members."[70]

Loyalties among party members in the US Congress may also be important. For instance, House Majority Leader Dick Armey, a staunch opponent of Communist governments who voted consistently over the years to maintain the embargo against Cuba, recently suggested that engaging Cuba and lifting the travel ban is the best way to undermine Fidel Castro. However, he noted that he had backed the restrictions

---

68 *Congress Daily*, "Nethercutt Cutting a Cuba Deal," (June 27, 2000).
69 Ghent and Hess, "Seeking an End to Sanctions."
70 *Congress Daily*, "Cuba Trade Backers Blast GOP Compromise," (June 29, 2000).

on travel and trade out of loyalty to two Cuban-American House members. In early August 2002, he said:

> What you see in the House of Representatives and what you see by way of individual vote – my own is an example – is loyalties to our friends. Sometimes on an issue like Cuba, my particular loyalty to Lincoln Diaz Balart and Ileana Ros-Lehtinen is not counterbalanced by focused interest in my district.

While the case of Armey may not constitute learning (He may have always believed that sanctions do not work), his declaration suggests that loyalties among party members can prevent the implementation of some lessons learned. Commenting on Armey's statement, Representative Jeff Flake, a leading opponent of the embargo, noted: "If the House had a secret ballot, there would be an additional 75 or 100 votes in favor of lifting restrictions."[71]

Despite their disappointment with the final version of the bill on food and medicine sales to Cuba, several legislators have continued to push for lifting of the embargo. On June 12, 2001, the Bridges to the Cuban People Act was introduced in both chambers. This legislation aimed to promote a peaceful transition to democracy on the island and produce benefits for both the United States and Cuba by removing some restrictions on trade, travel, and cultural exchange between the two countries. All legislators listed in Table 3.1 were among the co-sponsors of the bill.[72]

Forces that support an easing of sanctions have gained momentum in the wake of the announcement of the first sale of US food products to Cuba in December 2001. That same month, a group of 15 US Senators including Max Baucus, Byron Dorgan, Pat Roberts, and Arlen Specter sent a letter to President Bush soliciting his help on relaxing financing and shipping restrictions. In addition to mentioning that sales to Cuba would help to assist that country's recovery from the devastation caused by hurricane Michelle earlier in November, the letter observed that, "given the crisis in American agriculture, the prospect of selling to a new market is welcome news to U.S. farmers and exporters."[73] On June 26, 2002, a group of 37 Representatives, including Nethercutt and Stenholm, co-sponsored the Freedom to Travel to Cuba Act of 2002. The bill, introduced in the House by Jeff Flake, intended to eliminate restrictions on travel to Cuba for US citizens and facilitate transactions incident to travel such as the importation into Cuba or the United States of accompanied baggage for personal use only, the payment of living expenses, and the acquisition of goods and services for personal use.[74]

---

71 Paul Richter, "Armey Urges End to Cuba Sanctions," *Los Angeles Times* (August 9, 2002).

72 *House Record*, HR 2138, "Bridges to the Cuban People Act of 2001," (June 12, 2001), <http://thomas.loc.gov/cgi-bin/query/D?c107:16:./temp/~c107TbkTyv::>.

73 *Embargo Update*, "Senators Offer President Support on Sales to Cuba," (December 7, 2001), <www.giraldilla.com>.

74 *House Record*, HR 5022, "Freedom to Travel to Cuba Act of 2002," (June 26, 2002), <http://thomas.loc.gov/cgi-bin/query/D?c107:17:./temp/~c107YNbO9p:: >.

Until now, supporters of a hard line against Cuba have been able to thwart attempts to ease restrictions on trade and travel. The future of the Cuban embargo and the implementation of a new policy that better reflects current learning within the US Congress will mainly depend on the ability of the aforementioned Senators and their allies in the House of Representatives to build a wider coalition around their ideas. Admittedly, such a task has been greatly complicated by the recent behavior of Fidel Castro. Between late March and early April 2003, the Cuban government imprisoned 75 political dissidents and executed three men who hijacked a ferryboat in Havana bay to flee the island. As a result of the outrage provoked by these actions, on April 8, 2003, the House of Representatives approved a resolution (with 414 votes in favor and no dissenting vote) that condemns the systematic human rights violations in Cuba committed by the Castro regime, calls for the immediate release of all Cuban political prisoners, and supports the right of the Cuban people to exercise fundamental political and civil liberties.[75]

There is no doubt that the Cuba's latest crackdown on internal dissent has meant a real setback for anti-embargo initiatives in Congress. For instance, on April 25, 2003, George Nethercutt, reflecting the view of many House Representatives, admitted that easing restrictions now "would be perceived the wrong way, somehow condoning what Castro has done."[76] Nevertheless, several US legislators still support a policy of engagement with Havana, as demonstrated by their attempts to remove the travel ban for American citizens. It should be noted that the movement in Congress for the lifting of financing restrictions on trade with Cuba had already lost momentum before the events in Havana. Surprisingly, the Cuban government has proved its ability to buy significant amounts of US products on a cash-basis. Although purchases would certainly be higher in the absence of restrictions, by the end of 2004 Cuba had become the 23rd largest food market for the United States, and probably the safest one because of the cash-only conditions of trade.[77]

On April 30, 2003, 27 Senators, including Daniel Akaka, Max Baucus, and Byron Dorgan, co-sponsored the Freedom to Travel to Cuba Act of 2003, which aims to eliminate any restrictions on travel to Cuba for US citizens.[78] A few weeks later, 65 Representatives, including George Nethercutt, Charlie Stenholm, and Jim Leach, introduced the same bill in the House under the name of Export Freedom to Cuba Act of 2003.[79] In presenting the legislation on the Senate floor, Baucus stated:

---

75 *House Record*, HR 179, "Expressing the sense of the House of Representatives regarding the systematic human rights violations in Cuba," (April 7-8, 2003), <http://thomas.loc.gov/cgi-in/query/D?c108:11:./temp/~c108JqqVxE::>.

76 Pablo Bachelet, "Embargo foes in disarray as U.S. mulls Cuba options," *Reuters* (April 25, 2003).

77 Paolo Spadoni, "Don't change export rules on Cuba," *Orlando Sentinel* (December 27, 2004).

78 *Senate Record*, S 950, "Freedom to Travel to Cuba Act of 2003," (April 30, 2003), <http://thomas.loc.gov/cgi-bin/query/D?c108:6:./temp/~c108hDpDfn:: >.

79 *House Record*, HR 2071, "Export Freedom to Cuba Act of 2003," (May 13, 2003), <http://thomas.loc.gov/cgi-bin/query/D?c108:12:./temp/~c108hDpDfn:: >.

"After forty-three years, it ought to be clear to everyone that the embargo has failed to weaken Castro. A better approach is to reach out to the Cuban people. Ending the travel ban is the first and best way to do this." He then highlighted the benefits that open travel would provide to US farmers and the US economy by noting that, while Americans are currently allowed to sell food and medicine to Cuba on a cash-basis, the majority of potential sales are not realized due to the travel ban and trade embargo. In his conclusion, he said: "If we truly care about the Cuban people, if we care about democracy…let us travel to Cuba and show them democracy in action."[80] In July 2003, in remarks on the floor of the Senate, Dorgan declared:

> The issue of trade and travel is important. It is not in any way supportive of Fidel Castro for us to say a 40-year embargo does not work and that the same strategy we use with respect to China and Vietnam does work, and that is engagement through trade and travel. It undermines the ground on which dictators sit. It undermines their capability to govern, and that is what we ought to do.[81]

Between September and October 2003, both chambers of Congress voted strongly in favor of identical provisions to ease restrictions on American travel to Cuba. The amendments to the travel ban, attached to the Treasury, Transportation, and General Government appropriations bill, were approved by the House 227 to 188, and by the Senate 59 to 38. However, leaders of a House-Senate conference committee removed the travel provisions before sending the bill to the President, who had threatened to veto any legislation that weakened economic sanctions against Cuba.[82] As Cuban American leaders in Congress like to say, "our best insurance policy is the veto pen of George W. Bush."[83] In August 2003, a group of Florida Republican state Representatives (most of Cuban origin) sent a letter to the US president warning he risked losing their support and the votes of the Cuban American community for the 2004 elections unless he adopted a tougher Cuba policy. Although they asked for specific measures such as a review of current migration policy and increased assistance to dissidents in the island, the letter specified: "It is absolutely critical that you express as soon as possible, once again, that you will never permit any weakening of the embargo while you are president."[84] In short, domestic politics considerations and pressures exercised by the Cuban American community and their

---

80 Senate Press Release, "Baucus Introduces Legislation to Eliminate Cuba Travel Ban on Senate Floor, Senator Urges Opening Doors, Bringing Democracy to Region," (April 30, 2003), <http://216.239.33.104/search?q=cache:7of5ytx5AD4J:>, <www.senate.gov/~finance/press/Bpress/2003press/prb043003.pdf+cuba+baucus&hl=en&ie=UTF-8> .

81 *Senate Record*, S 9368, "Travel to Cuba," (July 15, 2003), <http://thomas.loc.gov/cgi-bin/query/D?r108:2:./temp/~r108ayxQ7O:: >.

82 Christopher Marquis, "Bush's allies plan to block effort to ease ban on Cuban travel," *The New York Times* (November 13, 2003).

83 Ken Guggenheim, "Lawmakers temper bid to ease Cuba embargo," *Associated Press* (April 22, 2003).

84 Cubanet, "A letter to the president," (August 12, 2003), <http://www.cubanet.org/CNews/y03/ago03/12e7.htm>.

allies on George W. Bush are additional examples of how political factors can prevent learning from being translated into policy change. While there has not been a need for the President to exercise his veto power, it is conceivable that his position on Cuba has played a role in the political struggles between different groups in the US Congress. Prospects for a relaxation of US economic sanctions against Cuba appear even slimmer after Bush won re-election in November 2004 and carried Florida with a comfortable margin.[85]

Conclusion

This chapter has analyzed the current debate within the US Congress about the role and usefulness of economic sanctions with respect to Cuba in order to provide some evidence for a potential learning process. The qualitative case study is mostly based on Levy's notion that individual policymakers learn when they change their beliefs as a result of the observation and interpretation of experience. He also claims that failures of previous policies, in particular those that were unanticipated, are more likely to lead to learning than are successes.

During the 1990s, the United States reinforced its embargo against Cuba through the implementation of the Torricelli law in 1992 and the Helms-Burton law in 1996. To some degree, both legislations were conceived as effective instruments for exerting economic pressure on the Cuban economy, hastening the collapse of the Castro government, and offering positive inducements to democratic reforms in Cuba. The Torricelli law prevented US subsidiaries from trading with Cuba, put restrictions for any vessel that touched Cuban ports, and allowed humanitarian donations for specific medical products. The Helms-Burton law has attempted to undermine Cuba's opening to foreign investment by allowing lawsuits and the imposition of travel restrictions against foreign companies or other entities that "traffic" in US properties expropriated during the early days of the Revolution.

We can fairly say that economic sanctions against Cuba have mostly failed to reach their goals. Fidel Castro remains firmly in power, the economy has slowly but steadily recovered from the deep recession of the early 1990s, and there are no signs of significant democratic reforms or changes to Cuba's economic and political model. In the last few years, an increasing number of Senators and Representatives have pushed for a change in US policy toward Havana and promoted legislations aimed to lift the restrictions on food and medicine sales to Cuba as well as increase people-to-people contacts with the island through the lifting of the travel ban for US citizens. They mostly argue that the current embargo did little to alter the behavior of the Castro government and eventually hasten its collapse, while negatively affecting US producers who are prevented from exporting their products to Cuba. The fact that they had previously voted in favor of strengthening the embargo, and sometimes publicly declared their support for economic sanctions, suggests that changes of

---

85 Anthony Boadle, "Little cheer in Cuba over Bush's U.S. election win," *Reuters* (November 3, 2004).

beliefs (and therefore learning) as a result of policy failures might be taking place among them.

The aforementioned learning process has led not only to a change of behavior among Congressmen but also to an important change of policy. In October 2000, the US Congress enacted legislation that relaxed the economic sanctions against Cuba by allowing the sale of US agricultural products to the island. However, there is some evidence that not all learning has been translated into policy change. Supporters of greater opening toward Havana have faced resistance from anti-Castro groups in the Cuban American community, Cuban American Congressmen, and the House leadership. In the end, they were forced to make a compromise with these groups and submit a revised version of the bill that not only prohibits US financing institutions from providing credit for sales to Cuba, but also codifies into law existing travel restrictions. So far, pro-embargo forces have been able to thwart any attempt to further relax US economic sanctions with respect to Cuba.

Admittedly, while making the case that a number of US legislators might have learned from the failures of previous policies toward Cuba, this study still presents several limitations. First, one is left wondering whether changes of beliefs among legislators are simply the result of the lobbying efforts promoted by US business groups rather than learning. These legislators (especially Senators) are mostly from big farm states and respond to particular interests of the agricultural community. As suggested before, policymakers whose changes of beliefs are correlated to economic interests still learn if those changes are the result of new information made available to them. It is conceivable that US legislators might have learned from new data on the loss of opportunities for American producers. Since the mid-1990s, when the Cuban economy began to recover, an increasing number of countries are exporting their products to Cuba and taking advantage of the lack of US competition. Nevertheless, in order to test this assumption, a study of the role of epistemic communities in US policy toward Cuba and eventually a series of interviews with selected US Congressmen would be useful.

Second, the research design should have incorporated elements that allow us to establish whether variations in beliefs among legislators are correlated with changes in their political position or institutional role. Different roles in Congress might link legislators to different economic and political interests, thus undermining the learning hypothesis. A longitudinal study of selected Congressmen over time that focus on this aspect is needed. Finally, although it provides a few cases, the empirical analysis should have included more declarations of legislators before the enactment of the Torricelli and the Helms-Burton law in order to demonstrate what they believed when they voted in favor of a strengthening of the embargo. In fact, policy preferences expressed through votes in Congress do not necessarily reflect individual beliefs.

Notwithstanding these limitations, the analysis presented in this study remains a useful one for several reasons. First of all, it enriches the current debate on the effectiveness of economic sanctions by offering the perspective of a group of legislators in a country, such as the United States, that continues to use them to reach major foreign policy goals. In addition, it improves our understanding of the role of learning in US foreign policy toward Cuba, which has been characterized so far more by failures than successes. This is also particularly important for the future of the relations between the two countries. With the enactment of the Helms-Burton legislation, economic sanctions against the regime of Fidel Castro are codified in law and can be repealed only by Congress. If successful, legislators' attempts to promote a gradual easing of tension and a more constructive approach toward Havana (through a new policy that relies less on isolation and more on the influence of the American society) will increase the likelihood that some significant changes might take place in Cuba. Otherwise, the United States will have no choice but to wait until Castro passes from the scene by natural causes, and hope his successor will be less resilient than he or more inclined to introduce democratic reforms.

Chapter 4

Epistemic Communities and the Russian Energy Sector

Eric A. Morgan

Russia's energy industry, one of the most autonomous sectors of the Soviet era, has finally begun to emerge from the doldrums. Russia's production of oil and gas rivals that of Organization of Petroleum Exporting members, and its electrical grid is among the most sophisticated in the world. The sector is increasingly integrated into the global economy, and its policies and activities are increasingly coordinated with global intergovernmental agencies. However, the stability and future success of these trends will be affected by Russian and global energy officials' ability to engage in mutual learning in a competitive context.

For centuries, there have been gaping disparities in policies and practices employed by corresponding institutions in Russia and the West. However, harmonization occurred on many levels among Western countries, even among bitter rivals, suggesting that competitive learning processes drove Western institutions to actively adapt[1] and learn from one another, despite religious, linguistic, and political differences. But the rapid and tumultuous changes that regularly swept across the West rarely stirred Russia.[2] Recently, however, the end of the Cold War and globalization have removed many obstacles to communication and coordination between Russia and the West. As sectors and organizations with corresponding functions began to coordinate their activities, Russian policymakers and experts have reevaluated traditional assumptions and practices and revised values, goals and procedures. The end of the Cold War and globalization present new learning opportunities for Russian energy sector officials[3] but it must be asked to what extent

---

1   See a discussion of analysts' distinctions between organizational "adaptation" and learning in Chapter 1, p. 6.

2   One example of this trend was Russia's use of the Julian calendar long after the West adopted the Gregorian system. In fact, if one measures time with the Gregorian calendar, the October Revolution occurred in November 1917. Other examples include Russia's late abolition of serfdom and its difficulties creating a modern legal code.

3   Russia's harmonization with the West extends beyond the energy sphere. Several examples include attempts to reform the Russian army by ending the practice of conscription and the adoption of free media practices during the Boris Yeltsin era. The movement toward ending use of the death penalty may also be seen as an attempt to bring Russian criminal justice in line with European Union views.

are new Russian policies a consequence of organizational learning (knowledge acquisition and policy change resulting from interaction with Western energy sectors and global organizations), or are they instead a response to other compelling political, economic, and technological stimuli?

To investigate potential learning processes between the Russian and global energy sectors, this study draws upon organizational and social learning theories, particularly Peter M. Haas' conceptualization of the importance of "epistemic communities."[4] In this study, firstly I hypothesize that discrete, consensus-based Russian and global energy epistemic communities influence information and knowledge acquisition and policy decisions. Secondly, due to the troubled history of policy coordination between the global and Russian energy sectors, I hypothesize that the two epistemic and policy communities both cooperate and compete in their efforts to learn. Data for the study are drawn primary from documents generated by Russian and global energy organizations and personal interviews with global energy experts. The evidence suggests that Russian officials seek to reform and modernize energy production, increase profitability and make the sector attractive to global investors. However, the Russian community also seeks to acquire the expertise necessary to solidify control over the fledging portions of the sector domestically and in the former Soviet republics. In contrast, the global epistemic community's objectives are to erode Russian autonomy and regional influence and to promote Russian cooperation and integration with global energy organizations and markets. We begin exploration of these hypotheses by revisiting the epistemic communities literature.

Conceptualizing Epistemic Communities

Peter Haas defines an epistemic community as a...

> network of professionals with recognized expertise and competence in a particular domain and an authoritative claim to policy-relevant knowledge within that domain or issue-area. Although an epistemic community may consist of professionals from a variety of disciplines and backgrounds, they have (1) a shared set of normative and principled beliefs, which provide a value-based rationale for the social action of community members; (2) shared causal beliefs, which are derived from their analysis of practices leading or contributing to a central set of problems in their domain and which then serve as the basis for elucidating the multiple linkages between possible policy actions and desired outcomes; (3) shared notions of validity—that is, intersubjective, internally defined criteria for weighing and validating knowledge in the domain of their expertise; and (4) a common policy enterprise—that is, a set of common practices associated with a set of problems to which their professional competence is directed...[5]

---

4   See Chapter 1, pp. 8-10.

5   Peter M. Haas, ed., *Knowledge, Power, and International Policy Coordination* (Cambridge, MA: World Peace Foundation and Massachusetts Institute of Technology, 1992), p. 3.

Haas embraces Burkhart Holzner and John Marx's definition of knowledge as, "…the communicable mapping of some aspect of experienced reality by an observer in symbolic terms."[6] An epistemic community is created when "communicated mapping" draws a varied set of actors into a dialogue that results in a set of shared understandings, expressed in a standardized manner, regarding the discipline or activity in question. The epistemic community's application of this consensual knowledge within a political and legal setting may well influence policy.[7] Epistemic communities do not simply generate policy alternatives or policy. Instead, they work to actively coordinate policy by developing a wide-ranging knowledge-based consensus that serves as the intellectual basis for coordinated action by multiple parties. Policy coordination is a course or method of action among an assemblage of organizations with an epistemic objective or set of objectives that is reached through consensus. Haas writes, "Policy coordination is, ultimately, based on consent and mutual expectations."[8] Epistemic communities differ from more inclusive policy communities in that their contribution to policymaking is knowledge-based, and they are commonly constituted by nongovernmental as well as governmental actors.

The Russian Energy Sector

Currently, the Russian Federation is the only industrialized country in the world self sufficient in energy.[9] It is the world's largest exporter of natural gas, and second largest exporter of oil.[10] More than thirty percent of Russia's export revenues derive from sales of gas on the world market.[11] Thus, energy accounts for a large portion of the Russian economy. The Russian energy sector is a large, formal and informal entity with a diverse set of actors: political leaders, regulators, technicians, scientists, and financial experts.[12] Some of its members extract and produce gas, oil, and coal; other participants operate power plants and distribution networks. Government regulators deal with issues such as planning, pricing, taxation, licensing and environmental safety. Despite the diversity of participants, Russia's energy sector is a coherent unit of analysis because its members are linked by the infrastructure to which they all

---

6 Haas, *Knowledge, Power, and International Policy Coordination*, p. 21.

7 "Policy" may be conceptualized as a definite course or method of action selected from among alternatives, in light of given conditions, to guide and determine present and future decisions.

8 Haas, *Power, and International Policy Coordination*, p. 371.

9 Caroline Kuhnert, "More Power for the Soviets: Perestroika and Energy," *Soviet Studies* vol. 43 (1991), p. 495.

10 <www.eia.doe.gov/emeu/cabs/russia2>

11 Andrew L. Baldwin and Ilka Lewington, "Russia," *Utility Regulation, 1997: Economic Regulation of Utilities and Network Industries Worldwide* (London: Centre for the Study of Regulated Industries, 1997), p. 278.

12 Civil servants provide expert knowledge in specific fields as well as represent other governmental interests.

contribute, are accountable to the Russian government, and wrestle with many of the same political, legal and financial challenges.

The influence of the current Russian epistemic community may be traced to the Soviet era. In 1920, the Soviet Union's first comprehensive economic plan, the State Plan for the Electrification of Russia (GOELRO), laid the foundations for the centrally-planned economy. The primary ideas of GOELRO, including the centralization of the energy system and prioritization of thermal stations and massive power units, shaped the Soviet energy system for more than 30 years, and to some extent continue to do so.[13]

Paul Josephson provides an excellent depiction of the political importance of energy experts during the Nikita Khrushchev era:

> Khrushchev invited Kurchatov[14] to speak at the XXth Party Congress in 1956. In that speech, which promoted a nascent engineering culture, Kurchatov showed the authority that physicists had come to command and the hubris of their research and development program. He spoke about a "strong, powerful, young, and capable army of scholars, engineers, and designers" who were ready to commence the construction of…atomic power stations…[15]

The energy sector of the Russian Federation has been the target of reform since the collapse of the Soviet Union in 1992.[16] These reforms have occurred in two phases: a radical change in ownership of energy infrastructure assets and an attempt to reform the legal environment that has severely limited the ability of the new ownership to make necessary changes. Soviet-trained technical experts, public and private energy producers, and the new political leadership engage in decision making within the context of a new, incomplete and evolving constitutional and institutional framework. Reform efforts have been described variously as overly radical, insufficiently aggressive, corrupt, and as surrender to Western corporate encroachment. Most Russian and global experts agree that a lack of competition, an aging infrastructure, inefficiency, safety and environmental concerns, an unsupportable domestic price regime, and debt continue to dog the sector.[17] Despite significant reform and a great deal of attention from global energy and financial experts, the Russian energy sector is not nearly as productive, efficient, and profitable as it might be. Energy is a highly controversial political issue in Russia. In 2001, for example, Andrei Illarionov, economic advisor to Russian President Vladimir

---

13 Kuhnert, "More Power for the Soviets: Perestroika and Energy," p. 494.

14 Igor Vasilyevich Kurchatov (1903-1960) is remembered as the father of the Soviet atomic bomb; he managed the development of the first hydrogen bomb.

15 Paul R. Josephson, "Atomic-Powered Communism: Nuclear Culture in the Postwar USSR," *Slavic Review* vol. 55 (1996), p. 301.

16 Sergey I. Palamarchuk, Sergei V. Podkovalnikov and Nikolai I Voropai, "Getting the Electricity Sector on Track in Russia," *The Electricity Journal* (October 2001), p. 53.

17 Palamarchuk, et. al., "Getting the Electricity Sector on Track in Russia," pp. 55-56.

Putin, accused the Russian Parliament of wasting and mismanaging the country's oil revenues as a consequence of "euphoria."[18]

The Russian energy epistemic community is made up of two levels of actors: those who make policy and those who implement it. Members of the first level are primarily top officials from the federal and regional governments and private corporations. Russian federal government officials in this first tier include people like Viktor Borisovich Khristenko (Minister of Industry and Energy), Aleksandr Yuryevich Rumysantsev (Minister of Atomic Energy), and Yuriy Trutnev (Minister of Natural Resources). Russian firms that directly affect energy policy-making include Gazprom, Unified Energy Systems of Russia (UES), Lukoil, and Itera (a gas trader).[19] Examples of first tier officials in private firms include Anatoly Chubais (Director of UES), Valery Otchertsov (General Director and Chairman of the Management Board of Itera Oil and Gas Company), and R. I. Vyakhirev (Chairman of the Management Committee of Gazprom). The second level of epistemic community members includes less politically-powerful but more knowledge-based contributors such as industry specialists, regulators, academics, lawyers and journalists.

The second level of membership within the Russian epistemic community exerts less influence than their global counterparts because lawyers and journalists play a less important role in the Russian energy sector than they do in the West. The reduced importance of legal experts is due to the fact that Russia's judiciary is more susceptible to political influence than in the West. The International Energy Agency reports, "Concerns of investors have turned increasingly to non-legislative aspects of the Russian investment climate. The judiciary's dependence on the executive branch of government and private interests remains a key issue."[20]

Due to the current lack of independent media in Russia, journalists are also less relevant to Russian energy epistemic activity. The news media is controlled by the state,[21] and the state has been captured by the powerful energy sector. Balmaceda writes:

> The influence of Russian oil and gas groups in Russian politics is growing rapidly, in part because of their ability to earn vast amounts of much-needed hard currency..., their potential to act as a powerful player outside of Russia, and their links to the highest levels of the Russian government. In many ways, as the Russian Military-Industrial Complex is losing some influence because of its economic problems, the oil and gas complex is taking over some of the prestige and influence.[22]

---

18 <www.eia.doe.gov/emeu/cabs/russia2>

19 Itera has become famous for its ability to collect payments from non-paying clients, especially the Ukraine.

20 Organization for Economic Co-operation and Development/International Energy Agency, *Russia Energy Survey*, 2002 (2002), p. 35.

21 <http://www.washingtonpost.com/ac2/wp-dyn?pagename=article&node=&contentId =A5722-2002Feb26>

22 Balmaceda, Margarita Mercedes. "Gas, Oil and the Linkages between Domestic and Foreign Policies: The Case of Ukraine," *Europe-Asia Studies* vol. 50 (1998), p. 265.

This assessment of the state of Russian epistemic influence was confirmed by several interviews with economists, engineers, and lawyers attending a World Bank-sponsored international energy regulation conference convened at the University of Florida during June 2002. [23]   When asked whether lawyers and journalists are important members of the Russian energy community, Xavier Aguirre (Vice President of Strategic and Regulatory Affairs for Tractebel S.A., the energy division of the Belgium-based Suez Company) replied, "UES hires US and British law firms! They don't even use their own [Russian] lawyers. Yes, it is true that lawyers and journalists are more important internationally than in the Russian energy sector."

The normative and causal beliefs of Russia's epistemic community are similar to those of the global community in that they derive from the same technical and economic considerations. But there are important differences. Consensus within the Russian epistemic community is more tenuous. Conflict obtains between reformers such as Chubais, who lead the newly-privatized firms and who wholeheartedly embrace the paradigm of the global epistemic community, and actors like Gazprom, who remain still strongly influenced by the country's particular history and experience. Path dependency factors' influence[24] on the Russian energy sector is profoundly different from those of the West. Josephson writes:

> Soviet technological style differed from that of other countries. First, there was an exaggerated level of interest in mass production…, which led to premature fixing of design parameters; and there was gigantomania, which grew out of the fascination with and the commitment to the development of a public culture of technology. These characteristics conspired with political forces to create a style noteworthy for bland, functional designs in which safety and comfort played a secondary role, and environmental issues were rarely raised. Standardization also contributed to Soviet engineers' lack of accountability to society.

Josephson notes the importance of standardization on the Russian nuclear industry:

> In nuclear technologies, the "Moscow model" was adopted for the entire USSR. Irrespective of local cultural, political, or geological considerations, experimental and commercial reactors, particle accelerators and training programs developed in Moscow were transferred wholesale to physics institutes, industries, and agriculture throughout the nation.[25]

---

23 Thanks to Professor Sanford V. Berg, Distinguished Service Professor of Economics and Director of the Public Utility Research Center of the University of Florida, for his interest and support for this project.

24 Adapted from a 1999 Public Utility Research Center brochure, Warrington College of Business Administration, University of FL, Gainesville, FL.. See <www.purc.org>.

25 Josephson, "Atomic-Powered Communism: Nuclear Culture in the Postwar USSR," p. 300.

Standardization and mass production characterized all Soviet energy sector technologies.

Aguirre is skeptical that a consensus obtains among Russian energy sector personnel of today:

> Russia is an interesting country because the political world is included in the energy sector community. There are really two sets of people: the political appointees and the engineers and other business or technical people associated with the industry. So, in a way, you could say it is a little schizophrenic.

He continued, "There is some tension between the reformers and those who prefer the old system."

When asked whether personnel across the Russian energy sector share a common set of objectives for the industry as a whole, Aguirre replied:

> Yes, at the top level they do. At the top level, they have a clear view of the next ten years. And they have surrounded themselves with consultants that are further insulating them from old ways of doing things. But they do not have complete control. From the perspective of the top management, Gazprom is behind many of the problems in the Russian energy sector.

Armenak Yayloyan, an engineer, and Anoush Markaryan, an economist, from the Licensing Activity Monitoring Division of the Republic of Armenia's Energy Regulatory Commission and Ruzanna Zarantsyan, an economist with the Commission's Tariff Department, are less tentative in their assessment. They believe that a common set of beliefs unite Russian energy sector personnel.

The Global Energy Epistemic Community

Membership in the global energy epistemic community is extensive. Again, members may be divided into two levels of import---those with the political authority to take policy decisions and those who create, draft, implement, monitor, study and report on policy. First level members include personnel from (particularly Western) governments, global intergovernmental agencies, and global corporations. Examples of first tier governmental personnel at the time of this writing include Wolfgang Clemant (the German Minister of Economics and Labor),[26] Joan MacNaughton (Director General for Energy, Department of Trade and Energy in the United Kingdom),[27] or Samuel W. Bodman (the US Secretary of Energy).[28] A partial list of intergovernmental agencies whose personnel constitute the global epistemic community includes the International Energy Agency (IEA), the International Atomic Energy Agency of the United Nations, and the Energy Regulators Regional

---

26 <www.eia.doe.gov/emeu/cabs/germany>.

27 <www.eia.doe.gov/emeu/cabs/uk>.

28 <www.eia.doe.gov/emeu/cabs/usa>.

Association.[29] Examples of global energy firms include Calpine, British Petroleum, or *Electricite de France*. Academics, lawyers, industry experts, and journalists who cover energy sector activities also number among second tier members of the global community.

The principled and causal beliefs of the global energy community are extensive and comprehensive and relate to industry conditions (including factors like technology, demand, knowledge and ownership); market structures for the various sub-sectors (electricity, gas, oil, nuclear and coal) including factors like quantity of firms and entry conditions; market performance (including factors like prices, investment, quality of service, and earnings), and regulatory governance including concerns like accountability, transparency, predictability, and environmental responsibility.[30] Despite the fact that the global energy sector and associated epistemic community are sub-divided by energy types, a variety of regulatory regimes, and a vast range of technical, geographical, or financial constraints, significant evidence exists that consensus obtains regarding fundamental principles and causal beliefs as well as "notions of validity" among the global energy sector.

How sector performance is evaluated provides a robust example of one aspect of this consensus. According to the University of Florida's Public Utilities Research Center, any International Energy Agency regulator would consider the following questions to assess the present and future performance of an energy sector.[31]

The first area of inquiry focuses on the political and legal context of the sector: Is the state or region politically stable? Is management culture reliable, corrupt, and/or competent? What kind of monitoring or other forms of control or sanctions exist to correct poor decision-making among energy sector organizations?

A regulator would also examine the conditions of the industry itself: What is the quality of technology in use? What is the level of demand for energy? Is it easy to obtain information about the energy industry? To what extent is it transparent? Is it easy to learn the ownership of industry components? What type of ownership prevails?

Next, a regulator would examine the market structure of the energy sector: Does it produce wholesale or retail electricity? Is it powered by oil, natural gas, nuclear energy, or coal? How many firms are competing with one another? How difficult is it for a new firm to startup and compete for business? To what extent are the firms differentiated?

Regulators would then want to know about market behavior: What is the level and quality of investment and service provided? Do their services meet all needs

---

29 The Energy Regulators Regional Association is a voluntary organization of independent energy regulators from the Central/Eastern European and Newly Independent States that provides research services, publishes issue papers, and organizes training and exchange programs. See <http://www.erranet.org>, last accessed July 10, 2005.

30 Public Utility Research Center brochure, Warrington College of Business Administration, University of Florida, Gainesville, FL, 1999 (<www.purc.org>).

31 Beyond this concern, of course, lie a variety of technical measures for developing a deeper knowledge of the energy sector's performance.

of the market? Is the pricing structure was optimal given the consumer population? Does the pricing encourage energy saving or energy use? Are the energy firms become more productive and profitable?

Yet another important area of consideration when evaluating the performance of an energy sector is regulatory governance. The design of regulation is crucial and this is one area where epistemic consensus may not yet exist. Some regulatory designs focus on incentives, others on penalties or compulsion. What is the nature of the tax structure and to what extent must different institutions share their resources? Are there price caps or a limit on permissible revenues? The degree to which accountability is built into an energy sector and its regulation is also very important. Energy firms, the government, regulatory agencies should all know exactly what is expected of them and what they are responsible for; and each should have the autonomy to carry out their work. Of course, in many countries the regulatory process itself is difficult to understand, unfair, or corrupt. Someone hoping to evaluate the performance of an energy sector would examine the regulatory process to learn how participatory, transparent, and predictable it is.

Secondary markets are also important to sector performance. Regulators would want to examine which natural resources are available, how entrepreneurship is facilitated, and the types and availability of capital and labor. History and path dependency are important factors to be understood to evaluate decision-making and performance of an energy sector. Other important factors to be studied include global and national economic and political conditions and perceptions. It is possible that the energy sector itself is working well, but is limited by factors at the national or global level.

When asked whether a consensus obtains regarding how things should be done among technicians, financial experts, politicians and others who work internationally in energy industries, Xavier Aguirre replied:

> This was especially true a few years ago. It was called the Washington consensus of the early 1990s. But it has weakened recently because of what happened in California. For example, Thailand was planning to adopt many of the same reforms, but they are now delaying. So the consensus is questioned by intellectuals, but it is still accepted among private firms.

Common standards and means of evaluating procedures and new ideas are another important area of consensus characterizing epistemic communities. Internationally, Aguirre said, "There is more diversity now, after the crisis in California." Yayloyan, Markaryan, and Zarantsyan, however, perceive a consensus internationally and in Russia in the area of standards and means of evaluation. Interviews with global energy officials indicate that cooperative and competitive organizational learning is occurring within and between the two epistemic and policy communities.

Aguirre summarized the objectives of the global epistemic community: "To gain economic efficiency, that is to reduce costs while maintaining or increasing productivity, to abolish monopolies, increase competition, and increase investment from [other countries]."

Recent examples of global agreements reflecting the consensus and coordination of the global energy epistemic community are the 1997 Kyoto Protocol,[32] the Implementing Agreement for the Establishment of Coal Combustion Sciences,[33] and an Implementing Agreement for the Establishment of an International Center for Gas Technology Information.[34]

Cooperative and Competitive Learning among Russian and Global Energy Experts

Primary and secondary literature and interviews provide strong evidence of a fundamental global consensus around a paradigm that includes support for relatively unhampered global energy markets ("the Washington Consensus"),[35] profit and price stability, industry and market conditions, and accepted regulatory practices.[36] However, it is clear that the Russian energy sector is less cohesive and agreement among Russian energy experts more tenuous. This brings us to the final concerns of this study: Is the Russian energy sector "learning" from the global energy epistemic community? Or, instead, does "competitive learning" along two parallel tracks characterize relations between the Russian and global energy sectors?

Interviews with energy sector specialists suggest that the experts themselves do not necessarily conceptualize or describe their roles or the activities of the Russian and global energy actors as theorized by Haas. However, interviewees confirm that many of the criteria necessary for epistemic learning are apparent in each sector.

Global epistemic community involvement in the Russian policy making processes began with Russian independence in 1992 and was most strongly felt during the implementation of former Russian Federation Prime Minister Egor Gaidar's "Shock Therapy" economic program.

As was noted, the influence of the global energy community is primarily exerted via agreements designed to harmonize regulatory procedures. Because the regulatory institutions of the Russian energy sector are still extremely undeveloped, it is difficult for global experts and agencies to influence developments and shape Russian responses to specific problems. The Organization for Economic Cooperation and Development (OECD) advises,

---

32 Organization for Economic Co-operation and Development, *Russia Energy Survey*, p. 28.

33 <http://iaem.osti.gov/CFDOCS/CF_Apps/IAM_Docs/subject-frame>.

34 <http://iaem.osti.gov/CFDOCS/CF_Apps/IAM_Docs/subject-frame>.

35 Responding to recent events in California, one interviewee suggested that the consensus-based international energy sector community had been challenged recently on the issue of domestic deregulation. Based on a January, 2003 interview in Gainesville, FL with Igor E. Artemiev, Senior Private Sector Development Specialist, World Bank.

36 Public Utility Research Center brochure, Warrington College of Business Administration, University of Florida, Gainesville, FL, 1999 (www.purc.org).

The [Russian] government should strengthen and ensure the independence of federal and regional regulatory bodies. The Federal Energy Commission and its regional counterparts, the newly established Commission on Oil and Gas Pipeline Use and the Anti-Monopoly Ministry all need to be strengthened. This will ensure a "level playing field" for competition in all natural resource sectors and in the electricity and heat industries. This new system should include third-party access, transparent tariff-setting based on full costs and licensing rules for new players in the markets.[37]

Other international energy sector experts make similar observations. *The Electricity Journal* comments: "...the system of state regulation...is not effective."[38] And the Centre for the Study of Regulated Industries reports, "Current regulation by the Regional Energy Commissions is far from achieving the aims and following the principles [of Law No. 41-FZ concerning tariffs]."[39] And, important agreements between Russia and the global epistemic community have not been ratified—despite years of lobbying—indicating that the influence of global epistemic actors is not very strong in Russia.

State control over the dissemination of ideas in Russia also hampers substantive debate of new policy ideas. Haas points out the importance of a free exchange of information for epistemic actors to exert influence in the policy process:

As demands for information arise, networks or communities of specialists capable of producing and providing the information emerge and proliferate. The members of a prevailing community become strong actors at the national and transnational level as decision makers solicit their information and delegate responsibility to them. A community's advice, though, is informed by its own broader world view. To the extent to which an epistemic community consolidates bureaucratic power within national administrations and international secretariats, it stands to institutionalize its influence.[40]

Evidence suggests that a cadre of politicians, corporations, and industry specialists dominates the paradigm of the Russian epistemic community and insulates it from outside influences, including the global epistemic forces, by controlling the news media.

Aguirre cautiously supports the assertion that international agencies exert relatively weak influence on the Russian energy sector: "Organizations such as the International Energy Agency don't have as much influence in Russia, but organizations such as the IMF [International Monetary Fund] or the European Bank for Reconstruction do have influence there."

Interviews with global energy officials indicate that some cooperative and competitive organizational learning is occurring within and between the two epistemic and policy communities.

---

37 OECD, *Russia Energy Survey*, p. 25.

38 Palamarchuk "Getting the Electricity Sector on Track in Russia," p. 55.

39 Baldwin, "Russia," p. 277.

40 Haas, *Knowledge, Power, and International Policy Coordination*, p. 4.

When asked how closely Russian energy sector objectives match those of the global energy sector, Aguirre said, "The Russians have the same objectives as the international community, but additionally, they hope to raise money through privatization."

Despite the difficulties, important policy coordination is ongoing between the global and Russian energy epistemic communities as illustrated by the Joint Declaration of Co-operation, signed by representatives of the International Energy Agency and the Russian government in July 1994. Russia participates in the IEA's international technology collaboration activities and is a Contracting Party to seven implementing agreements: Solar Power and Chemical Energy Systems; Stellarator Concept; International Center on Gas Technology Information; Environmental, Safety and Economic Aspects of Fusion Power; Fusion Materials; Nuclear Technology of Fusion Reactors; and Enhanced Oil Recovery.[41] However, the Joint Declaration of Cooperation has yet to be ratified by the Russian Parliament.[42]

Illustrative of how knowledge-, political-, and economic-motivations commonly interact to affect actors' behavior, is the global community's influence (in this case the European Union) upon the Russian policymaking with regard to its relationship with Ukraine. This influence has little to do with the persuasiveness of the global community's paradigm or worldview. Pressing market concerns drive Russian Federation policy toward Ukraine:

> The Russian energy complex gets most of its hard currency revenue from exports to Europe (nearly 100% of gas exports to the "far abroad" go to Europe, and 85% of energy exports overall), the issue of how to transport gas and oil from their deposits (most of them in Siberia) to Western Europe is of enormous importance. Ukraine plays an important role here, because currently 95% of Russia's energy exports pass through the Ukraine. Because the Western European demand for gas is increasing, Gazprom is especially interested in securing a gas transport infrastructure as quickly as possible. There is certain urgency here, because by around 2015, new European Union environmental regulations are to come into effect which would limit the use of coal and other fuels, thus boosting gas consumption rates. Gazprom's sense of urgency has to do not only with the desire to tap into this new demand, but also to secure its markets before competing suppliers can offer comparable prices.[43]

A significant area of disagreement is how each epistemic community conceptualizes the potential and goals of the Russian energy sector. The global energy community views Russia as a backward country, struggling to master the technical and managerial nuances of modern energy sector activity in a global market. However, some believe that the Russian energy community is conscious of its present and future mammoth potential, and conceptualizes the Russian and former Soviet realm as in transition, the territories and characteristics yet to be fully

---

41 OECD, *Russia Energy Survey*, p. 21.

42 OECD, *Russia Energy Survey*, p. 43.

43 Balmaceda, "Gas, Oil and the Linkages between Domestic and Foreign Policies," p. 268.

determined. Some Russian energy sector actors do not yet view energy assets in the former republics as legitimate autonomous legal entities, to be respected and competed with according to globally recognized norms and practices. For this reason, Russian energy sector enterprises seek to remain their current monopolistic forms—ideal for aggressively expanding the Russian portfolio of assets, sidelining those that will remain out of reach, and strong enough to withstand the long winter of the Russian economic, political and legal transition. Margarita Balmaceda describes an aggressive Russian energy sector:

> Russia is pursuing a policy of parallel strategies: ...one of them is accelerated development of the oil and gas infrastructure on its own territory, and the other—the establishment of control of objects of the oil and gas infrastructure in the former Union republics. In particular, the second strategy is aimed at seizing the rights of ownership of the most important objects of the oil and gas complex during the process of privatization and acquiring them as compensation for state debts arising as a result of importing Russian energy resources.[44]

Russia's conceptualization of the former republics as part and parcel of its mission is illustrated by the Chairman of Gazprom's Board of Directors' (R. I. Vyakhirev) discussion of his company's business environment: "Ever new international economic alliances, organizations, and institutions are coming into being and developing."[45]

However, Aguirre does not regard the Russian energy sector as aggressively seeking to consolidate its control over former Soviet Energy assets. In fact, he does not believe that Russia's large gas, oil, and utility companies allow it to exert influence and control over the other former Soviet Republics. He said, "On the contrary, Russian oil firms that operate according to Western business principles are able to take much more initiative than Gazprom. So the large size of Russian energy firms does not work to the advantage of Russian influence abroad."

Yayloyan, Markaryan, and Zarantsyan concur. While acknowledging a joint partnership with Gazprom, Yayloyan said that Armenia has had a "good experience" with Russian energy firms. He also said that that the Russian energy sector was not trying to control the energy assets of the other former Soviet Republics. Zarantsyan said that Russian energy firms with business in Armenia had "met all of [the Armenian Regulatory Commission's] expectations."
Aguirre observed:

> My perception of the Russian energy sector is that it is rather unorganized at the moment. So I don't think that there is a specific policy aimed against the surrounding countries. In fact, the Ukrainians are ahead of the Russians in the way that they are managing their energy activities.

---

44 Balmaceda, "Gas, Oil and the Linkages between Domestic and Foreign Policies," p. 267.

45 < http://www.gazprom.ru/eng/welcome/>.

Aguirre concluded his remarks by predicting that Russian firms would become more competitive. He said:

> Eventually they will be unbundled. In fact, Chubais recently invited investors to come to Russia and make bids on a variety of assets—he did this without any sort of mandate or political support. It caused quite a stir. I think he did this to send a signal to the old energy community that change is coming. Additionally, UES is implementing new accounting standards in preparation for further privatization.

Conclusion

Convergence is apparent between global and Russian energy experts and policy-makers in terms of values, knowledge, beliefs and goals. There is increasing coordination between Russia and the West in technical, legal, financial, and environmental aspects of policy. However, a mixed record of learning is discernible between the Russian and global epistemic communities. The undeveloped state of Russian's legal and economic environment makes it difficult for Russian reformers to adopt global paradigms. Russian energy actors are divided between reformers such as Anatoly Chubais and actors who remain resistant to Western ideas, such as Gazprom. Many Russian firms remain committed to monopolistic, aggressive practices particularly in relation to energy assets in the former Soviet republics rather than those advocated by the global epistemic community. However, it is likely that over time even large, powerful organizations such as Gazprom will be forced to alter their procedures to conform to the global knowledge-based consensus. At this time, neither the Russian nor global epistemic community is fully capable of conveying its paradigm to the other through cooperation or persuasion in a deliberate, strategic and systematic manner.

PART 2
Social Learning

Chapter 5

US Telecommunications Policy:
A Process of Social Learning

Michael J. Zarkin

During the last three decades United States (US) telecommunications policy has undergone a transformation. Prior to that time, government regulation separated the telecommunications industry into technologically distinct niches. The telephone and cable television industries were treated as natural monopolies and subject to public utility style regulation. In contrast, the broadcasting and data processing industries were allowed to engage in marketplace competition. Whether treated as monopolies or competitive enterprises, however, the various sectors of the telecommunications industry were barred from directly participating in each other's markets.

Since 1980, telecommunications regulation in the US has changed in two significant ways. First, the telephone and cable television industries have been opened to competition. Second, the formerly separate niches are integrating and competing with one another. The turning point came when the US Federal Communications Commission (FCC) issued its second computer decision, allowing telephone companies and data processing providers to compete with one another. A series of subsequent FCC decisions in the 1980s and 1990s moved the telephone and cable television industries toward competition. Finally, in 1996, Congress passed the Telecommunications Act, removing the major regulatory barriers to competition among the telephone, cable television, broadcasting, and information service markets.

This chapter will demonstrate that the transformation of US telecommunications policy is a consequence of social learning. The empirical parameters of the study revolve around the relationship between three sectors of the telecommunications industry: telephony, data communications,[1] and cable television. The study begins with a detailed discussion of the pertinent theoretical propositions. These propositions are then tested against evidence drawn from several major instances of telecommunications policymaking undertaken by the FCC and US Congress between 1934 and 1996.

---

1   For the purposes of this study, data communications generally includes those services integrating computers and telephone technology.

Social Learning and Policy Change

The notion that government policymaking can be viewed as a process of social learning was first introduced in Hugh Heclo's study of social policy in Britain and Sweden.[2] Heclo concludes that variables such as societal change, electoral politics, and interest group pressure do not fully account for policy change. While important, these factors generally serve as environmental stimuli, making issues more salient within policy circles. Instead, Heclo argues that substantive policy change occurs across time because state actors become dissatisfied with previous policy and undertake intellectual searches for new policy solutions. These intellectual searches are the core component of social learning.

While Heclo outlines the notion of social learning in general terms, subsequent scholarship has more systematically described processes through which it occurs. In particular, Richard Rose argues that policymaking is often the result of "lesson-drawing," i.e., state actors use previous experience to develop solutions to current policy problems.[3] Peter Hall and Lawrence Dodd further suggest that the experiential learning of policymakers is sometimes guided by broad patterns of ideas referred to as policy "paradigms" or "epistemologies."[4] Building on these theoretical specifications, three propositions to guide this study are developed below:

1) *Discrete instances of telecommunications policymaking between 1934 and 1996 were shaped by experiential lesson-drawing.* Experiential lessons are particularly crucial during the policy formulation stage. Policymakers fashion policy instruments either by drawing on the past experiences of their organizations, or by borrowing from the experiences of actors in other jurisdictions.[5] Drawing lessons from past experience is a particularly useful way to make relatively minor adjustments in existing policies, such as varying spending levels from one year to the next or adjusting rate structures for public utilities. Occasionally, however, policymakers draw upon past experience by taking a policy instrument developed for a completely different purpose and applying it to a new situation. This second

---

2   Hugh Heclo, *Modern Social Politics in Britain and Sweden: From Relief to Income Maintenance* (New Haven, CT: Yale University Press, 1974).

3   Richard Rose, *Lesson-Drawing in Public Policy: A Guide to Learning Across Time and Space* (Chatham, NJ: Chatham House, 1993). It should be noted that Rose does not restrict lesson-drawing to state actors. For the purposes of this study, however, lesson-drawing by state actors will be the specific focus.

4   Peter A. Hall, "Policy Paradigms, Social Learning and the State: The Case of Economic Policymaking in Britain," *Comparative Politics* vol. 25 (1993), pp. 275-296; Lawrence C. Dodd, "Political Learning and Political Change: Understanding Development Across Time," in Lawrence C. Dodd and Calvin Jillson, eds., *The Dynamics of American Politics*, (Boulder, CO: Westview Press, 1994), pp. 331-364.

5   Richard Rose, "What is Lesson-Drawing?" *Journal of Public Policy* vol. 11 (1991), pp. 3-30.

scenario is most likely to occur when policymakers draw conceptual analogies between previous problems and the current situation.[6]

Other times, however, situations arise that are completely unprecedented. In these instances, policymakers often turn to the experiences or expertise of those in other policy venues engaged in similar problems. These individuals may include academics or researchers, or they may include policymakers in other cities, states, or nations. This second type of lesson-drawing takes place through such venues as hearings, professional conferences, academic journals, and informal contacts, and involves the transfer of a policy instrument or idea from one jurisdiction to another. These policy transfers may include simply copying verbatim a policy already in place in another jurisdiction, synthesizing components of programs in place in two or more places, or using a program from another region as an intellectual inspiration for devising an analogous policy.[7]

2) *Telecommunications policy between 1934 and 1996 was guided by one or more "policy epistemologies."* Following the work of Dodd, a policy epistemology is a general belief system or set of shared ideas that frames the policy learning process.[8] In its most developed form, a policy epistemology resembles the kind of coherent theoretical belief system described by Hall as a "policy paradigm."[9] More often, however, a policy epistemology consists of a shared language, a set of loosely coupled ideas and rules that provide a way of interpreting new policymaking situations. Whether tight theories or more diffuse intellectual constructs, policy epistemologies reflect the social, technological, and political environment and prevailing ideas regarding state-market relations.

Policy epistemologies are likely to take hold in areas that are highly knowledge based, requiring the complex understandings of economic, technological, and social circumstances that accompany professional expertise. For that reason, enduring epistemologies are found in areas where administrative agencies have significant discretion over policy. While professionals in different fields may adhere to very different views of the world, administrative policymaking is an instrumental process in which experience provides a strong justification for policy effectiveness. Furthermore, as March and Olsen point out, individuals in organizations tend to work within a "logic of appropriateness" in which institutional norms and routines become very important.[10] Thus, within administrative agencies, policy epistemologies become enmeshed with the standard operating procedures that guide decision-making on a

---

6   Rose, "What is Lesson-Drawing?" p. 13.

7   Rose, "What is Lesson-Drawing," pp. 19-24.

8   Here, I adapt Dodd's broader notion of a political epistemology; see Dodd, "Political Learning and Political Change," p. 333.

9   Hall, "Policy Paradigms, Social Learning, and the State," p. 279. I explain more fully why I use the policy epistemology concept instead of Hall's "policy paradigm" in Michael Zarkin, *Social Learning and the History of US Telecommunications Policy, 1900-1996* (Lewiston, NY: The Edwin Mellen Press, 2003), pp. 32-34.

10   James G. March and Johan P. Olsen, *Rediscovering Institutions: The Organizational Basis of Politics* (New York: Free Press, 1989), pp. 160-161.

daily basis. Because bureaucrats tend to be rigid in their behavior, policy change and institutional change are interrelated. Significant policy change may require reorganization and new personnel who are able to break with old procedures and find new patterns of action.

While the existence of a stable administrative authority aids the institutionalization of an epistemology, policymaking in the US is rarely confined to a single venue. Instead, policy is made within the broader context of a policy community consisting of the political actors engaged a specific issue area. Members of the policy community may include policymakers in multiple governmental institutions as well as interest groups and academic researchers. Policy communities may be very cohesive entities, consisting of a relatively small group of like-minded actors, or they may be very fluid and conflictual, representing multiple interests and decision arenas.[11] Furthermore, policy communities are subject to evolution across time as interest groups and institutional actors move in and out of the policy process.

Given the diverse and changing nature of policy communities, the institutionalization of an epistemology frequently requires the presence of a like-minded group of professionals comprising an epistemic community. As is discussed more fully in Chapters 1 and 4, an epistemic community is "a network of professionals with recognized expertise and competence in a particular domain and an authoritative claim to policy-relevant knowledge."[12] Epistemic communities typically consist of a diverse group of professionals that possess a shared set of normative and causal beliefs regarding the nature of policy problems and the most appropriate policy instruments to resolve them. If an epistemic community comes to dominate a particular policy community, its members are called upon for advice and granted positions of authority.

Lacking such a cohesive group of professionals, the institutionalization of any single policy epistemology is not imminent. In some instances there may be several competing epistemologies coexisting within a policy community.[13] If the governing authority is fragmented over several institutions or jurisdictions, multiple epistemologies may simultaneously guide policymaking and conflict may ensue. Furthermore, the existence of an entrenched policy epistemology does not guarantee path dependency or preclude significant policy change. Policy epistemologies become outmoded across time and must be reassessed, revised, and replaced, a process here referred to as "epistemology reconstruction."

---

11 R.A.W. Rhodes and David Marsh, "New Directions in the Study of Policy Networks," *European Journal of Political Research* vol. 21 (1992), pp. 181-205.

12 Peter Haas, "Epistemic Communities and International Policy Coordination," *International Organization* vol. 46 (1992), p. 3.

13 This point is made by Paul Sabatier and Hank Jenkins-Smith in their work on policy-oriented learning in policy communities. See Hank C. Jenkins-Smith and Paul Sabatier, "The Dynamics of Policy-Oriented Learning," in Paul A. Sabatier and Hank C. Jenkins-Smith, eds., *Policy Change and Learning: An Advocacy Coalition Approach*, (Boulder, CO: Westview Press, 1993), pp. 41-56.

3) *There was a telecommunications epistemology reconstruction between 1980 and 1996.* Epistemology reconstruction typically accompanies broader shifts in the ideas that structure expectations about the relationship between the state and private sector.[14] Epistemology shifts may be stimulated by electoral realignments, shifting patterns of interest group power, changes in institutional leadership, and crises and focusing events. In many instances, however, a shift in policy epistemology involves an intellectual crisis in which elites are forced to break with long-standing patterns of action and embrace radically new policy alternatives.

While the process of epistemology reconstruction varies by policy area, it is possible to identify some of the political circumstances that characterize these shifts. Epistemology reconstruction generally ensues when new economic, technological, or social circumstances emerge that cannot be fully comprehended or resolved within the logic of entrenched ideas and standards. Policymakers may initially respond by applying policy instruments that fail to solve the problem, and in some instances make the situation worse. In the wake of policy failure, decision-makers are left casting about for new solutions to resolve previously unforeseeable dilemmas.[15]

Within this context, a window of opportunity opens for members of the policy community to articulate broad new patterns of policy action. These "policy entrepreneurs" that step forward to advocate new epistemologies may be bureaucrats, legislators, interest group leaders, or academics. Regardless of their immediate institutional origins, however, policy entrepreneurs most likely belong to an epistemic community of the type discussed above. In the instances where epistemology change is conflictual, policy entrepreneurs may emerge in rival venues, challenging existing lines of authority.

Regardless of their institutional origins, policy entrepreneurs face the difficult task of overcoming the political and intellectual commitments that continue to surround the old epistemology. To succeed, policy entrepreneurs must be able to define the problems faced by society and explain why the solutions prescribed by the new epistemology are the most feasible. Claims to technical expertise aid the entrepreneur in the quest to advance her views. In many instances, however, the policy entrepreneur must also be someone who possesses the political clout to raise her voice above others in the policy debate.[16]

While policy entrepreneurs are important, the exact timing and nature of epistemology change differs from one policy area to another. Epistemology reconstructions may occur suddenly with extensive public involvement, or they may take place incrementally within elite circles. The circumstances surrounding

---

14 Examples include such things as "regulatory regimes." See Marc Allen Eisner, *Regulatory Politics in Transition* (Baltimore, MD: Johns Hopkins Press, 1993).

15 This is similar to the process of policy "paradigm shift" described by Hall in "Policy Paradigms, Social Learning, and the State," pp. 280-281.

16 On policy entrepreneurs, see John Kingdon, *Agendas, Alternatives, and Public Policies*, 2d ed. (New York: Harper Collins, 1995), pp. 179-183.

epistemology reconstruction ultimately depend upon the political environment that characterizes the policy in question.[17]

In concluding this section, it should be noted that preliminary evidence supports each of the three propositions discussed above. Between 1934 and 1971, telecommunications policy was guided by an epistemology here referred to as *regulatory separation*, which involved strict regulation and structural separation of different sectors of the industry. Policymaking during this time drew on past experiences that were consistent with the existing epistemology. By the 1970s, however, a number of forces including technological change, interest group pressure, and macroeconomic conditions placed the existing epistemology under strain. The foundations of a new policy epistemology, here referred to as *competitive integration*, grew out of ideas advanced by economists from the Chicago School and related intellectual traditions. Over the next twenty-five years, policy entrepreneurs in multiple governmental venues brought these ideas to the forefront, gradually enacting policies based in the principles of competition. During this time, patterns of lesson-drawing reinforced the new epistemology.

The First Epistemology: Regulatory Separation

Roughly between 1900 and 1934, a policy epistemology for the regulation of the US telecommunications industry developed around two tenets: 1) the telephone industry was treated as a rate-regulated public utility, and 2) kept structurally separate from other sectors of the industry including broadcasting. This strategy, here referred to as *regulatory separation*, was defensible on two grounds.

First, most economists and state regulators during this period concluded that the telephone industry was a natural monopoly, i.e. an industry in which one firm provides the most efficient service.[18] Because monopolies' market share tends to

---

17 Policy scholars employing a variety of theoretical approaches note that "policy determines politics." See Theodore J. Lowi, "American Business, Public Policy, Case Studies, and Political Theory," *World Politics* vol. 16 (1964), pp. 687-691; James Q. Wilson, *Political Organizations* (New York: Basic Books, 1973); and Paul Pierson, "When Effect Becomes Cause: Policy Feedback and Political Change," *World Politics* vol. 45 (1993), pp. 595-628. With respect to social learning, this point is well-articulated in William D. Coleman, Grace D. Skogstad, and Michael M. Atkinson, "Paradigm Shifts and Policy Networks: Cumulative Change in Agriculture," *Journal of Public Policy* vol. 16 (1996), pp. 273-301. I borrow liberally from these authors in reaching this conclusion.

18 Economists during the Progressive Era provided a modern definition of natural monopoly and suggested government control as a solution. On the telephone problem, see Richard Ely, *Monopolies and Trusts*, (New York: The Macmillan Company, 1912). The need for regulatory control of industrial capitalism was also stated in broader terms several years earlier by Henry Carter Adams; see his "Relation of the State to Industrial Action," in Joseph Dorfman, ed., *Two Essays by Henry Carter Adams* (New York: August M. Kelly, 1969), pp. 59-133. Regulators reached similar conclusions through their experiences with competition in the telephone industry; see Alan Stone, *Public Service Liberalism* (Princeton, NJ: Princeton

yield excessively high profits, government regulation was seen as a way to ensure that telephone companies earned a fair rate-of-return. Furthermore, it was feared that participation by monopolies in competitive lines of business lead to predatory pricing and other anticompetitive abuses. Acting on these fears, Congress included a provision in the Federal Radio Act of 1927 aimed at keeping telephone companies and broadcasters out of each other's markets.[19]

Second, regulation was justifiable because the telephone industry was viewed as a public utility: a good or service deemed so essential to the community that it must be provided on a non-discriminatory basis. To this end, government regulation served as a way to make telephone service available to the population without sacrificing industry profits. Through regulation, the telephone industry was guaranteed stable earnings and insulated from competition. In exchange for these protections, telephone companies were expected to make basic telephone service widely available at reasonable charges.[20]

These basic principles were codified in the Communications Act of 1934, which created the FCC and gave it broad powers to regulate interstate telecommunications. Title I of the Communications Act established the goal of "[making] available, so far as possible, to all the people of the United States, a rapid, efficient, nationwide and world-wide wire and radio communications service with adequate facilities at reasonable charges." Title II, sec. 202 made it illegal for any licensed telephone company to discriminate "in charges . . . facilities, or services." Title II, sec. 204 empowered the commission to investigate proposed telephone rate changes, and sec. 205 authorized the prescription of "just and reasonable" rates when necessary. Finally, Title II, sec. 214 gave the FCC the authority to grant entry into the telephone business by approving the extension of new lines.

As the provisions mentioned above indicate, the Communications Act outlined broad policy goals that were consistent with the logic of regulatory separation. Between 1934 and 1971, the FCC used its policymaking authority in a manner consistent with the regulatory separation epistemology, even as the societal conditions upon which the epistemology was originally formulated changed dramatically.

FCC Policymaking under Regulatory Separation

A core component of public utility regulation was the setting of rates and profit levels through a methodology known as rate-of-return regulation. Rate-of-return regulation was based around the assumption that the firm needed to set rates at a level that covered the operating costs contained in its rate base while at the same

---

University Press, 1991), p. 127; and Jeffrey E. Cohen, "The Telephone Problem and the Road to Telephone Regulation, 1876-1917," *Journal of Policy History*, vol. 3 (1991), pp. 51-52.

19 Robert B. Horwitz, *The Irony of Regulatory Reform: The Deregulation of American Telecommunications* (New York: Oxford University Press, 1989), p. 119.

20 For a further discussion of the public utility concept see Stone, *Public Service Liberalism*, pp. 31-38.

time earning sufficient profits to allow for expansion and technological innovation. Generally speaking, profits were measured as an appropriate level of earnings above the value of the rate base. Thus, for regulators, the rate-of-return methodology proceeded in two stages: establishing an appropriate overall profit level for the firm and then creating a schedule of charges for individual services that both maintained profit levels and prevented cross-subsidization and other anticompetitive behaviors.[21] Far from novel at the time, the rate-of-return methodology was a long-standing instrument of public utility regulation, employed by the Interstate Commerce Commission and state regulators to set railroad rates since the turn of the twentieth century.[22] Rate-of-return regulation was also consistent with the Progressive logic of state intervention, representing an attempt to use government to approximate market conditions in an otherwise monopolistic industry.

Aside from the monitoring of finances, the FCC's regulatory strategy during this period consisted of keeping telephone service structurally separate from other sectors of the telecommunications industry. Between 1956 and 1971, technological developments threatened to alter the telecommunications marketplace by subjecting the telephone industry to greater competition. Rather than moving decidedly in the direction of competition, however, the FCC implemented policies consistent with the existing policy epistemology. As a result, competition was minimized and the new technologies were isolated within niches.

One such technological development was microwave-based communication. Because microwave technology employs high frequency radio waves instead of a wire infrastructure, it gradually became more cost-effective for multiple firms to provide long distance offerings. The FCC, however, responded to these technological developments with extreme caution, choosing to sustain the wire-based long distance telephone monopoly and treat microwave providers as "specialized" carriers. In 1959, the FCC began authorizing businesses to build private microwave systems for their internal corporate communications.[23] Over the next decade, the FCC gradually began licensing commercial microwave providers, but only for the provision of "specialized" telecommunications offerings that differed significantly from traditional long distance telephone service.[24] In essence, the FCC dealt with the development of microwave technology by limiting it to the prescribed parameters of its own industry niche.

The second major technological shift confronted by the FCC during this time was the development of computer-based data communications services. Data

---

21 Charles Phillips, *The Regulation of Public Utilities: Theory and Practice* (Arlington, VA: Public Utilities Reports, Inc., 1985), p. 187; Charges for Interstate and Foreign Communications Services, 9 FCC 2d. 30 (1967), pp. 51-54.

22 Martin G. Glaeser, *Outlines of Public Utility Regulation* (New York: Macmillan, 1927), p. 275; Thomas K. McCraw, *Prophets of Regulation* (Cambridge, MA: Belknap Press, 1984), pp. 31-40.

23 Microwave Frequencies in the Band Above 890 Mc., 27 FCC 359 (1959), p. 388.

24 MCI Telecommunications Corp., 18 FCC 2d 953 (1969); Specialized Common Carriers, 29 FCC 2d 870 (1971), recon. Denied, 31 FCC 2d 1106 (1971).

communications integrated computer and telephone technologies in ways that frequently made it difficult to separate the two.[25] Data communications showed the potential to be a highly competitive enterprise if left unregulated. Much like broadcasting several decades earlier, FCC officials believed that regulatory boundaries needed to be drawn to prevent the telephone industry from using its market power to leverage a monopoly in data communications. Because telephone technology was an integral component of data communications services, however, FCC officials recognized that it would be unrealistic to completely prevent telephone companies from participating in data communications markets. In response to these considerations, in 1971 the FCC adopted a *maximum separation* policy under which telephone companies could only provide data communications offerings through a fully separate subsidiary that had virtually no business ties to the parent company. The separate subsidiary requirement was intended to curb the market power of the telephone companies.[26] In imposing this requirement, however, the FCC made an assumption that telephone and data communication services could be treated as distinct niches for the foreseeable future.

The final technological development that the FCC had to contend with during this period was cable television. In the mid-1960s, cable television served principally as a mechanism for delivering television signals to rural areas, just as the telephone acted as a "carrier" for the voice messages of others. Recognizing this similarity as well as the economic potential of cable technology, telephone companies began building and operating cable systems in competition with independent cable service providers. By 1966, independent providers were complaining to the FCC that telephone companies were engaging in business practices that were aimed at developing a cable television monopoly. Following an administrative inquiry, the FCC concluded in 1970 that cable television should be allowed to develop as an independent sector of the communications industry and issued an ownership ban prohibiting telephone companies from providing both cable television and telephone services in the same geographical areas. In the instances where telephone companies did provide cable television service, they were required to do so through a fully separate subsidiary of the type mandated for the provision of data communications. In essence, through its cable-telephone cross-ownership restrictions, the FCC recognized cable television as another technologically distinct industry niche.

In this section it has been argued that the FCC did not stray far from the logic of the "regulatory separation" following the passage of the Communications Act of 1934. The rate-setting methods chosen by the commission grew out of well-established precedents consistent with the logic of public utility regulation. Furthermore, between

---

25 Today we associate data communications with the Internet and other methods of delivering video and data content over the telephone lines. In the 1960s, however, data communications assumed more primitive forms, such as the transmission of stock quotes over telephone lines into a special computer device. See Alan Stone, *Wrong Number: The Breakup of AT&T* (New York: Basic Books, 1989), pp. 202-205.

26 Computer I, 28 FCC 2d 267 (1971).

the 1950s and the early 1970s, technological changes threatened to significantly alter the landscape of the telecommunications marketplace. In spite of these new realities, however, the FCC dealt with technological change by fashioning policies that were logically consistent with the existing epistemology. The evidence seems to indicate that regulators drew lessons from pre-existing patterns of action in deciding to keep microwave communications, data communications, and cable television structurally separate from the telephone industry. During the 1970s and 1980s, however, further technological changes combined with a changing political environment would cause regulators to fundamentally reconsider regulatory separation, opting instead for a more competitive telecommunications policy.

The Move toward Competition, 1971-1980

The period between 1971 and 1980 is best characterized as the beginning of an epistemology reconstruction in US telecommunications policy. During this time, policymakers gravitated toward "deregulation" as a means of achieving economic efficiency, combating inflation, and lowering consumer prices. Against the wishes of industry giants like The American Telephone and Telegraph Company (AT&T), decisionmakers in all three branches of the federal government considered policy changes designed to make the telecommunications industry more competitive.

This sea change in US telecommunications policy was in part related to changes in the political environment that accompanied further technological developments. By the early 1970s, microwave competition gave small firms like Microwave Communications, Inc. (MCI) the opportunity to expand into new markets and develop services that chipped away at the established telephone monopoly. In addition, further advances in data communications technology undermined the FCC's maximum separation policy for data communications and created the possibility of further competition in this area as well. As smaller firms clamored to compete in telecommunications markets, a new group of interests began to enter the telecommunications policy community and lobby for the dissolution of the telephone monopoly.

As noted above, however, the FCC attempted to walk a fine line with respect to technological change, gradually introducing competition while at the same time remaining true to established regulatory principles until well into the 1970s. The result of this strategy was that neither traditional telephone companies nor their new competitors were satisfied with the outcomes. AT&T, for instance, believed that the FCC had gone too far by introducing even limited competition, while the newly emerging competitors sought more rapid changes in policy.

Thus, by the mid-1970s, both sides sought out alternative decision-making venues to resolve political conflict. In 1976, AT&T turned to Congress in an effort to gain passage of legislation to restore its monopoly, a move that ultimately backfired when Congress instead considered legislation that would have extended competition. AT&T's competitors, especially MCI, turned to the courts and the US Department of Justice, seeking to end the AT&T long distance monopoly and force the firm to compete on even footing. Ultimately, the efforts of AT&T's competitors paid off, leading to the end of the long distance telephone monopoly and the structural dissolution of the firm under an antitrust consent decree in 1984.[27]

Yet neither technological change nor interest group politics fully explained why the regulatory separation epistemology began to crumble in the 1970s. The move to deregulate telecommunications in the 1970s was shaped by new policy ideas advanced by Chicago School economic analysts. Beginning in the early 1960s, scholarship emanating from the Chicago School and related lines of economic thinking advanced the argument that government rate regulation of utilities was wasteful. Specifically, Chicago School analysts theorized that rate-of-return regulation was a potential cause of economic inefficiency and anticompetitive behavior in the long distance telephone industry. Because rate-of-return regulation measured profits as a percentage above operating costs, firms had the incentive to overcapitalize to increase dollar earnings. Furthermore, because additional capitalization contributed to the overall rate base, regulated firms had an incentive to expand into new markets. If the markets were competitive, and if regulators were ineffective at monitoring charges for individual services, cross subsidization and anticompetitive behavior might occur.[28] Efficiency and anticompetitive behavior had long been concerns of telecommunications policymakers. When viewed through the lenses of Chicago School thinking, however, regulation was the *cause* of these problems rather than a solution to them. For Chicago School analysts, promoting greater competition within the telecommunications industry was the solution to inefficiency and anticompetitive behaviors.

In the early 1970s, economists and lawyers schooled in these ideas became a part of the Washington community. Many of them worked in think tanks where their research was uniquely accessible to policymakers. Others found employment in government, working in such venues as the US Congress, the Department of Justice, and numerous regulatory agencies, including the FCC. Forming a kind of epistemic community, these Chicago School devotees used their positions of influence to advocate deregulation as the basis of a new economic policy.[29]

By 1980, this new "free market" epistemic community had infiltrated the FCC and was successfully fostering policy change. Personnel changes at the FCC beginning in the late 1970s led to the creation of an environment in which these new policy ideas were more actively considered. In 1977, President Jimmy Carter appointed Charles Ferris, a strong advocate of deregulation, to chair the commission.

---

27 For a good overview of the events discussed above, see Peter Temin, *The Fall of the Bell System: A Study in Prices and Politics* (New York: Cambridge Press, 1987), pp. 70-191.

28 For the classic Chicago School criticism of public utility regulation, see Harvey Averch and Leland Johnson, "The Behavior of the Firm under Regulatory Constraint," *American Economics Review* vol. 52 (1962), pp. 1052-1069.

29 Martha Derthick and Paul J. Quirk, *The Politics of Deregulation* (Washington, DC: Brookings Institution, 1985); Temin, *Fall of the Bell System*, p. 38.

Presidents Ronald Reagan and George Bush, Sr. appointed FCC Chairmen Mark Fowler, Dennis Patrick, and Alfred Sikes, who were also committed to the free market philosophy. These chairmen, in turn, appointed bureau chiefs and other key senior staff members who shared their views. Also during this time, the FCC's Office of Plans and Policy, a policy analysis division dominated by economists, became highly active in advocating pro-competitive policies, some of which were ultimately adopted by the commission.[30]

Between 1980 and 1992, several major policy changes were undertaken by the FCC to make long distance telephone service, data communications, and cable television more competitive enterprises. In addition, the changing technological realities of these industries forced the FCC to abandon the notion that these regulatory "niches" were distinct enterprises. As a result, some of the FCC's most prominent policy changes during the 1980s were aimed at fostering competition *among* the industry niches. For these reasons, the new telecommunications policy epistemology that began to develop through FCC policymaking during the 1980s is here referred to as *competitive integration*.

The Second Epistemology:　Competitive Integration

The move toward competition and industry niche integration at the FCC between 1980 and 1992 may be seen in key policy decisions relating to data communications regulation, long distance telephone rate regulation, and cable television. In each of these decisions, the FCC's actions were not only informed by a new policy epistemology, but were also in many instances shaped by "lessons" the agency drew from experience.

With respect to data communications, the FCC experimented with two different policies between 1980 and 1986. Both decisions were prompted by the realization that technological changes had rendered the "maximum separation" policy adopted a decade earlier unworkable. Increasing technological integration between telephones and computers in the provision of data communications services necessitated that the FCC find a more flexible regulatory system that did not insist on absolute structural separation.[31]

30　With respect to the influence of free market thinking within the agency during this time, see Derthick and Quirk, *Politics of Deregulation*, pp. 64-85; Douglas Webbink, "The Recent Deregulatory Movement at the FCC," in Leonard Lewin, ed., *Telecommunications in the US: Trends and Policies* (Dedham, MA: Artech, 1981), p. 62; and, Zarkin, *Social Learning and the History of US Telecommunications Policy*, pp. 117-143.

31　An important consideration for the FCC here was the rapid replacement of mainframe computer terminals with a larger number of "smart" terminals that collected, processed, and sent data over the telephone lines. This was probably the beginning of what we think of today as the "PC revolution." See AT&T Revisions to Tariffs 260 and 267 Relating to Dataspeed 40, 62 FCC 2d 21 (1977).

In response to these considerations, the FCC issued a decision in 1980 that partially abandoned the maximum separation policy in favor of a "resale" mechanism that allowed for greater competition and technological integration in the provision of data communications services. The resale mechanism was an adaptation of a policy instrument tried several years earlier to foster competition in long distance telephone service.[32] The resale mechanism allowed telephone companies to abandon fully separate subsidiaries for the provision of data communications and replace them with resale subsidiaries that had greater flexibility to integrate technologies. Through resale, the FCC hoped that telephone companies could integrate telephone and computer technologies in more innovative ways while providing competing data communications service providers with the same opportunities.[33]

By the mid 1980s, however, the FCC had concluded that the resale mechanism, though more flexible than maximum separation, was an inefficient mechanism given rapid technological change. Furthermore, resale still required telephone companies to use a separate subsidiary to provide data communications services in an effort to prevent anticompetitive behavior. Free market advocates at the commission believed that such a mechanism was inefficient because it imposed economic costs on telephone companies to address problems that could be handled through less invasive regulatory mechanisms. In response to these considerations, in 1986 the FCC issued an order aimed at replacing subsidiaries with "non-structural" regulatory mechanisms of the kind developed several years earlier in an inquiry dealing with long distance competition.[34] Telephone companies could abandon separate subsidiaries once they demonstrated to regulators that they were providing competitors with non-discriminatory access to their networks and facilities. FCC regulators hoped that these non-structural regulatory safeguards would enable telephone companies and other service providers to compete more vigorously and become more innovative in their data communications offerings.[35]

Data communications aside, the free market philosophy also influenced the FCC's decision to implement a new system of long distance telephone rate regulation during the late 1980s. By that time, decades of experience suggested to FCC regulators that rate-of-return regulation was an unworkable methodology. For more than fifteen years, regulators had amassed evidence suggesting that rate-of-return regulation was providing AT&T with incentives to engage in rate-padding and anticompetitive conduct of the kind that Chicago School critics had predicted years earlier.[36] Seeking to find a method of rate regulation that would promote greater

32 Resale and Shared Use of Common Carrier Services and Facilities, 60 FCC 2d 261 (1976).

33 Second Computer Inquiry, 72 FCC 2d 420 (1980).

34 Gerald Brock, *Telecommunications Policy for the Information Age: From Monopoly to Competition* (Cambridge, MA: Harvard University Press, 1994), p. 224.

35 Third Computer Inquiry, 104 FCC 2d 968 (1986).

36 Gerald Brock, *Telecommunications Policy for the Information Age*, pp. 259-260.

efficiency and deter anticompetitive conduct while the long distance industry made the transition to competition, FCC regulators turned to "price caps" in 1989.

Originally proposed by two FCC economists in 1987,[37] price caps regulation drew heavily on the British experience, where a similar methodology was implemented several years earlier.[38] Rather than trying to control prices through profit ceilings, the price caps method separated different classes of services into "baskets" and set average prices within each grouping to increase at a rate of inflation minus 3% to allow for productivity gains. The regulated firm was then allowed to keep any profits generated as a result of increased economic efficiency. In this respect the price caps approach spoke directly to the efficiency concerns of Chicago School critics. Furthermore, grouping services into different "baskets" reduced the opportunity for cost shifting and other anticompetitive practices. Thus, FCC officials saw implementation of price caps regulation as a regulatory "bridge" to full competition within the industry.

Finally, during this period, the FCC became dissatisfied with the cable-telephone cross-ownership ban. The growth and development of the cable television industry combined with a changing economic and technological environment made competition with telephone companies seem more desirable. By the late 1980s there was a growing belief among some members of the telecommunications policy community that the marketplace demands of the information age were causing the two technologies to converge.[39] Telephone companies, in particular, promoted deregulation in this area, arguing that their entrance into cable television markets would provide them with the economic incentive to build a national fiber optics network with the capacity to carry the kinds of high-capacity data and video communications that information age industries would demand.[40]

Technically the FCC could not completely abandon the cable-telephone cross-ownership ban because Congress has written it into law in the early 1980s. Instead, the FCC settled on a strategy for promoting competition and technological integration through a policy instrument known as "video dial-tone." Originally suggested by

---

37 John Haring and Evan Kwerel, *Competition Policy in the Post-Equal Access Market*, Working Paper 22, Office of Plans and Policy, 2 FCC Rcd. 1488 (1987).

38 The price caps idea was developed by Stephen C. Littlechild as a more efficient way to regulate the recently privatized British Telecom. See *Regulation of British Telecommunication Profitability* (London: Department of Trade and Industry, 1983). In the working paper referenced in footnote 38, Haring and Kwerel cite a trade journal article as the source of their knowledge about the British price caps plan. The notice of proposed rulemaking in the price caps inquiry, however, cites Littlechild's report at length. See Policy and Rules Concerning Rates for Dominant Carriers, 4 FCC Rcd. 2873 (1989).

39 Indicative of this belief was a report published by the US Department of Commerce called *NTIA Telecom 2000: Charting the Course for a New Century* (Washington, DC: Government Printing Office, 1988).

40 Telephone Company Cable Television Cross-ownership Rules, 2 FCC Rcd. 5092 (1987); 3 FCC Rcd. 5849 (1988).

the Department of Commerce in a 1988 report,[41] video dial-tone allowed telephone companies to serve as a neutral carrier of video programming for cable companies, much as they delivered the voice messages of private individuals. When Alfred Sikes moved over from the Department of Commerce to become FCC Chairman in 1989, he sought to bring the video dial-tone concept into the cable-telephone debate, ultimately implementing it through a rulemaking completed in the 1990s.[42]

Thus, the video dial-tone rulemaking was the last major step in the direction of competitive integration during this time. The issues raised during these years, including the need to promote competition, technological integration, and infrastructure development were revisited later in the 1990s by Congress as it considered rewriting the country's telecommunications laws.

The Telecommunications Act of 1996

By the end of the 1980s, the Chicago School revolution had significantly altered the terms of debate over telecommunications policy in Washington. The move toward competition, while painful at first, caused telecommunications companies to restructure their business practices. By that time, formerly entrenched monopolies sought opportunities to compete in new markets. Furthermore, as noted above, technological advances such as fiber optics promised to make possible formerly unheard of new "information age" services that combined voice, video, and data transmission. For many industry players, the only obstacles standing in the way of these economic realities were regulatory barriers to competition.[43]

It was within this context that several members of Congress, including Representative Edward Markey (D-MA) and Senators Ernest Hollings (D-SC) and Conrad Burns (R-MT) began actively considering legislative proposals for policy reform. The need to maintain competitiveness in the information age was a particularly important topic between 1989 and 1993. Numerous legislative hearings in the late 1980s and early 1990s revealed that the US was falling behind other industrialized countries in the telecommunications sector.[44] France, for example, was making public

---

41 US National Telecommunications and Information Administration, *Video Program Distribution and Cable Television: Current Policy Issues and Recommendations*, (Washington, DC: Government Printing Office, 1988).

42 See, for instance, Telephone Company-Cable Television Cross-Ownership Rules, 7 FCC Rcd. 5781 (1992).

43 Mike Mills, "Spirit of Cooperation Breaks Media Industry Gridlock," *Congressional Quarterly Weekly Report* vol. 52 (1994), p. 426; "A Digital Breakthrough," *Congressional Quarterly Weekly Report* vol. 52 (1994), p. 66.

44 See Congress, House, Subcommittee on Telecommunications and Finance of the Energy and Commerce Committee, *Modified Final Judgment*, 100th Congress, 1st Session, July 30, 1987, pp. 89-198; Congress, House, Subcommittee on Telecommunications and Finance of the Committee on Energy and Commerce, *Networks of the Future*, 101st Congress, 2nd Session, October 4, 1989, pp. 1-2; Congress, Senate, Subcommittee on Communications of the Committee on Commerce, Science, and Transportation, *Telecommunications Equipment*

investments in information services through its "minitel" system, while Japan was investing billions of dollars in the construction of a fiber optic telecommunications infrastructure.[45]   With rising federal budget deficits and a general bias against large-scale industrial policy ventures in the United States, public investment in the telecommunications infrastructure seemed infeasible. Nevertheless, the industrial policy efforts of other countries influenced Congressional policymakers who sought ways to remain globally competitive as the country entered the information age.

For many policymakers and interest group leaders, the solution to this dilemma seemed to be increased competition within the telecommunications industry. In many of the ensuing legislative debates, some telephone companies reiterated their argument that removing barriers to competition in high-tech telecommunications markets would provide them with the incentive to invest in information services and rapidly deploy a fiber optic infrastructure. By that time, their claims were backed up by several government reports that highlighted the need for a more proactive telecommunications policy.[46]   From a rhetorical standpoint, the idea of using competition to promote infrastructure development worked perfectly – it was easily understood by legislators, promised results without public investment, and fit neatly with the already established trend of competition and deregulation in US telecommunications policy.

With the newly-elected Clinton Administration promising to make the "information superhighway" a top priority, telecommunications policy reform emerged as a prominent issue on the Congressional agenda in 1993. Legislation was introduced both in the House and Senate to allow local telephone companies, long distance telephone companies, and cable television companies to openly compete with one another.[47]   While two bills passed the House in June of 1994, Senate Republicans and Democrats were unable to reach a compromise and no legislation was passed that year.[48]

Research and Manufacturing Competition Act, 101st Congress, 2nd Session, April 25, 1990; Congress, Senate, Subcommittee on Communications of the Committee on Commerce, Science, and Transportation, *Communications Competitiveness and Infrastructure Modernization Act of 1990*, 101st Congress, 2nd Session, July 24, 1990.

45 On France, see House, *Modified Final Judgment*, pp. 89-198; on the Japanese situation, see Heather E. Hudson, *Global Connections: International Telecommunications Infrastructure and Policy* (New York: Van Nostrand Reinhold, 1997), p. 116.

46 On the general need for infrastructure development, see Congress, Office of Technology Assessment, *Critical Connections: Communication for the Future* (Washington DC: Government Printing Office, 1990); on competition and infrastructure development, see US Department of Commerce, National Telecommunications and Information Administration, *The NTIA Infrastructure Report: Telecommunications in an Age of Information*, NTIA Special Publication 91-26 (Washington, DC: Government Printing Office, 1991).

47 H.R. 3626 (1993), H.R. 3636 (1993), S. 1822 (1994).

48 Jon Healy, "New Telecommunications Age Hits a Snag in the Senate," *Congressional Quarterly Weekly Report* vol. 52 (1994), p. 1776.

Throughout 1995, Congress gradually pieced together the compromise that became the Telecommunications Act of 1996. The stated goal of the new law was to establish "a pro-competitive, deregulatory national policy framework" in order to make available to all Americans "advanced telecommunications and information technologies and services by opening all telecommunications markets to competition." The specific provisions of the Telecommunications Act would eventually allow local and long distance telephone, cable television, and data processing enterprises to compete with one another. Rhetorically, at least, the bill was portrayed as an open doorway to the information age.[49] Competition and technological integration would encourage the development of new products and services that would maintain US global competitiveness in the coming century. For consumers, competition was expected to provide lower prices and technological advances that would make life better for all. The practical implications of the law, however, still remained to be determined.

In the end, the Telecommunications Act of 1996 was the result of nearly two decades of change in the direction of competition. Technological changes, interest group demands, and electoral alignments caused the dissolution of regulatory separation. Ultimately, however, the acceptance of competitive-integration as an alternative epistemology was solidified by new policy ideas first advanced by economic analysts as early as the 1960s. As these ideas were advanced and accepted by policy entrepreneurs within the FCC, Congress and other policy venues, they became the shared language that justified a new course of action in telecommunications policy. While the authors of the Telecommunications Act did not draw directly on Chicago School critiques during the policy formation process, by the mid-1990s the logic of competition pervaded the political debate. The debate was no longer between monopoly and competition, but between competition and more competition.

Conclusion

This study indicates that social learning was an important factor in telecommunications policy change between 1934 and 1996. In nearly all cases, policy change was motivated by dissatisfaction with the status quo. While interest groups and power politics frequently played a role in pushing change forward, changing economic and technological circumstances created confusion and dissatisfaction among policymakers. This confusion led policymakers to undertake an intellectual search for solutions. Following the theoretical parameters established at the beginning of the study, it is now necessary to ask whether intellectual searches resulted in "lesson-drawing," and whether they were conditioned by a "policy epistemology." Finally, it is necessary to examine whether broad-based policy change in the 1980s and 1990s was conditioned by an epistemology reconstruction.

---

49 Dan Carvey, "Congress Fires its First Shot in Information Revolution," *Congressional Quarterly Weekly Report* vol. 54 (1996), pp. 289-294.

First, it is evident that lesson-drawing took place in a number of these cases. In employing the rate-of-return methodology, the FCC drew on the accumulated wisdom of the ICC and state regulators. Furthermore, the microwave, first computer, and cable-telephone inquiries that took place between 1956 and 1971 all indicated a kind of lesson-drawing. In each of these three cases, the FCC emulated past practices by keeping these new technologies structurally separate from the telephone industry. The later computer decisions and price caps inquiry of the 1980s also contain substantial evidence of lesson-drawing. In the computer inquiries of the 1980s, the FCC drew on the lessons of past experience, borrowing policy instruments such as resale and equal access from earlier inquiries to promote competition in data communications markets. Furthermore, in the price caps decision, FCC economists drew lessons from the British experience in their search for a new method of telephone rate regulation. Finally, in the years leading up to the passage of the Telecommunications Act of 1996, Congress drew lessons from the experiences of countries like France and Japan in concluding that the US would soon lose its competitive edge if action were not taken. The case of video dial-tone is somewhat less clear. Ultimately, the implementation of video dial-tone appears to have resulted less from experiential reflection and lesson-drawing than from the personal agenda and policy views of Chairman Alfred Sikes.

Second, there is evidence that two distinct "policy epistemologies" existed between 1934 and 1996. The evidence suggests that between roughly 1934 and 1971, a policy epistemology here referred to as *regulatory separation* prevailed. All of the major policies examined during this time, including rate-of-return regulation and the microwave, first computer, and cable television decisions, conformed to the logic of regulatory separation, which consisted of government regulation along with structural separation of the different industry niches. Between the late 1970s and 1996, regulatory separation gave way to another epistemology called *competitive integration*, which was characterized by increasing competition and a gradual dissolution of the industry niches. All of the policy decisions examined during this time conformed to the basic logic of competitive integration.

Finally, the existence of two distinct policy epistemologies during the timer period examined in this study indicates that there was an epistemology reconstruction. The transformation occurred during the 1970s and was motivated in part by technological change and interest group pressure. Chicago School analysts shaped the new competitive integration epistemology; by the mid-1970s, they were forming a powerful "epistemic community" within Washington policy circles. Chicago School ideas were influential in a string of regulatory decisions undertaken by the FCC between 1980 and 1992. The Telecommunications Act, while not a direct outgrowth of Chicago School thinking, built on earlier experiences with competition and technological integration that were influenced by these ideas.

Ultimately, the case of telecommunications policy illustrates the importance of ideas and experiential learning as variables in the policy process. In some areas, policymaking is not only a struggle to exert political power, but an intellectual enterprise as well. The ability to wield power in a democratic society is related to the ability to advance policy proposals that make "good sense" to both elites and masses. Whether or not a policy instrument is perceived as being workable, however, depends on the intellectual parameters within which decision-makers operate. These parameters, when widely agreed upon, chart the course of policymaking.

Chapter 6

Lesson-Drawing, Policy Transfer and Social Learning: What can the Economic Historian Learn?[1]

Michael J. Oliver

Over the past thirty-five years, the historian of contemporary economic policymaking has increasingly had to share his research agenda with the sociologist, economist and political scientist.[2] However, the political scientist, in particular, has begun to encroach on the most hallowed of historical terrain, lesson-drawing. Theorists of the state increasingly focus analytical attention on specific historical episodes and discuss the political, social and economic lessons associated with each. Examples of these studies include Hugh Heclo's 1974 examination of social policy in Britain and Sweden, Lloyd Etheredge's 1985 investigation of United States (US) foreign policymaking and David Dolowitz' 1990s studies of welfare reform transfer to the United Kingdom (UK).[3] During the past fifteen years, the literature on lesson-drawing has proliferated at an incredible pace. Three particular works should be noted as making a significant contribution to this literature: Richard Rose's 1993 book entitled *Lesson-Drawing in Public Policy*, Peter Hall's 1993 *Comparative Politics* article, and the work on policy transfer by Dolowitz and Marsh.[4]

---

1   The author would like to thank the following people who have read and made comments on this chapter: Mark Blyth, David Ellis, Ian Greener, John Greenaway, Lars Jonung, Hugh Pemberton, Gordon Pepper and Peter Von Doepp.

2   A. Britton, *Macroeconomic Policy In Britain 1974–1987* (Cambridge: Cambridge University Press, 1991); Peter A. Hall, *The Political Dimensions of Economic Management* (Ann Arbor, MI: University Microfilms International, 1982); W. G. Runciman, "Has British Capitalism Changed since the First World War?" *British Journal of Sociology* vol. 44 (1993), pp. 53-67.

3   Hugh Heclo, *Modern Social Politics in Britain and Sweden* (New Haven, CT: Yale University Press, 1974); Lloyd Etheredge, *Can Governments Learn?* (New York: Pergamon, 1985); David P. Dolowitz, "British Employment Policy in the 1980s: Learning from the American Experience," *Governance* vol. 10 (1997), pp. 23-42, and *Learning from America: Policy Transfer and the Development of the British Workfare State* (Brighton: Sussex Academic Press, 1998).

4   Richard Rose, *Lesson-Drawing in Public Policy: A Guide to Learning Across Time and Space* (Chatham, NJ: Chatham House Publishers, Inc., 1993); Peter A. Hall, "Policy Paradigms, Social Learning, and the State: The Case of Economic Policymaking in Britain,"

Unfortunately, in the United Kingdom the work on policy transfer has come to dominate the public policy research agenda. Several years ago when policy transfer was on the ascendancy, I argued that it would ultimately yield political scientists limited returns as it was only a fairly static description of processes.[5] Despite Evans and Davies' best efforts,[6] the policy transfer literature is unable to address some of the key questions that learning models need to explain: under what conditions, why and how do state actors learn? It is still impossible to talk about a policy transfer "learning model." Among other things, a learning model should allow social scientists to differentiate between rational and non-rational policymaking; it should recognise that history matters (Policymakers may draw negative or positive lessons from policies promulgated in another time or place.), and it should conceptualise learning as a dynamic process. The should also be flexible enough to allow for the fact that actors may learn the wrong thing and/or policy outcomes may be ineffective due to influences beyond the learning process. Is such a comprehensive model possible?

Arguably, the social learning model offered by Peter Hall contributes more to the debate than has been acknowledged by the majority of British political scientists. Ironically, after a ten- year hiatus, economic historians are now recognising the value of this model for their own work. This chapter will apply Hall's model to a particular case study---macroeconomic policymaking in the UK since 1945, with particular emphasis on the post-1979 period. The first segment of the chapter discusses lesson-drawing and policy transfer and provides an exegesis of Hall's social learning model. Section two considers the process of macroeconomic policymaking in post-1945 Britain within the context of the model. This is followed by a discussion on fourth order learning and an examination of the extent to which policymakers in the United Kingdom "learnt how to learn" during the 1980s.

Comparative Politics vol. 25 (1993), pp. 275-296; Dolowitz, *Learning from America* and "A Policy–maker's Guide to Policy Transfer," *Political Quarterly* vol. 74 (2003), pp. 101-108; David Dolowitz and D. Marsh, "Who Learns What from Whom: a Review of the Policy Transfer Literature," *Political Studies* vol. 44 (1996), pp. 343-357, and "Learning from Abroad: the Role of Policy Transfer in Contemporary Policy Making," *Governance* vol. 13 (2000), pp. 5-24; David Dolowitz, S. Greenwold and David Marsh, "Policy Transfer: Something Old, Something New, Something Borrowed, but Why Red, White and Blue?" *Parliamentary Affairs* vol. 52 (1999), pp. 719-730; David Dolowitz, R. Hulme, M. Nellis and F. O'Neal, *Policy Transfer and British Social Policy: Learning from the USA?* (Philadelphia, PA: Open University Press, 1999).

5   Michael J. Oliver, "Social Learning: A Necessary Precondition to Policy Transfer?" Paper presented to the *Policy Transfer Conference*, University of Birmingham (October 26-27, 1999).

6   M. Evans and J. Davies, "Understanding Policy Transfer: A Multi-Level, Multi-Disciplinary Perspective," *Public Administration* vol. 77 (1999), pp. 361-385.

Lesson-Drawing, Policy Transfer and Social Learning

Richard Rose defines a "lesson" as:

> more than a symbol invoked to sway opinion about a policy and more than a dependent variable telling a social scientist what is to be explained. A lesson is a detailed cause-and-effect description of a set of actions that government can consider in the light of experience elsewhere, including a prospective evaluation of whether what is done elsewhere could someday become effective here.[7]

Rose suggests that policymakers draw lessons subconsciously across time and space, and that lessons can be negative or positive. James and Lodge are critical of Rose's conception of lesson-drawing for not departing from a conventional rational account, where "decisions are based on searching for the means to pursue goals in a systematic and comprehensive manner."[8] As Neustadt and May recognize, drawing lessons across time and space is difficult for policymakers. Some problems occur because the supply of history is inexhaustible but the demand is limited; policymakers seek lessons that can be used in dealing with current problems, but do not engage in extensive search. This implies that policymakers do not always engage in rational lesson-drawing and often fail to optimize their choices.[9]

At first glance it appears that Dolowitz and Marsh have avoided the difficulties associated with the bifurcation between rational and non-rational policy making by providing another way of thinking about lesson-drawing through a concept known as "policy transfer." They define policy transfer as "a process in which knowledge about policies, administrative arrangements, institutions etc. in one time and/or place is used in the development of policies, administrative arrangements and institutions in another time and/or place."[10] They contend that the policy transfer framework can encompass "lesson-drawing,"[11] "policy band-wagoning,"[12] "emulation" and

---

7 Rose, *Lesson-Drawing in Public Policy*, p. 27.

8 O. James and M. Lodge, 'The Limitations of 'Policy Transfer' and 'Lesson Drawing' for Public Policy Research," *Political Studies Review* vol. 1 (2003).

9 R. E. Neustadt and E. R. May, *Thinking in Time: The Uses of History for Decision Makers* (New York: Free Press, 1986).

10 Dolowitz and Marsh, "Who Learns What from Whom," p. 34.

11 Rose, *Lesson-Drawing in Public Policy*.

12 J. G. Ikenberry, "The International Spread of Privatization Policies; Inducements, Learning and Policy Bandwagoning," in E. Suleiman and J. Waterbury, eds. *The Political Economy of Public Sector Reform* (Boulder, CO: Westview Press, 1990).

"harmonization,"[13] "policy convergence,"[14] "policy diffusion,"[15] "policy learning,"[16] and "systematically pinching ideas."[17] Dolowitz and Marsh, however, have stepped into another potentially explosive area, as Evan and Davies point out:

> These studies encompass a host of disciplines ranging from domestic and international political science to comparative politics; the study of policy transfer has a truly multi-disciplinary character. Yet what is commonly viewed as a strength can also be identified as a weakness. As a consequence of the diffuse nature of this field of study, policy transfer analysts do not have the benefits of a common idiom or a unified theoretical or methodological discourse from which lessons can be drawn and hypotheses developed. Indeed, despite complementary research agendas, these disciplines have continued to speak past each other.[18]

Unfortunately, many scholars have followed the lead of Dolowitz and Marsh and have given policy transfer an important role as the explanatory variable in the lesson drawing literature. Evans and Davies' quotation neatly identifies all the problems associated with this approach. First, policy networks, lesson-drawing and policy transfer cannot be lumped together under a single heading. Secondly, these disciplines continue to "speak past each other" precisely because they do not share the same methodological frameworks, and policy transfer is not sufficient to redress the disciplinary divide. Thirdly, the loose methodological framework proposed by Dolowitz and Marsh does not provide an explanatory theory for lesson-drawing across time and space. Recognising this, Evans and Davies suggest that "policy transfer analysis…may be viewed as an analogical model in the sense that it refers to the suggestion of substantive similarities between two entities. For example, likening an organisation to a machine or an organism."[19] This is rather a puzzling sentence. A theory is usually a statement or set of related statements about cause and effect, action and reaction. A model is a formal statement of theory (usually it is a mathematical representation of a presumed relationship between two or more variables). It is possible to provide a theory of learning and to develop a "learning model" – this is precisely what Peter Hall has done---but Evans and Davies essentially offer two *processes* of policy transfer, one voluntary and the other coercive. While this is a shift away from the composite literature on policy transfer and lesson-drawing "which

---

13 C. J. Bennett, "Review Article: What is Policy Convergence and What Causes It?" *British Journal of Political Science* vol. 21 (1990), pp. 215-233.

14 W. Coleman, "Policy Convergence in Banking: a Comparative Study," *Political Studies* vol. 42 (1994), pp. 274-292.

15 G. Majone, "Cross-national Sources of Regulatory Policymaking in Europe and the United States," *Journal of Public Policy* vol. 11 (1991), pp. 79-106.

16 Peter Haas, "Knowledge, Power and International Policy Coordination," *International Organisation* vol. 46 (1992).

17 A. Schneider and H. Ingram, "Systematically Pinching Ideas: a Comparative Approach to Policy Design," *Journal of Public Policy* vol. 8 (1988), pp. 61-80.

18 Evans and Davies, "Understanding Policy Transfer," p. 361.

19 Evans and Davies, "Understanding Policy Transfer," p. 362.

make up definitional criteria and a check list of categories," it leaves many questions unanswered.[20] For example, can policy transfer account for how the state, interest groups and other actors initiate shifts in policy? Are some actors more influential than others at shaping policy? More crucially, once policy has been transferred, how are lessons drawn and how does policy change occur? In short, policy transfer is essentially process driven, with dodgy mechanics. It is not a substitute for lesson-drawing, but rather a complement to social learning, with policy transfer sitting more comfortably as an *ex post* justification rather than a formalised model with *ex ante* consequences.

Despite Evans and Davies' claim to have created a heuristic model, there is an ominous silence on the role social learning plays in the policy transfer process. Diane Stone notes that:

> "social learning" or "policy learning" is yet another label connected with policy transfer, but this concept is analytically different. Here the emphasis is on cognition and the redefinition of interests on the basis of new knowledge that affects the fundamental beliefs and ideas behind policy approaches. Consequently, learning could just as likely lead to policy innovation or termination as well as policy transfer and/or convergence.[21]

Although the mainstream literature on social learning has been growing steadily over the past thirty years,[22] until recently it has excited little interest amongst political scientists. There have been only a few criticisms of Hall's 1993 model and relatively few attempts to introduce social learning to a wider audience.[23] While Rose did not consider social learning, he ended his study by claiming that "the critical issues of lesson-drawing are not whether we can learn anything elsewhere, but when, where and how we learn."[24] In this chapter, I contend that because of its heuristic composition, social learning gives social scientists a tool to address the "when, where and how" of lesson drawing by offering a structure through which levels and processes of learning can be assessed. This is in marked contrast to traditional learning models that describe "who learns what from whom."

---

20 Evans and Davies, "Understanding Policy Transfer," p. 366.

21 Diane Stone, "Learning Lessons and Transferring Policy across Time, Space and Disciplines," *Politics* vol. 19 (1999), p. 52.

22 Chris Argyris and Donald A. Schon, *Organizational Learning: A Theory of Action Perspective* (Reading, MA: Addison-Wesley Publishing Company, 1978); A. Bandura, *Social Learning Theory* (Englewood Cliffs, NJ: Prentice-Hall, 1977); John Steinbrunner, *The Cybernetic Theory of Decision* (Princeton, NJ: Princeton University Press, 1974).

23 See, for example, R. Deeg, "Institutional Transfers, Social Learning and Economic Policy in Eastern Germany," *West European Politics* vol. 18 (1995), pp. 38-63; J. Greenaway, "Policy Learning and the Drink Question in Britain, 1850-1950," *Political Studies* vol. 56 (1998), pp. 903-918; A. Jordan, "'Private Affluence and Public Squalor?' The Europeanisation of British Coastal Bathing Water Policy," *Policy and Politics* vol. 26 (1998), pp. 33-54; M. Lodge, "Institutional Choice and Policy Transfer: Reforming British and German Railway Regulation," *Governance* vol. 16 (2003), pp. 159-178.

24 Rose, *Lesson-Drawing in Public Policy*, p. 157.

Hall's concept of "social learning" was clearly influenced by Hugh Heclo's concept of "political learning." From his studies of Sweden and Britain, Heclo asserts that much of the time, policymaking is a process of "collective puzzlement" in which political parties, interest groups and state bureaucracy cogitate to solve policy problems. Heclo argues that this "political learning" is shared among a small group of autonomous experts (largely administrators), and that political power is exerted only when the consensus process fails. The demotion of the politician and promotion of the role of the specialist in detailed areas of policymaking implies that parties entering government make changes to policy only at the margin thereby advancing a policy consensus. Policy at time-1 is invariably affected by policy at time-0; i.e., policymakers respond to past successes or failures in policy and conduct future policy with regard to policy legacies.[25] While Heclo and Sacks emphasize that governments act independently from societal pressure, Hall assigns a greater role to actors outside the traditional policy community.[26] Thus, rather than political learning, Hall utilises the concept "social learning" defined as "a deliberate attempt to adjust the goals or techniques of policy in response to past experience and new information. Learning is indicated when policy changes as the result of such a process."[27]

Hall states that policymaking should be seen as a process that usually involves three central variables: goals that direct policy in a certain area; the policy instruments used to attain those goals; and the precise settings of these instruments. If goals, instruments or instrument settings are altered, then four "orders of change" potentially occur. First order change occurs when the levels of the basic instruments of policy are altered. Second order change is denoted when the instruments of policy as well as their settings are altered in response to past experience. Both first order and second order changes retain the existing policy paradigm. When the instrument settings, instruments and the goals behind policy shift, this process is known as third order change. Third order change is the most fundamental since it represents a marked shift in the intellectual framework within which policy is made by processes that "spilled well beyond the boundaries of the state to involve the media, outside interests, and contending political parties."[28] Hall mentions a fourth order of change in a footnote, wherein "policymakers learn how to learn."[29]

---

25 Heclo, *Modern Social Politics in Britain and Sweden*, pp. 304-315; P. M. Sacks, "State Structure and the Asymmetrical Society: An Approach to Public Policy in Britain," *Comparative Politics* vol. 12 (1980), pp. 349-376; M. Weir and Theta Skocpol, "State Structures and the Possibilities for 'Keynesian' Responses to the Great Depression in Sweden, Britain and the United States," in Peter Evans, D. Ruescheneyer and Theta Skocpol, eds., *Bringing the State Back In* (Cambridge: Cambridge University Press, 1985).

26 Heclo, *Modern Social Politics in Britain and Sweden*, p. 318; Sacks, "State Structure and the Asymmetrical Society," p. 35.

27 See Hall, "Policy Paradigms, Social Learning, and the State," p. 293.

28 Hall, "Policy Paradigms, Social Learning, and the State," p. 288.

29 Hall, "Policy Paradigms, Social Learning, and the State," p. 293.

This framework is like a *gestalt*, Hall argues, embedded in the minds of policymakers shaping not only the goals of policy and the choice of instruments and settings to achieve these goals, but also policymakers' "framing" of the problems they are addressing.[30] This is a "policy paradigm," – a deliberate evocation of Thomas Kuhn's argument that scientific paradigms "gain their status because they are more successful than their competitors in solving problems that the group of practitioners has come to recognize as acute."[31]

Macroeconomic Policymaking in the United Kingdom

While Hall has done much to carry the debate forward, his account of social learning is not entirely convincing. As has been partly shown elsewhere, Hall's conceptualisation of the model is rather unsatisfactory as is its application to macroeconomic policy in the UK.[32] In places, the perfunctory composition of the model tends to understate the complex relationships between political actors and policymakers, and greater importance should be placed on contextual factors (social pressure via cultural factors, interest groups or even political parties). Hall seems to draw away from Heclo's characterisation of the politician as idiosyncratic in the first and second order change process but does not give us much idea on why and how certain politicians influence the direction of policymaking at the important third order change stage. Moreover, there is no discussion on fourth order learning and how it relates to the first three orders of change. Hall's model is rather static, although its potential for dynamism is indisputable. To consider these criticisms in more detail, it would be instructive to first examine the evidence that provides the case study for Hall's model before turning to reflect on how the process of learning occurs.

From 1945 until the mid-1970s, British economic policy was conducted within a Keynesian framework, which was broadly endorsed by both Conservative and Labour governments. Post-war economic policy was dominated not by the specific ideas of Keynes but by an "actually existing Keynesianism" that drew on the logical development of Keynes' ideas.[33] At the heart of this framework was the commitment

---

30 Hall, "Policy Paradigms, Social Learning, and the State," p. 279.

31 Thomas S. Kuhn, *The Structure of Scientific Revolutions* (Chicago: University of Chicago Press, 1962/1996), p. 23.

32 M. Blyth, "'Any More Bright Ideas?': The Ideational Turn of Comparative Political Economy," *Comparative Politics* vol. 29 (1997), pp. 229-250; Michael J. Oliver, "Social Learning and Macroeconomic Policymaking in the United Kingdom Since 1979," *Essays in Economic and Business History* vol. 14 (1996), pp. 117-131 and *Whatever Happened to Monetarism? Social Learning and Macroeconomic Policymaking in the United Kingdom since 1979* (Aldershot, UK: Ashgate, 1997), pp. 11-17; I. Greener, "Social Learning and Macroeconomic Policy in Britain," *Journal of Public Policy* Vol. 21 (2001), pp. 133-152; Michael J. Oliver and Hugh Pemberton, "Learning and Change in Twentieth Century British Economic Policy," *Governance* vol. 17 (2004), pp. 415-441.

33 D. Winch, *Economics and Policy: A Historical Study* (London: Hodder and Stoughton, 1969), p. 107; P. Clarke, ed., *The Keynesian Revolution and its Economic Consequences*

to maintain "a high and stable level of employment," enshrined in the 1944 *Full Employment White Paper*. This commitment required extensive changes to, and re-prioritisation of, policy instruments. Yet while both parties accepted the use of monetary and fiscal policy in managing the economy, it would be more accurate to identify the Conservatives as "reluctant Keynesians" although both parties readily seized on the suggestion by the Radcliffe Committee in 1958 that monetary policy should be responsible for the external balance whilst fiscal policy should be employed to maintain the domestic balance.[34]

Post-war British economic policy was determined by a central government decision-making network, which consisted of Treasury ministers, officials from the Treasury and revenue departments and the Bank of England. As Hugh Pemberton explains, the core executive did not operate in a policy vacuum.[35] The actors and institutions involved in the policy process are embedded in other networks while the network is characterised "by specific configurations of perceptions which are related to [its] history and nature."[36]

Pemberton's very instructive schema, reproduced as Figure 6.1, illustrates how these institutions and actors shaped the policymaking process post-1945. There are two boxes and a feedback loop. The policymaking "terrain" is identified by the smaller of the two boxes, with the actors represented by circles and the "networks" represented by octagons. Each actor is linked to one or more networks, except the media where the links are so numerous that no attempt has been made to illustrate them. The linkages are dynamic, non-exhaustive, and can be formal, informal or a mixture of both. For instance, the Cabinet is a formal institution and is a network because it brings together actors to discuss and decide policy.

The actors and networks are divided into five groups. The groupings are self-explanatory, but it should be noted that political advisors straddle the political and administrative groups. Also, the administrative grouping is based in Whitehall, and excludes external civil servants, local government or government agencies staffed by non-civil service employees.

(Northampton, MA: Edward Elgar, 1998), p. 303; A. Booth, "Britain in the 1950s: a 'Keynesian' Managed Economy?" *History of Political Economy* vol. 33 (2001), pp. 283-313 and "New Revisionists and the Keynesian Era in British Economic Policy," *Economic History Review* vol. 54 (2001), pp. 346-366.

34 A. K. Cairncross, *The British Economy Since 1945: Economic Policy and Performance, 1945-1990* (London: Routledge, 1992), p. 95.

35 Hugh Pemberton, "Policy Networks and Policy Learning: UK Economic Policy in the 1960s and 1970s," *Public Administration* vol. 78 (2000), pp. 777-779.

36 E. H. Klijn, J. Koppenjan and K. Termeer, "Managing Networks in the Public Sector: a Theoretical Study of Management Strategies in Policy Networks," *Public Administration* vol. 73 (1995), p. 440.

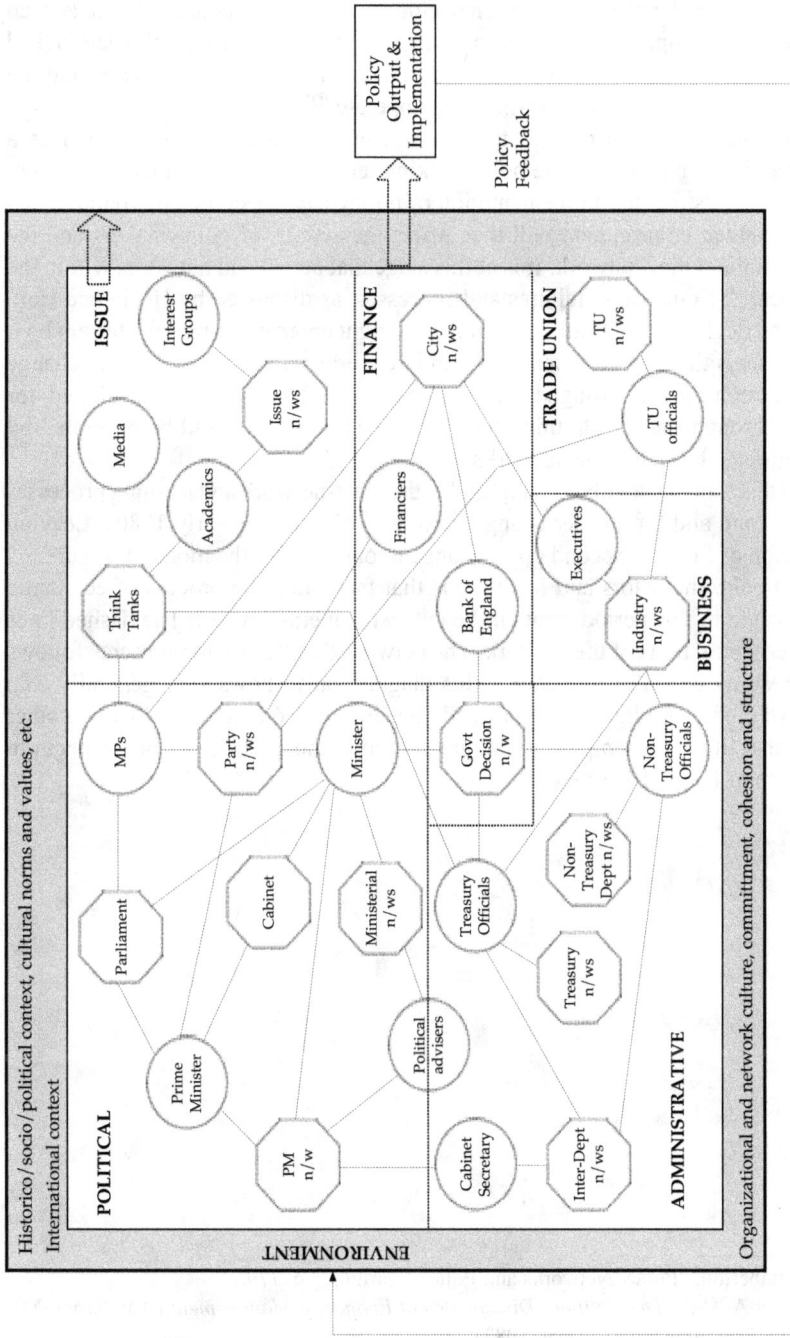

Historico/socio/political context, cultural norms and values, etc.
International context

Organizational and network culture, commitment, cohesion and structure

Figure 6.1 A Policy Network Schema

The larger box is where the policy-making terrain is embedded, which Pemberton simply labels the environment, or context. Although the diagram is unclear, the context has three levels: organizational culture, the international context (which for purposes of simplicity, is treated as exogenous) and the historical, sociological and political context "that shapes and constrains individual policy makers and the institutions and networks within which they operate."[37]

Finally, there are two devices that allow environmental change to occur as a result of actions taken within the policymaking terrain. The first is a feedback loop, which recognises that the implementation of policy can affect the environment and that the changed environment will then affect the actions of policymakers and the structure of the policy network. It is at this stage that actors and networks within the terrain "learn" from policy failures and successes, as discussed by Heclo and Hall. The second device is the small arrow at the top right emanating from the terrain box. This represents the way in which actors and networks within the terrain can change the policy environment through the influence of ideas. New ideas are developed, for example, through the media, think tanks and academia and could be promoted by interest groups through issue networks.

From this schema, Pemberton highlights the meta-network and learning processes of first, second and third order change between 1970 and the early 1980s. Leaving a discussion of first and second order change to one side for the moment, Figure 6.2 shows, in bold, the actors and institutions that facilitated the process of economic policy change in this period through the extensive meta-network. The dashed lines are the peripheral parts of the network. The network that Pemberton presents follows a close reading of Hall.[38] However, this diagram only shows very generally *who* was active in the paradigm shift and really needs to be complemented with another diagram that illustrates *how* the paradigm shifted in the 1970s if we are to begin to make sense of Hall's 1993 model.

---

37 Pemberton, "Policy Networks and Policy Learning," p. 779.

38 Peter A. Hall, *The Political Dimensions of Economic Management* (Ann Arbor, MI: University Microfilms International, 1982).

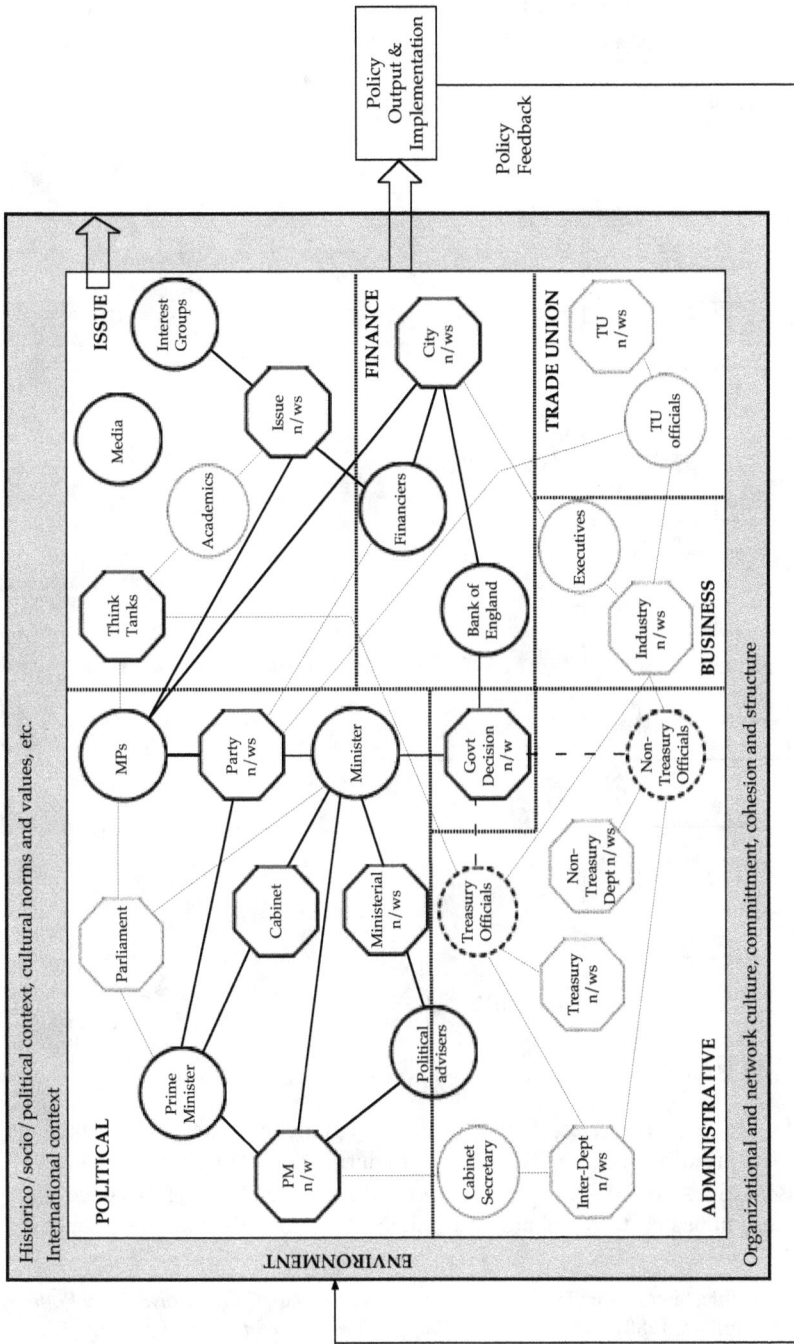

Historico/socio/political context, cultural norms and values, etc.
International context

POLITICAL

ISSUE

FINANCE

TRADE UNION

BUSINESS

ADMINISTRATIVE

ENVIRONMENT

Organizational and network culture, commitment, cohesion and structure

Interest Groups
Media
Academics
Issue n/ws
Think Tanks
City n/ws
Financiers
Bank of England
TU n/ws
TU officials
Executives
Industry n/ws

MPs
Party n/ws
Minister
Govt Decision n/w
Non-Treasury Officials
Non-Treasury Dept n/ws.
Treasury Officials
Treasury n/ws

Parliament
Cabinet
Ministerial n/ws
Political advisers
Cabinet Secretary
Inter-Dept n/ws

Prime Minister
PM n/w

Policy Output & Implementation

Policy Feedback

Figure 6.2 First and Second Order Change During the 1970s and early-1980s

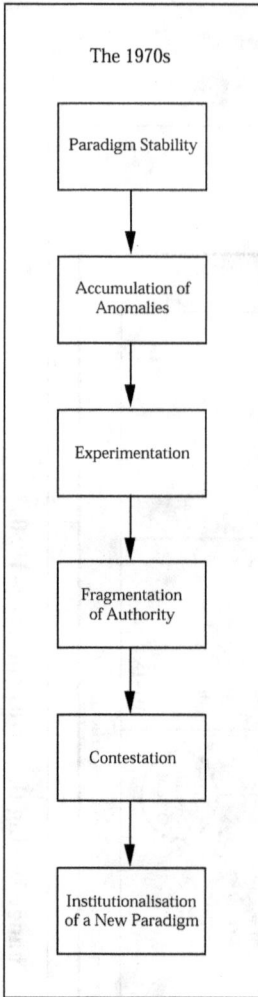

Figure 6.3 The 1970s Paradigm Shift

Source: Hall 1990, p. 68.

As Figure 6.3 illustrates, the Keynesian paradigm shifted in a six-stage process. The promises made by Edward Heath during the 1970 election (if elected, the Conservatives would cut taxes, reform industrial relations and reduce state intervention) appeared to repudiate past policies.[39] The reality was less sanguine

---

39 A. Gamble, "Economic Policy," in Zig Layton-Henry, ed., *Conservative Party Politics* (London: Macmillan, 1980); Martin Holmes, *Political Pressure and Economic Policy, British Government 1970-74* (London: Butterworth, 1982).

and the "Barber boom" coupled with industrial conflict effectively ended Heath's Premiership. The accumulation of anomalies (commodity prices rises in 1972-73, high inflation in 1973-75, Treasury forecasting errors in 1974-75) led to experiments such as attempts to keep sterling down on the foreign exchanges in 1976 and the introduction of severe incomes policies in 1975-77. As Hall notes:

> In the face of these developments, the Treasury lost its virtual monopoly of authority over matters of macroeconomic management. The chancellor himself lost faith in the view of his own officials, and an unusual number of senior officials left the Treasury shortly thereafter.[40]

During the early 1970s, there had been a number of widespread reforms to the operation of UK monetary policy and by the mid-1970s, monetary policy in the form of targets for monetary aggregates had become a major element of macroeconomic policy, introduced by the Labour Government just before the UK began negotiations with the International Monetary Fund (IMF) after the sterling crisis of 1976. The period between 1974 and 1979 was a time of intense debate about economic policymaking. In opposition circles, a number of prominent politicians in the Conservative Party conducted a root and branch analysis of economic policy following the disastrous election of November 1974.[41]

This debate was not confined to government and opposition circles. As captured by Figure 6.2, the debate spilled out beyond the core executive to include key actors and networks in the "issue" and "finance" boxes, with think tanks (in particular the Institute of Economic Affairs and the Centre for Policy Studies), the media (for example, *The Times*, *Financial Times* and the *Economist*) and City firms (notably W. Greenwell & Company). This "marketplace in economic ideas" helped to explain the course of real world events to a wider audience, allowed the public to respond (through, for example, the letters pages of *The Times* and *Financial Times*), and offered solutions to the decisionmakers that went beyond the established Keynesian boundaries.[42] In so doing, these ideas helped shape and were shaped by public opinion, which steadily moved away from the Keynesian paradigm by the end of the decade.

But what replaced the Keynesian paradigm? The shorthand description, and one which is readily taken up by Hall, is that it was replaced by a "monetarist" paradigm. Post-1979, the Conservative administration moved decisively away from the "false trails of post-war social democracy, with its profound faith in the efficacy

---

40 Peter A. Hall, "Policy Paradigms, Experts and the State: the Case of Macro-Economic Policy Making in Britain," in Stephen Brooks and Alain G. Gagnon, eds., *Social Scientists, Policy and the State* (New York: Praeger, 1990), p. 69.

41 M. Garnett and Michael J. Oliver, "The Art of Learning and Forgetting: the Conservative Party, 1974-79," *Twentieth Century British History* (2006).

42 Oliver, *Whatever Happened to Monetarism?*, pp. 52-54.

of government action."[43] However, it is misleading and inaccurate to describe policy as monetarist throughout the 1980s. Monetarism was only one of the theoretical strands that made up the economic *gestalt* of the 1980s; the other two parts were supply side economics and public choice theory. The more accurate description of British economic policy-1979 is neo-liberal.[44]

Herein lies one of the biggest weaknesses of Hall's application of the model. His account concentrates on the development of economic policy in the 1970s through to the early-1980s, yet by failing to consider developments in policy throughout the 1980s (particularly after 1985), the scope of his thesis is limited. Hall argues that changes in the setting of instruments do not automatically lead to policy and paradigm changes, but the evidence suggests that first and second order change led to a movement away from the monetarist paradigm by 1983. Moreover, this was followed post-1985 by the adoption of an eclectic economic policy and an *attempt* to shift the policy paradigm (third order change).

Throughout the 1980s, there were frequent first order changes. However, the seemingly routine first order changes (instrument settings) in economic policy during the early 1980s were part of a wider dissatisfaction with the policy instruments and this led to the adoption of alternative instruments. Between 1979 and 1983, the Government's monetarist economic experiment faced two difficulties. First, the monetary aggregate that the government had chosen to target (£M3) wandered outside its target band. This gave the impression that monetary policy was loose when in fact it was very tight and encouraged a continuation of tight policies. Secondly, the domestic economy underwent a period of rapid contraction, which was exacerbated by the tight monetary regime. A debate opened in policymaking circles as to whether the government should adopt a different monetary target or abandon monetarism altogether.

Between 1981 and 1985, there were several second order changes: the introduction of a new monetary aggregate, M0; the greater emphasis put on the exchange rate by Chancellor Nigel Lawson and the ending of overfunding in 1985.[45] The government began to get bogged down with the sterling issue and money technicalities. Some economists who had previously supported the government began to argue for joining the European Communities' Exchange Rate Mechanism (ERM) as a means of stabilizing currency fluctuations and for controlling inflation. There were also widespread arguments beginning to appear in the monetarist camp over which

43 Nigel Lawson, *The New Conservatism* (London: Centre for Policy Studies, 1980), p. 3.

44 Michael J. Oliver, "British Economic Policy and Performance Since 1945: an Early 21st Century Assessment, " in Michael J. Oliver, ed., *Studies in Economic and Social History* (Aldershot, UK: Ashgate, 2002).

45 With the introduction of targets for broad money, the Bank of England sold more gilt-edged stock to the non-bank private sector than was needed to cover the Exchequer's funding requirement in attempts to prevent broad money from exceeding its target. Such "overfunding" grew greatly in size and its suspension in 1985 was most significant for the demise of monetary targeting.

money aggregates to target. Chancellor Lawson was left with the problem of having to choose between conflicting advice from the experts. From 1985, money targets were finally abandoned and policy became more pragmatic.

Between 1986 and 1990 (when the UK joined the ERM), macroeconomic policies returned to a traditional "stop-go" (boom and bust) pattern that had bedevilled previous governments. Conflicts in policy and personality became widespread including the disagreements among Prime Minister Margaret Thatcher, Lawson and Professor Alan Walters over whether the UK should join the ERM. There was also a failure on the part of the Treasury to predict the boom of the late-1980s. Despite the accumulation of anomalies, experimentation, fragmentation of authority and contestation in the 1980s, a new paradigm was not institutionalised by the end of the decade.[46]

Fourth Order Learning

Thus far, we have identified the actors and institutions that were responsible for economic policy change in the 1970s and early 1980s (Figure 6.2). And, we have established that during the 1970s, the paradigm shifted through three orders of change (Figure 6.3), and that first order change and second order change do not necessarily result in third order change, as the experience of the 1980s showed. Despite this analysis, it is difficult to escape the conclusion that these three orders of change are rather mechanistic ways of understanding learning, and as such might be better described as a *process* of learning. If we consider one further order of change, however, we can also view learning as an *outcome*.[47]

Although he does not develop his idea of fourth order change, Hall contends that fourth order learning is where "policymakers learn how to learn."[48] There is no definitive explication of fourth order change in the academic literature, although Argyris and Schön and Larry Dodd attempt to extrapolate the idea of "deutero-learning" from Bateson.[49] What is fourth order change and how does it fit with the other three orders of change?

---

46 Oliver and Pemberton, "Learning and Change in Twentieth Century British Economic Policy."

47 Argyris and Schön summarize the process-outcome debate well: "'Learning' may signify either a product (something learned) or the process that yields such a product. In the first sense, we might ask, what have we learned?, referring to an accumulation of information in the form of knowledge or skill; in the second sense, how do we learn?, referring to a learning activity that may be well or badly performed." See Chris Argyris and Donald Schön, *Organizational Learning II: Theory, Method and Practice* (Reading, MA: Addison-Wesley Publishing Company, 1996), p. 3.

48 Hall, "Policy Paradigms, Social Learning, and the State," p. 293.

49 Argyris and Schön, *Organizational Learning*, pp. 26-28; Lawrence C. Dodd, "Political Learning and Political Change: Understanding Development across Time' in Lawrence C. Dodd and Calvin Jillson, eds., *The Dynamics of American Politics: Approach*

A visual representation of social learning is offered in Figure 6.4. The fourth order of change (learning) brings dynamism to the model, illustrating the relationship between instruments, instrument settings and policy changes. Fourth order learning is the *sine qua non* of the learning process: it is portrayed as overarching the other three orders of change. In this way, learning is a process (three orders of change) and outcome (fourth order learning) driven, with the slightest policy change being a result of learning (whether it is positive or negative lesson drawing). Lesson-drawing is about continuous change: the ultimate goal of policymakers is to bring stability to a paradigm and it is very hard to envisage how a paradigm could exist that did not require continuous adjustment. Fourth order learning is also perpetual because policymakers inhabitant a world where human actions and real world events force them to adapt and respond to new ideas. Thus while we can identify negative or positive lessons and describe policy as either a failure or success, we need to bear in mind that social learning is more than an "error correcting process."[50]

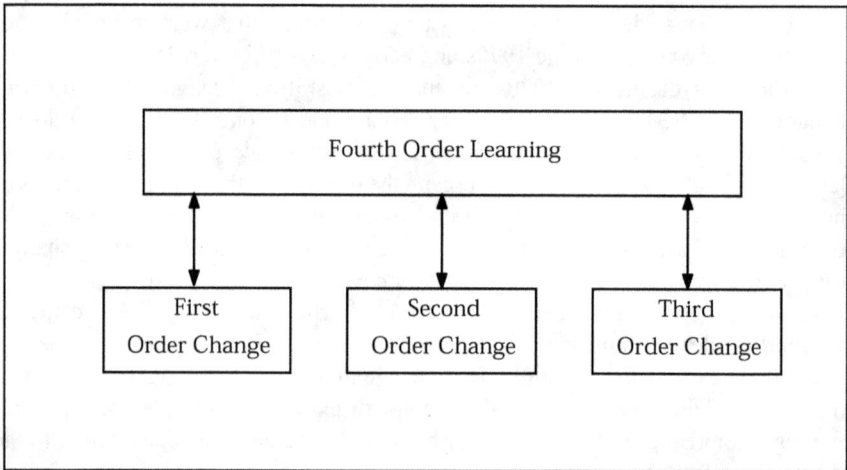

Figure 6.4 The Social Learning Model

To ascertain the full extent of fourth order learning in our case study on the 1980s we would need to investigate the role of officials in Treasury and Bank of England. However, economic historians have been prevented from examining key documents because of the 30-year rule laid down by the Official Secrets Act. The 2000 Freedom of Information Act which came into force January 1, 2005 could offer opportunities for researchers to obtain some documents within the thirty year rule, but it will be

---

and Interpretations (Boulder, CO: Westview Press, 1994); G. Bateson, *Steps to an Ecology of Mind* (New York: Ballantine, 1972). See also Chapter 1, pp. 13-14.

50 Ralph D. Stacey, *Complex Responsive Processes in Organizations: Learning and Knowledge Creation* (New York: Routledge, 2001), p. 26.

a considerable time before the 1980-1990 period yields a comprehensive series of primary documents. There are, however, published accounts written by politicians central in the development of neo-liberal policies during the 1980s, which can give valuable insights into their mindset. Focusing on the role of politicians raises further questions: How important is the political leader in the learning process? Which factors influence how a politician learns how to learn?

In the US context, Dodd fleshes out the idea of fourth order learning through an exploration of the careers of US senators during the 1980s, which exhibit a degree of "learning how to learn:"

> ...they (and we) come to believe in their inner resources and intuitive capacities – to believe that they can learn through experience to respect the open and serendipitous nature of politics and to reassess their political preconceptions in the light of new conditions and expanding awareness. Such politicians . . . may not be the most immediately successful . . . but they may ultimately become the most "real," the best "tested," the most genuine or empathetic, the sort of leader one would "trust."[51]

Dodd's observations and arguments can be applied to British macroeconomic policymaking and the role played by several senior politicians, for example, Margaret Thatcher (Prime Minister 1979-1990), Geoffrey Howe (Chancellor of the Exchequer 1979-1983) and Nigel Lawson (Chancellor of the Exchequer 1983-1989). For instance, Dodd notes that the senators who reflect and reassess new ideas and information enjoy a fair amount of developmental learning. Both Lawson and Thatcher acknowledge that their years in Opposition between 1974 and 1979 were crucial for the development of post-1979 policies.[52] Once in power, it becomes more costly to experiment, fail and reassess. Moreover, Lawson was keen to flirt with other money aggregates and explore currency shadowing in 1987 and 1988, while Prime Minister Thatcher saw any deviation in economic policy as a sign of failure and wished to avoid the policy reversals that had beleaguered Prime Minister Edward Heath in the early-1970s.[53]

Dodd notes that facilitative personal circumstances are central to a politician's success. If informed staff, "in touch with reality," surround a politician, he or she is much more likely to learn. From the mid-1970s, monetarists such as Gordon Pepper and Keith Joseph guided and developed Thatcher's thoughts. In government, Thatcher's monetarist economic strategy did not enjoy widespread support even amongst her own Cabinet colleagues, and she was surrounded by many hostile to her economic policies (the "wets"). During the early 1980s, she replaced several senior

---

51 Lawrence C. Dodd, "Learning to Learn: the Political Mastery of US Senators," *Legislative Studies Section Newsletter* (1992), p. 10.

52 Nigel Lawson, *The View From No. 11* (London: Bantum Press, 1992); Margaret H. Thatcher, *The Path To Power* (London: HarperCollins, 1995).

53 Margaret H. Thatcher, *The Downing Street Years* (London: HarperCollins, 1993), p. 14.

appointments with people more sympathetic to the monetarist cause and selected Alan Walters as her economic adviser.

Geoffrey Howe learned from bitter experience what happened when Prime Minister Edward Heath followed a permissive economic policy. Howe was determined that the UK should adopt voluntarily the sort of policy that the International Monetary Fund had imposed in 1976. Howe states: "One of the greatest challenges of the Chancellor's job is the extent to which he has to make judgements and reach conclusions about a huge range of technical subtleties…in the last resort in the name of common sense."[54] He was not a technical expert, and appears not to have realised that different weight should be placed on different monetary aggregates depending on the circumstances.

Dodd also argues that politicians who exhibit reflective self awareness "are prepared to listen to their intuitive feelings, to re-examine their personal and political preconceptions, and thus to learn and change."[55] Lawson is a fascinating example of a politician who not only adjusted his mind-set throughout the 1980s while keeping a core of central beliefs, but who was so self-confident in his ability to manage the economy that he persuaded senior Treasury officials that their mindset was incorrect.[56] Lawson describes, for example, how "I gradually brought my officials round to my way of thinking on the ERM."[57] During meetings with the Prime Minister, only the agreed position was articulated, with individual participants not putting forward their personal views.

By Dodd's definition, it is more difficult to label Thatcher as "self aware;" as the 1980s unfolded the Prime Minister refused to shift from her beliefs and particularly how her paradigm was influenced. It is interesting to note that when Sir Alan Walters returned as Thatcher's Personal Economic Adviser in May 1989, he did so in a part-time capacity and after spending a considerable amount of time in the United States where he was not directly exposed to many of the arguments in the UK on ERM. Thus, even before his return to the UK, Walters possessed a different mindset, in conflict with Lawson who surrounded himself with pro-ERM advisers while distancing himself from the monetarist experiment. The implications of this were that Margaret Thatcher persisted alone in the Cabinet with her monetarist views. Moreover, as the advisers either left office or became minority voices, their ability to influence the Prime Minister weakened. Howe also suggests that the resignation of Ian Gow as the Prime Minister's Parliamentary Private Secretary "may be seen in retrospect as one of the prime causes of her slowly developing isolation."[58]

Yet even if these prerequisite factors are in place, there is no guarantee that policymakers will learn how to learn. What could prevent "learning how to learn?"

---

54 Geoffrey Howe, *Conflict of Loyalty* (London: Macmillan, 1994), p. 172.

55 Dodd, Learning to Learn," p. 11.

56 Helen Thompson, *The British Conservative Government and the European Exchange Rate Mechanism, 1979-1994* (London: Pinter, 1996), p. 46.

57 Lawson, *The View from No. 11*, p. 486.

58 Geoffrey Howe, *Conflict of Loyalty*, p. 146.

One possible explanation might be found if we consider a simple analogy: learning how to drive. After taking a number of driving lessons, the individual will take a test that they successfully pass. A few weeks later, while out driving in the city, the driver ignores a "stop" sign. In failing to heed this, he crashes into another vehicle. Our new driver forgot a basic lesson: heed road signals. Just because he has learnt how to drive does not mean that he will never make mistakes. He will always be vulnerable to accidents, either because of mechanical failure, but more likely, because he will occasionally forget his highway code, however many times it was drilled into him on his driving lessons.

The point of this example can be seen when we consider the evolution of British monetary policy since 1970. From the mid-1970s, policymakers were learning about monetarism. By the early 1980s, they could put into practice the lessons of Milton Friedman. Instead of following Friedman to the letter, however, policymakers combined a mixture of theoretical and political monetarism.[59] In a way they were like a driver who has passed his test but who has yet to experience the "real world" situation on the roads, where other people's driving and the odd hazard force him to modify his driving skills. During the 1980s, policy-makers came across several "hazards" (for example, financial liberalization and currency problems) not to mention mechanical failures (the failure of sterling M3 to indicate the economy was in recession in 1980). On several occasions the policymakers were required to question the lessons they had learnt and ultimately had to end the monetarist experiment by the mid-1980s. As in our earlier example, however, there are some lessons that a driver must not ever forget and British policymakers ignored the signs that monetary policy was too loose between 1986 and 1987 and an inflationary boom followed. Although it looked as if the authorities had learned little from monetarism by the late-1980s, following the UK's brief disastrous encounter with the ERM between 1990 and 1992, there was greater monetary stability in the period after 1992. Concomitantly, the sustained emphasis on supply-side economics and public choice theory during the 1980s and 1990s showed that policymakers had absorbed many lessons from new growth economics. By the end of the 1990s, there was a far greater consensus between policymakers and politicians about economic policy than there had been for a generation.

Conclusion

Despite the popularity of policy transfer in the United Kingdom, this chapter argues that this framework does not provide a satisfactorily explanation of how policy learning takes place. The attraction of policy transfer is its catchall nature, but political scientists have been putting the cart before the horse by examining policy transfer without discussing or resolving the basic concepts of lesson-drawing.

---

59 Gordon T. Pepper and Michael J. Oliver, *Monetarism Under Thatcher – Lessons For The Future* (Northampton, MA: Edward Elgar, 2001).

They are mistaken to assume that all lesson drawing can be lumped under the policy transfer banner.

The chapter contends that Peter Hall's social learning model offers a more rigorous framework to explore lesson drawing. Drawing on the case study of British macroeconomic policy post-1945, it has shown that for much of the post-war period, mistakes with monetary and fiscal policy, the persistence of a "stop-go" mentality and inadequate consideration of the supply-side of the British economy persisted until the underlying Keynesian paradigm finally disintegrated. While Hall's account of the fall of Keynesianism and the rise of monetarism sits comfortably within the model, his account of social learning in the 1980s is problematical.

Although Hall did not explore how fourth order learning impacts the model, I have shown how it unifies the three orders of change and places the policymaker and politician center stage in the model. Despite the claims made by the "monetarist" government of Margaret Thatcher that they had learned from the mistakes of past administrations, this chapter suggests that their capacity to learn was checked in the 1980s and has drawn on Dodd's work to explain why.[60] Although there are restrictions on the availability of primary material in the public sphere, a more complete picture has yet to emerge about the accumulation of policy failures, anomalies and the propensity of actors to engage in learning in the 1980s and 1990s. Such frustrations should not prohibit the contemporary economic historian from providing a preliminary assessment of the changes in economic policy post-1979 although it is essential to remember that understanding of recent economic policymaking is enhanced by reference to historical experience.

---

60 Dodd "Learning to Learn."

Chapter 7

An Ecology of Learning: Concepts, Methods, and the United States 1992 Somalia Intervention

David C. Ellis

James March notes four outstanding issues impeding the development of a coherent and robust learning theory: (1) "whether decisions are to be viewed as *choice-based* or *rule-based*;" (2) "whether decision making is typified more by *clarity* and *consistency* or by *ambiguity* and *inconsistency*;" (3) "whether decision making is an *instrumental* activity or an *interpretive* activity;" and (4) "whether outcomes of decision processes are seen as primarily attributable to the actions of *autonomous actors* or to the systematic properties of an *interacting ecology*." He advises that each of these concerns is part of the learning process and decisionmaking that theorists should "weave...together in a way that allows each to illuminate the others" rather than choose among them.[1]

What is an *interacting ecology of learning*? Despite a few tentative explorations,[2] learning scholars have yet to develop the concept in a coherent and comprehensive way. Indeed, an ecology of learning has been conceptualized almost exclusively from an individualist rather than a social-structural ontology which perpetuates two epistemological and methodological shortcomings. Epistemologically, an individualist ontology leads scholars to look exclusively for causal relationships when they should also be searching for constitutive ones. Methodologically, it guides scholars to focus on individual actors as learners at the expense of their requisite counterparts – teachers. Since most learning theory scholars conduct their research within the positivist-empiricist tradition, and since they value parsimony and causal logic, it is little wonder that ecologies of learning have been neglected.

Traditionally, learning theorists have studied organizational learning, social learning, and societal learning as separate phenomena in order to orient their

---

1   James March, *The Pursuit of Organization Intelligence* (Malden, MA: Blackwell Business, 1999), p. 14.

2   Barbara Levitt and James March, "Organizational Learning," *Annual Review of Sociology* vol. 14 (1988), p. 31; Lawrence C. Dodd, "Political Learning and Political Change: Understanding Development Across Time," in Lawrence C. Dodd and Calvin Jillson, eds., *The Dynamics of American Politics: Approaches and Interpretations* (Boulder, CO: Westview Press, 1994), pp. 331-364.

research toward a specific unit of analysis. As a result, the literature has remained largely divided along these three research projects. In this chapter I posit a simple thesis: the individuals, organizations, bureaucracies, leaders, and societies routinely designated as distinct units of analysis constitute a holistic *ecological learning system*. An ecological learning system derives its logic from the understanding that, for each issue, there are relevant public and private organizations and bureaucracies, interested leaders and advocacy groups, and publics who participate in and influence how ideas and information are interpreted and promoted. They interact to mutually construct social reality and political meaning through various forms of ideational communication, including speech. Understanding how these actors interact to shape, influence, direct, prescribe, and proscribe information and ideas is the fundamental focus of this study.

The chapter is divided into three segments. The first describes the importance of idea creation and transmission within an ecological system rather than a stratified and disaggregated reality. The primary foci of this analysis are the competition of ideas and the relative strength of discourses promoted by various actors as they define reality, the issues and the range of policy options. Second, the paper develops some hypotheses as to how an ecological learning system functions and describes how a learning system might be studied employing March's "logic of appropriateness" concept. Finally, a case study of the 1992 United States (US) humanitarian intervention in Somalia is presented to demonstrate the utility of an ecological model.

An Ecology of Learning

Ideas as Intersubjective Phenomena

Although learning theory purports to be an ideas-based model of politics, its research concerns most commonly are: "who learns?," "what is learned?," and "how does learning affect policy?"[3] However, these foci leave unexplored the origins of the ideas and information learned, why some ideas gain currency while others fall by the wayside, and who serves as advocates and/or teachers of these ideas. Ideas do not exist in a vacuum, untouched by time and space, rather they are debated, negotiated, championed, ridiculed, acted upon, repressed, and forgotten.[4] If we are to formulate an ideas-based political theory, we must explain *how and why* certain ideas and information gain primacy over others *at a given place and time*. An ecological learning system approach allows us to consider actors' interactions and discourse

---

    3   Colin J. Bennett and Michael Howlett, "The Lessons of Learning: Reconciling Theories of Policy Learning and Policy Change," *Policy Science* vol. 25 (1992), p. 278.
    4   Peter L. Berger and Thomas Luckmann, *The Social Construction of Reality: A Treatise on the Sociology of Knowledge* (New York: Anchor Books, 1966), pp. 48 and 116.

that articulate, develop and choose among an array of ideas and policy options[5] within the constraints of paradigmatic beliefs and logics of appropriateness.[6]

Ralph Stacey argues that

> [t]he underlying theory of learning is a systems view of learning as basically an error correcting process. Knowledge creation is thought of as a sender-receiver system in which knowledge is created by converting tacit knowledge into explicit, transmitting that explicit knowledge to others, who convert it back into tacit knowledge.[7]

The problem with this view, he observes, is that:

> this systems perspective cannot succeed on its own as an explanation of how new knowledge is unfolded by the system...it simply assumes that [new knowledge] arises as tacit knowledge in the heads of some individuals, or exists in a common pool of meaning....[8]

Instead, Stacey contends that people live and work in social settings and structures, making uniquely independent thought unusual at best. Ideas and knowledge are developed by the interaction of people who share worldviews, logics, symbolic meanings and emotions in a constant, unending process of social communication. Stacey's critique underscores the fact that idea and knowledge creation and learning rely on intersubjective communication.[9]

Since ideas are intersubjective by nature, and are interpreted and acted upon based on the basis of identity constructs and institutional socializations, learning theorists should embrace an ontology that draws out and problematizes these relationships. By making the learning system the unit of analysis, the ecology of learning model avoids analyzing learning actors and processes in isolation. This perspective particularly allows us to focus on factors that make ideas in an issue area influential and advantaged relative to others.

---

5   Roxanne Lynn Doty, "Foreign Policy as Social Construction: A Post-Positivist Analysis of U.S. Counterinsurgency Policy in the Philippines," *International Studies Quarterly* vol. 37 (1993), pp. 297-320.

6   Peter A. Hall, "Policy Paradigms, Social Learning, and the State: The Case of Economic Policymaking in Britain," *Comparative Politics* vol. 25 (1993), pp. 275-296. On the creation of logics of appropriateness, see Berger and Luckmann, *The Social Construction of Reality*, pp. 39-41, 65-67, 121 and Graham Allison and Philip Zelikow, *Essence of Decision: Explaining the Cuban Missile Crisis* (New York: Longman, 1999), Chapters 3 and 5.

7   Ralph D. Stacey, *Complex Responsive Processes in Organizations: Learning and Knowledge Creation* (New York: Routledge, 2001), p. 26.

8   Stacey, *Complex Responsive Processes in Organizations*, p. 28.

9   While not embracing all social constructivist assumptions, learning theorists such as Allison and Zelikow, Paul Sabatier, and Peter A. Hall have long acknowledged the importance of social interaction in the learning processes. See Allison and Zelikow, *Essence of Decision*, p. 255, Paul A. Sabatier, "Knowledge, Policy-Oriented Learning, and Policy Change: An Advocacy Coalition Framework," *Knowledge: Creation, Diffusion, Utilization* vol. 8 (1987), p. 652; and Hall, "Policy Paradigms," pp. 288-289.

A Mutually Constituted Learning Ecology

The core concept behind the ecology of learning is that each actor in a learning system affects others in both a causal and constitutive manner. Hence, organizational learning includes such corporate entities as companies, churches, governments, governmental bureaucracies, and other general collectives; social learning includes political, economic, cultural, intellectual, and social leaders and elites who work within the aforementioned organizations; and societal learning includes the groups and individuals from which leaders are drawn. These three groups cannot be fully understood as autonomous actors.

Understanding idea generation, transmission, and learning as part of a broader process of social interdependence requires analysis conducted in terms of exploring constitutive relationships. Constitutive analysis is concerned with how actors create and/or define themselves and others through interaction and discourse, and how their identities and ideas become meaningful within the social context. Individuals process and understand ideas through the lens of collective or common knowledge, which makes their actions understandable to society at large.[10]

The identities and preference sets that condition human interests and the interpretation of ideas ensue from patterns of socialization that result in a shared "social stock of knowledge."[11] The social stock of knowledge comes about through the successive transmission of symbols, myths, narratives, imputed relationships, and languages across generations. Two types of socialization make this possible, primary and secondary. Primary socialization refers to the worldview instilled in a child from the perspective of his parents, with all its attendant assumptions, relationships, value judgments, and expectations. This is the most fundamental store of ideas leading to the core identity development of a person because it gives him the vocabulary that informs him of his place, station, and role in society. Secondary socialization refers to the subsequent, more specialized stores of knowledge relating to ideas pertinent to institutional settings, such as school, work, and sports.[12]

In the course of primary and secondary socializations, individuals are exposed to many social institutions, and, over time, these institutions are accepted as natural and are many times unquestioned. Such is the case with political, economic, and legal systems, as well as systems of socio-cultural hierarchy like religion. In this sense, institutions become social reality and form the rules, standards, and patterns of behavior for society. These social institutions contain within themselves a shared history, and when institutions exist prior to one's encounter with them, they assume the form of a crystallized and autonomous reality.[13] The point here is that organizations, leaders, and societies are first and foremost *social ideas* that are not

---

10 Wendt, Alexander, *Social Theory of International Politics* (Cambridge, MA: Cambridge University Press, 1999), pp. 180-181.

11 Berger and Luckmann, *The Social Construction of Reality*, p. 41.

12 Berger and Luckmann, *The Social Construction of Reality*, p. 138.

13 Berger and Luckmann, *The Social Construction of Reality*, pp. 55, 58.

just causally related, but more importantly, are constituted by one another.[14] There are myriad forms of social structures within which leaders and societies function, and the various uncountable permutations in social structures lead to equally uncountable variations in logics of appropriateness throughout the world.[15] Thus, organizations, leaders, and societies are both idea recipients and idea presenters; in the words of learning theory, they are both learners and teachers, and they are mutually dependent for social and ideational meaning.

Constructivist analysis seeks to explicate how social reality is created and sustained. This in turn, permits a deeper analysis of the social institutions, ideational constructs, and discursive relationships shaping social interaction and intersubjective communication. Discourse is the single most important vehicle for reality creation and maintenance and ideational competition because defining and discussing things establish values and expectations concerning them.[16] Discourse, speech, and language structure the world and are necessary to mutually constitute reality and understanding, one in which ideas can compete in an intelligible fashion.

Friedrich Kratochwil summarizes the importance of speech and conversation:

> Different from the world of signals, which keeps their beings in dependence on the here and now, speech not only frees humans from the immediacy of the situation – we can talk about a situation that has already passed, or has not even arisen – it also allows us to make choices rather than merely respond to a stimulus. With speech, an assessment of actions and events in terms of common values and through recollection and comparison becomes possible. We also can now "learn" not only from our own experiences, but – through our conceptual grasp – even from those of others.[17]

Approaching learning from an ecological model, then, requires that scholars explore the nature of ecological relationships. Doing so helps them determine the most important sources of information and idea exchange, and it also assists them in developing an accurate picture of how each actor's logic of appropriateness stands in relation to the others. This method requires an interpretive methodology, at least initially, but it does not preclude the use of other methods in the analysis since empirical data and rational methods might still be useful because an actor's logic of consequences is in part determined by his logic of appropriateness.[18]

---

14 Wendt, *Social Theory of International Politics*, pp. 49, 68. Wendt calls these "social kinds."

15 Allison and Zelikow, *Essence of Decision*, pp. 145-146, 153-158.

16 Berger and Luckmann, *The Social Construction of Reality*, p. 152.

17 Friedrich V. Kratochwil, "Constructivism as an Approach to Interdisciplinary Study," in Karin M. Fierke and Knud Erik Jorgensen, *Constructing International Relations: The Next Generation* (New York: M. E. Sharpe, 2001), p. 19.

18 James March suggests that a logic of consequence is a different behavioral motivator than a logic of obligation or appropriateness. However, Alexander Wendt convincingly demonstrates that a logic of consequences, prompting rational and instrumental behavior, is subordinate to the logic of appropriateness. March, *The Pursuit of Organization Intelligence*, p. 228; Wendt, *Social Theory of International Politics*, Chapter 3.

Logics of Appropriateness

An ecology of learning model facilitates our understanding of the range of possible policy options for entities within the learning system deriving from their worldviews, institutional imperatives, identity and normative orientations. Again following March, the range of options for each learning entity derives from its "logic of appropriateness." March asserts that "[m]uch of the decision-making behavior we observe reflects the routine way in which people seek to fulfill their identities." In contrast to rational models of decision-making, logic of appropriateness decision-making comes from matching a changing and often ambiguous set of contingent rules and identities to a changing and often ambiguous set of situations. Actions reflect conceptualizations of "proper behavior," and decision-makers routinely ignore their own fully conscious preferences. They act not on the basis of objective or subjective calculations of consequences and preferences but on the basis of rules, routines, procedures, practices, identities, and roles. Thus, decisionmakers interpret, learn and act upon information based on (1) the situation in which they find themselves (which influences relevant identities, roles and norms), (2) the identities, roles and norms chosen to deal with the situation (such as their personal, professional, or bureaucratic capacity), and (3) the match between the identity they adopt and the situation as they recognize it.[19]

Logic-of-appropriateness analysis within an ecology of learning model assumes that each entity in the learning system possesses a unique perspective on an issue deriving from its identity, norms, roles and rules, that shapes its policy ideas and range of preferred actions. This conceptualization is congruent with the constructivist argument that socialization and identity are foundations for the distinctive and idiosyncratic ways individuals and organizations develop interests and preferences. An ecology of learning model analyzes the range of discourse on an issue by identifying the ideas that predominate or enjoy the greatest competitive advantage. Leaders, governmental organizations and societal entities interact and may constrain each other when their logics of appropriateness diverge.[20] When ideas converge (i.e. when they are defined similarly, are assigned similar values, expectations, and yield similar policy preferences), there is little resistance to action, but when ideas diverge there must be discussion and resolution of differences. The divergence of worldviews, beliefs and norms results in a competition of ideas and the need for learning. The preceding assumptions lead to the principal hypothesis of this paper: Policy outcomes in ecologies of learning are a consequence of competition and convergence of the constituent entities' logics of appropriateness through discourse.

In essence, then, political discourse (including framing and spin) is an attempt to construct lenses through which others interpret events so as to legitimize a given

---

19 March, *The Pursuit of Organization Intelligence*, p. 21.

20 Allison and Zelikow, *Essence of Decision*, pp. 145-146; Berger and Luckmann, *The Social Construction of Reality*, pp. 55-60.

logic of appropriateness. Efforts to control the language and discourse associated with an issue, including affixing norms and principles, are part and parcel of defining the range of possible policy options. Within an ecology of learning, entities (leaders, governmental bureaucracies non-governmental organizations, media elites, political parties, cultural leaders, etc.) vie for control over the discourse through which policy ideas are articulated and evaluated. Entities within an ecology of learning bring different ideational and well as institutional and power assets to the discourse.

Leaders within an Ecology of Learning

As is emphasized in several chapters in this volume, leaders and executives play important roles in an ecology of learning by virtue of their station – they are privileged providers of ideas and information, persuaders and teachers, and they commonly have significant power to affect promulgation and implementation of their ideas and policies. The latter source of power is better examined via other theoretical approaches, such as those based on the logic of consequences (rationalist methods), rather than from an ideational perspective. However, the former sources of influence are critical to understanding the importance of ideas in learning. Leadership theory recognizes two functions of leaders: instrumental and expressive leadership. Instrumental leadership is oriented toward achieving specific tasks, such as acquiring resources. Expressive or relationship-oriented leadership maintains group identity, morale, cohesion, and motivation. [21]

Most contemporary analyses view leadership as a process of social influence whereby the leader attempts to mobilize the followers to achieve a common goal or task. [22] James M. Burns notes that leadership is

'[d]issensual' because it is 'rooted in conflict and power over authoritative allocation of values for a society,' 'collective in that it involves leaders and follower interaction,' and 'purposeful and causative in that it leads to the creation of ideas, movements, institutions, nations.' [23]

Discourse is a process of "sensemaking" by political leaders, a term Karl Weick uses to describe the cognitive processes of placing items into frameworks, "comprehending, redressing surprise, constructing meaning, interacting in pursuit of mutual understanding, and patterning." [24] Leaders are central to these cognitive and

---

21 Amitai Etzioni, "Dual Leadership in Complex Organizations," *American Sociological Review* vol. 30 (1965), p. 689; Fred E. Fiedler, *A Theory of Leadership Effectiveness* (New York: McGraw-Hill Book Company, 1967), p. 13.

22 Martin M. Chemers, *An Integrative Theory of Leadership* (Mahwah, NJ: Lawrence Erlbaum Associates, Publishers, 1997), p. 1.; Etzioni, "Dual Leadership in Complex Organizations," p. 690.

23 Mostafa Rejai and Kay Phillips, *Leaders and Leadership: An Appraisal of Theory and Research* (Westport, CT: Praeger, 1997), p. 3.

24 Karl E. Weick, *Sensemaking in Organizations* (Thousand Oaks, CA: Sage, 1995), p. 6.

political processes within ecologies of learning. Indeed, constructivists increasingly conceptualize leaders as occupying a critical role in the construction of social and political reality. For example, Jutta Weldes, et. al. argue that "certain agents or groups of agents play a privileged role in the production and reproduction of these realities."[25] Leaders may enjoy potential relative power in the competition of ideas because of some admixture of the quality of their ideas, the trust and authority invested in their positions, their ability to persuade and/or teach, their ability to appeal to group identity, to generate morale, cohesion and motivation. These attributes are related, of course, to a host of issues including legitimacy, trust, effectiveness, decisiveness, charisma, and popularity. Perhaps most important to a leader's role within in the context of this study, a trusted, charismatic, and effective leader may wield great influence in the construction of reality, the creation of ideas and the framing of policy issues.

Organizations and Bureaucracies within an Ecology of Learning

Organizations' influence within an ecology of learning derives from the fact that institutions are created specifically to organize human activity to achieve collective goals. To function effectively and coherently, organizations must be "rule-governed ways of deciding, delegating and setting the boundaries of membership..."[26] Organizations convey to individuals predetermined, organization-specific logics of appropriateness that influence how they interpret information and make decisions with the organizations' identities, roles, interests and preferences in mind. They also develop routines and socialize individuals to simplify decisionmaking and guarantee consistency in outcomes. Thus, to a significant degree, organizational logics of appropriateness replace individual ones. An important source of the relative power of organizations on ideas, issue framing and policymaking derives from their ability to create and shape the ideas and knowledge to which their members pay attention and upon which they act.

Historical and sociological institutionalism offer the clearest analysis on this form of influence. Both variants in the new institutionalism literature stress the fact that institutions shape or define the goals and preferences actors adopt based on the institutions' enforcement mechanisms, opportunity structures, and power relationships.[27] Sociological institutionalism goes one step further, however, and

---

25 Jutta Weldes, Mark Laffey, Hugh Gusterson, and Raymond Duvall, "Introduction: Constructing Insecurity," in Jutta Weldes, Mark Laffey, Hugh Gusterson, and Raymond Duvall, eds., *Cultures of Insecurity* (Minneapolis, MN: University of Minnesota Press, 1999), p. 13.

26 Chris Argyris and Donald A. Schön, *Organizational Learning II: Theory, Method, and Practice* (Reading, MA: Addison-Wesley Publishing Company, 1996), p. 9.

27 Peter A. Hall and Rosemary Taylor, "Political Science and the Three New Institutionalisms," *Political Studies* vol. 44 (1996), p. 939; Paul Pierson, "The Path to European Integration: A Historical Institutionalist Analysis," *Comparative Political Studies* vol. 29 (1996), pp. 123-163.

posits that institutions constitute individuals' identities by molding their culture.[28] Institutions create the "scripts" that individuals follow to interpret the world around them.[29] In this way, institutions influence individuals by determining what is appropriate or culturally legitimate.

The literature suggests that organizations and institutions derive their influence and power in the competition of ideas by creating mechanisms that force or encourage individuals to follow strict logics of appropriateness in their daily routines and to interpret new ideas, information, and knowledge in specific ways. Consequently, issue framing, policy analysis, decisionmaking, and implementation are undertaken within an environment designed to limit the range of ideas from which individuals choose in order to achieve meaning and cognitive consistency. Organizational, institutional, and cultural norms, rules and procedures ensure the collective ability to act in a coherent and meaningful way and to produce and reproduce collective realities, identities, logics of appropriateness and policies over time.

An Ecology of Learning and US Humanitarian Intervention in Somalia

US government policy learning that yielded the decision to intervene in Somalia in 1992 was characterized by very distinctive organizational and societal discourses. The policy choices of then-President George H.W. Bush were significantly constrained by the discourses associated with the public's understanding of the United States' appropriate role in humanitarian crises and by the Defense Department's operational doctrine. President Bush's deliberations and inquiries mostly focused on whether the United States should and could positively influence the crisis in Somalia, a country whose problems ran directly counter to the conditions societal and Department of Defense discourses portrayed as appropriate for US military action.

Throughout the 1970s and 1980s, Somalia, under the leadership of Siad Barre, was embroiled in Cold War politics, first siding with the Soviet Union and later with the United States. As the Cold War ended, U.S. support for the Barre regime was withdrawn, and a movement removed him from office in January 1991. Throughout 1990-1991, the United Nations (UN) tried to minimize the impact of the Somali civil war on the population, but by 1992, starvation became a serious threat. International aid to civilians fell hostage to clan fighting, and mass starvation in Somalia became an international crisis. Although the UN deployed a small contingent of armed troops to protect food shipments, it became clear by the summer of 1992 that US military assistance was necessary. Indeed, the crisis found its way into American

---

28 Mark D. Aspinwall and Gerald Schneider, "Same Menu, Separate Tables: The Institutionalist Turn in Political Science and the Study of European Integration," *European Journal of Political Research* vol. 38 (2000), pp. 8-9; Hall and Taylor, "Political Science and the Three New Institutionalisms," pp. 946-947.

29 Bo Rothstein, "Political Institutions: An Overview," in Robert E. Goodman and Hans-Dieter Klingemann, eds., *A New Handbook of Political Science* (New York: Oxford University Press, 1998), p. 147.

homes on the television throughout the summer and fall, and became an issue in the 1992 presidential election.

The Societal Discourses – Public Opinion and the Media

While Americans overwhelmingly supported maintaining a strong military and an assertive foreign policy during the Cold War, their attitudes changed dramatically once that conflict officially ended. Americans became concerned primarily with domestic issues, and the salience of foreign policy declined with the loss of an identifiable enemy.[30] By 1992, the majority of the public was wary of the United States acting as the world's sole policeman and providing significant international economic assistance. Americans preferred multilateral action over unilateral intervention and expected the US's major Western allies and the United Nations to address international security issues.[31] US public opinion favoring unilateral humanitarian intervention dropped to its lowest levels in two decades.[32]

Two additional factors colored the public's logic of appropriateness at the time of the intervention. First, the experience of the Vietnam War continued to divide the public on what constituted legitimate intervention in other countries. Garnering coherent and widespread public support for US intervention abroad was therefore a difficult task.[33] In addition, Americans were intolerant of casualties following Vietnam, and the first Gulf War's remarkably low casualty rate reinforced the public's demand for relatively bloodless wars.[34] In effect, the first Gulf War taught the public that limited casualties in military engagements were now possible.

Some have characterized Somalia as a situation in which media coverage of destitute and dying Somalis compelled President Bush to launch a humanitarian operation.[35] This argument portrays Bush's choices as driven by the so-called *CNN Effect* whereby the

> professional policy expert and diplomat [are] undermined by media. To the degree that foreign policy is reactive to news content, the key decisions are those made by reporters,

30 John E. Reilly, "The Public Mood at Mid-Decade," *Foreign Policy* vol. 98 (1995), p. 76; Steven Kull, "What the Public Knows that Washington Doesn't," *Foreign Policy* vol. 101 (1995-96), p. 103.

31 Kull, "What the Public Knows that Washington Doesn't," pp. 102-105.

32 Reilly, "The Public Mood at Mid-Decade," p. 81.

33 Charles A. Stevenson, "The Evolving Clinton Doctrine on the Use of Force," *Armed Forces and Society* vol. 22 (1996), p. 515.

34 Stevenson, "The Evolving Clinton Doctrine on the Use of Force," p. 526.

35 Jonathan Mermin, "Television News and American Intervention in Somalia: The Myth of a Media-Driven Foreign Policy," *Political Science Quarterly* vol. 112 (1997), p. 385; Steven Livingston and Todd Eachus, "Humanitarian Crises and US Foreign Policy: Somalia and the CNN Effect Reconsidered," *Political Communication* vol. 12 (1995), pp. 413-414.

producers, and editors. In this view, foreign policy decision making has become epiphenomenal to news decision making.[36]

Recent content and time-series analyses by Livingston and Eachus and by Mermin raise serious doubts about the validity of this view. Both assert that the media did not control the policy discourse regarding the Somalia intervention; instead savvy politicians and bureaucrats used the media to shape the discourse and promote their ideas.

In fact, media coverage of the crisis began in earnest in July 1992, more than a year after key State Department officials began efforts to direct the government's attention to the growing disaster in Somalia.[37] Nevertheless, the media was an important entity in the ecology of learning because of its ability to frame the issue and to transmit images. The media acted as a principal teacher on the Somalia issue; its discourse and interpretation of events influenced the way the public and the administration understood and responded to the crisis. Indeed, the media framed the Somalia crisis as one in which the US should and could play a pivotal role.[38] The media, as teacher within the ecology of learning, invoked a discourse that indicated the moral obligation of the United States to intervene in Somalia.

Organizational Discourses – The Departments of Defense and State and the US Congress

At the outset, the US Department of Defense opposed humanitarian intervention in Somalia. The Pentagon's logic of appropriateness, discourse and general orientation toward military intervention were outlined in the force utilization doctrine developed in the wake of the Vietnam War. The doctrine stated that (1) the state may protect the nation's vital interests but must use overwhelming force to deliver a quick, decisive victory; (2) important but not vital interests merit limited military force commensurate with limited political objectives; (3) political leaders must provide military commanders with clear political objectives and clear, achievable mandates; (4) measures of operational success and an exit strategy must be identified before committing troops; and (5) the operation must have public and congressional support before implementation. To this list, practical requirements in the planning of missions included ensuring the operation to be not just quick, but casualty rates needed to remain low.[39] Stevenson summarizes well the discourse of the doctrine:

> While most [principles] are phrased positively, the underlying thrust is often negative: don't embark on high risk operations that have a less than overwhelming chance of success;

---

36 Livingston and Eachus, "Humanitarian Crises and US Foreign Policy," p. 415.

37 Livingston and Eachus, "Humanitarian Crises and US Foreign Policy," p. 426; Mermin, "Television News and American Intervention in Somalia," pp. 392-393.

38 Mermin, "Television News and American Intervention in Somalia," pp. 388-389, 396.

39 Stevenson, "The Evolving Clinton Doctrine on the Use of Force," pp. 511-513.

don't start something without a clear idea of how to end it; don't use force incrementally or gradually...The [civilian leaders] must provide clear objectives and criteria for success, along with an assurance of public support; the military, in contrast, must be the calculator of costs and risks as well as the judge of what forces and tactics to use.

The major principles of military doctrine shaping the Pentagon's position on Somalia were derived from lessons learned in Vietnam (clear objectives and overwhelming force) and Lebanon (exit strategy). To these principles, General Colin Powell, Chairman of the Joint Chiefs, added the need for popular support, a lesson drawn from his experiences in Vietnam.[40]

The Joint Chiefs of Staff are the President's primary advisors on military issues, and observers suggest that in many cases they wield a veto over decisions to use force. Stevenson notes, "Instead of exercising that veto directly, however, the chiefs have used their influence to impose key conditions on military operations, such as exit strategies and the freedom to make operational decisions." Thus, Department of Defense officials and bureaucrats contribute to policymaking discourse in terms of the force utilization doctrine and specific operational preferences. The Pentagon objected to intervening in Somalia because there was no clear mandate or objective, there was the real potential for mission creep, and there was no expectation of resolving the political situation.[41] Despite the Department of Defense's general orientation against intervention, Powell, as Chairman of the Joint Chiefs, was a major catalyst in moving the operation forward. He believed that a mission should and could be launched to ameliorate the humanitarian problem. Powell's discourse framed intervention in Somalia in terms of the force utilization doctrine. Humanitarian intervention in Somalia should and could be undertaken with a limited objective, utilizing overwhelming force, and with a quick exit strategy. This formula, he argued, would preclude the operation's deteriorating into another Vietnam.[42]

The State Department, however, participated in the ecology of learning regarding Somalia with a different logic of appropriateness, discourse and policy recommendations. State Department officials (specifically Ambassador Morris Abram, Jon Fox, Andrew Natsios, and Jan Westcott) had been working on the crisis as early as March of 1991 and were essential to raising public and Congressional awareness of the starvation in Somalia.[43] Throughout 1991 and early 1992, Somalia received very little press coverage, predominantly because the Bosnian crisis and the 1992 presidential election campaign dominated the news. It was only after a number of political entrepreneurs from the State Department and Congress were able to capture the attention of the press that public discourse focused on the Somalia crisis.

---

40 Stevenson, "The Evolving Clinton Doctrine on the Use of Force," p. 514.

41 Stevenson, "The Evolving Clinton Doctrine on the Use of Force," p. 523.

42 Herbert S. Parmet, *George Bush: The Life of a Lone Star Yankee* (New York: Scribner, 1997), p. 509.

43 Livingston and Eachus, "Humanitarian Crises and US Foreign Policy," p. 418.

Andrew Natsios and Congressman Tony Hall staged a hearing on Somalia in November 1991, describing it as one of the gravest humanitarian crises in the world. Although media coverage remained sparse, in June 1992, President Bush directed Ambassador Smith Hempstone to visit a refugee camp across the border in Kenya to gather information, and Hempstone's subsequent report increased Bush's interest in the growing crisis. Sensing the potential for military action, the Department of Defense objected to the State Department's increased involvement in the crisis.[44] State Department discourse framed intervention in Somalia to ameliorate profound human suffering as morally imperative. This survey of the logics of appropriateness, discourse and policy recommendations of the various participants in the ecology of learning about Somalia explains the possible and probable policy ideas and options available for consideration by the most important member of the ecology, the President, the actor primarily responsible for US foreign policy and the Commander in Chief.

Presidential Leadership in the Ecology of Learning

Somalia, as a major foreign policy issue with which the President had to contend, did not arise until well into the 1992 presidential campaign. President Bush was aware that the State Department was working to stabilize the humanitarian crisis, but Somalia was not considered newsworthy until mid-year. The President received a report by Senator Nancy Kassebaum who returned from Somalia in July 1992 advocating US intervention. Congruent with Department of Defense doctrine, Bush opposed becoming involved in Somalia until a UN-brokered cease-fire had been obtained, but Kassebaum disagreed and began a series of public appearances to pressure the administration, urging the appropriateness and necessity of action.[45] Other political figures, such as Senators Edward Kennedy and Paul Simon, began openly criticizing the Bush administration for its inaction, and media coverage intensified dramatically. More importantly, legislators began openly challenging Bush's decision to wait for a UN cease-fire before intervening.[46] In August, President Bush announced a US airlift of emergency supplies to Somalia and press coverage spiked, as did references to Somalia in campaign rhetoric in the 1992 presidential election.[47]

Once the election was over, President Bush considered US action in Somalia. He had been under pressure from United Nations Secretary-General Boutros Boutros-Ghali who begged for US assistance.[48] The United States indicated to the United Nations on Thanksgiving its willingness to participate in the distribution of food

---

44 Livingston and Eachus, "Humanitarian Crises and US Foreign Policy," pp. 424-425.

45 Livingston and Eachus, "Humanitarian Crises and US Foreign Policy," pp. 425-426; Mermin, "Television News and American Intervention in Somalia," pp. 392-393.

46 Mermin, "Television News and American Intervention in Somalia," p. 393.

47 Mermin "Television News and American Intervention in Somalia," p. 395; Elizabeth Drew, *On the Edge: The Clinton Presidency* (New York: Simon and Schuster, 1994), p. 139.

48 Parmet, *George Bush*, p. 508.

in Somalia, but only with its own military playing the lead role.[49] There was no question that President Bush was the most important entity in the Somalia ecology of learning; indeed, Andrew Natsios credits the movement on Somalia exclusively to Bush's change of heart.[50] On foreign policy concerns, Bush was known to be flexible and open to negotiation, but any negotiation occurred within the range of options he deemed appropriate.[51]

When Bush decided to undertake the humanitarian intervention, he adopted a policy consistent with Pentagon force utilization doctrine, principles he learned as a top member of White House administrations for twelve years. Bush approved a mission that would only last 2-4 months and that would be transformed into a UN peace operation after that time. Moreover, in keeping with Pentagon discourse, the mission was to use overwhelming force, maintain a small, off-shore contingent once the mission was transformed into the UN operation, and did not include among its missions the reestablishment of a stable government in Somalia.[52] The deployment of troops was specifically designed to be "limited in scope, time, and objective."[53] This limited deployment of US forces actually put the administration at cross-purposes with the United Nations, which favored an extended disarmament campaign.[54] Bush refused to expand the mission beyond the provision of food and stability because he knew he did not have public or congressional support for a more aggressive mission, nor did he think it the proper role for the US military.[55] Despite these operational limitations, the Pentagon had to be "dragged along" on the mission.[56]

The Bush plan was consistent with the logics of appropriateness of both the American public and the Pentagon, since it called for a minimal, quick operation, and it satisfied Americans' sense of international duty and morality.[57] Bush did not feel inaction was possible given the persuasiveness of media and congressional discourses,[58] and now the Pentagon proposed an operation with a high probability of success. In addition, State Department notions of appropriateness would be satisfied by some action being taken to deal with the crisis.

---

49 Clement Adibe, *Managing Arms in Peace Processes: Somalia* (New York: United Nations Institute for Disarmament Research, 1995), p. 49.

50 Adibe, *Managing Arms in Peace Processes*, p. 49.

51 Larry Berman and Emily O. Goldman, "Clinton's Foreign Policy at Midterm," in Colin Campbell and Bert A. Rockman, eds., *The Clinton Presidency: First Appraisals* (Chatham, NJ: Chatham House Publishers, 1996), pp. 298-299.

52 Stevenson, "The Evolving Clinton Doctrine on the Use of Force," pp. 523-524.

53 Adibe, *Managing Arms in Peace Processes*, p. 58.

54 Adibe, *Managing Arms in Peace Processes*, p. 60.

55 Adibe, *Managing Arms in Peace Processes*, p. 60; William G. Hyland, Clinton's World: Remaking American Foreign Policy (Westport, CT: Praeger, 1999), p. 54.

56 Parmet, *George Bush*, p. 509.

57 Kull, "What the Public Knows that Washington Doesn't," p. 113.

58 Hyland, *Clinton's World*, p. 53.

A Linear Depiction of the Various Logics of Appropriateness within the Ecology of Learning

Having recounted the various perspectives, it is now possible to graphically depict the consequences of the several logics of appropriateness represented within the ecology of learning. Figure 7.1 represents the spectrum of possible policy options toward Somalia given the nature of the crisis, with the various societal and organizational actors' policy positions given their logics of appropriateness.

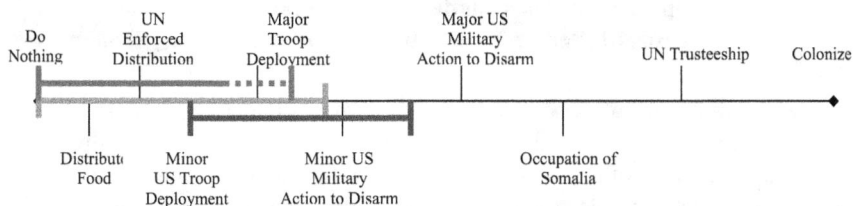

Figure 7.1 Logics of Appropriateness: US Society (the least shaded bar), the Pentagon (the medium shaded bar), and the State Department (the darkest bar)

In the case of society and the Pentagon, doing nothing was a viable policy option, but the discourse from the media made a convincing case that the United States should and could do something positive for Somalia.[59] Although the Pentagon was generally against an intervention, its primary commander and principal advisor to President Bush, General Powell, decided that an intervention was possible, but that it would only take place with overwhelming strength (Powell's policy position is represented by the dotted lines). The State Department strongly supported the commitment of troops and was prepared for a more extensive political operation. Doing nothing receded as a possible option given the persuasiveness of State Department, congressional and media discourse in an election year.

President Bush's logic of appropriateness followed the Pentagon's, but was very mindful of public support. Figure 7.2 represents President Bush's understanding of the policy options available to him.

---

59 Mermin, "Television News and American Intervention in Somalia," pp. 388-389, 396.

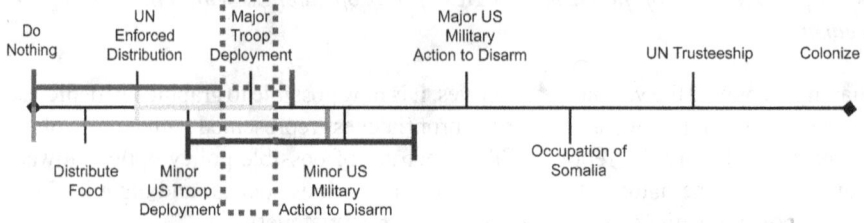

Figure 7.2 Logics of Appropriateness: Bush's Understanding of the Appropriate (the least shaded bar), and the Area of Policy Consensus (dotted area) within the Somalia Learning Ecology

Clearly the confluence of these logics of appropriateness demanded a quick mission with overwhelming force as advocated by General Powell. While Bush preferred that the UN take care of the situation without US forces, he became conscious that this option was not feasible. Only US troops could bring some measure of stability to the country. By virtue of Bush's understanding of his policy options, particularly as presented by General Powell, the deployment of a major force was the appropriate policy alternative. Humanitarian intervention should enjoy fairly high levels of legitimacy given that it conformed to the public and media's understanding of the crisis and discourse of what they regarded as appropriate.

Here the ecological nature of the learning system can be most readily observed. Both President Bush and the public were largely affected by the Somalia crisis through the reporting and discourse of the media, but President Bush was cognizant of the limitations placed on him by public opinion on military deployment. Indeed, the mission logic he explained (taught) to the public stressed the fact that the military was there only to stabilize the country and to eliminate the threat of starvation faced by the Somali people; the military was not to become involved in a political settlement as it later did. Thus, the key phrases in the discourse of the intervention were: limited in time and scope, altruistic, and incurring few casualties. When the mission altered its purpose and activities in 1993, the logics of appropriateness diverged and legitimacy for the mission was lost. In this case, each entity in the learning system advocated, taught, and learned, i.e., each was a learner and a teacher.

Conclusion

The purpose of this chapter has been to illustrate that learners do not simply learn information, ideas, and beliefs but instead interpret and reflect upon them via discourse among other policy actors. Ideas are not equal. Some enjoy real and measurable competitive advantages over others. For this reason, before beginning analysis, learning theorists should identify the most important ideas which, of course, are related to the persuasiveness and relative importance of their advocates.

Collectively these ideas, discourses and their advocates can be described as an ecological learning system. Moreover, this study describes how to incorporate the ecology of learning model within a broader research program. By analyzing the range of preferred policy options deriving from the logic of appropriateness of each of the actors in a learning system, it is possible to identify the policy option most congruent with the various logics of appropriateness. Each actor comes to the table with a logic of appropriateness, a broad set of ideas and policy preferences that are created and articulated via discourse. By comparing them graphically, it is possible to determine the most likely set of ideas and policy options to emerge from the ecology of learning.

The ecology of learning model is not designed to predict political outcomes. Rather it is offered to demonstrate how social scientists can begin to understand which ideas are most likely to be adopted, and to develop hypotheses as to when policy options are most likely or unlikely to receive high degrees of support. President Bush's decision to intervene was designed to maintain the support of all the major actors concerned and did in fact enjoy widespread support. An interesting question, however, is what happens when the logics of appropriateness of the most important actors diverge or do not overlap at all? This study suggests that the decision would enjoy limited public support and would not receive the best effort of the entities charged with implementation. This question deserves serious attention in order to show that the logic of appropriateness model is in fact theoretically useful and robust.

On a more theoretical level, the ecology of learning model highlights the fact that learning is constitutive as well as causal in nature. Scholars should devote attention to this fact because much political teaching is related to actors' identities. It was no accident that the media portrayed the Somalia crisis as one in which the US was morally obligated to intervene. The decision to intervene was almost purely based on humanitarian interest, and given the limited material interest in Somalia, such a motivation could only come from asking, "what is the right thing to do in this situation?" This is a constitutive rather than causal question. Moreover, the discourse used by the media, some important State Department officials, and several legislators defined the crisis in terms that the Bush administration should and could intervene, which required President Bush to *justify inaction* rather than action. Images of starving people raised issues of morality among the public, the various bureaucracies, and the White House – bringing to the fore discourse directly associated with their logics of appropriateness.

Returning now to the issues raised by James March, it is possible to resolve a number of the challenges facing learning theory. Beginning with the question whether learning outcomes result from the actions of autonomous actors or from a systemic ecology, the answer is – "yes." Actors are influenced by the ecological system, but they have the capacity to make decisions independent of it. The ecology is not deterministic although it conditions responses by filtering out all but a few dominant ideas and discourses. Learning is a never-ending process – a dialectic of information, ideas, discourse, reflection, expectations, choices, re-evaluations, learning, and teaching.

This analysis indicates that an instrumental versus interpretive dichotomy of decisionmaking is counterproductive. By participating in a set of discourses, people are immersed in an interpretive environment. The identities they bring with them, the roles they play out, the interests and preferences that guide their activities all contribute to how they interpret their daily lives. Myriad instrumental logics of consequences could result from this reality, but humans are thoughtful enough to produce organizations, institutions, cultures, and taboos to ensure consistency and simplicity in the decision making process. The empirical question is how well the organizations and institutions direct the logics of consequences of individuals. The stronger the socialization to institutions and organizations, the greater the predictability of organizational outcomes. Predictability of collective outcomes allows us to reify organizations without having to reduce them to the individuals inhabiting them.

Approached from a social-structural ontology, many of learning theory's problems become less overwhelming; the difficulty merely becomes one of matching the proper analytical tools with the question under investigation. Understanding whether the research question asked is causal or constitutive in nature is the first step in picking the most useful epistemological approach and methodological tools. Many of the ideas learning theorists have developed have, in fact, been rooted in a social-structural ontology though they have been approached from an individualist one. This chapter was dedicated to integrating social-structural logic with learning theory and developing a methodological approach rigorous enough to redress some of its weaknesses. This does not imply that individualist ontology and positivist-empiricist methodologies lack utility. Instead, the ontology and methodology should be driven by the research question. A healthy competition of ideas, assumptions and models will enhance our understanding the complex phenomena that is organizational learning.

PART 3
Learning by Illicit Actors

Chapter 8

Organizational Learning Processes in Colombian Drug Trafficking Networks

Michael Kenney

Since the late 1970s, Colombian trafficking networks have provided a steady flow of illegal drugs to American and European consumers. Successive Colombian governments, with ample prodding and *matériel* from Washington, have sought to curtail this illicit commerce by destroying several hundred thousand hectares of drug crops and thousands of processing labs, seizing tons of illegal drugs, freezing millions of dollars in drug profits, capturing hundreds of suspected traffickers, and extraditing dozens of "kingpins" to the United States (US). While the names of these counter-drug programs change periodically—from Operation Stopgap to Operation Snowcap, from the Andean Strategy to the Kingpin Strategy, from Plan Colombia to Plan *Patriota*—their basic strategy remains the same: to reduce the consumption of illegal drugs in the United States by eliminating their supply in Colombia.

Vigorous efforts to eliminate the drug trade by targeting its source have essentially failed. Notwithstanding modest reductions in drug production in Colombia in 2002 and 2003, the country remains the source of approximately 90 percent of the cocaine and 50 percent of the heroin entering American drug markets.[1] In recent years prices for both drugs have remained remarkably stable in the US, where millions of Americans remain "current" consumers of cocaine, heroin, and other illegal drugs.[2]

---

1   Due to the illicit, clandestine nature of cocaine and heroin production and consumption, these data should be interpreted with caution. I use them to illustrate broad trends rather than to suggest perfect knowledge of these activities. Bureau for International Narcotics and Law Enforcement Affairs, US Department of State, *International Narcotics Control Strategy Report 2005* vol. 1, "Drug and Chemical Control" (March 2005), p. 126, <http://www.state.gov/documents/organization/42867.pdf>, last accessed April 12, 2005.

2   The *National Survey on Drug Use and Health*, administered regularly since the mid-1970s, defines a "current" user as someone that has used an illegal drug during the month prior to the survey interview. The 2003 Survey estimates that 2.3 million persons are current cocaine users, while 119,000 persons are current heroin users. These numbers pale in comparison to other drugs consumed illegally in the United States, including marijuana (with an estimated 14.6 million current users in the 2003 *Survey*), and the non-medical use of psychotherapeutic drugs (6.3 million estimated current users). Substance Abuse and Mental Health Services Administration, *Overview of Findings from the 2003 National Survey on Drug Use and Health* (Rockville, MD: Office of Applied Studies, NSDUH Series H-24, DHHS Publication No.

At best, supply-reduction programs have produced temporary ripples in the Colombian narcotics industry that stabilize quickly as traffickers establish alternative sources of supply, move their drug plantings and processing labs, introduce new production methods, and create fresh transportation routes. In the face of intensive counter-drug enforcement efforts, Colombian trafficking enterprises have proven to be remarkably adaptive and innovative. These skills have enabled many trafficking groups to maintain the profitability of their activities while surviving government efforts to destroy them.

While a number of government officials and independent observers have recognized the flexibility and resilience of Colombian trafficking organizations, there have been few attempts to develop a systematic, learning-based explanation for how these criminal enterprises respond to government counter-drug efforts. This chapter offers such an explanation. Drawing on the work of James March and other scholars, I argue that Colombian smuggling networks alter their behavior in response to past experience and new information, store this knowledge in practices and procedures, and select and retain innovations that produce satisfactory results.[3] In other words, traffickers "learn;" they acquire skills and improve practices, becoming increasingly difficult for law enforcers to eliminate.

But if drug traffickers learn, they do not learn equally well. Similar to legally sanctioned organizations, smuggling groups face a number of impediments to learning, including limited attention spans, bounded rationality, and mental models that bias interpretation. These difficulties are compounded in clandestine organizations that, for reasons of operational security, compartment their participants into separate working groups and restrict communication among different parts of the larger network. Even the most sophisticated Colombian trafficking organizations, such as the infamous cocaine networks headquartered in Medellín and Cali, have not proven immune to these difficulties, which have been exploited by US and Colombian law enforcers to rather modest effect. Following a discussion of the three-fold process of organizational learning as applied to trafficking groups, I consider the numerous impediments to this process. I conclude by examining some of the implications of learning by drug traffickers for counter-narcotics policy, suggesting that better

SMA 04-3963, 2004), pp. 3-4, <http://oas.samhsa.gov/NHSDA/2k3NSDUH/2k3OverviewW. pdf>, last accessed April 12, 2005.

3   See Barbara Levitt and James G. March, "Organizational Learning," *Annual Review of Sociology* 14 (1988), pp. 319-340; Richard M. Cyert and James G. March, *A Behavioral Theory of the Firm* (Englewood Cliffs, NJ: Prentice-Hall, 1963); Chris Argyris and Donald A. Schön, *Organizational Learning II: Theory, Method, and Practice* (Reading, MA: Addison-Wesley, 1996); Herbert A. Simon, *Administrative Behavior: A Study of Decision-Making Processes in Administrative Organizations*, 4th ed. (New York: The Free Press, 1997); and Karl E. Weick, *The Social Psychology of Organizing*, 2nd ed. (New York: Random House, 1979).

results in America's long-standing "war on drugs" will not be forthcoming until policymakers engage in some strategic learning of their own.[4]

Collecting Information

Colombian trafficking organizations use a variety of methods to gather information about their tradecraft and government counter-narcotics efforts. Some trafficking groups send their participants on fact-finding missions to learn about practices in other parts of the network or the narcotics industry in general. Traffickers also gather information about new smuggling practices and technologies they can use to remain a step ahead of law enforcement. Groups may ask their participants to develop smuggling innovations or utilize outside consultants who, in the words of Peter Lupsha, "beat a path to their door with new ideas, technologies, techniques, and investment opportunities."[5] More exotic smuggling methods, such as molding cocaine into plastic suitcases, developing semi-submersible vessels that glide along the surface of the Caribbean Sea, or constructing submarines capable of transporting upwards of ten metric tons of cocaine often come from "independent folks" that sell innovations to established smuggling groups.[6]

Trafficking groups hire engineers, chemists, lawyers, even former law enforcers, military officials, and paramilitary operatives, to obtain specialized knowledge of criminal law, weaponry and explosives, drug production practices, and counter-surveillance technologies. When numerous Colombian cocaine traffickers diversified into heroin in the 1990s, they hired refining specialists from Mexico and the Far East to teach them how to process opium latex into heroin.[7] More recently, at least one Colombian enterprise hired chemists to teach their participants to process potassium permanganate, an essential precursor chemical for refining cocaine base.[8]

---

4   This chapter stems from a larger research project which includes interviews conducted with more than eighty US and Colombian informants, including government counter-drug officials, academic researchers, and a small sample of former drug traffickers. See Michael C. Kenney, *From Pablo to Osama: Trafficking and Terrorist Networks, Government Bureaucracies and Competitive Adaptation* (University Park, PA: The Pennsylvania State University Press, forthcoming 2007).

5   Peter A Lupsha, "Transnational Organized Crime versus the Nation-State," *Transnational Organized Crime* vol. 2, (1996), p. 34.

6   Author interview with Drug Enforcement Administration intelligence analyst, Washington, DC, July 22, 1999; "'Made in' Colombia," *Cambio* (July 24, 2000), pp. 36-37; Sidney Zabludoff, "Colombian Narcotics Organizations as Business Enterprises," *Transnational Organized Crime* vol. 3 (1997), p. 29.

7   Author interviews with various Colombian and US officials, Bogotá, Colombia and Washington, DC (various dates 1999 and 2000); Rosso José Serrano Cadena, *Jaque mate: De cómo la policía le ganó la partida a "el ajedrecista" y a los carteles del narcotráfico* (Bogotá, Colombia: Editorial Norma, 1999), pp. 50-51.

8   "'Made in' Colombia," p. 36.

Colombian trafficking organizations have been known to direct many of their information gathering activities towards government counter-narcotics efforts. During the 1980s, several cocaine transportation rings established listening posts in Miami and other coastal areas to monitor the radio frequencies of US Customs interdiction flights and local counter-drug agents. Some groups stationed observers at federal facilities in South Florida, including the Homestead Air Force Base and Boca Chica Naval Air Station, in order to monitor drug interdiction flights. Trafficking organizations acquired lists of the radio frequencies used by the Drug Enforcement Administration, the Federal Bureau of Investigation, and other law enforcement agencies from radio shops and public documents. Some enterprises even purchased flight schedules for US Customs and Coast Guard planes from corrupt US officials.[9]

In Colombia, some Cali-based enterprises developed sophisticated intelligence networks with the help of active collaborators from a variety of public and private institutions, including numerous law enforcement agencies, national and regional legislatures, prosecution offices, telephone companies, newspapers, taxi cab companies, law firms, hotels, and other service industries. Through these informants, the Cali traffickers were able to acquire valuable information regarding government drug enforcement policies and programs, as well as impending legislation and criminal proceedings.[10]

The diffusion of knowledge and experience among participants in trafficking enterprises is often fairly informal. Participants meet in informal settings, such as restaurants, bars, and dance clubs, to discuss impending activities, business problems, and recent developments in the industry. Private social gatherings, including birthday parties, baptisms, and weddings, provide participants additional opportunities for swapping stories and exchanging trade rumors. In this manner, veterans socialize less experienced colleagues to the norms and practices of drug trafficking. The latter then draw on this shared knowledge to develop their own trafficking skills.[11]

---

9   Roy Thomas Dye, *A Social History of Drug Smuggling in Florida*, unpublished PhD dissertation (Tallahassee, FL: Florida State University, 1998), p. 239; Max Mermelstein, *The Man Who Made it Snow* (New York: Simon and Schuster, 1990), p. 118; and Berkeley Rice, *Trafficking: The Boom and Bust of the Air America Cocaine Ring* (New York: Charles Scribner's Sons, 1989), pp. 83, 148.

10   Guillermo Pallomari, "Direct Testimony of Guillermo Pallomari," *Trial Transcript in the United States of America vs. Michael Abbell, William Moran, Luis Grajales, Eddy Martinez, Ramon Martinez, J.L. Pereira-Salas, et al, Defendants*, Case No. 93-470-CR-WMH, vol. 39 (US District Court, Southern District of Florida, Miami Division, July 23, 1997), pp. 6312, 6319; Serrano Cadena, *Jaque mate*, p. 154.

11   Author interview with former drug traffickers, journalists, and government officials (various dates and locations 1999 and 2000).

Interpreting Information

Colombian trafficking enterprises give meaning to information they have collected through interpretation—or what Karl Weick and his colleagues term "sensemaking." Sensemaking is a retrospective social process through which participants share perceptions of past events and construct inter-subjective understandings of reality.[12] It is triggered when expectations are interrupted by unforeseen events that prevent the organization from satisfying its aspirations. For trafficking groups that operate in dynamic, hostile environments, such events include intercepted drug shipments, destroyed processing laboratories, dismantled transportation routes, seized profits, arrested participants, and impending legal proceedings that disrupt ongoing smuggling activities and threaten the physical integrity of the group. To make sense of these problematic situations, traffickers communicate, share knowledge, and interpret past and present circumstances through conversations, storytelling, and meetings. These meetings allow managers and participants to share perceptions, analyze problems and identify potential solutions.[13]

The discovery process offers an illuminating example of how some Colombian trafficking networks engage in organizational sensemaking.[14] During the 1990s, several Cali smuggling groups manipulated discovery procedures to obtain access to criminal indictments, search warrant affidavits, wiretap affidavits, criminal complaints, law enforcement intelligence reports, and other government documents that described in detail how US counter-drug authorities carried out their criminal investigations. US-based lawyers representing the traffickers obtained these documents through discovery and sent them to Colombia, where they were analyzed in meetings between traffickers and their lawyers. The purpose of these sensemaking sessions was to determine how law enforcers penetrated the group's operations, identify confidential informants, learn about the latest tactics in criminal investigations, and devise strategies to avoid similar mistakes in future operations. On occasion, network leaders ordered mid-level participants to read these materials to learn from their predecessors' mistakes. Following the arrest of a prominent cell manager in Miami, Miguel Rodríguez Orejuela had his replacement study documents obtained through discovery to determine how the US government had penetrated the cell's communications system. When it became clear that law enforcers had

---

12 Richard L. Daft and Karl E. Weick, "Towards a Model of Organizations as Interpretation Systems," *Academy of Management Review* vol. 9 (1984), p. 286; and Weick, *Sensemaking in Organizations*, pp. 45-46.

13 Author interviews with US and Colombian officials (various dates and locations) and "Homero" [pseudonym], former drug trafficker, Federal Correctional Complex, Coleman, FL, September 19, 2000; Pallomari, "Direct Testimony of Guillermo Pallomari."

14 Discovery refers to a set of procedures in the US legal system that allows parties in a civil or criminal dispute to see information prior to trial that is likely to be used against them in court. Discovery is designed to help disputants prepare for trial, encourage pre-trial settlement by informing all parties of the efficacy of their claims, and expose insubstantial claims that do not merit the full resources of a formal trial.

wiretapped the cellular phones of several participants, Rodríguez Orejuela decreed new communication rules for his organization, telling cell workers to avoid using cellular phones when discussing business.[15]

Applying Knowledge and Experience: Adapting Transportation Routes

Colombian trafficking enterprises change practices, procedures and performance programs in response to information gathering and interpretation at virtually every stage of the production, transportation, and distribution of psychoactive drugs. Frequently, though not inevitably, these adaptations occur in response to feedback from a hostile environment. Facing challenges from counter-drug law enforcement agencies and other illicit competitors, including smuggling groups, guerrilla fronts and paramilitary organizations, Colombian trafficking enterprises adjust their practices and protocols as quickly and often as circumstances warrant. Their survival as illegal organizations demands it. Much of this behavioral adjustment occurs at the level of tactical routines. Trafficking enterprises routinely tinker with the practices and procedures used in their day-to-day activities. Routines that help trafficking groups meet their targets tend to be retained and incorporated into existing performance programs; those that fail to do so are often discarded. In this section I discuss changes in transportation routines, which represent some of the most common, and consequential, adaptations by Colombian smuggling networks.[16]

Drug transportation routes contain practices, procedures, and technologies for transporting supplies, resources, and other materials from one location to another. These routines are a critical component of the international drug industry. Without secure and effective transportation routes, rapid movements of capital, precursor chemicals, equipment, refined narcotics, illicit profits, and personnel are infeasible. Recognizing the significance of trafficking routes, government interdiction strategies often prioritize their disruption.

Over the last two decades, Colombian trafficking enterprises have consistently responded to law enforcement pressure by refining existing transportation routes and developing new ones. Indeed, changing routes have become one of the most predictable outcomes in the competitive adaptation struggles between "narcs" and

---

15 Author interview with numerous US and Colombian officials (various dates and locations 1999 and 2000); Edward J. Kacerosky, "Search Warrant Affidavit of Special Agent Edward Kacerosky," Case No. 93-470-CR-WMH (September 1 and 5, 1994), pp. 36, 53, 67-68; Jim McGee and Brian Duffy, *Main Justice: The Men and Women who Enforce the Nation's Criminal Laws and Guard its Liberties* (New York: Touchstone, 1997), pp. 65-66, 147; Third Superceding Indictment, *United States of America vs. Michael Abbell, William Moran, Luis Grajales, Eddy Martinez, Ramon Martinez, J.L. Pereira-Salas, et al, Defendants*, Case No. 93 470-CR-WMH (no date), pp. 36-38.

16 For additional examples of trafficking adaptations, including changes in drug processing, drug distribution, and money laundering routines, see Michael C. Kenney, *From Pablo to Osama.*

narcos. When law enforcers identify and dismantle a particular transportation route, large trafficking enterprises usually require only ten to fourteen days to re-organize their operations, although smaller operations with fewer transportation options may require more down time.[17] In some cases, trafficking enterprises have other routes already in place or under investigation, which reduces the time necessary to activate these alternatives. Whether starting from scratch or pre-existing substitutes, during re-organization participants gather and interpret information relating to the problematic situation, and adjust the location of their routes to areas where drug enforcement efforts are less intense. With one sea, two oceans, dozens of international airports, hundreds of clandestine airstrips, and thousands of miles of secluded coastline from which to choose, traffickers are limited only by their own resources and ingenuity.

In addition to changing the geographic locations of their routes, trafficking enterprises adjust their transportation technologies and practices to avoid government surveillance and interdiction. One common adaptation is to vary the mode of transportation. When law enforcers identify and intercept a particular air-, sea-, or land-based vessel used to transport narcotics, transportation rings change vessels, again following a period of re-adjustment in which participants gather and analyze the requisite information. Over the last two decades, traffickers have used a variety of aircraft, including single-engine propeller planes, twin-engine jets, and multi-engine passenger planes, seafaring vessels, such as high-speed "cigarette" boats, sport fishermen's yachts, commercial fishing boats, freighters, "semi-submersible vessels" and submarines, and overland vehicles, including tractor trailers, trains, pick-up trucks, minivans, and sedans, to transport illicit drugs, switching among different vehicles to avoid interdiction efforts.

Smuggling rings also alter conveyance methods. Containerized cargo are particularly useful for drug traffickers because they provide dozens of options to hide illicit drugs within shipments of legitimate Central and South American exports to the US and Europe, including vegetables and flowers, fruits and fruit juices, coffee and seafood, mechanical equipment, and an assortment of other commodities. When law enforcers discover a particular scheme, enterprises quickly change to other containerized cargo routes already in operation, or develop new ones, sometimes by purchasing established companies in Central and South America that export these commodities.

As these examples demonstrate, Colombian trafficking enterprises respond to government interdiction pressures by changing transportation practices and programs. These adaptations allow them to continue to transship narcotics to consumer markets even as law enforcement efforts intensify. The expectation that all routes, no matter how creative or ingenious, will eventually "heat up" or run into problems prompts smugglers to continually refine existing transportation programs and develop new ones, even when current arrangements are performing satisfactorily. As traffickers develop these and other innovations, they expand their operational

---

17 Drug Enforcement Administration (DEA), *The Illicit Drug Situation in Colombia* (Publications Unit, Intelligence Division, DEA Headquarters, November 1993), p. 14.

repertoires, providing participants with a greater range of routines to draw upon when transporting psychoactive drugs, money, supplies or other materials. The more transportation programs within an organization's repertoire, the greater its ability to adapt to the vicissitudes of counter-drug law enforcement. A network with ten established routes for shipping cocaine to the US possesses a greater variety of practices, technologies, and geographies from which to choose than an organization with only one route. The more diversified enterprise will be better positioned to respond to the constant flow of problems, including seizures, arrests and theft that characterize its dynamic, hostile environment.

Strategic Adaptations

While Colombian trafficking enterprises routinely tinker with techniques and tactics, it is less clear whether they change their long-range objectives as a result of acquiring and interpreting information. Data gathered in this research suggest that some trafficking enterprises adjust their strategies in response to feedback. Prominent examples of strategic learning include diversifying into new products and markets, and restructuring criminal operations.

Colombian trafficking groups have expanded into new markets and products on numerous occasions. In the 1960s and 1970s, contraband smugglers specializing in emeralds, cigarettes, whiskey, and domestic appliances established themselves in marijuana exports, fueling the short-lived *bonanza marimbera*. By the late 1970s, some marijuana smugglers diversified their product lines to include methaqualone and cocaine, in effect becoming polydrug organizations.[18] Smugglers kept transportation costs low by exporting these less bulky psychoactive substances with their marijuana shipments. Some traffickers required their wholesale customers to purchase fixed quantities of their new commodities along with the more popular marijuana.

By the mid-1980s, Colombian methaqualone and marijuana declined, in part due to intensified drug interdiction by US and Colombian authorities. However, the Colombian drug industry experienced considerable growth as the amount of US- and European-bound cocaine exports rose substantially. In the middle of the cocaine boom, numerous trafficking enterprises diversified into the heroin trade. Similar to the *marimberos*, cocaine traffickers piggybacked heroin on their cocaine

---

18 Methaqualone is a nonbarbiturate sedative better known by the trade names Quaalude, Mandrax, and Sopors. In the 1970s it was manufactured in Germany and Hungary and imported to Colombia in powder form, where it was packaged and re-exported to the US. There are also reports that the drug was at least partly manufactured within Colombia by the country's legitimate pharmaceutical industry. See *New York Times*, "Jersey Police Arrest 4 in Alleged Plot to Sell 555,000 Pills," (August 3, 1980), <http://web.lexis-nexis.com/universe>, last accessed June 4, 2001; Peter Reuter, "After the Borders are Sealed: Can Domestic Sources Substitute for Imported Drugs?" in Peter H. Smith, ed., *Drug Policy in the Americas* (Boulder, CO: Westview Press, 1992), p. 170; and Francisco E. Thoumi, *Political Economy and Illegal Drugs in Colombia* (Boulder, CO: Lynne Rienner Publishers, 1995), p. 127.

shipments and required US wholesalers to accept small amounts of the new product. Using distribution systems developed by large cocaine networks, trafficking groups marketed Colombian heroin in major US markets. In an aggressive strategy to undercut their competitors and increase market share, Colombian enterprises offered a low-priced product at high levels of purity.[19]

Colombian trafficking organizations have also expanded to new markets. In the 1980s and 1990s, a number of smuggling groups expanded into the lucrative European and Japanese markets, where wholesale cocaine prices were approximately two to three times the average US price. To facilitate their entry, trafficking groups formed partnerships with criminal organizations established in these markets, including Italian Mafiosi and Japanese Yakuza. This expansion increased in the latter half of the 1990s, following the break-up of several large Colombian trafficking networks based in Medellín and Cali. In recent years, Colombian traffickers have exported cocaine and heroin to Western and Central Europe, Russia and the Newly Independent States, Japan, Australia, as well as the United States.[20]

When shifting to new markets and products, trafficking enterprises use existing stores of knowledge and experience. Smuggling expertise is often fungible across product lines. *Contrabandistas* found that many of the practices and procedures for smuggling black market emeralds, cigarettes and liquor could be used, with few modifications, to transport marijuana. *Marimberos* subsequently determined that their transportation and distribution routines could also be applied to cocaine smuggling. *Cocaleros* discovered they many of their cocaine distribution and marketing techniques worked well for heroin.

Obstacles to Network Learning

Colombian trafficking networks learn as participants gather, interpret and apply information to practices and procedures. However, not all trafficking enterprises are equally adept at these information-processing activities. The ability of Colombian and US law enforcers to identify and eviscerate dozens of Colombian smuggling groups over the past two decades belies facile interpretations of trafficker learning.

---

19 Author interviews with U.S. and Colombian informants (various dates and locations 1999 and 2000); Darío Betancourt and Martha L. García, *Contrabandistas, marimberos y mafiosos: Historia social de la mafia colombiana (1965-1992)* (Bogotá, Colombia: *Tercer Mundo Editores*, 1994), p. 107; Drug Enforcement Administration, *Colombian Opiate Assessment* (Publications Unit, Intelligence Division, DEA Headquarters, 1994), pp. 6-7; "La flor maldita," *Semana*, (September 10, 1999).

20 Author interviews with US and Colombian informants (various dates and locations 1999 and 2000); Douglas Farah, "New Threat From Colombia: Heroin Traffickers Aggressively Marketing Nearly Pure Drug in U.S.," *Washington Post* (March 27, 1997), <http://www.washingtonpost.com/wp-srv/WParch/1997-03/27/053F-032797idx.html>, last accessed April 1, 1997; Thoumi, *Political Economy and Illegal Drugs in Colombia*, endnote 18, p. 150; Zabludoff, "Colombian Narcotics Organizations as Business Enterprises," p. 24.

If trafficking impresarios develop such effective learning organizations, why have government authorities dismantled so many? One reason has to do with the variety of impediments facing criminal enterprises as they seek to adapt to change and uncertainty in hostile environments. Similar to participants in legally sanctioned organizations, traffickers make decisions based on imperfect information and limited cognitive abilities; they are prone to mental biases when interpreting feedback; and they fail to modify entrenched practices even when experience suggests that change is warranted. Moreover, as illegal organizations trafficking groups face additional obstacles to organizational learning. The need to maintain operational secrecy in the face of a hostile law enforcement environment hampers their ability to gather, interpret and apply knowledge and experience.

Some learning difficulties are due to basic limitations in human cognition and organizational behavior. As Herbert A. Simon recognized long ago, human decision-making operates under conditions of information uncertainty and bounded rationality.[21] Individuals lack perfect information and face significant cognitive constraints in analyzing feedback from complex environments. To compensate, they use mental short cuts to make sense of the overwhelming abundance of incoming stimuli, but these cognitive schemas are based on prior beliefs that bias interpretations in subtle ways.[22]

Within organizations, attention is a scarce resource, limiting the time and effort participants may direct towards information processing.[23] When attention is forthcoming, organizations remain vulnerable to a host of "learning disabilities" in analyzing information, including blind spots and filtering. Blind spots occur when information collection is narrow or misdirected, leading managers to miss or misinterpret feedback. Filtering occurs when critical information is ignored or downplayed because it is inconsistent with decision-makers prior beliefs, or powerful interests within the organization.[24]

When organizations overcome these information-processing difficulties, the knowledge they gain may still fail to impact organizational behavior in productive ways. Inertia may prevent the organization from adopting innovative technologies and routines that could improve task performance. Organizations often face large sunk costs with existing technologies, and therefore may be hesitant to embrace new practices and procedures. Organizations may also face internal political constraints

---

21 Herbert A. Simon, "A Behavioral Model of Rational Choice," *Quarterly Journal of Economics* vol. 69 (1955), pp. 99-118.

22 Dan Reiter, *Crucible of Beliefs: Learning, Alliances, and World Wars* (Ithaca, NY: Cornell University Press, 1996).

23 James G. March, "Introduction: A Chronicle of Speculations About Decision-Making in Organizations," in James G. March, ed., *Decisions and Organizations* (New York: Basil Blackwell, 1988), pp. 1-21; James G. March and Johan P. Olsen, "The Uncertainty of the Past: Organizational Learning under Ambiguity," *European Journal of Political Research* vol. 3 (1975), pp. 147-171.

24 David Garvin, *Learning in Action* (Boston, MA: Harvard Business School Press, 2000), pp. 28-29.

to adaptation. When powerful interests within the organization support established routines, decisionmakers may feel that their interests will suffer if they adopt new strategies or routines, becoming less likely to do so. In such circumstances, decisionmakers may learn but changes in their individual beliefs are not translated into changes in organizational routines.[25]

Beyond these broad limitations affecting virtually all human collectivities, Colombian trafficking groups face additional obstacles to organizational learning due to their status as illicit organizations operating outside the rule of law. To protect the integrity of their operations from law enforcers, trafficking groups employ a number of risk-reduction strategies that constrict information flows and disrupt feedback loops, impeding organizational learning. While all organizations lack access to perfect and complete information, knowledge surrounding clandestine trafficking operations can be particularly hazy and opaque. Trafficking groups contribute to this uncertainty by using code words and aliases to communicate sensitive transactional details and maintain strict secrecy about impending operations. Lack of clarity in communications can impede learning. In particular, the judicious use of ciphers can lead to frequent misunderstandings among loosely coupled participants as they struggle to make sense of transactions and problematic situations. Interpretations based on miscommunication are likely to be distorted and may lead to ill-suited tactical and strategic adaptations.

Trafficking enterprises conduct their activities with the utmost secrecy. In addition to camouflaging their operations and monitoring law enforcement activities, they maintain secrecy by restricting communication among participants and providing them with the minimal knowledge they need to perform their immediate tasks. Many trafficking groups compartment their participants into "cells" to limit communication between groups. While these strategies may be necessary to protect core technologies from exploitation by law enforcers and illicit competitors, secrecy and compartmentation hinder organizational learning by preventing different parts of the network from sharing information and experience with each other. When participants from different groups fail to communicate, useful knowledge about the latest law enforcement efforts or innovations in smuggling technologies may fail to spread across the network. While different cells may engage in their own trial-and-error learning, compartmentation may prevent them from drawing on other cells' experiences. Learning remains localized, with different groups from the same organization essentially re-learning the same lessons. Compartmentation also plays into the hands of law enforcers by preventing participants from different parts of the network from sharing information about ongoing criminal investigations. Police agents occasionally capitalize on this by arresting participants from one cell, without

---

25 Argyris and Schön, *Organizational Learning II*, p. 17; Michael T. Hannan and John Freeman, "The Population Ecology of Organizations," *American Journal of Sociology* vol. 82 (1977), p. 931; James G. March and Johan P. Olsen, "The Uncertainty of the Past: Organizational Learning under Ambiguity," *European Journal of Political Research* vol. 3 (1975).

the knowledge of other groups that continue their illegal activities, oblivious that the police are closing in.[26]

Still, we should be careful not to overemphasize the impact of compartmentation on organizational learning by trafficking groups. While numerous respondents I interviewed recognized the negative repercussions this risk reduction strategy can have on organizational communication, none suggested that it actually prevented traffickers from adapting to external pressure. Compartmentation does not stop information flows within smuggling groups but channels them through the decision-making hierarchies of the organization. In many trafficking networks, compartmentation tends to restrict communication across functional sub-units, such as between drug transportation and drug distribution cells, not between subordinates and supervisors within the same group. Moreover, as suggested above, private social gatherings provide opportunities for members from different cells—and even separate smuggling groups—to swap "war stories" and smuggling tips. If many of these informal exchanges are infused with jocularity and bravado, they still provide useful information that transcends the immediate experiences of individual cells.[27]

Another way that trafficking groups limit their ability to learn is by restricting their use of "organizational memories" to document their activities. Record keeping is a double-edged sword for smuggling enterprises that operate in hostile environments. On the one hand, criminals involved in numerous transactions need some sort of record-keeping system to monitor the myriad details involved in their activities. Documentation of transactional details, such as code words, prices, quantities, telephone numbers, and the like, is essential to conducting complex transactions and monitoring participant behavior. However, as soon as this information is stored in ledgers, notebooks, and computer files it becomes vulnerable to capture and exploitation by law enforcers and illicit competitors. As one former high-ranking Drug Enforcement Administration official explains, "The worst thing a trafficker could possibly do is store and document and put in some form of ledgers his activity. Because when I seize that, it becomes evidence that puts the noose around his neck."[28] The meticulous records maintained by Miguel Rodríguez Orejuela and the managers of his trafficking network eventually came back to haunt the cocaine "kingpin" as US and Colombian law enforcers exploited records seized in raids on his office and other properties to expand their criminal investigation and develop material evidence for prosecution.

Experienced traffickers understand the danger of record keeping. Indeed, they often attempt to mitigate this liability by minimizing their formal documentation, relying instead on the unaided human memories of their participants. While this

---

26 Author interview with Drug Enforcement Administration Resident Agent in Charge, Los Angeles Field Division, Los Angeles, CA (April 29, 2003).

27 Author interviews with various Colombian and US officials, Bogotá, Colombia and Washington, DC (1999 and 2000).

28 Author interview with former Drug Enforcement Administration Special Agent-in-Charge, Miami Division, Miami, FL, August 3, 1999.

practice reduces one source of vulnerability, it creates others. Information that is stored only in the minds of individual traffickers is more likely to be forgotten, manipulated, or subject to faulty recall. Dishonest participants, of whom there are a few in this illicit industry, may be tempted to manipulate undocumented knowledge to their own benefit. But even honest, well-intentioned traffickers may simply not remember telephone numbers, code words, or prices, leading to miscommunication and confusion in conducting transactions.

To the extent that information is stored in the minds of individual traffickers, their removal from the enterprise means that this knowledge, which may represent years of accumulated wisdom and experience, is likely to be lost. When the individual occupies a position of authority in the enterprise, or contains specialized knowledge that few personnel possess, his or her loss is likely to be all the more disruptive. High rates of personnel turnover, a common feature in many smuggling enterprises, make the accumulation of experience problematic, particularly when coupled with a lack of formal organizational memories. Trafficking enterprises that lack files and documents for recording experience have difficulty learning from experience, particularly when there is little continuity among personnel. These criminal organizations are more likely to repeat critical errors, increasing their exposure to counter-drug law enforcers.

Irrespective of personnel turnover, knowledge that is not accessed for long periods can also be lost. After all, human beings not only gather, interpret and apply information, they also forget. Forgetting is problematic in organizations when knowledge lies dormant for extended periods, as during times of low productivity.[29] The business of drug smuggling is fundamentally episodic, with long periods of dormancy punctuated by brief spikes of frenzied activity, as traffickers hustle to move their illicit merchandise to the next link in the transnational commodity chain, thereby eliminating their culpability to unforeseen events, such as drug busts and arrests. Colombian smuggling enterprises go through frequent periods with little activity due to lag times between drug shipments and the need to reduce or suspend their criminal operations to avoid counter-drug law enforcers. During these intervals, participants may forget important details in their day-to-day activities. When operations start back up again, traffickers must brush up on their roles, causing further delay before the enterprise returns to "peak" productivity. The problem of organizational forgetting is exacerbated in groups that lack formal memories participants can retrieve when necessary. Without accounting ledgers, manuals and oral traditions to remind them of the innumerable details involved in their daily operations, traffickers will require more time, and be susceptible to more mistakes, as they relearn their roles and responsibilities.

---

29 C. Lanier Benkard, "Learning and Forgetting: The Dynamics of Aircraft Production," *Research Paper No. 1560* (Stanford, CA: Graduate School of Business, Stanford University, 1999).

Conclusion

In spite of these impediments, Colombian trafficking networks learn. Traffickers gather, interpret and apply information with an eye towards reducing risk, while reaping satisfactory profits. Over the years, Colombian smugglers have developed numerous mechanisms for recording, sharing, and constructing knowledge, while facilitating the diffusion of information among different participants and groups. While much trafficker learning is focused at the level of tactical routines, including simple adjustments in transportation routes and shipping methods in response to law enforcement pressure, some smuggling groups do engage in strategic learning by expanding their criminal activities to new markets and products. When enterprises draw on knowledge and experience to alter existing routines or create new ones, they expand and diversify their repertoires, allowing them greater flexibility in adapting their operations to counter-drug law enforcement.

But drug traffickers also face a variety of obstacles to learning, including imperfect information, mental models that bias interpretation, the need to maintain secrecy, compartmented organizational structures, and personnel turnover. While none of these factors inevitably prevents learning, each of them can, and they are all found—to varying degrees—in Colombian smuggling groups. Due to the intense hostility of the US and Colombian counter-drug environment in recent years, trafficking enterprises that fail to adjust their tactical and strategic routines on a regular basis often do not survive for long periods. Poor learners are selected out of the transnational drug trade relatively quickly, leaving behind organizations with structures and strategems more conducive to productive learning. However, even the most successful trafficking groups need to balance fundamental trade-offs between protecting the integrity of their criminal operations and engaging in practices that would enhance their ability to learn as organizations. Clearly, many smuggling groups would benefit from having more robust—and accessible—organizational memories, but records that would presumably improve their ability to learn from experience would also increase their exposure to law enforcers. For this reason, trafficking groups will never be, in the parlance of prescriptive, practice-oriented treatments of organizational behavior, model "learning organizations."[30]

Unfortunately, neither are government officials, which cling to discredited supply-reduction strategies in the face of several decades of overwhelming evidence of their ineffectiveness. To achieve better results in the so-called "war on drugs," US policy makers should look beyond militarized law enforcement initiatives such as Plan Colombia and its recent off-shoot, Plan *Patriota*, and reconceptualize the country's drug problem as a public health issue first and a law enforcement issue second. This will involve transformative policy innovation on the part of American officials, or

---

30 Argyris and Schön, *Organizational Learning II*, p. xix.

what Peter Hall describes as "third order" learning, requiring substantial changes in the basic assumptions and values underlying US drug control programs.[31]

Preeminent among such assumptions is the dubious notion that supply-reduction programs are capable of eliminating, or even substantially reducing, an international trade in psychoactive substances that, by dint of their addictive properties, enjoy persistently robust demand in consumer markets. At the level of policy instruments, what Hall refers to as "second order" change, government learning would include expanding drug treatment programs to offer a variety of modalities suitable to the cultural and individual needs of all substance abusers, annual school-based prevention programs that provide credible information and peer resistance training to all children and teenagers, and broader social policies dealing with such drug-abuse related issues as urban development, job training, child care, housing, and health care.[32] The history of American drug control and learning theory suggest that such far-reaching changes are not likely soon. The US will likely require much greater experimentation in failed supply-reduction strategies before its policy makers—and public—embrace such "radical" alternatives. Meanwhile, Colombian trafficking groups will be content to continue their own organizational learning.

---

31 See Peter A. Hall, "Policy Paradigms, Social Learning, and the State: The Case of Economic Policymaking in Britain," *Comparative Politics* vol. 25 (April 1993), pp. 275-296.

32 Eva Bertram, Morris Blachman, Kenneth Sharpe, and Peter Andreas, *Drug War Politics: The Price of Denial* (Berkeley, CA: University of California Press, 1996), pp. 207-219.

Chapter 9

Organizational Learning and Terrorist Groups

Brian A. Jackson

The potential for any terrorist organization to stage acts of political violence and intimidation is directly related to the group's technological and organizational capabilities. Prominent among such capabilities is the terrorist group's ability to learn from experience and store this knowledge in routines to guide subsequent behavior. Terrorist groups do not automatically or immediately gain the ability to use given tactics or carry out particular types of operations. Capabilities, including those that facilitate learning, must be developed. In designing attacks, selecting targets, and using technologies for violent ends, terrorist groups gather information, integrate it with their past experience, and put it to use. The strengths and weaknesses of these learning processes not only help explain what a terrorist group is capable of doing today, but also help anticipate what it might be capable of tomorrow. With sufficient understanding of a group's learning processes, new policy interventions may be designed to undermine these efforts. Directing analytical attention not to *what* terrorists do, but *how* they learn to do it may provide counter-terrorism officials with the opportunity to degrade the capabilities of extremist groups and reduce the effectiveness of their attacks.

Although generally not an explicit focus of analysis, learning by terrorist groups has always been an element in the study of terrorism. Within the terrorism studies literature, scholars have disagreed over whether terrorist groups should be viewed as innovative or imitative organizations.[1] Some researchers discount the desire of terrorist groups to innovate and learn since they tend to be operationally conservative and use a limited set of tactics, including bombings and firearm attacks.[2] Other authors characterize terrorist organizations as fiercely innovative, adapting their strategies and routines as a result of pressures by law enforcement and counter-terrorism forces. For example, the Provisional Irish Republican Army (PIRA) evolved their explosive designs initially to incorporate crude timers, then radio control, and finally triggers using radar detectors or remote photographic flash units,

---

1   For a discussion of this debate, which comes down resoundingly on the side of terrorist innovation, see Paul Wilkinson, "Editor's Introduction: Technology and Terrorism" in Paul Wilkinson, ed., *Technology and Terrorism* (London: Frank Cass, 1993), pp. 1-11.

2   Jeffrey D. Simon, *The Terrorist Trap: America's Experience with Terrorism* (Bloomington, IN: Indiana University Press, 1994), p. 348.

in response to British efforts to jam or defeat their methods of bomb detonation.[3] One source of this disagreement about terrorist innovation is a focus on the *results* of their actions rather than the learning processes undertaken to attain them. The literature on organizational learning, with its consideration of the different incentives and behaviors that influence learning, represents a source of new insight into these processes within terrorist groups and a means to resolving the apparent contradiction between these two views.[4]

This chapter discusses a range of organizational learning issues relevant to terrorist groups, including learning by doing, learning through training, and the role organizational memories play relative to knowledge diffusion within terrorist groups. Throughout the analysis, my primary focus is the specific learning involved in technology adoption, as a terrorist group's ability to carry out successful terrorist attacks is closely related to its ability to enhance existing operations and develop new ones through technology adoption. Mindful, like the other contributors to this volume, that organizational learning is problematic, I also consider numerous impediments to terrorist learning, including compartmentalized organizational structures that impede the flow of information and experience feedback among terrorist cells.

Terrorist Group Learning

Concepts of organizational learning may be usefully applied to various aspects of terrorist groups' knowledge and decisionmaking from the broad strategic level to the most specific tactical level. A terrorist organization bases its plans and actions on an overarching religious, ethno-nationalist, political, or philosophical paradigm or model of reality. This paradigm is then likely combined with knowledge and ideas about global and domestic political and economic systems, actions and reactions of governments, and effective ways to act against enemies within existing systems. For example, left wing terrorist groups active in Europe in the 1970s, embraced particular visions of Marxism including the assumption that acts of terror could catalyze broader revolution. More recently, *Al Qaeda*'s belief structures include a radical interpretation of the teachings of Islam and strategic assumptions about how inflicting casualties on military and civilian targets may modify the behavior of the

---

3   Bruce Hoffman, *Inside Terrorism* (New York, NY: Columbia University Press, 1998), pp. 180-182.

4   Some recent efforts have sought to include the process of learning into analysis of terrorist group activity. See, for example, Brian A. Jackson with John C. Baker, Kim Cragin, John Parachini, Horacio R. Trujillo, and Peter Chalk, *Aptitude for Destruction, Volume 1: Organizational Learning in Terrorist Groups and its Implications for Combating Terrorism* (Santa Monica, CA: RAND Corporation, 2005), Michael Kenney, "From Pablo to Osama: Counter-terrorism Lessons from the War on Drugs," *Survival* vol. 45 (2003), pp. 187-206, and James J. F. Forest, ed., *Teaching Terror: Strategic and Tactical Learning in the Terrorist World* (Lanham, MD: Rowman & Littlefield, 2006).

United States. These paradigms and strategic assumptions are developed via stories and frames that serve as the groups' "collective understandings of history."[5] The Revolutionary Armed Forces of Colombia (FARC) provide an example of strategic learning when they altered their strategy from a strongly anti-state military orientation to undertaking activities that portray themselves as a legitimate alternative to the Colombian government.[6] Other examples of such strategic learning can be found in al Qaeda which altered its recruiting practices to include multiple branches of Islam as it transitioned its activities toward a global perspective, and the Egyptian Islamic Jihad's shift from targeting institutions and individuals within Egypt to attacking United States (US) and Jewish institutions internationally based on their assessment of the effectiveness of their activities.[7]

Moving from paradigmatic and strategic concepts to the opposite end of the terrorist group "knowledge continuum," one finds detailed factual information needed to carry out individual operations. In military terms, this knowledge is the tactical intelligence involved in selecting a target, planning an attack, identifying and avoiding obstacles to operational success, and, if it is called for in the group's strategy, allowing the attackers to escape. Developing this information is a learning process involving data collection and interpretation about the world at a very high degree of resolution. As in governmental security organizations, terrorist organizations' intelligence development relies on particular learning processes that define what information is desired, how much and how current it must be, how it is interpreted, and how the finished intelligence will influence operational planning and decision-making. For example, the Abu Nidal Organization, a violent Palestinian group that splintered from Yasser Arafat's Fatah, devoted considerable resources to intelligence gathering on targets.   The organization's Intelligence Directorate reportedly maintained operations in dozens of countries monitoring security measures and collecting information on potential targets.[8]

Knowledge that supports a terrorist organization's use of particular attack and weapons technologies falls somewhere between strategic and tactical knowledge. These routines combine both sorts of considerations and address a range of questions about the particular characteristics of the group's operations: Which targets will the group attack? How does the group prepare for an attack? Which tactics and weapons are used? How are they used? Beyond the particular details of attacks, a body of routines also govern the internal practices of the group in the induction,

---

5   See Barbara Levitt and James G. March, "Organizational Learning," *Annual Review of Sociology* vol. 14 (1988), p. 324.

6   Román D. Ortiz, "Insurgent Strategies in the Post-Cold War: The Case of the Revolutionary Armed Forces of Colombia," *Studies in Conflict and Terrorism* vol. 25 (2002), p. 131.

7   Rohan Gunaratna, *Inside Al Qaeda: Global Network of Terror* (New York: Columbia University Press, 2002), p. 100; and Ayman al-Zawahiri, "Knights under the Prophet's Banner," *Al-Sharq al-Awsat* (December 4-7, 2001).

8   Patrick Seale, *Abu Nidal: A Gun for Hire* (New York: Random House, 1992), pp. 23, 185-191.

training, and use of group members: Are there standard processes associated with bringing new members into the group? How are they trained? What is required of them? Is a standard body of knowledge provided or taught? Whether they are aimed at personnel or operational plans, the routines addressing these topics are intimately tied to the capability of a group and the ways they use particular technologies. As a result, organizational learning processes aimed at altering or improving routines in these areas will potentially advance a group's ability to use new weapons, carry out new attacks, or improve their skill and expertise in already fielded tactics and techniques. The learning process associated with this class of knowledge can be broadly labeled "technology adoption" and is the focus of the remainder of this chapter.[9]

Organizational Learning through Technology Adoption

A terrorist group's technological sophistication and tactical expertise to a great extent define the lethality, scale, and effectiveness of the organization's attacks. A group's access to technology – from basic firearms to weapons of mass destruction (WMD – define the boundaries of its operations. The skill level in using any given tactic or weapon then contributes to some portion of the effect a group achieves when it uses a technology or operational scheme. For example, a group targeting a specific building may place a bomb in many different locations. Depending on the intelligence, engineering know-how, and other types of knowledge available to the group, the consequences of the bombing may range from a nuisance to a highly lethal attack. Technology adoption is the organizational learning process through which groups learn about useful technologies and techniques, acquire them, integrate them into group operations, and experiment and/or train sufficiently to use them well. As such, it is necessary for groups to upgrade their skill in their current attacks, transition from more basic to potentially more lethal technologies, develop or deploy highly lethal weapons including WMD, and improve their ability to operate in the face of law enforcement and counter intelligence pressure. Therefore, technology adoption must be a constant and central focus in terrorist threat assessment and counter-terrorist planning.

In studies of technology-related learning in organizations, scholars have sought to better explain the process of acquiring and learning to use new technologies by drawing a distinction between *types* of knowledge that are involved. The first is *explicit knowledge*, information or data that can be readily written down or embodied in physical objects. Relevant examples of explicit knowledge include blueprints for a building a terrorist group seeks to target or a weapon obtained by the group. The second type is *tacit knowledge*, generally unrecorded expertise such as internal "know-how" developed by individuals through experience or implicit organizational

---

9   For a more lengthy treatment of this topic, see Brian A. Jackson, "Technology Acquisition by Terrorist Groups: Threat Assessment Informed by Lessons from Private Sector Technology Adoption," *Studies in Conflict and Terrorism* vol. 24 (2001), pp. 183-213.

knowledge about how techniques or technologies are best used for particular purposes. Terrorism-related examples of tacit knowledge include the intuition developed by soldiers over their operational careers and the expertise needed to be a "marksman" rather than simply fire a firearm. Unlike explicit knowledge, which is easily transferred among individuals or groups because it is encoded in written form or technological objects, tacit knowledge is more difficult to transfer and may require face-to-face communication and hands-on contact to transfer the knowledge from one individual to another. An organization must bring together the necessary tacit and explicit knowledge (for example, the explicit recipe for the explosives, the tacit knowledge required to manufacture them safely, the explicit engineering knowledge needed to place them well, and the tacit operational expertise to successfully carry out the operation) to use a technology most effectively.

Understanding the learning processes that increase technological sophistication and the effectiveness of terrorist attacks is critical. Acquiring this understanding is not straightforward, however, because many different knowledge and technology sources are involved in a group's technology adoption efforts. Relevant learning processes include obtaining explicit knowledge from sources of codified information, acquiring explicit and/or tacit knowledge from other organizations or individuals, and developing relevant explicit or tacit knowledge within the terrorist group. These processes can involve organizational search for relevant existing knowledge or appropriate knowledge sources, communication and acquisition activities to obtain knowledge from these external sources, and/or trial-and-error experimentation.

Search activities may be directed at particular problems encountered by groups but can also be initiated without a clearly defined tactical problem in mind. Because of their illicit nature, terrorist organizations must constantly devise new and better methods to avoid law enforcement or intelligence penetration of the group. In addition, anti-terrorism measures taken at terrorists' potential targets can also present problems that become the subject of group search activities. The challenge posed by diplomatic buildings or more rigorous border security, for example, may lead terrorist groups to explore larger explosives or stand-off weapons to overpower or circumvent the obstacles. The PIRA's explosives innovation in response to improvements in countermeasures is a prime example of such problem-directed search. On the other hand, some terrorist search activities are not intended to resolve specific problems. Research to acquire certain types of weapons, including chemical or biological agents, is often undertaken for reasons independent of particular tactical challenges. This discussion of technological learning is intended to capture both types of search activities.

The characteristics of the knowledge sources identified by the group, the nature of the technologies it is seeking to acquire, and the particular learning processes it undertakes will influence whether the organization will gain the explicit and tacit knowledge needed to use a particular technology effectively. These factors will also influence governments' counter-terrorist strategies to disrupt the learning processes of their terrorist adversaries.

Learning by Doing

A major area of interest in the study of organizational learning is how knowledge and performance improves as an organization gains greater experience in routine activities, sometimes referred to as "learning by doing." The progress of such learning activities is often plotted in learning or experience curves relating performance variables, such as increasing productivity or decreasing costs, against the number of units produced by a firm or other measure of operational experience. Because learning by doing focuses on existing technologies and organizational routines, this source of learning more likely derives from exploitation rather than exploration.[10]

Learning by doing among terrorists groups suggests that they may become more effective with particular tactics and technologies as they accumulate relevant operational experience. An example of how a "learning curve" showing such an increase in capability might be constructed for a terrorist group is included in Figure 9.1 below. The graph, which plots the average fatalities caused by Hamas suicide bomb attacks between May 2001 and May 2002 (a convenient length time period containing a significant number of attacks), shows that operations that were later in this time period resulted in higher average fatalities than earlier attacks. The number of attacks included in each average is included below the graph.[11]

Although the small number of data points and range of factors that could influence the fatalities resulting from an attack make it impossible to unambiguously assign a reason for the increase, tactical learning through experience may be a contributing factor. The potential for groups to learn during their operations makes it clear that understanding the impact of a group's longevity and its operational tempo on tactical expertise should be included in judgments about the threat posed by particular organizations. All other variables being equal, a group with a longer operational history with a particular tactic or weapon will pose a greater threat than one that has only recently adopted it.

Although learning by doing can help terrorist groups build expertise, there is a significant risk for organizations that rely solely on such experiential learning. Each individual terrorist operation, in addition to representing an opportunity to learn and refine operational routines, also represents an opportunity for group operatives to be captured or killed and the security of the group compromised. As a result, relying

---

10 James G. March, "Exploration and Exploitation in Organizational Learning," *Organization Science* vol. 2 (1991), pp. 71-87.

11 Due to difficulty in attributing attacks to groups (with or without claims of responsibility) and inconsistent reporting of the effects of attacks in different information sources, Figure 9.1 should be viewed as illustrative rather than conclusive. The reader should also keep in mind that for many terrorist operations total fatalities may not be an appropriate quantitative metric for success. In some cases, groups may seek to minimize casualties while still gaining attention for their causes. In the case of these suicide bombings, which were strongly motivated by a desire for revenge and have aimed to inflict as much damage as possible, use of the average number of fatalities per attack is an acceptable proxy for effective learning by doing.

only on learning by doing to improve group performance could be a costly strategy as failed "experiments" in tactical or weapons innovation have to be paid for through large human or organizational costs. In the case of suicide operations, the members of the group involved in the action will be lost by definition. Organizations that use this tactic must concentrate their relevant operational experience in members that do not carry out such attacks themselves, which requires separating the functions of planning and logistics from actual operations. Al Qaeda has developed a number of routines to help reduce the costs of experiential learning. These include having overt group members perform certain tasks that might compromise the more valuable covert members of the group, and evacuating important members of operations cells from targeted areas prior to an attack.[12]

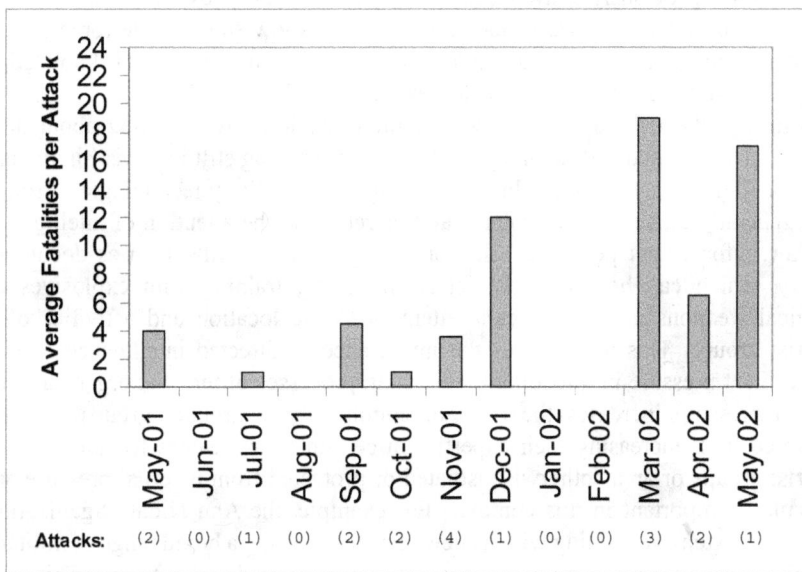

Figure 9.1 Average Fatalities Caused by Hamas Suicide Bombing Attacks, May 2001-May 2002

Source: RAND Terrorism Database and print media.

Learning through Training

Rather than simply relying on operational activities to produce the knowledge needed to improve group performance, many organizations take specific actions

_____

12 Rohan Gunaratna, *Inside Al Qaeda*, p. 77; Peter L. Bergen, *Holy War, Inc.: Inside the Secret World of Osama bin Laden* (New York: The Free Press, 2001), pp. 110, 115.

where knowledge acquisition is the primary goal. For military organizations such as terrorist groups, training activities are a central part of organizational learning activities. Operational training is the analog of learning by doing, but because techniques and strategies are tested under more controlled or simulated circumstances, the consequences of failure can be significantly reduced. For example, in the case of a terrorist organization perfecting a new tactic or mastering a new weapon, training is a chance to evaluate or "debug" the innovation away from the pressures of an actual operation. Controlled training can also be optimized to allow more learning in a shorter time than relying on experience.

Such training under more "relaxed" circumstances can result in developing greater expertise in an organization's existing practices and technologies, what James March identifies as "exploitation," or developing new technologies and practices with which the group was previously unaware, in March's terminology, "exploration."[13] While exploration may involve the creation of new explicit knowledge for a terrorist group, learning through training is often associated with developing the tacit knowledge groups require to use existing technologies well.

Although the risks associated with training are less than learning about new technologies and tactics through operations alone, training still involves significant risks for illegal organizations. In order to train with military technologies, groups must generally come "above ground" and thereby risk the attention of intelligence and law enforcement personnel. In contrast to learning skills such as document forgery, which can be done completely in hiding, training with explosives or chemical weapons necessarily calls attention to the location and activities of a terrorist group. This underscores the importance of directed intelligence or law enforcement pressure in impeding the learning processes of terrorist organizations. If such pressure increases the risks of coming above ground, groups may be prevented from increasing their expertise in certain areas. States friendly toward terrorist groups or areas otherwise isolated or protected from external pressure are particularly important in this context. For example, the Abu Nidal Organization carried out extensive training with its new recruits covering a broad range of military and clandestine techniques involving considerable operational activity. This was only possible because of the organization's access to a desert camp in Libya where the training could be carried out away from external pressure.[14] More recently, the expertise of the Al Qaeda fighters in Afghanistan was bolstered by their ability to train under the protection of the Taliban regime.[15] State sponsors or safe havens can give terrorist groups the opportunity to learn and increase their effectiveness.

---

13 March, "Exploration and Exploitation in Organizational Learning," pp. 71-87.

14 Seale, *Abu Nidal*, pp. 3-24.

15 C. J. Chivers and David Rohde, "Turning Out Guerrillas and Terrorists to Wage a Holy War," *New York Times* (March 18, 2002), p. A1.

Obstacles to Learning

As organizations learn, they make judgments about their efforts based on measures of the outcomes of their activities. These measures lead to conclusions about the perceived success of particular tactics, technologies, or routines, which serve as a guide to future learning. In general, routines that have been successful in the past will be used in the future, allowing the group to further increase expertise in that tactic or technology through repeated use. Although this behavior can result in a group becoming specialized and expert in a given tactic or technology, as March recognizes, there is a trade-off between exploitation and exploration. Exploitation of existing practices and technologies can become a barrier to learning new technologies and techniques that could improve the organization's performance, in a word: exploration. As an organization becomes more proficient in a given technology with which it is familiar, its competence can become a trap that blocks the organization from pursuing new tactics or techniques.[16] If a new and an established technology are compared in terms of effectiveness, the new technology will always be handicapped by the group's lack of familiarity and skill in its use. Such competency traps can serve as a partial explanation for why many terrorist groups have been operationally conservative and hesitant to adopt new tactics or weapons.[17] In the absence of compelling external reasons that change the apparent relative success of different attack forms, incentives work against displacing well established routines. Competency traps can be reinforced if the organization has made substantial resource investments in a particular tactic or technique. However, activities undertaken by Al Qaeda – ranging from car bombings, maritime operations, and the attacks of September 11, 2001 – demonstrate that such traps do not affect all groups equally.

Although it seems self evident that an organization would guide its actions and future learning activities based on an assessment of the success of its current operations, putting such an evaluation process into practice can be difficult. It is often difficult to impartially determine levels of organizational success or failure and even more difficult to tie changes in such a level of success with individual actions. Determining the success or failure of a particular action depends on an organization's defining the outcomes it expects and then comparing what actually happens to those targets. Such an assessment could be particularly difficult for an activity like terrorism. In the example of suicide bombings included earlier, success was measured based on numbers of casualties. For attacks motivated by religious fundamentalism or a desire for revenge, this is likely an acceptable, if imperfect, metric. Conversely, if the overall goal of a group is to induce political change by carrying out attacks, it may be difficult to determine the success of any given

---

16 See "Exploration and Exploitation in Organizational Learning," pp. 71-87; and Levitt and March, "Organizational Learning," pp. 322-323.

17 A number of groups have been singled out for their reticence to change their modes of operation, including the Palestine Liberation Organization, the Provisional Irish Republican Army, the Basque Fatherland and Liberty, the Japanese Red Army, and the Red Army Faction. See Hoffman, *Inside Terrorism*, pp. 197-198.

operation, much less compare the relative success of two operations using different tactics or weapons. In such campaigns, metrics based on numbers of causalities may be inappropriate. Success of an entire terrorist campaign might be discernable (for example, political recognition of the group's cause, obtaining an ethnic homeland, etc.), but the absolute success of a particular operation is not. Such a high level of ambiguity increases the potential for a group to reinterpret what constitutes success over time.

Terrorist Groups' Organizational Memories

Organizations learn when their participants learn and encode their experience in routines that can be passed on to other members of the group.[18] Whether learning by doing or through training, an increase in organizational capabilities will not be sustainable unless the knowledge embedded in routines pass from individuals into a collective organizational memory. This store of collective knowledge must be maintained over time and preserved by transfer to new group members through socialization and training. Depending on the characteristics of a group, organizational memories can be maintained in systems of rules, standard operating procedures, training manuals or materials, documents, usage of particular technologies, in addition to more abstract entities like group cultures, belief systems, and organizational stories and myths.

In the case of explicit knowledge, preservation of an organizational memory generally involves the archival collection of the relevant information, its preservation and maintenance, and transfer of the information to other group members. An example of such a collection of explicit knowledge is the multi-volume, 7000 page *Encyclopedia of the Afghan Jihad* assembled by Al Qaeda.[19] Tacit knowledge is not easy to identify and codify into formal documents, making organizational memories based on tacit knowledge far more difficult to construct. In fact, many organizations recognize that the tacit knowledge held by particular individuals is both critical and not "organizational" when those people leave the firm or group and the knowledge is lost. Methods to preserve tacit knowledge generally focus on structured training or interaction between organization members to promote information sharing. In addition, many organizations also devote considerable resources to capturing or recording tacit understandings as explicit knowledge in standard operating procedures or other organization documents. Although this process can preserve tacit knowledge in a more enduring form, it is difficult and resource intensive.

Although capturing the results of individual learning into an organizational memory is potentially costly for any organization, knowledge management activities have particular risks for terrorist groups. Because counter-terrorism forces are constantly seeking information about their illicit adversaries, any codified or explicit knowledge maintained by a group can represent a significant vulnerability. For

---

18 See Levitt and March, "Organizational Learning."
19 Gunaratna, *Inside Al Qaeda*, p. 70.

example, the wealth of papers, videotapes, and notes discovered in various al Qaeda sites in Afghanistan have provided US intelligence with significant information on the group's members, operations, and plans.[20] The seizure of documents by police in a raid on the Italian group, *Nuclei Armati Proletari*, also provided the authorities with significant amounts of information about the organization.[21] These risks are similar for other illegal organizations, such as drug trafficking networks.[22]

The risks posed by the maintenance of an explicit organizational memory once again underscore the importance of state sponsors or safe havens for terrorist groups. In addition to providing venues for learning and sources of knowledge, sympathetic states can also provide a haven for records and knowledge that might allow the terrorist group to maintain a more complete and effective organizational memory. It is likely that one reason so many Al Qaeda records and documents were found in Afghanistan is because the Taliban regime created a friendly haven for the group and Al Qaeda leaders believed that their state counter-terrorist adversaries would not be able to seize the organizational memory built there.[23] In general, however, one would expect that the high level of uncertainty faced by terrorist groups would lead them to avoid codifying knowledge and to rely on more informally shared understandings and tacit information.

Beyond the risks faced by terrorist groups from the potential compromise of their organizational memories, the construction and maintenance of collective knowledge also requires effective mechanisms for knowledge transfer within the organization. If significant barriers exist to information sharing, learning can not be successfully embedded in routines shared by the entire group. Within commercial organizations, barriers to transfer of knowledge have been observed between separate units or divisions within a firm, even if the individuals involved interact freely and frequently. In many cases, firms have had to restructure or drastically modify their corporate cultures and practices to stimulate the transfer of technology and learning within the organization. Because of the particular pressures and structural forms adopted by terrorist groups, even more serious barriers to knowledge transfer might be expected.

---

20 See, for example, Walter Pincus, "Seized Materials May Help Thwart Future Attacks," *Washington Post* (April 3, 2002), p. A14, <http://www.cnn.com/SPECIALS/2002/terror.tapes>, last accessed September 8, 2002.

21 Richard Drake, *The Revolutionary Mystique and Terrorism in Contemporary Italy* (Bloomington, IN: Indiana University Press, 1989), p. 30.

22 See Chapter 8 of this volume, and Michael Kenney, *From Pablo to Osama: Trafficking and Terrorist Networks, Government Bureaucracies, and Competitive Adaptation* (University Park, PA: The Pennsylvania State University Press, forthcoming 2007).

23 Pincus, "Seized Materials May Help Thwart Future Attacks," p. A14.

Terrorist Group Structure and Organizational Learning

To survive and continue operating, a terrorist organization must protect itself from infiltration and compromise by law enforcement or intelligence personnel. This stringent requirement to prevent knowledge transfer outside the group has led most terrorist organizations to structure themselves in ways to minimize the chances of such transfer and to reduce the potential damage if it does occur. A basic strategy adopted by many groups is to organize their activities based on a cell structure. A terrorist cell is a small group of individuals who operate together to plan and carry out attacks. The size of the group makes it possible for cell members to know each other well, thereby reducing the chances of infiltration. Depending on the size of the group, a terrorist organization will consist of one or more cells. For small groups, such as the Japanese Red Army or the Red Army Faction comprised of between 20 and 30 members, the entire group might consist of a single cell.[24]

For larger organizations, the entire group will contain a number of individual cells. In order to reduce the risk to a larger organization, these cells are compartmentalized – individual members may only know the identities of the others in their cell. Although this limits the damage if a cell is compromised, this structure creates inherent barriers to information flow within the organization and may handicap learning for the group as a whole, depending on whether communication exists between cells. When group leaders or other individuals serve as a bridge between different cells – through communication, direct interaction, or contact during the training of the cells – it may be possible for lessons learned by individual members or cells to be transferred to the larger organization. In this model, while most cell members are kept ignorant of the identity of other group members, a small number of individuals with broader knowledge of the group help offset the learning disadvantages of security. Evidence suggests that Al Qaeda utilizes this approach where most members are kept ignorant of the identities of others but interaction between organizational leaders and intermediaries allows transfer of information and knowledge among cells.[25] Given terrorists' interest in the Internet, it is relevant to consider the role that information technology also serves in reducing these information costs. If means exist for anonymous communication between individual cells, it is possible for the exchange of explicit knowledge among groups otherwise ignorant of each others' identities. In the absence of routes to allow interaction among cells of a larger group, it is debatable whether any organizational memory can be built. Cellular structures can also pose problems for command and control within terrorist groups, as individual cells may take actions in consistent with the overall goals of the group because compartmentalization makes it difficult to exert authority over them and guide their actions.

24 Bruce Hoffman, "Terrorism Trends and Prospects," in Ian O. Lesser et. al., eds., *Countering the New Terrorism* (Santa Monica, CA: RAND Corporation, 1999), p. 10.
25 Gunaratna, *Inside Al Qaeda,* pp. 76-77.

An even more isolated and segmented group structure is embodied in the strategy of "leaderless resistance" adopted over the past few years by certain terrorist groups. In leaderless resistance, an individual or small group prepares publications (either physically or on the Internet) espousing their philosophies and suggesting targets that would be appropriate to advance their agenda, under the assumption that like-minded individuals will accept this direction and carry out attacks. A variety of terrorist groups have adopted the strategy, including white supremacists, ultra-conservative militias, environmental and animal rights organizations, and violent anti-abortion activist groups.[26] In some cases, the founders or core leaders of the group give others permission to claim their attack in the name of the overall terrorist organization. For example, guidelines on the Animal Liberation Front (ALF) Internet site state that "Any group of people who are vegetarians or vegans and who carry out actions according to A.L.F. guidelines have the right to regard themselves as part of the A.L.F."[27]

Although leaderless resistance is advantageous from the standpoint of operational security, it has significant implications for organizational learning. Because the individual cells of these "groups" are completely unaware of the existence of each other and there is no contact between individual cells and any group leadership, there is no mechanism for sharing knowledge among groups, other than message board postings on the Internet or transmission in media reports. In such groups, it is difficult to envision how detailed, tacit knowledge gained by individuals in different locations of the loosely-coupled organization can be converted into organizational routines. This practical constraint may limit the level of tactical advancement one would predict for "groups" which adopt this structure.

Because of the significant pressures exerted on terrorist organizations by law enforcement and intelligence activities, these groups face particular challenges from the perspective of organizational learning. Efforts to capture and preserve knowledge, while helping to preserve group capabilities through turnover of individual members, can also compromise the group as a whole. In addition, the structures adopted by a terrorist group also can have a significant impact on their potential to learn at the organizational level. At one extreme, very small groups may be able to build organizational memories very effectively given the high degree of interaction among their members. However, large, compartmented groups put up intentional barriers to learning in the interests of security.

Conclusion

When considering the problem of terrorism and the design of counter-terrorist strategies, an understanding of organizational learning can clearly be an important

---

26 Jessica Stern, *The Ultimate Terrorists* (Cambridge, MA: Harvard University Press, 1999), pp. 83-84.

27 "History of the Animal Liberation Front," <http://www.animalliberationfront.com/ALFront/Premise_History/ALF_History.htm>, last accessed August 21, 2005).

component in successful law enforcement or intelligence activity. Whether examining learning associated with overarching strategic issues or the most detailed tactical concerns, insight into how extremist groups change over time is critical for devising counter-terrorist measures. Because technology and tactics affect the potential lethality of terrorist attacks, it is clear that the learning processes that make up technology adoption must be of particular concern.

While this chapter has sought to deepen our understanding of the various ways that terrorist groups learn, it is important to emphasize the exploratory nature of this research. There remains much that we do not know about how terrorist groups adopt technology to enhance their capabilities. To build a better, broader understanding of organizational learning in terrorist groups, more information is needed—particularly the first-person, internal information available in accounts of former group members or collected from current members when opportunities present themselves. In spite the need for further investigation, it is my hope that the results presented in this chapter will contribute to ongoing efforts against terrorist organizations and can assist in developing increasingly effective strategies to protect society from terrorist violence.

PART 4
Deterrents to Learning

Chapter 10

Changing Church: Middle Managers and Learning in Dogmatic Organizations

William J. Campbell

Much of the scholarly literature investigating sources of learning within organizations dichotomize these factors into either top-down or bottom-up influences; however, this simplification ignores the role of the middle manager in learning processes. Many instances of productive organizational learning credited to upper-level leaders may have failed without the transformative contributions of middle managers. Middle managers facilitate communication between upper- and the lower-level personnel. By synthesizing the principles and goals articulated by executives with the practical knowledge and demands of lower-level personnel, middle managers contribute to organizational learning.

In addition to this focus on middle managers, another issue inadequately addressed in the literature is how organizations with rigid rule structures learn and survive. Productive learning must be occurring if these organizations continue to exist, grow and achieve success. Dogmatic organizations that value and maintain the integrity of principles and rules over other organizational goals provide interesting contexts for possible learning. Middle managers may face special challenges in dogmatic organizations. The prioritization of principles within an organization may restrict learning and/or foster some types of learning and preclude others. This chapter explores the role of middle managers in facilitating productive organizational learning within dogmatic organizations. I suggest a model to help explain communication and learning among multiple organizational levels. I then apply this model to the Catholic Church in Latin America by examining the role of bishops as middle managers affecting learning associated with doctrinal changes deriving from the 1962-65 Second Vatican Council.

First, some explicit clarification of how "organizational learning," "the middle manager," and "dogmatic organizations" are conceptualized. One definition of organizational learning assumes that lessons drawn from past experience are encoded into routines, procedures and policies of an organization.[1] Others suggest that organizations' need for information, knowledge and skills beyond their current

---

1   See James G. March, *The Pursuit of Organizational Intelligence* (Malden, MA: Blackwell Publishing, 1999); and Peter Hall, *The Political Power of Economic Ideas: Keynesianism Across Nations* (Princeton, NJ: Princeton University Press 1989), p. 11.

capacity result in organizational "search" and the subsequent development of alternative procedures and policies. These learning processes may take personnel beyond accepted practices and policies to embrace new approaches, and in the most extreme cases may completely change the way the organization approaches problems (that is to say, they may elicit paradigmatic change).[2] Most organizational learning theory suggests that an active program of learning is required to achieve positive results. This leads many theorists to focus attention on executive leaders as actors powerful enough to articulate and implement large-scale organizational change. However, learning occurs at all levels of the organization.

Middle managers are human resources between lower-level personnel and executives. Middle managers must create positive outcomes from the broad principles and goals articulated by executive policy makers. To make this happen, they must select among, reframe and synthesize the broad goals of leaders into practical policies and procedures that lower-level personnel can implement. Middle managers serve as a bridge between the visionary ideas of the executive and the practical ideas and information of the lower-level personnel. The middle manager is therefore essential to the success of both the executives and lower-level personnel. Understanding how middle managers enhance or deter learning will be a valuable addition to the literature on organizational learning.

Dogmatic organizations regard certain beliefs or rules as authoritative and frequently beyond question. Dogmas may be incomplete, inconsistent, and supported by tradition or consensus rather then empirical "facts." Dogmas are commonly supported for reasons unrelated to market or political forces. There are different degrees of dogmatism within organizations. Some may be based on individual egos or defensive routines. Other dogmas may be the reason the organization was formed, are inherent to its identity, and will limit or restrain what the organization can do in the future, although even dogmatic organizations learn and change as their basic beliefs are redefined. Dogmas may act as constraints and incentives for the learning and actions that the organization may undertake. Learning within dogmatic organizations differs from the experiences of less rule-based organizations because information, routines and policies are measured against principles rather then their practicality or operational effectiveness. Dogmatic organizations may be vastly different; consider, for example, Greenpeace and the (United States-based) National Rifle Association.

The Catholic Church provides an interesting case study for scholars of organizational learning because it is slow to change, is often criticized for being inconsistent, but still occupies a powerful role in the world. The most recent and well-documented major change in the Church occurred during the Second Vatican Council in Rome from 1962 to 1965. Although there have been some change at the regional level, the hierarchical structure of the Church has experienced little change since Vatican II. Vatican II doctrinal changes were implemented on all levels, and

---

2   March, *The Pursuit of Organizational Intelligence*, pp. 115-117, and Chris Argyris, *On Organizational Learning* (Malden, MA: Blackwell Publishing, 1992), pp. 67-68.

this process involved learning on the pastoral, diocesan and papal levels. Policy change of this magnitude requires organization-wide understanding for success. After receiving direction from the executive papal authority during Vatican II, bishops acted as managers of lower-level change.

Since the Church is such a large organization, it will be beneficial to focus on a specific region. Latin America not only has the largest regional population of Catholics, but also possesses a Church viewed as conservative compared to Europe and the United States. In this chapter, I explore how Latin American bishops function as middle managers to facilitate and/or deter productive learning within the dogmatic organization that is the Church. Reinterpretation of doctrine resulted in changes in the structure of the Church that produced different experiences for religious leaders and parishioners. Vatican II created a stir in Latin America that produced new theological and social challenges for the Church particularly in the form of Liberation Theology. Some lessons drawn from Vatican II by Latin American Catholics were not supported or nurtured by Church executives, but were enthusiastically embraced by the laity. Drawing evidence from official documents from Vatican II and four conferences of Latin American bishops as well as scholarly analyses, I investigate how middle managers within the Church select among, reject and reframe policies put forth by the executive papal level while communicating information and demands from the lower-level allowing the organization to experience learning without changing its fundamental principles.

Middle Managers and Organizational Learning

Any analysis of organizational learning must take into account of the actions and interactions of different organizational levels.[3] Managers at different organizational levels act in response to both the principles and goals articulated by leaders and lower-level personnel's understanding and demands. The middle manager wears two organizational hats as a subordinate of the upper-most leadership within the organizational hierarchy and a superior for lower-level personnel. Studying the role of the middle managers allows us to understand the processes that reconcile differences within an organization. A selector, reframer and synthesizer of beliefs and information, the manager communicates information, but also creates new information that incorporates principles and practicalities within organizational understanding.[4]

Examining how middle managers work within organizations will help us identify which functions should be decentralized to make an organization learn more productively. Better use of the managerial knowledge and insights can make any organization meet its constituents' demands more efficiently. In large organizations,

---

3   Argyris, *On Organizational Learning*, pp. 97-98.

4   Ikujiro Nonaka and Hirotaka Takeuchi, *The Knowledge-Creating Company: How Japanese Companies Create the Dynamics of Innovation* (Oxford: Oxford University Press, 1995).

lower-level personnel do not participate directly in the creation of the goals of an organization and the middle manager, if sufficiently autonomous, can address this discrepancy by reorienting the ideas of the executive level to make them successful on the lower levels.

The importance assigned to these roles and responsibilities is fluid within and between organizations. Organizations in the marketplace experience changes in what is demanded of them and will tend to focus on the practical concerns such as efficiency and profitability. Organizations that deal in principled and ideological debates and goals are susceptible to fewer external demands and focus on reflective issues of definition and goal achievement.[5] Each organization values a different type of learning. Dogmatic organizations are concerned primarily with principles (ideology) and less concerned about outcomes. The middle manager is more likely to increase his influence through systemic validation rather than situational, goal-oriented performance. Because of this, policy implementation and evaluation are inconsistent and the organization is more likely to learn via leadership than by policy success or failure. Religious organizations fall into this category as well as other issue-driven organizations.

The middle manager works to achieve systemic validation and situational goals; he selects, reframes, synthesizes, and communicates principles and policies sent down from the leadership. These four tasks are informed by the middle managers' interaction with lower-level personnel. The middle manager selects from among the directives articulated by the leadership those that seem most applicable and/ or practical for implementation. A directive is accepted when the middle manager views no necessary change. Alternatively, a directive may be rejected if the middle manager views it as inapplicable or destructive for organizational goals or the lower-level personnel. The middle manger serves as a two-way conduit for communication. Input from lower-level personnel may inform the middle manager in his selecting, reframing, synthesizing and communicating. If questioned by the leadership, the middle manager may justify his action by reference to local knowledge. This communication may allow the organization to learn from the lower-level personnel's practical knowledge. Thus, middle managers may communicate information to justify their actions and to attempt to alter policies and directives issued by the leadership.

Since maintaining the integrity of organizational principles is the highest priority for leaders in dogmatic organizations, they prefer acceptance to all of the other managerial behaviors. Acceptance means that the least change will happen to the principle and the leadership can have the most control over how the principle is defined. Selection is less preferred because it may not retain the complexity and breadth of the leadership's definition of a principle. Reframing the principle changes the discourse and may risk misrepresenting the leader's original intent, but may make the principle more applicable to the lower-level situation. Rejection of the directive

5 To clarify, demands are placed on these institutions; however, they are not as instantaneous or as varied as those experienced by organizations more responsive to the needs of constituents or consumers.

is the least preferred middle manager behavior because it leaves the leadership with little power to affect policies at the lower levels. The leadership works to achieve acceptance of directives to protect and promote the principles and to maintain power within the organization.

To avoid rejection, executive leaders create broad principles and directives that allow flexible and inclusive definitions. However, intentionally vague definitions and directives defend the power of the leadership by not allowing middle managers and lower-level personnel to participate in changing the principles. Chris Argyris views such defensive routines as a system of anti-learning.[6] Subordinates push for autonomy while the central authority wants to maintain control. Top leaders' maintaining control suggests to middle managers that they are not trusted; if they feel they are not trusted they are more apt to reject definitions from the leadership. Mixed messages may seem clear and ambiguous simultaneously and are often constructed with knowledge about the receiver in mind.[7] Eventually, mixed messages will create dichotomous understandings and actions by the groups who act on the extension of these vague definitions. Mixed messages are most obvious when the tasks of selection and reframing are controlled through structural change, power and intimidation. This will decrease rejection of the principles that the dogmatic organization values while increasing inconsistencies in implementation, evaluation and situational validation. Dogmatic organizations may learn from lower-level personnel and policy success and failure, but the goal of the executive leadership is to protect the integrity of principles and goals and less importance is placed on the preferences of lower-level personnel or policy outcomes. Figure 10.1 on page 182 provides a summary of the roles, responsibilities and motivations associated with the executive leadership, middle managers and lower-level personnel in the Catholic Church.

The Catholic Church and Latin America: An Opportunity for Learning?

Organizational learning theories may shed some light on how and why bishops act as middle managers of learning and change within the Catholic Church, and why the slow process of change within the Church may be both beneficial and detrimental. The study begins with a description of the structure of the Church, and then turns to a consideration of the Second Vatican Council and the emergence of Liberation Theology in response to the Council. Several councils of bishops are then examined in terms of their potential for facilitating learning, beginning with the establishment of the councils in 1955 in Rio de Janeiro and concluding with the 1992 Santo Domingo meetings where the Church strove to impart a new evangelization to the people of Latin America. The intervening years are a period of revolutionary change within the Latin American Church and the continent, characterized by oppression and force, learning and liberation.

---

6   Argyris, *On Organizational Learning*, p. 141.
7   Argyris, *On Organizational Learning*, pp. 93-94.

Hierarchical Position	Roles and Responsibilities	Motivations
Leadership (the Vatican and the Pope)	Agenda setting Articulate principles and goals Give directives	Reflective principles
Middle Managers (bishops and regional conferences)	Select (accept and reject) Reframe Synthesize Inform Communicate	Reflective principles and practical outcomes
Lower-level Personnel (including pastors, priests and the laity)	Inform managers Articulate demands Implement Meet goals Use resources efficiently Evaluate	Practical outcomes

Figure 10.1 Hierarchy, Roles and Motivations

The Pope has multiple official titles and roles reflecting his place at the apex of the official structure and authority of the Church: "The pope is the bishop of Rome, the primate or chief bishop of Italy, the patriarch of the west, the absolute monarch of the Vatican City State, and the head of the college of bishops and of the Catholic Church."[8] Our primary concern in this chapter is the actions of the Pope as the head of the college of bishops. The Pope holds an interesting position as both the chief executive and a colleague of the bishops. The Pope's claim to primacy derives from history and organizational development that continues to be interpreted and challenged. Leo I introduced the primacy of the Pope's authority in the Church during his 440-461 AD reign. During the Medieval period, Gregory VII (1073-1085) laid out twenty-seven propositions that supported the primary authority of the Pope over the world. Innocent the III (1198-1216) introduced an all-embracing papal theocracy and declared the Pope the Vicar of Christ to both believers and unbelievers in the world.[9] Pope Boniface VIII asserted that Rome had established the entire Patriarchal, Metropolitan, and Episcopal sees, which was historically inaccurate. This was the time when the Pope as ruler of the Papal States asserted the

---

8   Thomas Reese, *The Politics and Organization of The Catholic Church* (Cambridge, MA: Harvard University Press, 1996), p. 10.

9   Patrick Granfield, *The Limits of the Papacy: Authority and Autonomy in the Church* (New York: Crossroads Publishing, 1987).

authority of a monarch and established a lineage for the divine right of the Church's monarchy.

The First Vatican Council (1869-1870) laid out four canons that reaffirmed papal authority and added that the Pope could be infallible. The Second Vatican Council reaffirmed the primacy of the Pope as the leader of the Church but changed the language used to justify that authority. The authority of the Church derived not from the power handed down from Peter, but from the legitimacy of the college of bishops as the successor of the apostles led by Peter, the predecessor to the modern Pope.[10] This approach expands the ecclesial authority of the bishops and deepened collegiality among the bishops. The Pope is placed within the college of the bishops as a fellow bishop and head of the college.[11] Vatican II also began to legitimize the local church as a valuable resource for insights into local theological perspectives. It emphasized the role of the bishops in their jurisdiction and their role to validate the universal jurisdiction of the Pope.[12] These ideas were introduced fully in the documents *Lumen Gentium* and *Gadium et Spes*.[13] Vatican II increased the value and appropriateness of input of information and ideas from local pastors and the laity that created a fertile environment for the emergence of the Liberation Theology movement.

The next organizational level of the Church is the level of the Cardinal Bishops. These bishops are advisors to the Pope and have more political power in the Vatican than bishops outside of Rome. Cardinals are priests or bishops who are appointed rather than ordained, and the College of Cardinals remains today an advisory arm to the papacy, similar to the cabinet of the Presidency in the United States. The Cardinals have little power without the Pope's backing, but because of their proximity possess great political influence.[14] Cardinals may also be ambassadors or representatives of the Pope and the Vatican to other countries.

The Pope, bishops and priests are all representatives of God and must defer to higher levels of leadership once it is deemed that the decision moves beyond their jurisdiction. The next level is the archdiocese that is a geographically distinct area overseen by an archbishop. The archbishop is also the bishop of the city after which his archdiocese is named. The bishops at the lower levels of the church enjoy a similar mixture of authority and powerlessness in relation to the Vatican.

---

10 Granfield, *The Limits of the Papacy*, pp. 32-36.

11 Granfield, *The Limits of the Papacy*, pp. 36, 43.

12 Reese, *Inside The Vatican*.

13 *Lumen Gentium* contained the idea of the Church as the people of God, a community characterized by a fundamental equality and a common responsibility. Before the hierarchy of office, power, and privilege among episcopate, clergy, and laity, there is their fundamental unity, equality, and solidarity as the people of God, and their common responsibility as a sign and instrument of God's kingdom. *Gadium et Spes* contained the principle of the church as servant, a community in service to humanity and the world. The Church partakes of the hopes, joys, grief and anxieties of all humanity, particularly the poor. M.D. Litonjua, *Liberation Theology: A Paradigm Shift* (Lanham, MD: University Press of America, Inc., 1989), p. 16.

14 Reese, *Inside the Vatican*, p. 26.

The bishops control the dioceses and churches and property therein. A diocese is usually a corporate entity unto itself; funding for the diocese comes from donations made at the parish level. Customarily 97 percent of funding stays in the parish from which it originated. For simplification purposes, this study will combine the roles of archbishops and bishops since both enjoy many of the same rights including participation in councils. The archbishop rarely intervenes unless asked by the diocese or the Vatican to intercede on their behalf. This means the bishops exercise a good deal of autonomy in the everyday functioning of the Church.[15]

The laity along with the lower-level religious can be considered supervised personnel. It is important to understand the actions taken by the laity so that we have the organizational context before Vatican II. During the 1930's, a Catholic Action Movement to make Catholicism a part of the adherents' everyday life arose in Europe and was transplanted to Latin America. Catholic Action emphasized an active role for lay persons, with significant consequence in Latin American where the cultural expectation was for the laity to be passive. By the 1950s, the Catholic Action Movement had organized in so many countries that they convened a conference in Chimbote, Peru on "Catholicism in Latin America." This conference declared that Latin American Catholics lacked instruction in the faith from their Church and that a great revitalization of the faith was needed.[16] While attempting to explain Catholicism's limitations in custom, the conferees described socioeconomic and political realities in Latin America, linking their faith with empirical reality.

Along with the Catholic Action Movement, there was a parallel concern that religion was becoming something practiced by women rather than men. Retreats were organized in Cursillo to help men become more active participants in their faith. The retreats were very selective, with preference given to community leaders likely to influence others in their social groupings.[17] Around this time, there was a great influx of missionaries and priests to Latin America bringing new ideas, lifestyles, cultural understandings and expectations. All of these factors contributed to a growing demand for a more responsive Church. These tendencies began with European ideas, movements and policies and were then applied to the Latin American experience, as the Vatican II doctrine would be later applied to the Latin American Church at a meeting of the Latin American Episcopal Council in Medellin, Colombia.

---

15 Under the diocesan bishops are the church pastors, fellow priests, diocesan sisters and brothers and if they chose to transfer under the domain of the diocese certain members of religious orders. Religious orders operate under a different structural hierarchy that has larger regions and the connection to the Vatican depends greatly on the historical formation of the group.

16 Edward Cleary, *Crisis and Change* (Maryknoll, NY: Orbis Books, 1985).

17 Cleary, *Crisis and Change*, p. 4.

Rio 1955: The Creation of Latin American Councils

The first *Consejo Episcopal Latinoamericano* (CELAM) was convened in Rio de Janeiro in 1955, but it is generally regarding as accomplishing little except establishing the organization. Although the Rio Conference is mentioned only briefly in most literature, it is important to note this beginning of the bishops' conferences as potential agents of organizational learning within the region. Before 1955, Church infrastructure was undeveloped in Latin American, such that dialogue was conducted between the Vatican and local dioceses rather than between the Vatican and the regional Church. [18] The bishops served as middle managers through their connections to the Vatican rather than via an organized regional entity. The creation of the regional council conferred upon the bishops regional authority and legitimacy in addition to the authority derived from the Vatican and allowed the them to identify concerns unique to Latin America. CELAM offered a "safety net" to allow lower-level Catholics to trust the mid-level leadership and begin to express their concerns. The CELAM allowed bishops to communicate horizontally, as well as vertically, facilitating learning on the national and regional levels. This allows the Latin American Church to reduce costs of policy implementation and strengthens the institutional bond among regional churches.[19] The creation of CELAM meant that the Latin American Church is not dependent exclusively on Rome for innovation and change.[20] CELAM increases the space for the bishops to exercise the managerial roles discussed previously. The power to reframe information and make corrections gives legitimacy to local concerns and allows an enhancement of the bishops' managerial roles to address the increased demands of the local Church as well as providing the Vatican with information. The bishops' communicative roles increased and conveyed legitimacy to local and regional concerns as justifications for pursuing policies exceptional to the region. The council also provided the bishops an avenue to select (accept or reject), reframe and synthesize doctrine and policies as a group without fear of individual retribution.

Vatican II and the Latin American Church

Earlier in the chapter, we discussed how the roles of the Pope and the college of bishops changed because of the Second Vatican Council, but specific conclusions as to the appropriate role of regional structures like the CELAM were not generated at those meetings. When Vatican II began in 1962, CELAM was still in its infancy; thus, much of Vatican II was spent defining how the regional body would interact with the executive body. A year before the Council began, Pope John XXIII convened a synod in Rome and recommended that other regional churches prepare similarly for

---

18 Cleary, *Crisis and Change*, pp. 5-11.

19 March, *The Pursuit of Organizational Intelligence*, pp. 86-89.

20 Penny Lernoux, "The Long Path to Puebla" in John Eagleston and Philip Scharper, eds., *Puebla and Beyond* (Maryknoll, NY: Orbis Books 1979), p. 11.

Vatican II.[21] This created informal networks of theologians and bishops to support future entrepreneurial actions taken by the Latin American church. Preparation for Vatican II also increased consultation among Latin American countries and active lay groups: "The four year experience of the council brought them together in a way that no other experience had."[22] When it was time for Vatican II, the Latin American countries made up the largest delegation with more than 600 bishops and 319 *periti*.[23] The *periti* proved invaluable in this process of learning because they were mainly young priests, recently graduated from seminaries in Europe, who acted as intellectual bridges to interpret the proceedings for the bishops. What the Latin American bishops learned as individuals during Vatican II would be the impetus for the changes at the subsequent Medellin Council. At this juncture, the Latin American Church was organized as a regional power in the form of the bishops' councils and had the benefit of the Vatican II experience that strengthened their understanding of how the church worked and how they might participant in doctrinal debates.

The papal leadership hoped that Vatican II could pave the way for the Church to move into the future including dealing with such issues as the challenge of science to the faithful. Although there was some concern about the relationship of regional churches to God and His authority through the Church, the relative youth of the CELAM and the papal focus on European and American issues neglected the concerns of the Latin American Church. The papal leadership was reflective about the church; however many of the challenges of developing countries went unaddressed.

After CELAM I in Rio and Vatican II, the bishops in Latin America had the capacity to act as middle managers for the Latin American church. The bishops now had privileged access to both executive and regional information that empowered them to become better middle managers. The bishops accepted Vatican II's new vision of the church to reframe it for the Latin American Church. However, the Latin American bishops' organization was younger then its European and American counterparts and less certain in its relationship with the Vatican. This limited the bishops' inclination to select or reject the Vatican's directives. The bishops would make Vatican II relevant to Latin America at their second conference in Medellin.

Medellin 1968: The Bishops Find their Voice

At their second conference at Medellin in 1968, the bishops reframed Vatican II doctrines to make them relevant to Latin America, a unique experience in that no other regional church had systematically applied Vatican II to the situation of their

---

21 A Synod is a meeting of bishops with their diocese to plan for the future of the diocese. Peter Wigginton, *The Popes of Vatican Council II* (Chicago: Franciscan Press, 1982).

22 Cleary, *Crisis and Change*, pp. 18-19.

23 *Periti* are theological and canonical law advisors. Thomas Reese, *Inside the Vatican*.

local churches.[24] This was particularly important because the influence of the Latin American Church in formulating Vatican II was weak, given that more developed countries' concerns dominated the agenda. The Latin American Church had far more temporal threats than science and modernity – poverty and inequality threatened parishioners' faith in God. Despite the fact that the CELAM was quite new, Vatican II innovations made the Latin Americanization of the Church a logical next step. The bishops' reframing of Vatican II was a consequence of their reflection on the documents and experiences at the Rome council and their knowledge of the socio-economic challenges faced by their parishioners.[25]

Unlike the initial Rio conference, made up of mostly of church dignitaries and intellectuals, the Medellin conference had pastoral representation that brought lower-level personnel, the priests and laity, into the decisionmaking.[26] Another major innovation occurred in the area of methodology; the Medellin conferees modeled their procedures on the thoughts of St. Thomas Aquinas and initiatives laid out in *Gadium et Spes* from the Vatican II council. This methodology entails a system of fact gathering (organizational search in the parlance of organizational learning theory), reflection on those facts, and, finally, the outlining of recommendations. Edward Cleary assesses this change in methodology as "monumental: a shift from a perspective that was dogmatic, deductive and top-to-bottom to one that was exploratory, inductive, and bottom-up."[27] This method also suggests a form of *praxis* that led many liberation theologians to find resonance in Marxism.[28]

The reframing of Vatican II had historical roots in the Catholic Action Movement's description of faith in Latin America as a distinct social reality. Latin American theology, Liberation Theology, is concerned about the material crisis of the faithful. "Latin American theology is more interested in the crisis within reality and less in the repercussions of this crisis on the subject of who may be affected." The bishops selected the *Gadium et Spes* reaffirmation of the Church's option for the poor from among the various Vatican II doctrines. The Jesuits of Latin America reframed *Progresso Popularium* and proclaimed their "desire to cooperate with the clergy and the laity in a joint pastoral effort, to look for a new collaborative structure on which our work might be based."[29] The bishops' only rejection of papal leadership was their lack of consultation. Vatican input at the Medellin conference was minimal except for the Pope's visit, which did not affect the conference's agenda.[30]

---

24 Edward Cleary, "Journey to Santo Domingo" in Alfred T. Hennelly, ed., *Santo Domingo and Beyond* (Maryknoll, NY: Orbis Books 1993), p. 3.

25 Cleary "Journey to Santo Domingo," p. 3.

26 Cleary, *Crisis and Change*, p. 17.

27 Cleary, *Crisis and Change*, pp. 22-23.

28 The method suggested by St. Thomas Aquinas is a form of praxis which may explain why many liberation theologians found resonance in Marxism. Jon Sobrino, *The Church and The Poor* (Maryknoll, NY: Orbis Books, 1984), p. 17.

29 Alfred T. Hennelly, *Theology: Documentary History* (Maryknoll, NY: Orbis Books, 1990), p. 121.

30 Cleary, *Crisis and Change*, p. 45.

The unusual organizing principles and methodologies of the council extended the collegiality of the bishops from the peasants to the archbishops legitimizing input from every stratum of the Church hierarchy.[31] The printing and diffusion of inexpensive copies of doctrine and *Bibles* facilitated a complex learning process in the Latin American church. The bishops funded think tanks, attended numerous meetings, and met with local groups to discuss the issue from a local perspective. The CELAM's reframing of Vatican II, Liberation Theology, was disseminated throughout the Latin American Church and the larger society.

It is important to note that all conferees did not approve the results of Medellin. Alfred Hennelly sees the period following Medellin as a period of great paradox. Most participants demonstrated enormous vitality in spreading the reframed doctrine and results of the conference to the far reaches of Latin America.[32] However, at least 130 bishops did not approve the Medellin conclusions; these dissenters began to mobilize against many of the key tenets of Liberation Theology. This group would work to change the structure of future councils of the bishops and promote a more conservative agenda within the Church. The bishops communicated their actions to the Vatican, but Liberation Theology was not positively received. In future conferences, the Vatican's negative reaction would result in retrenchment of upper-level management and the cooptation of Liberation Theology.

Puebla 1979: Conservative Backlash?

The bishops at Medellin promulgated an important theological treatise with high aspirations, but little guidance for implementation. Debate then shifted to the role of the Church in society: Should the Church be active politically and socially or should it limit itself to concerns of spiritual liberation?[33] The two factions differed on whether the Church's option for the poor referred to the materially poor or the "poor in spirit." This debate continued within CELAM in the period before the Third Conference of Latin American Bishops in Puebla, Mexico. The Vatican, however, began to criticize Liberation Theology and its supporters, encouraging conservative bishops who had not been vocal at the Medellin conference to express their concerns with Liberation Theology.[34] These bishops, with papal backing,

---

31 CELAM, "The Church in Present-day Transformation of Latin America in the Light of the Council" in Alfred T. Hennelly, *Santo Domingo and Beyond* (Maryknoll, NY: Orbis Books 1993), p. 89.

32 Although the term Liberation Theory may designate any theological movement laying emphasis upon the liberating impact of the gospel, it has come to refer to a movement developed in Latin America in the late 1960s, which stressed the role of political action and oriented itself toward the goal of political liberation from poverty and oppression. Alister E. McGrath, *The Blackwell Encyclopedia of Modern Christian Thought* (Malden, MA: Blackwell Publishers, 1995).

33 Cleary, *Crisis and Change*, p. 45.

34 Lernoux, "The Long Path to Puebla," p. 14.

secured the appointment of Archbishop Alfonso Lopez Trujillo, who interpreted the option for the poor as referring to the poor in spirit.

Before the Puebla conference, Archbishop Trujillo also made major changes to depoliticize the legacy of Medellin and increase the influence of conservatives.[35] The Vatican supported these changes by making their representative in the region more conservative and applying pressure. Trujillo next purged CELAM of Medellin supporters by eliminating programs that supported Liberation Theology. Citing budgetary concerns, he closed offices and staffed remaining offices with conservative European theologians.[36] The Pope also used his power of appointment to strengthen the conservative structure of CELAM and to move the Latin American church back to a more centralized model. During the interim between conferences, the poor experienced greater military repression. The Latin American Church's response to the repression was mixed: Argentinean bishops supported the military dictatorship, and parishioners were killed for protesting against dictators in Central America. At Puebla, conservatives' and liberals' contradictory interpretations of Church doctrine and passions came to a head.

The Puebla conference was held in a seminary and only invited guests and press had access to the proceedings. In contrast to the openness at Medellin, participants were upper-level church leaders and selected theologians. To insure success of the centralized agenda, the Pope appointed twelve additional conservative delegates.[37] Three conservative leaders were presiding officers. Before Puebla, Pope John Paul I died, and John Paul II was chosen his successor. John Paul II announced his goal to restore unity to the Catholic Church, interpreted by some as a preference for a return to the centralized authority of the Vatican.[38] At the same time, the Pope reaffirmed the Church's option for the poor with stronger language: "human beings are not pawns in the economic and political processes."[39] Thus, the Pope lent credence to both sides of the centralization-Liberation Theology debate; the Church must address social inequality but avoid cooptation into purely political processes that neglect the spiritual needs of humanity. Instead of mandating change within the Church, John Paul II asserted the power of the Pope but left room for the Latin American bishops to address their own problems.

"Evangelization in Latin America's Present and Future," the theme of the conference, limited the agenda to the spiritual realm. The Pope and Archbishop Trujillo selected theological advisors for the conference. The liberal bishops insisted that many of their theologians come, even though they were not allowed

---

35 Jose Maria Ghio, "The Latin American Church in the Wojtyla Era: New Evangelization or 'Neo-integralism'?" (Notre Dame, IN: Kellogg Institute, 1990), p. 3.

36 Lernoux, "The Long Path to Puebla."

37 Lernoux, "The Long Path to Puebla," pp. 12-13.

38 Ghio, "The Latin American Church in the Wojtyla Era," p. 6.

39 John Paul II, "Opening Address at the Puebla Conference" in John Eagleson and Phillip Scharper, eds., *Puebla and Beyond* (Maryknoll, NY: Orbis Books 1979), p. 63.

to participate directly.[40] The excluded theologians became dissenting voices to the discussion within the official conference, and issued reports to the media in response to announcements from the official conference. Official conferees then responded to the liberals' reports even as they continued to bar them from the meetings. The closed proceeding made it difficult for those representing the various pastoral and parishioner interests to meet with their officials. At the end of the proceedings, a clarification was issued as to the appropriate means to carry out the Medellin directives.[41] Liberation Theology and the primary insights of Medellin were not rejected outright, but bishops' domain to act on behalf of the Church was limited and the spiritual rather than socio-economic and political nature of the Church was reinforced.

As middle managers, the conservative bishops at this conference focused on making the Medellin doctrines compatible with the more centralizing principles of the Church. In hindsight, the unity aspired to by the Pope was not achieved at the very antagonistic conference. The closed doors of the Puebla conference make it difficult to assess which sects of the Church were represented in the debates. It is clear that there were two dissenting parties – those included in the conference and outside. The liberal group criticized the conference and the bishops within responded to this criticism with conservative reframing; thus, the bishops' reframing was very complicated because it reflected two opposing points of view. By contrast, the Medellin conference produced a unified statement that created the impression that the Latin American Church was speaking with one voice, making a reframing of Liberation Theology more difficult. Conservative bishops disagreed with many of the ideas found in Medellin final report, but instead of rejecting them and weakening the Church, they focused on gaining positions of power to change the framing of the debate. This allowed the conservatives to control the Puebla conference, but the debate outside the conference was more disparate. Trujillo attempted to limit the influence of liberal bishops by changing the conference methodology and reframing the agenda to focus on the more spiritual concerns of evangelization. This allowed the debate to be dominated by a spiritual rather than material interpretation of the option for the poor.

The greatest opportunity for creating common ground between these two factions was provided by the Pope, who offered vague admonishments on which everyone could agree. The Pope broadened the debate to be inclusive. The nuanced stance and seemingly inconsistent issues inherent in the option of the poor came from both the Pope and the bishops in the conference. However, the acceptance and selection done by Trujillo set the agenda and limited the scope of the debate. The Pope and Trujillo's appointment of conservative bishops to positions of power within the conference allowed for broad definitions of Liberation Theology in public. However, neither conservatives nor liberals were able to get exactly what they wanted from

40 Moises Sandoval, "Report from the Conference" in John Eagleson and Phillip Scharper, eds., *Puebla and Beyond* (Maryknoll, NY: Orbis Books 1979).

41 Sandoval, "Report from the Conference," pp. 35-36, 41.

the conference in Puebla. Trujillo's attempt to consolidate a conservative majority and turn back Medellin proved incomplete. The liberals made no great advances on their agenda, but still preserved the option for the poor. The bishops' opportunity at Puebla to facilitate organizational learning by combining input from below with executive aspirations was missed by the structuring of the conference. Though the Pope supported a conservative agenda through his appointed members, Trujillo missed an opportunity to strengthen organizational effectiveness and legitimacy on all levels by denying the liberals participation in official meetings.

Santa Domingo 1992: The Triumph of Top-Down Tendencies

Some of the insights of Medellin were legitimized by the final documents of Puebla. The Pope's broader definition of the option for the poor and Liberation Theology provided room for disagreement on how the bishops should proceed. The issue addressed at the 1992 Santo Domingo conference was how the Church might implement evangelization to respond to the realities in Latin America. Edward Cleary contends that the John Paul II leadership became more conservative and concerned with centralizing the power of the Church in the years following the Puebla conference:

> John Paul and the Vatican leadership have reversed many of these trends. Many more conservatives were appointed bishops; progressive experiments were questioned, controlled and quashed ... within a growing climate of control, many bishops and other church leaders occupying the center ground found self-censorship or inactivity preferable to outspoken prophecy.[42]

The Church did not directly opposed Liberation Theology, but shifted support to more conservative organizations rather than trying to seek a balance between the liberal and conservative stances. Most theology schools in South America do not teach Liberation Theology, even though the Pope referred to it as "useful and necessary."[43] The Pope mandated the major themes for the 1992 Santo Domingo conference: evangelization, human promotion, and Christian culture. The conservative leadership of CELAM produced some working documents that addressed the three themes and forwarded them to Rome for approval; they were returned with modifications. This confirms a trend over the three bishops' conferences wherein the Vatican exercised more and more control in setting the agenda. At Medellin the Latin American Church acted more autonomously. Through the appointment of Trujillo, the Vatican tried to control the Puebla agenda. With the Santo Domingo conference, the Vatican mandated the agenda and exercised a final review privilege. Evangelization and human promotion were issues with historical resonance, but the Christian culture theme lacked clarity.

---

42 Cleary, "Journey to Santo Domingo," p. 15.
43 Cleary, "Journey to Santo Domingo," p. 16.

The conference was held on October 12, 1992 the five-hundredth anniversary of the landing of Columbus and the symbolic beginning of evangelization of the Church to Latin America. The structure of the conference continued to include mainly bishops and Vatican officials, rejecting the pastoral focus of Medellin. Months before the meeting the Pope appointed a co-secretary to the proceedings, Bishop Jorge Medina Estevez, a staunch conservative, who had supported Augusto Pinochet in Chile and was opposed by the conference's Chilean bishops.[44] Estevez immediately threw out the working documents formulated by CELAM and approved by the Vatican. This act shows not only a lack of interest, but a strong distaste for any form of local knowledge. The quotation below well illustrates the new relationship between the Vatican and the bishops of Latin America:

> Instead of discussing that document (working document) in plenary sessions, the bishops were subjected for several days to long, primarily conservative and useless lectures that were already familiar to the audience. Finally, they were to break up into smaller working groups or committees, thirty in all that discussed specific issues and problems. Obviously, this division into committees, while useful and perhaps necessary, divided the bishops and further impeded strong leadership among the Latin bishops.[45]

The jettisoning of the working papers left the Latin American bishops no framework from which to work. They selected the Pope's opening address as a framework. The only original Latin American pieces came in the form of exploring the Pope's apology to the indigenous peoples of Latin America and the misuse of Church authority in the region during the first evangelization. While this apology to the indigenous is often interpreted as a continued interest in the ideas set forth in Medellin, it was more to do with recognition of past suffering, than an assessment of contemporary concerns of the lower-level Catholics.

The Vatican had successfully reversed the empowerment of CELAM coming out of the Medellin conference. The Santo Domingo conference was more a lecture on how the Vatican conceptualized the Latin American church rather than an interactive dialogue. The opportunities for bishops to make valuable contributions were minimized. The acceptance role was valued, involving strict interpretation of doctrine with little modification to take into account local input and knowledge. The reframing and selective application of Vatican directives were clearly sanctioned; the conference tolerated little autonomous thought, and communication from below was severely limited. The bishops reframed the Pope's apology to retain the option for the poor, but beyond that local information is so devalued that the bishops are unable to communicate local concerns.

It might now be asked whether the CELAM had become a false symbol of empowerment of the Latin American Church. The acceptance of the Vatican's will seem to be the purpose of the entire conference. The communication of regional concerns is unimportant to the Vatican, with their review, approval and eventual

---

44 Cleary, "Journey to Santo Domingo," p. 18.
45 Cleary, "Journey to Santo Domingo," pp. 26-27.

rejection of CELAM documentation. The bishops have now become a body for policy execution rather than management. Selection and reframing processes are minimized by the lecture (vertical) format of the conference and the demise of the working papers, forcing the bishops to rely on the framework of the Pope's address. The bishops' ability to reject the directives of the Vatican was reduced when the regional organization became hostile to debate, leaving those who rejected the directives of the Vatican open to personal repercussions. The potential for bottom-up learning supported by Vatican II and the Medellin conference was subverted by conservative elements in Rome and Latin America.

Conclusion: Anti-Learning after Medellin

Analyzing the roles of Latin American bishops as middle managers in organizational learning allows us to understand how selecting (accepting and rejecting) and reframing information (in this case doctrine) interacts with processes of empowering and disempowering lower-level input and information. This study also helps us better understand the struggles associated with decentralization of information and power within a dogmatic organization. As the bishops' opportunities for reframing and selection decreased in the policy process, power has become more authoritative and dogmatic within the organization. This study makes clear that the Church never really transferred middle-managerial roles and legitimacy to the Latin American bishops as suggested in the Vatican II documents. Instead, the Vatican participated in anti-learning by sending mixed messages with regard to Church policies.

The Vatican's reaction to the Medellin conference is an example of sustained anti-learning within the organization. The issue for the Church is who may legitimate information. The Pope traditionally had total power of interpretation until Vatican II expanded the power to the bishops. The Latin American bishops interpreted this change to mean that they could select and reframe doctrine to address their specific regional concerns. The Medellin conference legitimized information from lower-level Church personnel. Those embracing the Medellin perspective concluded that the Church's primary function was to address practical concerns of poverty and political disenfranchisement. The Vatican responded to this bottom-up input and interpretation as a threat to its authority to control the principles of the Church, and began to implement defensive routines to undermine the autonomy of the Latin American Church. Chris Argyris labels such defensive routines as a system of anti-learning. Subordinates push for autonomy while the central authority seeks to maintain control. However, efforts to maintain centralized control send the message to middle managers that they are not trusted. To avoid this dilemma, executive leadership uses mixed messages to include those who feel left out and thus maintain control while simultaneously creating an impression of decentralization.[46]

---

46 Argyris, *On Organizational Learning*, pp. 94 and 215.

Earlier in this chapter, we addressed the problem of deliberately vague, mixed messages sent by the executive to subordinates. Vatican II gave authority to the bishops to undertake initiatives for their local churches. This was supported at the official rhetorical level, but in practice, inconsistencies developed between real autonomy and executive control. Definitional changes and ambiguity about the option for the poor and Liberation Theology allowed the Church to promote a very conservative agenda without alienating moderate liberals. Instead of remaining an autonomous entity, the CELAM became an instrument of control for the Vatican, while ostensibly remaining an institution of empowerment for the Latin American Church.

The change in response to Vatican II over the last forty years was more a consequence of organizational control than productive organizational learning. Productive organizational learning was apparent at the Medellin conference when the Latin American Church responded to the changes of Vatican II. The possibility for productive learning existed in Puebla, but was never fully realized. At the Puebla conference, mixed messages were discernible as Trujillo foreclosed debate and reestablished centralized control under the guise of CELAM autonomous action. Successful regaining of control was apparent at the Santo Domingo conference where the discourse deviated from Medellin to the extent that localizing tendencies were not longer discernible. The literature confirms the importance of unrestricted flows of information throughout various organizational levels to optimize effective learning. Mixed messages and defensive routines eventually result in severe organizational dysfunction. The longer these defenses persist the more embedded they become and difficult they are to correct. Theory, thus, suggests the need for a new council to lend provide support to decentralization tendencies to foster a more effective learning Church.

This study may suggest that dogmatic organizations cannot learn for protracted periods of time. Dogmatic organizations may risk the principles they value if they create effective learning organizations. Learning in dogmatic organizations seems more driven by principles and directives from above than knowledge and input from lower-level personnel. Broadening the scope of their fundamental principles would allow dogmatic organizations to accept different and more diverse outcomes as indicators of success. Broadening the principles and indicators of success would, however, translate into less executive control over implementation. In this case, middle managers' ability to select and reframe principles and broaden the goals and indicators of success were restricted by the executive leadership wishing to protect the integrity of the principles.

The current executive leadership seeks to maintain control of the massive organization that is the Catholic Church, which deters productive learning. This allows little flexibility for the bishops to respond to the realities of their parishioners and the world, including problems like pedophilia, poverty, divorce and safe sex. These issues must be addressed at the pastoral level; if the Vatican gives guidance that does not apply regionally then the deacons, priests and bishops may be forced to address them without the Vatican's guidance. Evidence already exists that a duality exists between executive doctrine and practice on the parish level.

This possible dichotomous action within the church signals an extreme case in organizational learning, but provides a good case for critiquing the previous studies of organizational learning. An exclusive analysis of organizational leadership that focuses on the importance of leaders' ideology, charisma or power to persuade, neglects important factors at lower level of the organization particularly relating to practical information and implementation. Alternatively, an exclusive study of the importance of input from the lower levels of an organization may neglect the power exerted by the executive leadership. Both executive and lower-level factors must be taken into account as well as the role of middle managers. Understanding middle managers' role in information selection and reframing is essential to understanding organizational change. Large organizations have mid-level players that are more or less empowered to affect learning. A dogmatic organization, like the Catholic Church, leaves the middle managers with less space for action and fewer opportunities for fostering learning throughout the organization. The theoretical literature suggests that organizations that privilege principles over efficiency may lack the ability to respond to challenges in their ever-changing environment.

Chapter 11

"Getting it Right or Wrong": Organizational Learning about the Physical World[1]

Lynn Eden

In this chapter, I examine how organizations learn—and fail to learn—about the physical world. Of course, most organizations "get it right" about the physical world most of the time. We do not commonly encounter poison mushrooms in the supermarket, elevators hardly ever crash, buildings rarely collapse, and commercial airline operations are almost always safe. Yet, we can think of many cases of organizations "getting it wrong" about the physical world, that is, failing to understand physical processes relevant to their activities, some of which are exceedingly consequential. In November 1940, for example, the Tacoma Narrows Bridge, a large and graceful suspension bridge near Seattle, collapsed from the force exerted by a light wind. As it turned out, and odd as it might sound to us, professionals in the organizations responsible for designing and building the bridge had not sufficiently understood the aerodynamic forces involved. After a century of building suspension bridges, the question is: why not?

More recently, in the summer of 2000, the Forest Service accidentally burned 48,000 acres in Nevada. Evidently the information the Forest Service had about the expected course of a much smaller intentional burn (initiated, ironically, to reduce the probability of a large wild land fire) was incorrect. What had the foresters not understood, and why had they not understood it? More broadly, how do the Forest Service and other organizations experience their histories and draw inferences from them? How do they, as James March and his colleagues claim, encode inferences

---

1 Acknowledgements: I thank Neta Crawford, Ron Hassner, Michael Kenney, Ron Mitchell, Barry O'Neill, Scott Sagan and other colleagues at the Center for International Security and Cooperation, Freeman Spogli Institute for International Studies at Stanford University for brainstorming and trenchant comment. And, again, Michael Kenney for organizing the American Political Science Association panel that led to the earliest version of this chapter, and for excellent and extensive editing thereafter. Some of this chapter appeared in Lynn Eden, *Whole World on Fire: Organizations, Knowledge, and Nuclear Weapons Devastation* (Ithaca, NY: Cornell University Press, 2004).

from richly experienced histories into routines that guide behavior?[2]   What are the processes by which this happens?   We can think of many other instances of catastrophic failure to understand, from design flaws in airplanes, to the O-rings on the Challenger space shuttle, to thousands of gallons of jet fuel burning inside the World Trade Center in 2001.

To address these questions, this chapter analyzes two key concepts: "organizational frames" and "knowledge-laden artifacts and routines."[3] After explicating and briefly outlining the literatures that develop these ideas, I explore several cases of organizations getting it right and getting it wrong about the physical world.

Organizational Frames and Knowledge-Laden Artifacts and Routines

Organizational frames are approaches to problem solving used by organizational personnel.   They include what counts as a problem, how problems are represented, the strategies to be used to solve those problems, and the constraints and requirements placed on possible solutions.[4]

Organizational frames are social constructs. During the creation of organizations, and during periods of organizational redefinition or upheaval, actors articulate organizational goals and draw on and modify existing understandings, or knowledge, of the social and physical environment in which they operate. This creates frameworks for action that structure how those in organizations identify problems and find solutions.   Organizational frames encounter the present and look to the future.   At the same time, they embody the past: foundational understandings of organizational mission, long-standing collective assumptions and knowledge about the world, and earlier patterns of attention to problems and solutions.[5]

---

2   See Barbara Levitt and James G. March, "Organizational Learning," *Annual Review of Sociology* vol. 14 (1988), pp. 319-340; and James G. March, Lee S. Sproull, and Michal Tamuz, "Learning from Samples of One or Fewer," *Organization Science* vol. 2 (1991), pp. 1-13.

3   See Eden, *Whole World on Fire*.

4   My definition of organizational frame borrows from the sociologist of technology Wiebe Bijker's definition of "technological frame"—inflected by Herbert Simon.   I use a somewhat broader notion than Bijker, explicitly place it in organizational context, and emphasize the organizational determinants of what problems are to be solved. See Bijker's definition of "technological frame" in his *Of Bicycles, Bakelites, and Bulbs: Toward a Theory of Sociotechnical Change* (Cambridge, MA: MIT Press, 1995), especially pp. 122-127. Frames are a way to understand how organizations experience their histories: they carry those histories within them as they solve problems—in the form of understandings about their goals, and understandings of what is known and what is not, what is knowable and what is not, and what problems can and cannot be solved.

5   Like Bijker's notion of technological frames, the concept of organizational frames draws on Thomas Kuhn's "paradigms"—but neither technological frames nor organizational frames are encompassing conceptual world-views. They are, rather, paradigms writ small.

As organizations solve problems, they embed their solutions in artifacts and in knowledge-laden routines. Like Levitt and March, I'm suggesting that although organizations learn and solve problems based on their histories, these histories are interpreted through frames and story lines constructed by participants seeking to understand their experience. Once solutions are encoded into knowledge-laden routines and artifacts, they enable organizations to carry out new actions and at the same time sharply constrain what organizations can do. What is learned by organizations and guides their problem solving, is "influenced less by history than by the frames applied to that history."[6]

We know from the sociology of technology that artifacts—created and invented things—carry knowledge and social relationships within. Think of light bulbs, refrigerators, bicycles, bridges, and nuclear weapons. And, we know from organizational studies that routines store experience, that is, knowledge, but also that the cognitive content of routines is difficult to study.[7] This probably explains why nuanced empirical analyses of these phenomena are few. Powerful empirical analyses include Edwin Hutchins's widely reprinted discussion of the distributed knowledge immanent in the organizational shipboard routine for dead reckoning, and Diane Vaughan's rich analysis of cognition in organizational routines in *The Challenger Launch Decision*.[8]

There is a close relationship between frames and knowledge-laden artifacts and routines. Frames can be seen, or "read," in artifacts and routines. In *Whole World on Fire*, about how and why US nuclear weapons damage has been seriously underestimated, and, in particular, why blast damage has been well predicted but potentially more devastating mass fire (popularly termed "firestorm") damage has been largely ignored, I find that organizational concentration on predicting blast damage (the blast damage frame) resulted in increasingly refined predictions about such damage. That predictive knowledge is stored in both artifacts and organizational routines. The main artifact was a handbook, revised over many years and written in a kind of code; the main knowledge-laden routine is what war planners do with the

See Thomas S. Kuhn, *The Structure of Scientific Revolutions* (Chicago: University of Chicago Press, 1962 and 1996).

6   See Levitt and March, "Organizational Learning," p. 324.

7   Michael D. Cohen ad Paul Bacdayan, "Organizational Routines Are Stored as Procedural Memory," *Organization Science*, vol. 5 (1994), reprinted in Michael D. Cohen and Lee S. Sproull, *Organizational Learning* (Thousand Oaks, CA: Sage, 1996), pp. 405-407.

8   Edwin Hutchins, "Organizing Work by Adaptation," *Organizational Science*, vol. 2 (1991), reprinted in Cohen and Sproull, *Organizational Learning*, pp. 20-57; Diane Vaughan, *The Challenger Launch Decision: Risky Technology, Culture, and Deviance at NASA* (Chicago: University of Chicago Press, 1996); see also Martha S. Feldman and Brian T. Pentland, "Reconceptualizing Organizational Routines as a Source of Flexibility and Change," *Administrative Science Quarterly*, vol. 48 (2003), pp. 94-118; Martha S. Feldman, "Resources in Emerging Structures and Processes of Change," *Organization Science*, vol. 15 (2004), pp. 295-309; and James G. March, Martin Schulz, and Xueguang Zhou, *The Dynamics of Rules: Change in Written Organizational Codes* (Stanford, CA: Stanford University Press, 2000).

handbook as they plan nuclear war. Of course, the knowledge in the handbook is now stored in computer software, that is, computer programs or routines; the verb is now built into the artifact itself. The handbook and the routines represent organizational learning. They are solutions that we can analyze to see the problems that actors tackled, the knowledge base from which they worked, and the organizational goals that they pursued.[9]

Yet frames do more than shape organizational attention, knowledge, and action. The process of identifying problems and finding solutions shapes organizations themselves. As part of problem-solving activity, actors build organizational capacity to solve problems, and this, in turn, affects relatively enduring features of organizations: the expertise brought into or developed by organizations, specialized activity to carry out large-scale research, and routines developed within organizations, including knowledge-laden routines that embody and apply knowledge gained in research activities. Thus, frames can be discerned not only in organizational routines, but also in enduring features of organizations like organizational expertise and other specialized activities.

Learning about the Physical World

Being sensitive to organizational goals, existing states of knowledge, problem-solving approaches pursued by those in organizations, and artifacts and routines as solutions to those problems, what can we say about the determinants of organizations getting it right and getting it wrong about the physical world?

Table 11.1 below highlights four organizational approaches to problem solving. All involve organizational learning, that is, encoding inferences from history, or experience, into artifacts and knowledge-laden routines via specific problem-solving frames. But in some cases, organizations draw inferences from experience to accurately predict physical processes, in other cases not. In addition, organizations may adhere to very high contemporary standards of professional practice; they do not suppress evidence or disregard or distort a well-understood body of knowledge. In other cases, however, organizations do not adhere to best practice; they neglect, suppress, or lie about evidence and the state of knowledge.

Thus, we see four categories of organizational action. In the first category, physical processes are well understood by organizational problem solvers. In addition, organizational actions are consistent with best practice. Consequently, resulting technologies and knowledge-laden routines are reliable and safe. This is the world each of us hopes to live in all the time, a world in which ships float, buildings are structurally sound, elevators are safe, airplanes fly as expected, and mushrooms and meat in the supermarket are untainted.

---

9 Eden, *Whole World on Fire*; p. 33 illustrates a page from the war planners' handbook.

Table 11.1 Organizational Approaches to Problem Solving

Category	Physical processes well understood?	Organizational actions consistent with best practice?	Potential results	Examples
1) "Bright" side	Yes	Yes	Technologies and knowledge-laden routines are reliable and safe	Ships float; buildings stand up; food is safe
2) "Dark" side	Yes	No	Dire consequences as organizational actors neglect, suppress, or lie about the state of knowledge, usually for profit	Cigarette industry after 1960; Ford Pinto gas tanks; Firestone tires; Paxil time-release manufacture
3) "Dumb and dark" side	No	No	Dire consequences, but was there negligence in organizational actors' interpretation of evidence?	Mad cow disease; *Challenger* explosion; Cerro Grande fire; Johns Hopkins hexamethonium drug trial
4) "Ignorant but upright"	No	Yes	Dire or potentially dire consequences due to poorly understood physical processes reflected in knowledge-laden routines	*Titanic*; effects of burning jet fuel in World Trade Center; tsunami prediction in December 2004 Sumatra-Andaman earthquake; partial prediction of nuclear weapons damage; but disaster averted at Citicorp Center

Second, there is the "dark" side of organizations, the world of corporate wrongdoing and crime, in which physical processes are well understood, but organizational approaches to problem solving fly in the face of contemporary best practice: Organizational actors neglect, suppress, or lie about evidence and the state of knowledge. In these cases, the pursuit of craven organizational interests in profit or, rarely, organizational or national pride, cause people in positions of responsibility to ignore physical processes that they could, and should, understand. Examples include the cigarette industry after about 1960, when the connection between lung cancer and cigarette smoking had been clearly established and the industry both denied the state of knowledge and suppressed and twisted evidence; the suppression of evidence of danger in the Corvair automobile that rolled over; the decision not to change the design of the Ford Pinto gas tank that exploded; and the continued manufacture and sale of Firestone tires that shredded. Other examples include French officials who did not prevent contamination of their national blood supply by the HIV virus; builders in India who did not construct buildings to code which led to disastrous collapses in a large earthquake in early 2001; British manufacturers dumping in Europe thousands of tons of feed suspected of causing mad cow disease after the feed had been banned in the United Kingdom; and the GlaxoSmithKline drug company claiming that unresolved quality control problems with its "controlled release" version of Paxil, were, in the words of the *New York Times*, "unlikely ever to hurt patients. Patients who took an inert half of Paxil CR would be no worse off than if they had simply skipped a day's dose." This argument was not accepted by the US Food and Drug Administration, which said that it, and the Department of Justice "will not allow drug manufacturers to ignore our high public health standards for drug manufacturing,"[10] In these cases, organizations learned from experience, but their learning was harnessed for deeply self-interested purposes. (Chapters 8 and 9 discuss drug traffickers and terrorists learning for deeply malign purposes.) In terms of their knowledge and understanding of the physical world, they got it right; in terms of their acts, they then did wrong.

Third is the "dumb and dark" side of organizations in which problem solvers poorly understand relevant physical processes, and their approaches to problem solving are inconsistent with contemporary best practice. These cases often raise difficult questions about what could and should have been known, whether evidence was interpreted poorly, and if action was taken without proper precaution. Was there negligence, in other words, and if so, to what degree, and why? Examples include the profitable use of sheep remains in cattle feed in Britain in the 1970s in the face of some early warnings of risk, which resulted in what we now know as mad cow disease; and the conduct of clinical trials for an asthma study at Johns Hopkins medical school that resulted in the death of a participant. The study "failed to obtain published literature about the known association between hexamethonium [the drug

10 On corporate wrong-doing, see Robert Jackall, *Moral Mazes: The World of Corporate Managers* (New York: Oxford University Press, 1988); Diane Vaughan, "The Dark Side of Organizations: Mistake, Misconduct, and Disaster," *Annual Review of Sociology* vol. 25 (1999), pp. 271-305; and the discussion of power, interest, and production pressures in Charles Perrow, *Normal Accidents: Living with High-Risk Technologies*, with a new afterword (Princeton, NJ: Princeton University Press, 1999). On mad cow disease, see Suzanne Daley, "Mad Cow Disease Panicking Europe as Incidents Rise," *New York Times* (December 1, 2000). For discussion of Paxil, see Gardiner Harris, "F.D.A. Seizes Millions of Pills From Pharmaceutical Plants," *New York Times* (March 5, 2005).

used in the study] and lung toxicity," which was "readily available," and violated federal regulations that required, among other things, the convening of face-to-face meetings of medical review boards overseeing such studies.[11]

Another example of the dumb and dark side is the accidental burning by the U.S. Park Service of 48,000 acres (75 square miles) in the Cerro Grande fire near Los Alamos National Laboratory in May 2000. Eighteen thousand residents were evacuated, hundreds of homes were destroyed or damaged, and total damage was estimated at US$1 billion. In a contingency never planned for, the nuclear weapons laboratory itself was threatened, and forty laboratory structures were destroyed.[12] This gigantic wildland fire resulted from a deliberately set, or prescribed, fire going out of control. First, the prescribed fire burned beyond its boundaries and then, to contain it, a backfire was introduced that, in conjunction with the wind and seasonal conditions, was disastrous.[13] A National Park Service board of inquiry found that "questionable judgment was exercised" but that there were "no violations of policy."[14] It is clear that Park Service fire managers did not understand the risks, and this was due partly to procedural problems in risk assessment. The National Weather Service did not predict winds in their three- to five-day forecast due to constantly changing conditions, and Park Service personnel evidently took that to mean high winds were not expected. Indeed, the Park Service official in charge "said that if he had better information on the wind... he would not have introduced fire... into the burn area."[15] Yet, a General Accounting Office (GAO) study said, "This time of year typically brings high winds, [further,] the area was in the midst of a 3-year drought.... Also, during the 2-week period before the fire was started ... four prescribed fires got out of control in that region."[16] Another procedural problem was that the fire complexity ratings for prescribed fires had been mistranscribed on the website used by National

---

11 Office of Human Research Protections (OHRP), US Department of Health and Human Services, letter to Johns Hopkins University School of Medicine suspending all of the school's human subjects research (July 19, 2001); Thanks to Roz Leiser for a copy of this widely circulated e-mail message; see also James Glanz, "Clues of Asthma Study Risks May Have Been Overlooked," *New York Times* (July 27, 2001).

12 Barry T. Hill, General Accounting Office, Testimony before the Subcommittee on Forest and Forest Health, Committee on Resources, House of Representatives, "Fire Management: Lessons Learned from the Cerro Grande (Los Alamos) Fire and Actions Needed to Reduce Fire Risks," released August 14, 2000, GAO/T-RCED-00-273, pp. 1, 34. This and the two reports cited below are available at <http://www.nps.gov/cerrogrande>.

13 Report by a panel of the National Academy of Public Administration for the US Department of Interior, *Study of the Implementation of the Federal Wildland Fire Policy*, Phase I Report: *Perspectives on Cerro Grande and Recommended Issues for Further Study* (n.p., December 2000), pp. 14-15.

14 [National Park Service] Board of Inquiry, Final Report, *Cerro Grande Prescribed Fire* (n.p., National Park Service, February 26, 2001), p. i.

15 [National Park Service] Board of Inquiry, *Cerro Grande Prescribed Fire*, p. 33; Hill, "Fire Management," p. 11.

16 Hill, "Fire Management," p. 5.

Park Service fire managers, resulting in a significant underestimate of the difficulties that could be encountered. Given evident incompetence and inadequate procedures, the GAO recommended that prescribed burn plans "need to be 'peer-reviewed' by independent, knowledgeable individuals."[17]

A concluding example of the dumb and dark side of organizational problem solving is the US space shuttle program's understanding of the behavior of the O-rings that sealed in the hot propellant gases in the shuttle's booster rockets—the failure of which resulted in the explosion of the *Challenger* on January 28, 1986. The engineers did not understand the mechanisms of sealing in cold weather (although they thought they did), nor did they clearly see the correlation of cold temperature and erosion of the O-rings by hot gases. But were they negligent in not understanding these complicated processes? On the one hand, they believed they were following best practice, and in many respects they were. On the other hand, in part due to design compromises (and all projects have design compromises), the difficulty of understanding the sealing mechanisms, and the scale and complexity of the whole enterprise that caused them not to know what they did not know, they unwittingly departed from best practice in a process Diane Vaughan terms the "normalization of deviance." It appears that the catastrophic failure of the *Columbia* space shuttle on February 1, 2003, reflects a similar "incremental descent into poor judgment."[18]

In these examples, organizational history and goals contributed to incompetent problem solving for physical processes that were not well understood. Explicit or implicit pressure from the top to proceed seems likely. In addition, precaution can be mind-bogglingly expensive in the short term, though not as costly as the consequences that may result.[19]

Finally, let us turn to the fourth category in which poorly understood physical processes, embodied in knowledge-laden artifacts, technologies, and routines, combine with best contemporary practice to produce dire or potentially dire consequences. In addition to military planners' partial predictions of nuclear weapons damage, there are other striking examples. These include medical practitioners' ignorance about the spread of childbed, or puerperal, fever in the eighteenth and nineteenth centuries— "the most serious, deadly, and terrifying of all the complications of childbirth and the most common cause of maternal deaths" in this period;[20] shipbuilders' lack of

---

17 [National Park Service] Board of Inquiry, *Cerro Grande Prescribed Fire*, pp. 14-22; Hill, "Fire Management," pp. 4, 6.

18 Vaughan, *Challenger Launch Decision*, pp. 119-195; Diane Vaughan, quoted in John Schwartz with Matthew L. Wald, "Echoes of Challenger: Shuttle Panel Considers Longstanding Flaws in NASA's System," *New York Times* (April 13, 2003).

19 On the precautionary principle, see Commission of the European Communities, "Communication from the Commission on the precautionary principle," COM 2000, 1 (Brussels, February 2, 2000), <http://europa.eu.int/comm/dgs/health_consumer/library/pub/pub07_en.pdf>.

20 The definitive account is Irvine Loudon, *The Tragedy of Childbed Fever* (Oxford: Oxford University Press, 2000), quoted on p. 15. Thanks to Ron Hassner for telling me about this case and for finding sources for this and several of the cases discussed above.

knowledge about the *Titanic*'s steel plates, which proved tragically brittle in cold water; structural engineers' ignorance of the impact of dynamic loads on suspension bridges that resulted in the sudden collapse of the Tacoma Narrows Bridge on November 7, 1940; building engineers' failure to calculate certain forces on New York's Citicorp Center in the 1970s, which could have resulted in a catastrophic collapse; the failure of World Trade Center engineers to consider the damage that would be produced by thousands of gallons of jet fuel burning inside the building, even as they designed the building to withstand the impact of a Boeing 707, the largest jet airliner of the early 1960s; and the lack of scientific understanding of the catastrophic potential of a tsunami immediately following the Sumatra-Andaman earthquake on December 26, 2004.[21]

These examples—and there are many others—are especially troubling because they involve no willful misinterpretation of evidence or obvious deviation from best practice. This suggests that incentives to stimulate organizational learning will not necessarily result in valid knowledge since competent, even preeminent, practitioners are already doing the best they can and acting with integrity.

This does not mean that nothing can be done. These examples represent a wide range of outcomes in which greater understanding of the physical world developed from samples ranging from one to many. The learning that paved the way to solution occurred after persistent failure (childbed fever) or a single failure (the *Titanic*, Tacoma Narrows Bridge, and World Trade Center). The examples also suggest that dire consequences can be averted (Citicorp Center) or may remain unrecognized altogether (underestimates of nuclear weapons damage). Thus, the cases have implications both for understanding dire consequences and for preventing disaster.

Let us begin with a case of learning in the face of repeated failure, childbed fever. In the eighteenth and nineteenth centuries, lying-in hospitals for women in childbirth became widespread in Europe. These hospitals provided rest and nutrition for women, professional delivery by midwives and doctors, and training facilities for midwives and medical students. One problem associated with these hospitals was the very high rate of childbed fever. Within a few days after delivery, affected mothers began to suffer from terrible shivers and fevers, excruciating abdominal pain, and, often, death. Sometimes entire maternity wards would suffer epidemics in which "nearly every patient died."[22]

Drawing on current medical knowledge, doctors tried to understand the problem. French doctors who did postmortems on the affected women observed a milky white substance covering the intestines and omentum and theorized that breast milk had metastasized to the abdominal cavity. An English doctor thought it was due to the "putridity" of the indoor atmosphere in which, deprived of an essential ingredient, the air became "vitiated." Others thought childbed fever was due to miasmas—

---

21 Andrew C. Revkin, "Gauging Disaster: How Scientists and Victims Watched Helplessly," *New York Times* (December 31, 2004); Brooks Hanson, "Learning from Natural Disasters," and the articles following in *Science* vol. 308 (May 20, 2005), p. 1125 ff.

22 Loudon, *The Tragedy of Childbed Fever*, p. 22.

odorless materials in the air emanating from vegetable decomposition—or to "mental depression, malnutrition, or its opposite," gluttony.[23]

Outbreaks of childbed fever were sometimes associated with particular midwives and doctors, but until the early 1850s, no one thought that midwives and doctors themselves might play a role. However, as part of their training, medical students performed postmortem examinations and then routinely went from examining cadavers to delivering women—without washing their hands. And they went from mother to mother delivering babies—again without washing their hands.[24] Their knowledge-laden childbirth routines did not include hand washing for the same reason that we do not routinely stand on our heads before taking tests: They understood no causal connection. It was not until the last quarter of the nineteenth century, after the development of the germ theory and its incorporation into hospital practices of antisepsis and sterilization—thanks largely to the physician Joseph Lister—that incidents of childbed fever, caused primarily by streptococcal bacteria, declined dramatically.[25] Until germ theory was developed, the theoretical knowledge base from which medical practitioners could learn practical solutions for childbed fever simply did not exist.

The ship *Titanic*, which sank in 1912 when it hit an iceberg in the North Atlantic, is similar in one way: Knowledge of the time was inadequate to prevent catastrophe or to directly address it after. The proximate cause of disaster was the flooding of the forward five compartments in the ship, which as every moviegoer now knows, had been designed to withstand flooding in the first four. The design itself, which set new marks for safety, cannot be faulted by contemporary standards. For many years the prevailing theory held that the iceberg had torn a large continuous gash in the side of the ship. But when the ship was found at the bottom of the ocean many years later, it turned out that the iceberg had not forcefully punctured the side; rather, the pressure of the iceberg had caused the ship's inch-thick steel plates to buckle and to open in several thin discontinuous slits. The plates had buckled because they were brittle in cold water.[26]

Contemporaries understood that brittle metal was a problem in shipbuilding. For that reason the *Titanic*'s steel plates were not made by the Bessemer process, which produced brittle steel, particularly at low temperatures (due to its high nitrogen content). The only other manufacturing method available at the time was the open-hearth process, which was most commonly done in acid-lined tubs. The acid-lined tubs produced steel with a high sulfur content and other chemicals that,

---

23 Loudon, *The Tragedy of Childbed Fever*, pp. 18-19, 21, 79-82.

24 Loudon, *The Tragedy of Childbed Fever*, p. 89.

25 Loudon, *The Tragedy of Childbed Fever*, pp. 95, 130 ff.

26 This paragraph is drawn from *James Cameron's "Titanic" Explorer* (Fox Interactive CD-ROM, 1997); and Katherine Felkins, H. P. Leighly, Jr., and A. Jankovic, "The Royal Mail Ship *Titanic*: Did a Metallurgical Failure Cause a Night to Remember?" *JOM* [formerly *Journal of Metals*] vol. 50 (1998), pp. 12-18.

as it turned out, also embrittled steel and produced a hull "not suited for service at low temperatures."[27]

Given the lengths to which the *Titanic*'s builders went to design and build a safe ship, it seems highly unlikely that they were aware of the effects of their manufacturing methods. Whether steel makers and metallurgists did not understand how the acid-lined tubs interacted with the steel being produced, or could not analyze the steel content and/or the embrittling effects of certain chemicals, it seems likely that no one understood the vulnerability of the steel produced for the *Titanic*. If the required knowledge was not beyond the theoretical knowledge base of the time (and I do not know whether it was or was not), in all likelihood it was beyond the knowledge available to the organizations and practitioners involved in steel production.

Three other cases illustrate failure to understand physical processes within a context of high professional standards. In the Tacoma Narrows Bridge collapse in 1940 and in the serious design errors in the Citicorp Center in the 1970s, the required understandings of physical processes were well within the knowledge base of contemporaries and, hence, were more amenable to solution. In these cases, the failures lay in the problems engineers sought to solve, and the problems they did not.

At the time it was built, the Tacoma Narrows Bridge near Seattle was the third longest suspension bridge in the world (after the Golden Gate Bridge in San Francisco and the George Washington Bridge in New York). From the time it opened in 1940, the bridge, known as "Galloping Gertie," undulated in the wind. Flexible suspension bridges were not unusual in this period and were frequently stiffened after construction. Engineers observed the bridge and began to take steps to reduce the sway, but no one expected a catastrophic failure. A few months after it opened, in a light wind in early November, the bridge not only swayed but began to twist, the sides of the roadway seesawing. Within a short time, the bridge tore itself apart and collapsed.[28] Fortunately, the bridge was closed to traffic that day, and no one was killed.

Eminent engineer Leon Moisseiff designed the bridge within well-established suspension bridge design principles of the period. Modern engineers had developed what appeared to be robust design algorithms that calculated wind forces on bridges as static, or steady, forces rather than as dynamic forces. Using this method, they worked within a "design climate" in which they focused on principles of structural simplicity and aesthetics to produce "ever longer, slenderer, and lighter suspension bridges."[29] The methods they used had been successful in the George Washington

---

27 Felkins, Leighly, and Jankovic, "The Royal Mail Ship *Titanic*."

28 Matthys Levy and Mario Salvadori, *Why Buildings Fall Down: How Structures Fail* (New York: Norton, 1992), pp. 109-119; Henry Petroski, *Design Paradigms: Case Histories of Error and Judgment in Engineering* (Cambridge: Cambridge University Press, 1994), pp. 144-165, and *Engineers of Dreams: Great Bridge Builders and the Spanning of America* (New York: Vintage, 1995), pp. 294-308.

29 Petroski, *Design Paradigms*, pp. 151, 155.

Bridge, built in the 1920s, and in later suspension bridges. However, the algorithms poorly represented the forces on the bridges, although bridge engineers were unaware of it at the time. Engineers modeled the wind forces pushing sideways on the roadway, but they did not take into account the forces that could lift the road and drag it down, much like an airplane wing. It was these forces that would cause the Tacoma Narrows Bridge to twist and collapse.[30]

Clearly, the effects of dynamic forces on bridges were beyond bridge designers' understanding at the time. But the new field of aerodynamics, used in the design of airplanes in the 1930s, provided precisely the dynamic analysis that was needed for suspension bridge building. Indeed, engineer W. Watters Pagon published a series of eight articles on aerodynamics in the 1930s—the first titled "What Aerodynamics Can Teach the Civil Engineer." However, according to author-engineer Henry Petroski, "the whole series seems largely to have been ignored by the bridge builders," in large part because "bridge building was becoming so highly specialized that there was the 'danger of losing contact with the other branches of engineering and with allied sciences.'"[31] In this case, a fully developed knowledge base was available, but bridge builders did not make use of it.

A more recent case illustrates other oversights. In the early 1970s, to accommodate a church on a corner of the building site of the planned fifty-nine-story Citicorp Center in New York, the structural engineer William J. LeMessurier decided to support the building's steel skeleton on four massive columns placed at the center of each side rather than at the corners as was usually done; he also used an innovative system of steel braces to provide strength against the wind. But when an engineering student challenged the strength of the completed structure, LeMessurier found, to his great surprise, that the steel braces were not as strong as he had expected against winds hitting the building from the corners, called quartering winds. The New York City building code required only that the perpendicular winds pushing face-on to the structure be calculated, but LeMessurier had also calculated quartering winds in the design; in particular, the massive columns placed in the center of each side were unusually strong against them. Although the engineer's recalculations showed that the strain on the braces was greater than anticipated, it was well within the margin of safety, all other things being equal.[32]

But all other things were not equal. In his reexamination, LeMessurier also discovered that the joints that held together the building's steel girders had not been built to his original specifications. Instead, his office had approved a change recommended by the construction company that the joints be bolted instead of

30 The algorithm, based on "deflection theory," is explained in Petroski, *Design Paradigms*, pp. 158-159; and *Engineers of Dreams*, pp. 293, 298-303. The lift and drag on the Tacoma Narrows Bridge is most clearly explained in Levy and Salvadori, *Why Buildings Fall Down*, pp. 118-119.

31 Petroski, *Engineers of Dreams*, p. 302, and quoting Glenn Woodruff, an associate of Moisseiff's, p. 305.

32 The account in this and the following paragraphs is drawn from Joe Morgenstern's "The Fifty-Nine-Story Crisis," *New Yorker* (May 29, 1995), pp. 45-53.

welded, on the grounds that welds were stronger than necessary. This was not a question of improper procedure or shoddy construction. The problem was that in designing the bolts, LeMessurier's office had not considered the sensitivity to quartering winds. This, plus another "subtle conceptual error," meant that the Citicorp building could fail catastrophically in a "sixteen-year storm"—a storm with a probability of occurring once every sixteen years.

After contemplating silence or suicide, LeMessurier explained the problem to the building's lawyers, architects, insurers, and owners. Emergency repairs were made, and disaster averted. In this example at least, catastrophe was not necessary for the relevant actors to learn from history; rather, they simulated a hypothetical future history by calculating forces on the structure.

We might be tempted to say that the structural engineers in the Citicorp Center case were not adhering to best practice, since best practice would dictate that buildings not be so vulnerable to wind forces. Yet, as with the Tacoma Narrows Bridge, the engineers involved were at the top of their profession, they *defined* best practice, and their oversights were not obvious at the time. At the same time, the understanding of the physical processes involved was well within the knowledge base of civil engineering. The framing of problems caused a lack of attention to particular wind loads on these structures.

Finally, the effects of burning jet fuel inside the towers of the World Trade Center may seem like a failure to anticipate the social environment rather than the physical one. Retrospective analysis notwithstanding, I find it hard not to agree with then National Security Advisor Condoleezza Rice's statement that "I don't think anybody could have predicted that these people would take an airplane and slam it into the World Trade Center."[33] Yet, Leslie Robertson, the engineer in charge of the structural design of the towers, did consider the contingency of the largest jet aircraft at the time, a Boeing 707, hitting the building, and he designed the building to withstand its impact.

> I listed all the bad things that could happen to a building and tried to design for them. I thought of the B-25 bomber, lost in the fog, that hit the Empire State Building in 1945. The 707 was the state-of-the-art airplane then, and the Port Authority was quite amenable to considering the effect of an airplane as a design criterion. We studied it, and designed for the impact of such an aircraft.[34]

But for all their devotion to detail and historical contingency, Robertson and his engineering team did not design for thousands of gallons of fuel burning inside the

---

33 Rice, quoted in David Johnson and James Risen, "Traces of Terrorism: The Intelligence Reports; Series of Warnings," *New York Times* (May 17, 2002).

34 Robertson quoted in John Seabrook, "The Tower Builder," *New Yorker* (November 19, 2001), <http://www.newyorker.com/fact/content/articles/011119fa_FACT >.

building.[35] Why not? According to Robertson, after designing for the impact of an aircraft,

> The next step would have been to think about the fuel load, and I've been searching my brain, but I don't know what happened there, whether in all our testing we thought about it. Now we know what happens—it explodes. I don't know if we considered the fire damage that would cause. Anyway, the architect, not the engineer, is the one who specifies the fire system.[36]

Aircraft impact, force, and structural response were anticipated, but potential fire damage was overlooked.

We see in these examples a range of determinants for understanding physical processes. At one extreme are the spread of childbed fever and the brittleness of the *Titanic*'s steel plates, which were beyond the ability of every contemporary to understand. In such cases, the background state of knowledge about the physical world defines and delimits organizational learning, including how problems are cast and solutions developed.

In the other examples, the requisite knowledge base about the physical world was, at least in theory, available to contemporaries. In these cases, the key lay in how problems were represented and solutions were defined—organizational frames. For example, had the designers of suspension bridges been familiar with aerodynamics, they could have much more quickly understood the forces on the Tacoma Narrows Bridge and would have solved structural design problems differently. Had the *Challenger*'s engineers been deeply grounded in statistical analysis or graphical analysis, they would have seen the danger of launching the *Challenger* shuttle in record-cold weather.[37] Environmental feedback can indicate that a severe problem exists, but contemporaries may be unable to diagnosis the problem or solve it (childbed fever). On the other hand, contemporaries may have the ability to recognize a problem before there is any direct indication that a problem exists (Citicorp).[38]

We can see that feedback from the environment is *always* mediated through social expectations, whether at the organizational or societal level. For example, at the organizational and professional level, the flexibility of suspension bridges, even the galloping of Gertie, did not lead bridge designers to think there was a serious problem in their calculations of forces. They expected the swaying and thought

35 Abolhassan Astaneh-Asl, interviewed by Terry Gross, *Fresh Air*, National Public Radio (October 16, 2001), transcript available at <http://www.npr.org>.

36 Seabrook, "The Tower Builder."

37 Frederick Lighthall, "Launching the Space Shuttle *Challenger*: Disciplinary Deficiencies in the Analysis of Engineering Data," *IEEE Transactions on Engineering Management*, vol. 39 (1991), pp. 63-74; Edward R. Tufte, *Visual Explanations: Images and Quantities, Evidence and Narrative* (Cheshire, CT: Graphics Press, 1997), pp. 38-53.

38 On learning from failure, see Petroski, *Design Paradigms*; on learning from near failure, see March, Sproull, and Tamuz, "Learning from Samples of One or Fewer."

they understood its causes. Similarly, the *Challenger*'s engineers reinterpreted the increasing erosion of the O-rings as normal and not dangerous.[39] We might think that mobilization for safety occurs when the threat to life is obvious. But even potential or actual deaths are not good predictors of the social acceptability of failures. Why do important problems in airline safety not get addressed until after crashes bring them to public attention? Why have large numbers of deaths from routine medical mistakes persisted for so long?[40] If the Citicorp case suggests that catastrophe need not be a necessary condition for organizational learning from history, the Tacoma Narrows Bridge and the terrorist attacks on the World Trade Center demonstrate that catastrophe, and tragedy, can be powerful teachers. Yet in some cases organizations seem not to learn even then. The *Columbia* space shuttle disaster seems to have been a reprise of organizational assumptions and routines present before the *Challenger* disaster. Nor is it clear just what sort of organizational learning has resulted from September 11. Certainly, many organizations have tried to learn from the experience, including the Department of Homeland Security and the Federal Bureau of Investigation. But many critical vulnerabilities remain, and we do not know how well the United States can anticipate future catastrophic attacks nor how well prepared it might be in the event. And this stems in part from processes beyond the scope of this chapter: nature does not try to outfox us, but states, transnational criminal organizations, and terrorist organizations operate in what Michael Kenney writes about as "competitive learning systems."[41]

Nuclear Weapons Damage

These cases give us a comparative context in which to understand the past sixty years in which the US government has not fully developed or incorporated predictions of mass fire damage into the knowledge-laden organizational routines used in US strategic nuclear war planning. Clearly, the failure to predict fire damage lies at an extreme of persistence (not to say potential consequence), at least among known contemporary examples.

Prior to World War II, US military doctrine was based on a strategy of precision bombing using blast weapons. There was virtually no incendiary capability, and the prediction of damage from high-explosive bombs and the designing of aircraft and operations, that is, solving problems associated with blast damage—the "blast

---

39 Vaughan, *Challenger Launch Decision*, pp. 119-195.

40 Stephen Engelberg and Adam Bryant, "Warnings Unheeded—A Special Report: F.A.A.'s Fatal Fumbles on Commuter Plane's Safety," *New York Times* (February 26, 1995); Peter T. Kilborn, "Ambitious Effort to Cut Mistakes in U.S. Hospitals," *New York Times* (December 26, 1999).

41 Michael Kenney, "From Pablo to Osama: Counter-terrorism Lessons from the War on Drugs," *Survival* vol. 45 (2003), pp. 187-206; and *From Pablo to Osama: Trafficking and Terrorist Networks, Government Bureaucracies, and Competitive Adaptation* (University Park, PA: Pennsylvania State University Press, forthcoming 2007).

damage frame"—was utterly dominant in the air war community. During the extraordinary mobilization of resources in the war, some weapons and analytical capabilities were developed to carry out, predict, and retrospectively assess incendiary bomb damage—the "fire damage frame." Toward the end of the war, the US undertook significant incendiary operations, but they were generally understood as experimental excursions or as effective only under exceptional circumstances. Even at Hiroshima and Nagasaki, both of which suffered extensive damage from atomic firestorms, far more emphasis was placed on the damage caused by blast than by fire.

At the end of the war, as resources decreased dramatically, the Air Force built on its core notions of precision bombing doctrine and the overriding importance of blast as a cause of damage. What had been dominant before the war remained dominant after. The few fire experts employed during the war were demobilized, and went back to their private lives working for insurance companies and fire departments. At the same time, the Air Force hired several professors of civil engineering, from Massachusetts Institute of Technology and the University of Illinois, for example, as consultants to predict nuclear blast damage and to incorporate those predictions into quantitative analytical routines—charts, graphs, etc., the equivalent of a computer program today—to be used by officers in making nuclear targeting plans.

In the same early postwar period, a great deal of new knowledge was acquired regarding nuclear weapons effects in above-ground nuclear tests. But more was learned about blast than about fire. Indeed, in some cases fire effects were *suppressed*—for example, by making buildings highly resistant to fire—in order to better understand blast. By 1954, a sophisticated manual on the effects of nuclear weapons on different types of structures was developed for blast. No such manual was produced for fire.

Even for those who were aware of considerable fire damage from nuclear weapons, because no knowledge-laden artifacts and routines to predict fire damage were being developed, there was no way to take such damage into account. Fire damage was relegated to "bonus effects" which were not computed. Further, the differential development of the blast damage and fire damage frames after the war became self-reinforcing. For example, as military officers tried to make sense of the practices in which they were involved, they developed explanations about how fire damage was less important than blast damage, and how it was too complex to be calculated.

Thus, after World War II, organizational learning continued about blast damage—through retrospective analyses of war-time bombing and experiments in the post-war atmospheric nuclear weapons tests—and this knowledge was incorporated into increasingly sophisticated analytical routines used in war planning. Meanwhile, the very small group of experts who worked within the fire damage frame during the war was completely demobilized after, and a process of organizational forgetting began.

Yet, an understanding of the basic physical processes involved in nuclear fire damage was well within the contemporary physics knowledge base, and had been for many years. The applied knowledge required for damage prediction was not so ready-made as in the case of the Citicorp Center or even the Tacoma Narrows Bridge, i.e., it was not circulating among practicing professionals. Instead, it had to be created, just as all knowledge about nuclear weapons effects had to be made. The physics of the fire environment had to be modeled. The potential variables contributing to fire damage had to be analyzed. The results had to be translated into organizational routines that were consistent with and built on past damage-predicting routines. The key to such learning lay in organizational frames, which defined military planners' views of what mattered and what did not, influencing the mobilization of expertise, resources, and resulting knowledge-laden routines.

One might think that the mass fires at Hiroshima and Nagasaki would have been sufficient indication that fire damage mattered. However, the issue was not understood to be whether nuclear fire damage would sometimes occur, but whether it would occur with enough regularity that it could be robustly predicted. The answer among war planners was thought to be no, and nothing occurred after World War II to shake confidence in the adequacy of this answer. But an example or two demonstrates the role that a different hypothetical history could have played. Had one of the atomic bombs dropped over the Nevada Test Site gone astray and accidentally burned down Las Vegas—approximately 65 miles away—or had the United States inadvertently burned down Moscow in a "limited" nuclear exchange, it seems likely that war planners would have reevaluated the necessity and feasibility of predicting nuclear fire damage. Fortunately for the world, these catastrophes never occurred.

But unfortunately it is often catastrophes that cause us to rethink our understandings of history and to recalibrate how we learn from experience—by making known what was not known, or at least widely known, and putting the pressure of the public's demand for accountability on internal organizational processes. Although professional standards within the nuclear weapons effects community have been high, historically, the issue of nuclear fire damage has been nearly invisible to the public. The lack of visibility resulted from both formal secrecy and opacity. The world of nuclear war planning is a secret one separated from practicing professionals and ordinary citizens.[42] To a large extent, this is a self-policing system in which those with classified knowledge pledge not to divulge it.

Still, it may not be the formal secrecy that has kept the issue from public awareness so much as opacity: Even the available unclassified information is not widely understood. Unlike building design, the technical issues are not familiar to a broad community of practicing professionals. Few outside the government-

---

42 On secrecy and nuclear weapons, see Hugh Gusterson, *Nuclear Rites: A Weapons Laboratory at the End of the Cold War* (Berkeley, CA: University of California Press, 1996), pp. 68-100; Peter J. Westwick, "Secret Science: A Classified Community in the National Laboratories," *Minerva* vol. 38 (2000), pp. 363-391, Westwick's broader *The National Labs: Science in an American System, 1947-1974* (Cambridge, MA: Harvard University Press, 2003). On the implications of government secrecy for democracy, see Daniel Ellsberg, *Secrets: A Memoir of Vietnam and the Pentagon Papers* (New York: Viking, 2002). On the usefulness to technologists of maintaining separate "technical" and "political" spheres, see Donald MacKenzie, *Inventing Accuracy* (Cambridge, MA: MIT Press, 1990), pp. 409-417.

sponsored nuclear weapons effects community have paid attention to these issues or been available to explain them to journalists, scholars, and the wider public. The organizational processes that have determined which problems are solved and which are not are no less important, and these too have been hidden from the public.

No wonder, then, that the lack of prediction of nuclear fire damage has been so persistent. These are largely self-reinforcing organizational processes, sealed off from the public through secrecy and opacity. And since World War II, the consequences of these weapons have been in the realm of the hypothetical.

Conclusion

Thinking in terms of organizational frames, I have mapped out four different sets of organizations "getting it right" and "getting it wrong" about the physical world. When organizations have a poor understanding of the physical world, we want to know about the wider professional practice and state of knowledge, and the kinds of organizational processes operating. Both will matter, but in some cases, organizations will be found to have adhered to high contemporary standards of learning and in other cases not. When they have not—and determining this is likely to be difficult—we then have to figure out why not.

Of course, organizations do not think; people think and approach problems in ways that are structured by organizational history, capacity, and routines. As we have seen, it can be extremely difficult to change organizational approaches to problem solving. Dominant understandings (paradigms), not surprisingly, dominate. Organizations that do not encourage alternatives to, or questioning of, dominant approaches to problem solving may overlook important problems and impede their ability to learn. (In Federal Bureau of Investigation Agent Coleen Rowley's words after the September 11 attacks, this is the "don't rock the boat, don't ask a question" problem.)[43] Queries from the top of an organization, or from outside, regarding technology and the physical world may be answered in ways that simply reflect ongoing approaches to problem solving. Further, change cannot simply be mandated from the top or from outside. To be fully effective, change must be implemented at the level of knowledge-laden routines, algorithms that both represent problems and embody solutions.

In many of the cases discussed in this chapter, organizations developed the knowledge-laden routines that allowed them to get it right about the physical world only following repeated failures, some of them catastrophic. The only alternative to learning from disaster is learning from smaller failures, near failures, and scenarios of possible failure and unforeseen consequences. Precaution regarding the unforeseen is particularly important in a world in which the full consequences of our actions will not be fully known until much later. We have experienced many unforeseen consequences of twentieth-century innovation, from the miracle mineral asbestos

---

43 "Excerpts from Senate Judiciary Committee's Counterterrorism Hearing," *New York Times* (June 7, 2002).

that has proved dangerous to human health to the miracle drugs that are steadily losing their effectiveness in promoting human health. What will the twenty-first century hold? The consequences will be great indeed if, among other things, we do not anticipate the social and ecological consequences of huge construction projects (like the Three Gorges and Narmada dams), if we do not exercise precaution in proceeding with genetically engineered organisms, and if we do not understand the effects of our actions on global warming.

Chapter 12

Unlearning War:
US Military Experience with Stability
Operations

Karen Guttieri

In the first months of the occupation of Iraq, beginning in March 2003, the immediate burden of rebuilding and governance weighed heavily on the military forces of the United States (US)-led coalition. By June 2003, one month after US President George W. Bush declared major combat operations over, one might have expected the coalition's civil administration structure to take the baton of governance from the military. At 1,000 in number, however, the civilian administrators were too few and struggling to operate, even in Baghdad. Unfortunately, the US military teams that assumed much of the responsibility for getting Iraq on its feet also were understaffed and, reportedly, unprepared. A senior Civil Affairs officer – a soldier specifically trained for civil-military aspects of stability operations – told the Washington Post, "We've been given a job that we haven't prepared for, we haven't trained for, that we weren't ready for."[1] One hapless captain, a respiratory therapist from New Hampshire, attempting to get the electricity running in the town of Bani Sad and screening candidates for the new town council, complained, "What we're doing now is never something we expected to do."[2] US military history and field manuals suggest otherwise.

In 1942 in North Africa, General Dwight D. Eisenhower had similar frustrations. The Department of State lacked capacity to manage governance issues, and

---

1   Rajiiv Chandrasekaran, "Inexperienced Hands Guide Iraq Rebuilding," *Washington Post Foreign Service* (June 25, 2003), p. A01. Civil Affairs are "component forces and units organized, trained, and equipped specifically to conduct civil affairs activities and to support civil-military operations," essentially what the Army calls "stability operations." US Department of Defense, "DOD Dictionary of Military Terms," as amended through June 5, 2003, <http://www.dtic.mil/doctrine/jel/doddict/index.html>. According to Army doctrine, "The very nature of stability operations and support operations places our forces in direct contact with civilians, governments, and NGOs. This relationship makes CMO [Civil Military Operations] critical to any stability operation or support operation." United States Army, *Stability and Support Operations* Field Manual FM 3-07, 2003.
2   Chandrasekaran, "Inexperienced Hands."

Eisenhower reckoned with civil matters as "an essential part of active operations."[3] In 1943, the director of the Civil Affairs Division, General John H. Hilldring, expressed the Army's grudging recognition of its duties:

> The Army is not a welfare organization. It is a military machine whose mission is to defeat the enemy on the field of battle. Its interest and activities in military government and civil affairs administration are incidental to the accomplishment of the military mission. Nevertheless, these activities are of paramount importance, as any lack of condition of social stability in an occupied area would be prejudicial to the success of the military effort.[4]

Field manuals designed to guide American officers in war anticipate military operations that continue in the wake of combat. Stability operations are a factor in war and its aftermath. US military doctrine describes four generic campaign phases – deter/engage, seize initiative, decisive operations, and *transition*:

> During hostilities, stability operations help keep armed conflict from spreading, and assist and encourage committed partners. …. Following hostilities, forces may conduct stability operations to provide a secure environment for civil authorities as they work to achieve reconciliation, rebuild lost infrastructure, and resume vital services.[5]

The remarkable and costly gaps in US military preparedness for the demands of stability operations in Iraq are well documented.[6] Given the military's own history and doctrine and the obvious requirements of the mission, these gaps suggest an almost willful refusal to gain knowledge and skills needed for effective stability operations. This study identifies military organizational factors that facilitate or impede learning stability operations.[7] First, I consider the particular characteristics of the learning agent. Often overlooked, sub-divisions within the military affect organizational flexibility. Second, I consider issues pertinent to the operational

---

3   Eisenhower added that once military and civilian matters are separated "and I can be relieved of direct responsibility for most of these things [civil affairs]. I will be delighted." Message, Eisenhower to War Department, December 22, 1942, Operations Division Message files, Classified Message-Incoming 9542.

4   'Letter from Major General John H. Hilldring to Assistant Secretary of State Dean Acheson, November 9, 1943, Civil Affairs Division files, 400.38 (2-20-43) (I), section 3; cited in Harry L. Coles and Albert K. Weinberg, *Civil Affairs: Soldiers Become Governors* (Washington, DC: Office of the Chief of Military History, 1964), p. 153.

5   United States Army, *Stability and Support Operations*, pp. 1-2.

6   See, for example, James Fallows, "Blind Into Baghdad," *The Atlantic* (January/ February 2004) and Robert M. Perito, *Where Is the Lone Ranger When We Need Him? America's Search for a Postconflict Stability Force* (Washington, DC: US Institute of Peace Press, 2004);

7   Although all US military services address issues pertaining to civilians in war, stability operations particularly concern the Army and Marine Corps. The US Marine Corps possesses specialized Civil Affairs Groups and the US Army is the service primarily responsible for civil affairs. These forces are most relevant because they operate in civilian environments.

environment of stability operations. Designed for major conventional war, the US military machinery is cumbersome in peace and stability operations. Although military learning systems record and transmit lessons learned from experience and experimentation, these have not overcome the structural bias against civil affairs. For these reasons, United States military forces in Iraq must revise or unlearn some basic assumptions about war, and re-learn lessons from previous stability operations.

The Military as Learner

We might talk about a military learning just as we might talk about a team competing or a firm adopting strategies. At the organizational level, these entities perform cognitive functions like thinking, deciding and inter-relating that we otherwise think about as individual processes. Although I focus on the US military in general and its land forces in particular, these actors are nested in a national security system that structures organizational behavior. It is tempting to set the subject at a very broad level of aggregation for this reason, as do studies of state behavior or strategic culture, but this will be too broad to be useful in this case.[8] There are important distinctions between and within the military services that become important factors in organizational efforts to cope with stability operations. It might then seem reasonable to focus specifically on sub-organizational units within the Army, such as the Special Operations Forces (SOF) or even further to a particular entity within the SOF, such as the Special Forces (SF, or Green Berets), but this level of analysis is too limiting. The following discussion aims at the middle ground, to describe how the separation of civil from military institutions and sub-organizational specialization within the armed forces act in tandem to suppress information-seeking.

Militaries are ideal candidates for organizational analysis in part because they tend to be so well *organized*. Individual personnel are organized on two levels of collective action: the military organization as a whole is a social entity differentiated from the civilian sphere; and, the military in turn is comprised of specialized sub-divisions. Some civil-military differences are obvious. Active duty military personnel frequently live apart, such as on a military base, and wear distinctive uniforms. Although they are drawn from the civilian realm, individuals who join the military sacrifice many of the freedoms taken for granted by civilians. Several lines of authority separate the civilian and military spheres, and define relationships within the military organization itself. Below the level of the President and Congress, administrative and operational control over the military flows from the Office of the Secretary of Defense and includes civilian service secretaries providing direct civilian leadership. These include decisions about war and peace, and control of budgets

---

8   For example, Colin Gray, *Nuclear Strategy and National Style* (Lanham, MD: Hamilton Press, 1986); Alistair Iain Johnston, "Thinking About Strategic Culture," *International Security* vol. 19 (1995), p. 32.

and significant promotions.[9] Cultural differentiation between military personnel and civilians reflects some self-selection, but also has an organizational basis:

> Certainly there is a distance, if not a divide, between military personnel and civilians in terms of how they view their jobs. In part, this distinctive outlook is a reflection of the special nature of the military as an institution – a reflection, that is, of the specific tasks it is expected to accomplish and the manner in which it organizes to accomplish them. In part, it reflects a deeper-seated set of convictions about how the world works, and a set of core values about how people ought to behave.[10]

This perceptual dichotomy sets the stage for problems when military staffs try to translate policy goals into military objectives, and again when military personnel run up against the civilian realm in the midst of stability operations.

The size and missions of the US armed forces require coordination among an elaborately specialized system of components. Military structure is not merely complicated in the sense that it has many parts, it is also complex in that its parts mesh inextricably in ways that influence outcomes.[11] The scale of the US military, on the one hand, provides incentives to create a system for storing institutional knowledge, but, on the other hand, creates disincentives for and constraints on the dissemination of some types of knowledge. Rigid military hierarchy and lines of authority put greater responsibility on high-ranking officers as operational sub-units increase in scale. The responsibility of a staff sergeant or sergeant commanding an Army or Marine Corps squad of a dozen personnel is no small thing. A colonel commanding a brigade might be responsible for 750 to 4000. A lieutenant general commanding an Army corps holds authority over more than 50,000 troops.

The parts, an individual soldier or an entire brigade, are designed to be as interchangeable to facilitate troop rotations of six to twelve months in and out of theaters of operation. Professional military education is thus important to create a common knowledge base and to some extent, outlook on the world.[12] In some respects the military, unlike many civilian organizations, is surprisingly

---

9 The US Constitution establishes civilian control over the armed forces at the apex of the national administrative structure by naming the President as Commander in Chief and giving Congress exclusive authority to declare war and allocate funds. Operational control extends from the Secretary of Defense through unified geographic (US Central Command, US European Command, US Pacific Command, US Southern Command) and functional commands (for example, US Special Operations Command).

10 Daniel T. Miltenberger, "Part III: The Military," in Pamela Aall, Lt. Col. Daniel T. Miltenberger, and Thomas G. Weiss, eds., *Guide to IGOs, NGOs, and the Military in Peace and Relief Operations* (Washington, DC: United States Institute of Peace Press, 2000), p. 207.

11 Robert Axelrod and Michael D. Cohen, *Harnessing Complexity* (New York: Free Press, 2000), p. 15.

12 Karen Guttieri, "Professional Military Education in Democracies," in Thomas Bruneau and Scott Tollefson, eds., *Soldiers and Statesmen: Institutional Bases of Democratic Civilian Control* (Austin, TX: University of Texas Press, forthcoming). See also Sam C. Sarkesian

not jealous about information. This makes sense given that all elements need the best possible understanding of each other's roles to effectively cooperate in battle.[13] In other situations such as planning, however, military sub-organizations will compartmentalize information, prohibiting access to nongovernmental and international agencies working on common projects, and even prohibiting access to other military and government agencies.

Rotation creates demand for an organizational system to record both positive and negative experiences for future replacements. Continuous high personnel turnover generates demand for concrete measures of effectiveness that, on the face of it, would seem useful to determine the mission's progress. A top-down evaluation system and competitive climate, however, create equal or greater incentives to show immediate results and hide mistakes. This syndrome, as it is associated with the US military in particular, is known as the "zero-defects" culture. Such an eyes-closed attitude plagued the officer corps in the Vietnam War, leading to inflated optimism and outright deception about the course of the war.

Zero-defects cultures lead people to cut corners, because they focus on short-term goals and put a premium on expedience.[14] Innovation and honesty are punished. Zero-defects cultures are risk averse, as exemplified by the extreme focus on "force protection" that has characterized American conduct in stability operations, particularly since eighteen American Rangers were killed during a botched mission in Somalia in 1993. The culture inhibits flexibility, initiative and willingness to move among civilian populations – factors commonly cited as vital to success in stability operations.

Specialization creates rigid incentive structures. Promotions come to depend on "punching tickets;" for example, command experience is a typical prerequisite for promotion, making warfighting specialties like infantry command more attractive to ambitious officers than Army or Marine Corps Civil Affairs (CA) positions. Transfer to a military government company during World War II, for instance, was a punishment for incompetence.[15] Despite tremendous need for personnel trained in these areas, there is disincentive to specialize in civil affairs. This specialization also leads to false delegation in strategy. Although civil affairs have been a responsibility of command since World War II, commanders persistently treat the civil dimension of conflict as an afterthought. They may do so in the mistaken belief that civilian

---

and Robert E. Connor, Jr., *The US Military Profession into the Twenty-First Century* (London: Frank Cass, 1999), p. 21.

13 James B. Thomas, Stephanie Watts Sussman and John C. Henderson, "Understanding 'Strategic Learning': Linking Organizational Learning, Knowledge Management, and Sensemaking." *Organization Science* vol. 12 (2001), pp. 331-345.

14 In the 1990s, many worried that a zero-defects culture once again characterized the US military. The force downsizing that followed the collapse of the Soviet Union gave rise to the possibility that one unfavorable letter in a file could ruin a career. James Kitfield, "Zero Defects, Zero Initiative," *National Journal* vol. 28 (April 5, 1996), p. 793.

15 Martin Kyre and Joan Kyre, *Military Government and National Security* (Washington, DC: Public Affairs Press, 1968), pp. 19-21.

issues will arise only after the job of war fighting is done, and then can be handled by dedicated CA officers alone. Civil-military specializations within the active US services, however, are few and secondary and rarely mobilized effectively. Most CA personnel are reservists, and must be mobilized for duty. CA officers are further isolated by designation as part of Special Operations Forces.[16] The civilian component in the Pentagon responsible for stability operations and civil affairs activities in particular is, like the Special Operations Command, the product of congressional legislation – that is, an externally imposed structure. Civil affairs, and those dedicated to civilian-centric activities, are institutionally marginal:

> [Civil affairs] seems always to be wavering between two worlds: conventional versus special operations missions, a peacetime versus wartime chain of command, and active versus reserve component control. It has no champion, no sponsor, and therefore, in spite of its great potential, tends to be lumped together with the "ash and trash" units.[17]

Set within a broader national security structure, military officers do sometimes respond to signals from the civilian leadership. Presidential candidate George W. Bush declared in 2000, "…I don't think our troops ought to be used for what's called nation building."[18] President Bush's National Security Advisor and later Secretary of State, Condoleezza Rice, had long sought to limit exposure of American military forces to peacekeeping. Instead, she argued for a division of labor that left those chores to European and other allies. "Carrying out civil administration and police functions is simply going to degrade the American capability to do the things America has to do," she was quoted as saying in 2000. "We don't need to have the 82nd Airborne escorting kids to kindergarten."[19] US foreign policy interests in Afghanistan and Iraq soon dictated otherwise.

Unconventional Challenges of Stability Operations

Once the invasion of Iraq began in March 2003, US forces seized the initiative and quickly decided the war's outcome. As early as July, a colonel in charge of a combat-stress unit explained that he was mostly treating stress due to the frustration of stability operations. "Our people are not really trained for peacekeeping, and not equipped for riot control," he explained. "They are trained to fight the enemy and

---

16 Other SOF are Special Forces, Rangers, SEALs, Delta and Psychological Operations.

17 Dennis C. Barlow, "A Planner's Guide for the Employment of Civil Affairs in Latin America," in John W. DePauw and George A. Luz, ed., *Winning the Peace: The Strategic Implications of Military Civic Action* (New York: Praeger, 1992), pp.117-139.

18 "The 2000 Campaign: 2nd Presidential Debate Between Governor Bush and Vice President Gore," *New York Times* (October 12, 2000), p. A22.

19 Cited in William Drozdiak, "Bush Plan Worries Europeans; Removing U.S. Troops From Balkans Is Seen as Divisive," *Washington Post* (October 24, 2000), p. A07.

kill them."[20] The military is geared for war, but if it conceives of that environment as depopulated and interactions within it as linear, some conceptions may need to be unlearned.

The multi-dimensional, multi-national and multi-organizational efforts of humanitarian, peace, or stability operations present special problems for the US military. First, these rarely involve the kind of mechanized, maneuver warfare that cold warriors – the baby boomers now populating the senior officer corps – prepared their organizations to fight. Instead of mass and fire, stability operations tend to involve small units in repetitive patrols. Instead of stand-off strikes, stability operations tend to involve face-to-face contact.[21] Adversaries and benchmarks for success are not as easily identified as when enemy fighters, bombers and tanks lie smoldering in ruins. Second, achieving mission objectives depends on cooperation with other, non-military agencies, and a constant effort to fit military operations to shifting and sometimes intrusive or sometimes unavailable civilian political guidance. This reality creates a very different operational flow-chart from those with which US military forces are familiar, and presupposes a system of coordination rather than control.[22] Scholars of civil-military relations cite these challenges as contributing conditions for military organizational change.[23]

Although the Army portrays stability operations as an anomaly to its core organizational purpose, in many respects there is little new. Military forces in foreign territory are, as ever, obliged by international law to provide for civilians under their effective control.[24] American forces confronted these challenges in numerous occupations in the Caribbean and the Philippines, in Europe after World Wars, in the midst of the Korean and Vietnam conflicts, in the intervention in the Dominican Republic, in the Grenada and Panama invasions, in Kuwait after the first Gulf War,

---

20 Scott Peterson, "Fatigued, US Troops Yearn for Home," *Christian Science Monitor* (July 7, 2003), p. 1.

21 Institute for National Strategic Studies, National Defense University, *Strategic Assessment 1998*, (Washington, DC: National Defense University Press, 1998), p. 266.

22 The call to think "Beyond Jointness," i.e. toward integration of civil-military efforts, reflects this insight. See the National Defense University Symposium, "Beyond Jointness: The Civil-Military Dimensions of Peace Operations and Humanitarian Assistance," June 2-3, 1999 (Washington, DC: Institute for National Strategic Studies, 2000).

23 Charles C. Moskos, John Allen Williams and David R. Segal, *The Postmodern Military: Armed Forces After the Cold War* (New York: Oxford University Press, 2000).

24 See the 1907 Hague Convention (IV), "Respecting the Laws and Customs of War on Land;" the Fourth Geneva Convention of 1949, "Relative to the Protection of Civilian Persons in Time of War;" the 1954 Hague Convention for the "Protection of Cultural Property in the Event of Armed Conflict'" and discussions of customary international humanitarian law in Adam Roberts, "What is a Military Occupation?" *British Yearbook of International Law 1984* (Oxford: Clarendon Press, 1985), pp. 249-305; and Karen Guttieri, "Symptom of the Moment: A Juridical Gap for US Occupation Forces," *International Insights* vol. 13 (1997), pp. 131-157.

and in Somalia, Haiti and the Balkans.[25] American and other North Atlantic Treaty Organization (NATO) troops making up the Kosovo Force in 1999 were compelled to handle civilian problems.[26] Without much anticipated civilian support from either the United Nations or the Organization for Security and Cooperation in Europe, soldiers took up tasks of administration, maintaining law and order, and repairing infrastructure. Throughout, American political and military leadership attempted to put the ostensibly civilian tasks in the hands of civilian government and non-governmental agencies.

The Clinton Administration in the 1990s sensed military and public reluctance to engage in nation building. The multilateral approach of that era leaned heavily on international institutions, but questions of effectiveness plagued them, in particular the United Nations. After a peace accord in 1995, the civilian-managed UN mission in the former Yugoslavia (United Nations Protection Force, UNPROFOR) handed off to a much larger and military-driven NATO-led Implementation Force. The results-oriented military machine wrote its predecessor off as a failure. A UN official recalls, "Little note was taken of the fact that UNPROFOR had massive experience of working in the Yugoslav environment, and as a result the military had to re-learn, often at great expense, lessons already learned by their UN predecessors."[27] Current US operations show little evidence of lesson integration.

The Bush Administration has taken a markedly unilateral approach. Defense policy makers rejected the idea of an integrated political-military plan within the US government.[28] Early Central Command (CENTCOM) Afghanistan campaign planning after the 9/11 terrorist attacks provided little role for civil-military operations.[29] The focus instead was logistics, with a few CA officers at headquarters focused on humanitarian de-mining. This reflected a narrow conception of civil military operations, but the approach was consistent with a preference shared by the Bush Administration and many humanitarian agencies – a small military footprint.

---

25 Karen Guttieri, *Toward a Usable Peace: United States Civil Affairs in Post-Conflict Environments*, PhD Dissertation, University of British Columbia (July 1999).

26 Independent Commission on Kosovo, *Kosovo Report* (London: Oxford University Press, 2001), p. 105.

27 Opening speech by Deputy Special Representative of the Secretary-General of the United Nations for Bosnia and Herzegovina Julian J.R.C Harston, cited in "Civil-Military Co-operation Lessons Learned and Models for the Future," in Peter Viggo Jakobsen, ed., *Report from the DUPI Conference in Copenhagen, 1-2 September 2000* (Copenhagen: Danish Institute of International Affairs, 2000), p. 10.

28 Policy Presidential Decision Directive PDD-56, developed to guide interagency coordination during the William J. Clinton administration, was largely abandoned by the administration of George W. Bush. A draft version called NSPD XX was prepared for the Bush administration, but not implemented. The Bush administration uses the title National Security Presidential Directive (NSPD) rather than Presidential Decision Directive.

29 See the account in Olga Oliker, et. al., *Aid during Conflict: Interaction between Military and Civilian Assistance Providers in Afghanistan, September 2001–June 2002* (Santa Monica, CA: RAND, 2004), p. 39.

And yet, CENTCOM took extraordinary measures to give a voice to civilians during planning, and actually included them in sessions in Tampa, Florida in November 2001.[30] However, the nonmilitary participants at Tampa realized too late that civilian aspects of the war planning was the province of logisticians at US Army Central in Atlanta, Georgia.[31] Despite a promising start, the relationship between the US military and the international and non-governmental agencies on the scene in Afghanistan was problematic. Civil-military relations hit new lows over military drops of food rations, the delivery of aid by civil-military Provincial Reconstruction Teams, and CA personnel wearing civilian attire while on duty.

Given these experiences, it is particularly noteworthy that in the period leading up to the 2003 invasion of Iraq, US defense planners effectively ignored the input of international, non-governmental and most government agencies. Did American war planners draw the lesson from previous interaction with these organizations that it is best to avoid a "cluttered" battlefield? Many hoped that CENTCOM's Iraq planning would follow the Afghanistan model. Instead, direction from the Pentagon and White House called for a more exclusively military and compartmentalized approach.[32] CENTCOM staff worked at the "secret" and "top secret" levels, and were forbidden to interact with others within their own government, including those working on the State Department's Futures of Iraq Project.

One planner involved in both Afghanistan and Iraq believes that the greater urgency of Afghanistan planning had given CENTCOM more freedom to draw in other actors: "In the Afghanistan effort we were driven to make something happen, and massaged it after the fact."[33] Preparing to invade Iraq, some of the same soldiers understood the significance of civilian issues, but did not believe they had a mandate to address them. Responsibility for the civil dimension seemed to fall constantly to some other agency, first the State Department, next a planning agency called Joint Task Force IV, and then retired General Jay Garner's Office of Reconstruction and Humanitarian Assistance (ORHA).[34] In August 2002, for example, CENTCOM was informed that State was no longer the lead agency. They launched a Humanitarian Planning Team, but when Bush's National Security Presidential Directive put Garner in charge of reconstruction many of the major interagency players left the table.

Garner's appointment signaled to many outside the inner circles of the Pentagon that little serious reconstruction was planned for Iraq. His previous post-conflict experience was relief to the Kurds in Northern Iraq after the first Gulf War – a limited

---

30 Interview with Bear McConnell, Director of the Central Asia Task Force of the US Agency for International Development, during this period (February 2004).

31 Interview with humanitarian liaison to CENTCOM (September 2002).

32 See Workshop Proceedings: "Planning for Post-Conflict Reconstruction: Learning from Iraq," Institute for National Strategic Studies National Defense University (July 29, 2004).

33 Interview, March 2005.

34 CENTCOM, the Combined Forces Land Component Command, the Civil Affairs Command, JTF IV and the Pentagon (both the civilian OSD and the military Joint Staff) were engaged in different, separate, and sometimes uncoordinated planning efforts.

mission more than a decade ago. There had been many post-conflict reconstruction efforts in the interim, and there were many individuals with more experience. The selection of a retired general officer also sent a signal. Ironically, although Garner's previous military status would seem to be an asset if civilian ORHA needed a voice in a military-driven occupation, it was counterproductive. The ORHA director might have emphasized his direct order from President Bush (NSPD-24) empowering him to take charge of civilian implementation. One officer on the scene reports that CENTCOM Commander General Tommy Franks said, "What's an NSPD?" and put Garner under the operational control of the Land Forces Commander.[35] Garner, say insiders, was too loyal a soldier to challenge his position in the third tier or his late access to the Iraqi theater.

Without conceptualizing civil affairs as part of its strategy, it is difficult to imagine the US military creating an appropriate force structure for current missions, providing adequate education for forces confronting the civil dimension, and supplying career incentives for officers to specialize and serve in these roles. Although the US military is well-organized for institutional learning, singular features of the organization influence what is learned and how.

Military Learning Systems

Personal experience can be a deadly teacher for both personnel and military organizations, and soldiers typically spend small amounts of their time in actual combat. One would therefore expect to see highly-developed mechanisms within the military for learning. Indeed, five levels of military education coincide with the phases of an officer's career, progressively moving from the tactical to the operational and strategic levels of war.[36] This system is very highly scripted from the top down.

Various methods of knowledge acquisition such as searching, vicarious learning, and grafting are employed in after action reviews (AARs) and simulation exercises. Yet the Army confronts structural and cultural barriers to mining history (its own, let alone that of others) for lessons. One theory is that the learning system itself is a culprit, that soldiers are overwhelmed by information dictated from above. They memorize, but do not learn. Leonard Wong contends that the Army produces too many *cooks* who might carry out a recipe, but too few *chefs* able to pull together ingredients to make a meal.[37] Ironically, Wong blames the Army's attempts to adjust to the demands of operations other than war in the 1990s for this problem.

The US armed services do consciously seek to adapt to circumstances or experiences, using tracking systems and measures of effectiveness to judge

---

35 Interview, February 2004.

36 US Chairman of the Joint Chiefs of Staff Instruction 1800.01A, December 1, 2000, available online at <http://dtic.mil/doctrine>.

37 Leonard Wong, "Stifled Innovation?" (Carlisle Barracks, PA: United States Army War College Strategic Studies Institute, 2002).

strategies. For example, the United States military shifted its doctrine in the 1970s in response to new understanding of Soviet conventional strength. The development of AirLand Battle integrated service elements on the battlefield set the stage for the "system-of-systems" warfare that now gives the United States a technological edge. AirLand Battle doctrine also set requirements for intensive joint training and a training revolution across the military forces.[38] The Army opened the National Training Center at Fort Irwin in the Mojave Desert of California for training exercises on a large scale. These changes extended to the service academies and campuses, creating incentives for professional military education and prompting development of training and simulation exercises, particularly at the joint or multiple service level. The products of these exercises in turn played a role in the further development of doctrine. Likewise, direct American experiences with stability operations, including nearly a decade of peacekeeping in the Balkans, are discussed in doctrine.

Doctrine teaches, providing rules and guidance. Doctrine is a product of extensive dialogue and review. It is the primary guide to the soldier going into the field. Not only does it provide a common language and text for the education system, doctrine helps to make for a common professional culture. Formal doctrine takes the form of approved field manuals, and these provide the most visible evidence of doctrinal change.[39] Journal articles, field orders and personal letters constitute informal doctrine that may find its way into field manuals.

In 2001, the capstone manual JP 3-0, *Joint Operations* for the first time directly addressed stability operations rather than confining the topic to another more specialized volume such as JP 3-57, *Civil Military Operations*, as has been the case in the past. *Operations* now includes civilians in the so-called METT-T factors fundamental to battle command assessment and visualization:

> METT-TC refers to factors that are fundamental to assessing and visualizing: Mission, Enemy, Terrain and weather, Troops and support available, Time available, and Civil considerations. The first five factors are not new. However, the nature of full spectrum operations requires commanders to assess the impact of nonmilitary factors on operations. Because of this added complexity, *civil considerations* has been added to the familiar METT-T to form METT-TC. All commanders must use METT-TC to start their visualization.[40] [emphasis in the original]

This new doctrine seeks to incorporate civilian considerations into its organizational routine, and into the rote learning required for military officers. Unfortunately, according to the assessments of those responsible for its implementation in the field, recent doctrine nevertheless inadequately informs the war fighters. One problem is

---

38 Anne W. Chapman, *The Origins and Development of the National Training Center 1976-1984* (Fort Monroe, VA: Office of the Command Historian, US Training and Doctrine Command, 1992).

39 Keith B. Bickel, *Mars Learning: The Marine Corps Development of Small Wars Doctrine, 1915-1940* (Boulder, CO: Westview, 2001).

40 United States Army, *Stability and Support Operations*, pp. 3-5.

the compartmentalization of war planning. In the construction of operations plans, information is very jealously guarded. This has led to some mishaps. When the United States invaded Panama in 1989, it was noteworthy that commanders had a post-conflict plan in place before going in. Unfortunately, this plan was developed separately from the war-fighting plan and was not revised to fit with it when the latter was secretly changed.[41] The result was an unanticipated level of chaos and disruption in the aftermath of combat operations. A now-requisite civil affairs annex was intended to help make coordinated planning a matter of course. Unfortunately, recent operations have proven that this addendum was also insufficient to integrate civil-military considerations into the larger war-fighting plan.

Surprisingly, barely three pages of the Army Third Infantry Division's 290-page Iraq after-action review, produced in July 2003, address stability operations, widely acknowledged as the most problematic phase of the war. The review admonishes planners to better integrate war termination and stability operations in pre-combat planning. In military language, this would be a "lesson learned," except that this same lesson was also ostensibly "learned" in military reports dating at least to the 1920 Hunt Report documenting US failure to anticipate the magnitude of responsibilities in the Rhineland after World War I. The complaint that the modified table of equipment provided inadequate transportation and other equipment assets to CA personnel in Iraq is, lamentably, the same voiced after the invasion of Panama in 1989.

Peter Senge, known for promoting the concept of a "learning organization," declared, "The Army's After Action Review...is arguably one of the most successful organizational learning methods yet devised."[42] Nevertheless, more than one participant has reported "We don't learn or read previous 'lessons learned.'"[43] Even as one book on the AAR lauds the US Army for creating a "culture of learning," others claim that its strong organizational culture and, ironically, its reliance on written doctrine, make the US Army less capable than the British Army of conducting counterinsurgency or low-intensity and peace operations.[44]

The precursor to the AAR was the combat interview.[45] Such histories, often disseminated in field manual vignettes of "lessons learned," serve as a kind of informal memory for the organization. In order to capture lessons from field experience, the

41 John T. Fishel, *Civil Military Operations in the New World* (Westport, CT: Praeger, 1997).

42 Peter Senge, "Introduction" in Marilyn Darling and Charles Perry, eds., *From Post-Mortem to Living Practice: An In-depth Study of the Evolution of the After Action Review* (Boston: Signet, 2001).

43 United States European Command, *Operation Support Hope After Action Report*, 1994, Appendix A, 8-3.

44 On the positive side, see Darling and Perry, *From Post-Mortem to Living Practice*. For a more jaundiced view, see John A. Nagl, "Learning to Eat Soup with a Knife: British and American Army Counterinsurgency Learning During the Malayan Emergency and the Vietnam War," *World Affairs* vol. 161 (1999), p. 161.

45 John E. Morrison and Larry L. Meliza, *Foundations of the After Action Review Process* (US Army Research Institute for the Behavioral and Social Sciences, 1999).

Army Center for Lessons Learned (CALL), for example, normally sends a team on each operation to document events and make suggestions for improvement. The CALL process, according to Thomas, creates a "systematic capability to rapidly learn from ongoing practice and to create foreshadowed knowledge of future events" that is credited with giving the Army a strategic advantage.[46] The AAR and other systems for collecting lessons learned are not, however, particularly well organized. One problem is simply the volume of information to be processed in short military rotation cycles. The Army's CALL database is clumsy to access as is the Joint Universal Lessons Learned System (JULLS), and neither are comprehensive. Part of the difficulty for the end-user of these systems comes from the way they are constructed. The JULLS system provides a compendium of service and joint reports that can be searched by keyword, obliterating much of the context. Because the system is built around individual reports addressing specific problems and devoid of any analysis that puts them into a larger context, Kenneth Allard concludes that JULLS reports amount to a "science of single events."[47] Deeper problems with JULLS stem from the tendency to water down joint reports that show particular services or commands in an unfavorable light.

The literature on organizational learning emphasizes that "information acquisition depends in many instances on attention, which is directed by previous learning retained in memory."[48] In other words, we learn from the things we pay attention to, and we typically pay attention to what is familiar or rewarded. Senior managers by definition are well-steeped in organizational culture. Privileging their role in the allocation of learning resources has costs as well as benefits in terms of the freedom of the system to exploit serendipitous learning.[49] The wash of after-action reviews commissioned elsewhere in the military organization also can generate "vanilla" evaluations according to how they are disseminated and who responds to them. The second, more critical, of two reviews commissioned for operations in Bosnia-Herzegovina (known as BHAAR II), for instance, was published in the US Army War College's quarterly magazine rather than as an official learning document. Although it is good that the story was told, this example indicates that the much-lauded open "learning culture" within the military is not all that energetic.

The military sometimes buries its mistakes. In October 2003, Thomas Ricks of *The Washington Post* reported that a publication posted on the CALL website described soldiers in Iraq and Afghanistan as unprepared and low on analytic skills.[50]

---

46 Thomas, et. al., "Understanding 'Strategic Learning,'" p. 343.

47 C. Kenneth Allard, "Lessons Unlearned: Somalia and Joint Doctrine," *Joint Forces Quarterly* (Autumn 1995), p. 107.

48 George P. Huber, "Organizational Learning: The Contributing Processes and the Literatures," in Michael D. Cohen and Lee Sproull, eds., *Organizational Learning* (Thousand Oaks, CA: Sage, 1996), p. 150.

49 Thomas, et. al., "Understanding 'Strategic Learning.'"

50 Thomas E. Ricks, "Intelligence Problems in Iraq are Detailed," *Washington Post* (October 25, 2003), p. A01.

The Joint Readiness Training Center assessment of US military operations in Iraq and Afghanistan was promptly removed from the website. Fred Kaplan complained,

> The report and its suppression make clear that, in pre-war training, combat deployment, and after-action assessments, the Army hierarchy in the field and the political hierarchy in Washington devote woefully scant resources to analysis of what they're doing – and that they hold the analysts themselves in contempt, sometimes lethally so.[51]

The report's assessment was bleak. The message to the Afghan people was that the Americans would not help with food, reconstruction, "or anything else of importance to you." Although the authors credited the talent and dedication of the troops themselves, these CA and psychological operations reserve units received only marginal pre-deployment training and preparation at the Fort Bragg, NC mobilization site and the Home Station. They did not receive vital language and cultural training, and were told they would "learn the cultural stuff and TTP [tactics, technique and procedures] once they got there."[52]

Civilian humanitarian relief workers have expressed frustration that the military fails to incorporate even the lessons of its own exercises. A former director of the Office of Foreign Disaster Assistance commented:

> …there have been a great many military exercises – a lot of which I attended, and a lot I have heard of -- but I am not sure that as a result of these exercises there is real transferability of information… I don't know if that is built into the system. I know within the various [military and civilian] communities there is a lot of rotation of people. That is inevitable. But, how do we get around the recognition of the fact of rotation and make what you all spend your time learning something that really gets transferred? [53]

His question suggests that there is a dynamic organizational learning system in place, but no mechanism to stimulate the input and feedback learning loops. This disconnect is only likely to get worse, unless something – not necessarily positive – forces a change.

The high tempo of military operations impedes systemic learning in two ways: first, military personnel in operations are very much "on the go," and have little time to indulge in resource-intensive learning; and, second, rapid personnel turnover means that tacit knowledge is less likely to be shared. A new generation of military officers takes a new tact – they employ technology to overcome some of these limitations by communicating outside regular Army channels.[54] Two former

---

51 Fred Kaplan, "Err War," *Slate* (October 3, 2003). Kaplan refers to the dangerous placement of human intelligence agents in door-kicker raids, as "the #2 man, who statistically is the person who gets shot."

52 "Operation OUTREACH: Tactics, Techniques and Procedures," Center for Army Lesson Learned *Newsletter* No. 03-27 (October 2003).

53 National Defense University Symposium, "Beyond Jointness."

54 Dan Baum, "Battle Lessons: What the Generals Don't Know," *The New Yorker* (January 17, 2005), pp. 42-48.

West Point classmates launched Companycommand.com in March 2000 to allow captains to convey advice about anything from how to handle a subordinate who becomes pregnant, to how to sandbag the floor of a vehicle, to how to kick in doors. These officers evidently prefer to spend time on companycommand.com rather than the CALL website. Although the innovation and initiative are laudable, something is clearly broken. Either military doctrine is irrelevant, or the personnel lack the patience and skill to access the information they seek.

A military force that credits much of its current prowess to an extensive system of formal education has done surprisingly little to prepare its personnel for the most likely missions. A RAND report commissioned by the Army found insufficient attention in the curricula of the Command and General Staff College and the Army War College to stability operations.[55] Despite this finding, little has been done to enhance curricula at the war colleges. The Army War College in Carlisle, PA, for example, in 2004 offered only one elective course in peacekeeping.[56] The Army, in short, was not educating its people for the most likely missions, including the combined-arms cohesion that must be achieved quickly among disparate elements in peacekeeping and stability operations. Despite its extensive stability operations commitments in Afghanistan and Iraq, not to mention ongoing missions in Kosovo, Bosnia and elsewhere, the US Army closed its Peacekeeping Institute in 2003. The staff had vacated their offices and the lights were nearly off when lobbying by non-governmental organizations and other civilian agencies and congressional pressure saved the center, now called the US Army Peacekeeping and Stability Operations Institute.

On the other hand, in October 2003, the National Training Center (NTC) at Fort Irwin began construction on mock towns that will be used to train forces for stability operations. This is an important, if belated, shift in emphasis for the NTC, from large-scale armored battalions meeting in traditional-type engagements in the Mojave Desert to an emphasis on "the human side of warfare."[57] Nonetheless, stability operations training is still today provided by a cottage industry on a largely ad hoc basis in brief increments, such as a two-week course. The Naval Postgraduate School has developed a fifteen-month multidisciplinary master's degree in stabilization and reconstruction. This program will welcome more US students as official curricula participants when the military's senior leadership call for US officer education appropriate to post-conflict and counterinsurgency environments.

---

55 David E. Johnson, *Preparing Potential Senior Army Leaders for the Future: An Assessment of Leader Development Efforts in the Post-Cold War Era* (Santa Monica, CA: RAND, 2002). See also Army FM 3-0, pp. 9-10, available online at <http://www.adtdl.army.mil/cgi-bin/atdl.dll/fm/3-0/ch9.pdf>.

56 Max Manwaring, Karen Guttieri and Michael Dziedzic, *The Civil Dimensions of Military Operations Conference Report*. Co-sponsored by the US Army War College and Institute for National Strategic Studies, Washington DC, September 23-24, 1998.

57 Major General Robert Scales quoted in David Wood, "Training for The New Warfare," *Newhouse.com* vol. 19 (November 2003).

Effective programs in civil-military operations are needed for those personnel who, often at the lowest tactical levels, will be responsible for carrying out missions. Until this happens, it is unlikely the lessons of any amount of peacekeeping post-mortems will lead to more effective stability operations in the future.

Lessons from Organizational Learning

Learning has been defined in ways that emphasize its character as a remedial exercise, "a process of detecting and correcting error."[58] A cross-referenced study of "lessons learned" by the Peacekeeping Institute found astonishing similarities in the after-action reports on US operations in Haiti (April 1996), Bosnia-Herzogovina 1 (May 1996), Bosnia-Herzogovina 2 (April 1997), in Central America after Hurricane Mitch (September 1999), and Kosovo (2001). More recent US operations in Afghanistan and Iraq exhibit many of the same errors. In sum, one must give the military good marks for error detection but poor marks for correction.

Learning implies not only the ability to gain insight from experience but also to change strategies in light of that insight. Mechanisms we associate with learning, using trial-and-error or a model of success we can imitate, can lead to new strategy. Change in the population of agents (in this case, the officer corps) can bring similar effect. Interaction among members of an organization spreads and changes strategies. The emergence of expert-entrepreneurs to create momentum for organizational change is one possibility. General William Crouch, who led the Implementation Force into Bosnia, recalls, "I was on my own. I'd certainly never trained for something like this."[59] After retirement, General Crouch became a senior mentor for a program to provide some educational preparation to headquarters personnel deploying to Bosnia, Kosovo and now Afghanistan and Iraq.

Of course, both reformers and actors must agree on what is to be learned. General George Joulwan emerged from his experience in Rwanda in 1994 reporting a "lesson" to avoid taking on additional tasks, and praising the US military performance there because, in an environment where atrocious crimes were being committed against civilians, the military was "careful not to move beyond its explicit mission," making no move to arrest murderous Hutu militia members or complicit former government leaders.[60] Military officers in Afghanistan, by taking on many of the tasks normally reserved for non-governmental organizations, may have reflected a "lesson" that it is best simply to avoid dealing with such organizations altogether.

---

58 Chris Argyris, "Double Loop Learning in Organizations: Continuity and Change," *Harvard Business Review* vol. 55 (1977), p. 116.

59 Cited in Howard Olsen and John Davis, *Training US Army Officers for Peace Operations: Lessons from Bosnia*, Special Report, United States Institute of Peace (October 29, 1999), p. 2.

60 George A. Joulwan. and Christopher C. Shoemaker, *Civilian-Military Cooperation in the Prevention of Deadly Conflict: Implementing Agreements in Bosnia and Beyond* (New York: Carnegie Corporation, 1998), p. 19.

James March warns that although it is desirable for individuals to socialize to the organization, it is vital that individual insights that would benefit the organization not be washed out during that process.[61] This is the rub in a "zero-defects" culture, where the checklists in field manuals too easily become the criteria for success. Just as Joulwan met the requirements of his mission and called it a success while ignoring the disaster unfolding around him, officers may seek to insulate themselves from criticism by slavishly following rules when the requirements of the environment require initiative. Unfortunately, in this "error-free" climate, we are unlikely to witness stability operations doctrine, with its relative ambiguity and mutability, actually being implemented.

Cognitive development can be differentiated according to the scope of learning. As was discussed in Chapter 1, "single-loop" learning is situated within a frame of reference "without change in the underlying governing policies or values."[62] "Double-loop" learning, by contrast, involves the development of a new frame of reference. While "single-loop" learning processes are more common, we might expect military organizations especially to conform to this pattern. First, the norms of civil-military relations decree that military forces are political instruments, and the role of military leaders is to implement rather than develop or change policy. Second, military organizations tend to be highly routine-oriented, emphasizing incremental improvements in those routines over paradigm change. Third, military organizations tend to be tightly compartmentalized, making it difficult to see outside the institutional parameters of one's own service sub-unit, let alone across military services, into the interagency or alliance arena, and so on.

In September 2003, a secret report on "Strategic Lessons Learned" in Iraq, prepared for the Joint Chiefs of Staff, was leaked to the *Washington Times*. The document reportedly concedes inadequate preparation for stability operations (phase IV, as described earlier) blaming this paucity on the rush to plan the operation (the President approved the overall strategy in August 2002, seven months before the actual invasion began), and notes planners' failure to "integrate the interagency process," that is, coordinate the work of the Departments of State and Defense going into the war.[63] Such language is shorthand for an excuse common to a "zero defects" culture: the military has done only what its civilian masters required and no more.

March's distinction between application- and discovery-driven learning is particularly useful. In the former, the organization picks the low-hanging fruit. It exploits existing competencies, technologies and paradigms for more certain improvements in performance. In the latter, the organization explores new alternatives

---

61 James G. March, "Exploration and Exploitation in Organizational Learning," *Organization Science* vol. 2 (1991), pp. 71-87.

62 See Chapter 1, pp. 13 and 14 which discusses Argyris, "Double Loop Learning," p. 116.

63 Rowan Scarborough, "U.S. Rushed Post-Saddam Planning," *Washington Times* (September 3, 2003), available online at <http://www.washtimes.com/national/20030903-120317-9393r.htm>.

for less-certain gains but bigger pay-offs with potentially decisive competitive advantage.[64] The distinction between these types of learning recognizes that some forms of information processing are more taxing than others. It is less costly in the short run to go ahead and use readily available military competencies, such as patrolling, in new situations than it is to rework the structure or the nature of patrols to meet unusual requirements. This is a strategic choice, as many organizations inhabit a competitive world, and some learning processes take more effort and risk. The "long hard slog" of stability operations in Iraq is certainly a competitive environment. As failures manifest, conditions are ripe for the American military to rethink learning strategy and even its very conceptions of combat effectiveness.

Conclusion

The tactical knowledge gaps for American soldiers in Iraq today are the result of several levels of inattentiveness to the civil dimension of conflict. Because a lesson is considered to be *learned* only when it leads to an observable policy change, even a cursory study of its operational history shows the US military sometimes makes do simply with lessons *noted*. The question that crops up again and again in discussions of civil-military issues in peace operations and other complex contingencies is, what does it take to learn?

Scholarship on organizational learning helps to explain how the military can seek lessons and yet fail to learn. The US military is an organization that likes to institutionalize processes. This preference can focus attention or it can leave entire areas of learning locked away or under-utilized. Commanders of military operations repeatedly report in AARs that they did not appreciate the CA assets available to them until their field experience raised the need. They then lost precious time trying to learn how to exploit existing CA capabilities.

The military establishes elaborate learning systems, but fails to utilize them effectively. AARs might represent a response that successfully gathers knowledge but fails to translate it into policy and action. The review is only one component of a dynamic system that incorporates education, exercise, doctrine and field experience, all of which are potential venues for interpretation, diffusion, experimentation and action in preparation for future operations. If the test of actual military operations shows the military to be functionally ill-suited for use in peace operations, avenues for feedback are designed to enable personnel returning from the field to alert the wider organization to the misfit. Headquarters, alerted to environmental changes through such channels, unfortunately tends to respond by exploiting existing competencies rather than developing new ones, and engaging in selective lesson-seeking about the consequences. It is possible that the chosen solutions to identified problems thus still will not adequately address or resolve them. It also appears that

---

64 March, "Exploration and Exploitation in Organizational Learning," pp. 71-87.

there are institutional triggers for *forgetting* that operate within this system alongside those for learning.

There is some progress, with more involvement of civilian actors in military training, and requirements for civil affairs annexes to operations plans. Lamentably, the changes so far look better on paper than on the ground, and are not even close to becoming fully integrated into a comprehensive officer training and education program. The real test of learning will be whether civil-military initiatives generate organizational routines more appropriate to effective operations and better suited to the types of environments in which military forces today commonly operate. It is not enough to reconfigure the pathways through which information flows in the military, although that is clearly needed; policymakers must make clear that civilian concerns are a factor in war and paramount in the wake of it.

Chapter 13

Learning Problems in Foreign Aid Agencies

Goran Hyden

Donor agencies are responsible for distributing and channeling financial and other resources from the richer to the poorer countries of the world. As such, they constitute a unique type of organization because they are not only responsive to demands and pressures exercised in a specific national political arena, but also those originating outside the donor states' jurisdiction. Thus, the conflicting pressures brought to bear on these agencies are more complex than those experienced by bureaucracies operating within a single national jurisdiction. Particularly significant also is that these agencies carry out their responsibilities in social, economic and political environments where their individual administrators usually are strangers. They do not necessarily speak the native language, and they often have difficulties relating to the culture of these foreign places. Moreover, these agencies operate in a large number of countries that display important differences. As if this weren't enough to complicate learning, the agencies' policy experiences are often accorded second priority in policy design because donor governments provide foreign aid for political or moral reasons, rather than organizational effectiveness. Learning in donor agencies, therefore, has its own definite challenges.

This chapter draws on a study[1] that covers three bilateral agencies: the United States Agency for International Development (USAID), the Swedish International Development Cooperation Agency (Sida), and the Chinese Ministry of Foreign Economic Relations and Trade (MOFERT).[2] I have added here a comparison with the World Bank, an international finance institution that is the single biggest provider of foreign aid to developing countries. USAID and Sida are members of the Development Assistance Committee (DAC) of the Organization for Economic Cooperation and Development (OECD), the principal coordinating mechanism for donor agencies. The World Bank works closely with the OECD/DAC. Thus, these three agencies constitute what may be called "mainstream" donors. MOFERT, in contrast, works independently from the other agencies and reports exclusively to the Chinese Communist Party. In this sense, it constitutes a "control" case in this study.

---

1   Goran Hyden and Rwekaza Mukandala, eds., *Agencies in Foreign Aid* (London: Macmillan, 1997).

2   MOFERT is the principal agency through which the Chinese government channels its foreign aid. The agency has changed over time and was previously called something else.

The discussion below focuses on the problems these agencies experience in learning to achieve higher levels of policy effectiveness. The first section looks at the environment in which these agencies operate and learn, the second focuses on what these agencies have learned and how, while the concluding section tries to place this study in a comparative "learning" perspective.

The Learning Environment

A study of the learning problems that these organizations face is justified on several grounds. One is their significant role in the transfer of funds from the North to the South. Although trade has come to play a relatively more important role in the past decade, aid is still a very significant factor in public finance in many developing countries, especially in sub-Saharan Africa. In some of these countries, foreign aid is also a significant component of the Gross Domestic Product (GDP). Some time ago, Riddell estimated aid to constitute between 10 and 25 per cent of GDP in these African countries.[3] It is clear, therefore, that what these agencies do has broad implications for development in many countries of the world. A second reason is that aid agencies are rarely the subject of more academic studies. To the extent that they have been studied, it has been primarily as instruments of foreign policy.[4] A third reason, already alluded to above, is that aid agencies operate across national jurisdictions and, thus, are exposed to cross pressures from domestic and foreign sources. The latter is a major factor affecting learning in these organizations.

The dilemma that these agencies face in learning from experience can be captured as follows. The policy feedback they receive derives from specific project or program experiences, most of which are difficult to aggregate at the macro level. Therefore, aid agencies tend to formulate policies and disseminate funds based upon dominant ideas or paradigms circulating at the global level rather than as a response to policy feedback. While aid organizations participate in the creation of these paradigms, they are also their captives. Policy effectiveness and efficiency are measured against the standards of these paradigms. This chapter discusses how the aid agencies initially were unable to make sense of experiences at the downstream level of project management and program administration and ended up relying on beliefs shared by other aid agencies to chart new paths forward. As interventions shifted to the upstream level of policy and governance, the problem of learning was no longer "aggregating the disaggregable," but incorporating goals advocated by national governments insisting on their own sovereign perspective. Donor agencies have increasingly placed themselves in a position where they impose their perspectives on recipient governments, a state of affairs not congenial to mutual productive learning.

---

3   Roger Riddell, *Aid Dependency*, monograph produced for the 2015 Project of the Swedish International Development Cooperation Agency (Stockholm, 1995).

4   See, for example, Stephen Hook, ed., *National Interest and Foreign Aid* (Boulder, CO: Lynne Rienner Publishers, 1995).

Donor agencies simultaneously possess a certain measure of discretion and are members of a single aid community. The latter is a function of shared beliefs in certain development paradigms that change over time. As such, they constitute a community with shared epistemic beliefs.[5] Following Peter Hall, a policy paradigm is defined as a framework of ideas that not only specifies policy goals but also the instruments used to obtain them.[6] Evidence of policy paradigms and their importance for learning in aid agencies can be found by studying how these agencies have behaved since the 1950s when "development" became a global or international concern. It is possible to discern four specific paradigm shifts that all agencies have helped shape and embrace.

It all began with the Marshall Plan (1947-1951), the first major transfer of public capital to enhance the pace of international development. Influenced by the success of this plan in achieving reconstruction in Western Europe, economic analysts began to turn these Keynesian ideas into universal recipes. A new field, development economics, was born. Within this perspective, development in the emerging states or the "Third World" would be achieved through transfers of capital and technical expertise.[7] This paradigm prevailed during the last days of colonial rule and early years of independence in Africa. It was also applied to Asia and Latin America with few modifications. Lodged in a modernization paradigm that assumed that development is a move from traditional to modern society, this approach was characterized by great confidence and optimism. Although reconstruction rather than development was the goal of the Marshall Plan, adherents to these assumptions conceptualized the development challenge as an easy one. Defined largely in technocratic terms, development was operationalized with little or no attention to context. The principal task was to replicate institutions and techniques that had modernized the West.

The intellectual efforts were concentrated in two directions. One approach was to produce comprehensive national development plans as guides for which policies should be prioritized. These plans stated the anticipated macroeconomic conditions under which specific program and project activities should and could be developed. Projects took on special significance. They constituted the means by which macro goals could be realized. Good project design was the key to success. It is no exaggeration to suggest that in this first phase of development thinking that lasted into the latter part of the 1960s, the *project* level was regarded as most important. Project design, however, was the prerogative of technical experts. It was done on behalf of potential beneficiaries without their input. Government and other public institutions were identified as responsible for ensuring effective implementation.

---

5 Lawrence C. Dodd, "Political Learning and Political Change: Understanding Development Over Time," in Lawrence C. Dodd and C. Jillson, eds., *The Dynamics of American Politics*: Approach and Interpretations (Boulder, CO: Westview Press, 1994).

6 Peter A. Hall, "Policy Paradigms, Social Learning, and the State: The Case of Economic Policymaking in Britain," *Comparative Politics* vol. 25 (1993), pp. 279-280.

7 John Rapley, *Understanding Development: Theory and Practice in the Third World* (Boulder, CO: Lynne Rienner Publishers, 1996).

Private and voluntary sector organizations were ignored. Development, then, was a top-down exercise by public agencies *for the people.*

The second phase began in the latter part of the 1960s, when analysts and practitioners recognized that a singular focus on projects in the context of national plans was inadequate. The critique followed at least two lines: Firstly, projects designed with little attention to context typically had more unanticipated than anticipated outcomes. For instance, the assumption that development would "trickle down" from the well endowed to the poor, thus generating ripple effects, proved to be mistaken. Secondly, projects were inevitably "enclave" types of intervention with little or no positive externalities. Analysts concluded that the project approach failed to realize improvements, especially in the conditions of the poorer segments of the population. The new paradigm suggested the importance of meeting basic human needs. Convinced that something else had to be done to reduce global poverty, the international community decided that a sectoral approach would be more effective. In operational terms, this meant designating *programs* rather than projects as the principle concern.

The important thing in this second phase, therefore, became how to design integrated programs that addressed not a single dimension of human needs but the whole range of them. For example, integrated rural development programs became very fashionable instruments of action. As a *sequitur*, governments also engaged in administrative reforms that stressed the value of decentralizing authority to lower levels of government in order to enhance coordination and management of these new sectoral programs.[8] Another thing that happened in this second phase was the growing emphasis on education and training of the general population. Human capital mattered. While capacity building in the first phase had been concentrated on elites, the second focused on such areas as adult education and universal primary education, the assumption being that these measures were integral parts of a poverty-oriented approach to development.[9] That is why during this phase the main idea can be said to have been development *of the people.*

At the end of the 1970s there was another shift, this time of even greater consequence than the first. It was becoming increasingly clear that governments typically could not administer the heavy development burden that had been placed on their shoulders. This was most apparent in sub-Saharan Africa, where the state lacked the technical capacity, but it was acknowledged also elsewhere because of bureaucratic shortcomings.[10] Government agencies simply did not work very efficiently in the development field. Placing all "development eggs" in one basket,

---

8   Gerald E. Caiden, *Administrative Reform Comes of Age* (New York and Berlin: Walter de Gruyter, 1991).

9   This first phase devoted to poverty reduction was very much inspired by the works of Simon Kuznets, who argues that the central factor in equalizing income is the rising income of the poorer segments of the population. See, e.g. his article on "Economic Growth and Income Inequality," *American Economic Review* vol. 45 (1955), pp. 17-26.

10   See, for example, R. B. Jain, ed., *Bureaucratic Politics in the Third World* (New Delhi: Gritanjali Publishing House, 1989).

therefore, was being increasingly questioned as the most useful strategy. So was the role of the state compared to the market as an allocative mechanism of resources.[11] As analysts went back to the drawing board, the challenge was no longer how to administer or manage development but instead how to identify the incentives that may facilitate it. The strategic focus shifted to the level of *policy*.

The World Bank, as mandated by its governors, took the lead on this issue and with reference to sub-Saharan Africa, the most critical region, produced a major policy document outlining the proposed necessary economic reforms.[12] This report served as the principal guide for structural adjustment in Africa in the 1980s, although the strategy was also applied in other regions of the world. These reforms, in combination with parallel financial stabilization measures imposed by the International Monetary Fund, were deemed necessary to "get prices right" and to free up resources controlled by the state that could be potentially better used and managed by other institutions in society – particularly the private sector. This period, however, also witnessed the increase in voluntary organizations around the world and preliminary efforts to bring such organizations into the development process. With more responsibilities delegated to the market, private and voluntary organizations could play a more significant role in working with people to realize their aspirations, whether individual or communal.[13] Even though the economic reforms tended to create social inequities, the basic premise was that nongovernmental organizations could do with the people what the government had failed to do for the people. Again, the perception of development had changed, this time to being an exercise done *with the people.*

The new thing in the 1990s has been the growing recognition that development is not only about projects, programs and policies, but also about *politics*. For a long time, politics and development were seen as separate and distinct activities. Out of respect for national sovereignty, donors and governments upheld this dichotomy for a long time. Only in the last ten to fifteen years has this approach been challenged. Although it is controversial in government circles in the Third World, there is a growing recognition that "getting politics right" is, if not a precondition, at least a requisite of development. The implication is that conventional notions of state sovereignty are being challenged and undermined by the actions taken by the international community, notably the international finance institutions and the bilateral donors. United Nations agencies also find themselves caught in this process. For example, human rights violations, including those that limit freedom of expression and association, are being invoked as reasons for not only criticizing governments but

---

11 Marshall W. Meyer, et. al., *Limits to Bureaucratic Growth* (New York and Berlin: Walter de Gruyter, 1985).

12 World Bank, *Accelerated Development in Sub-Saharan Africa* (Washington, DC: The World Bank, 1981).

13 Path-breaking for this new move toward greater emphasis on voluntary action by people themselves were E. Schumacher, *Small is Beautiful* (New York: Harper & Row, 1973) and David Korten and Rudi Klauss, eds., *People-Centered Development: Contributions Toward Theory and Planning Frameworks* (West Hartford, CT: Kumarian Press, 1985).

also for withholding aid if no commitment to cease such violations and improvement is made. Underlying this shift toward creating a politically-enabling environment is the assumption that development, after all, is the product of what people decide to do to improve their livelihoods. People, not governments (especially those run by autocrats), constitute the principal force of development. They must be given the right incentives and opportunities not only in the economic but also the political arena. Governance – the name that best describes this most recent paradigm – involves not only government, but civil society as well. Development is no longer a benevolent top-down exercise, not even a charitable act by nongovernmental organizations, but a bottom-up process, seen primarily in terms of something done *by the people*. The discussion so far is summarized in Table 13.1.

Table 13.1 Shifts in Development Paradigms, 1950s-Present

Paradigm	Period	Focus	Emphasis
Modernization	1950s-1960s	Project	For the people
Basic Needs	1960s-1970s	Program	Of the people
Economic Reform	1980s	Policy	With the people
Governance	1990s-Date	Politics	By the people

These changes, occurring about every ten years, suggest that the donor community is a rather turbulent entity, in which paradigmatic shifts take place fairly frequently. The rest of the chapter will examine the role learning has played in moving the community from one paradigm to the next. It will also discuss what these agencies learn and how. In order to distinguish between the variations that exist among member agencies, it may be helpful to introduce the concept of "autonomy," the extent to which these agencies enjoy legally or constitutionally determined discretionary authority. The agencies included here vary according to degree of autonomy, as shown in Figure 13.1 below. They also vary by *value orientation*, notably the extent to which they are driven by economic or political considerations.

The positions identified in the figure above reflect their core assumptions. The World Bank, as a lending agency, is mandated to give loans of various kinds that are expected to give an acceptable rate of return. The USAID is not a bank, but US foreign aid has always been driven by cost-benefit considerations (even though these calculations may at times have included also political, e.g. foreign policy, values). Chinese aid has been given, not because the country is rich (It considers itself a developing country.), but because it regards foreign aid as an important instrument to gain influence in the developing world. Sida has also acted more on political than economic grounds. Swedish foreign aid is justified on moral grounds; it is an international obligation that politicians regardless of ideological persuasion consider to be right. For example, even when for budgetary reasons, domestic programs have been cut, foreign aid has registered an increase. What I will show in the rest of the chapter is that despite these original diverse orientations, paradigmatic convergence has occurred among these aid agencies.

Figure 13.1 Autonomy and Value Orientation Distinctions among Donor Agencies

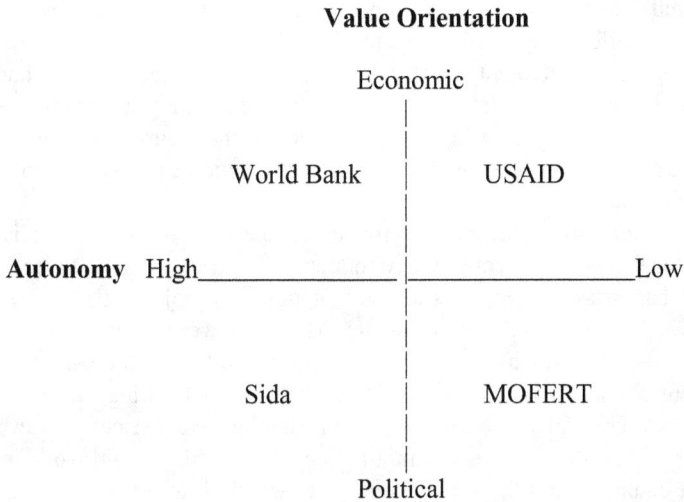

Value Orientation

Economic

World Bank | USAID

Autonomy High_____|_____Low

Sida | MOFERT

Political

What and How Aid Agencies Learn

The first hypothesis guiding this analysis is that agencies with a high degree of autonomy are more likely to adapt and learn, and perhaps even transform their strategy and behavior, than those with low degrees of autonomy. In short, Sida and the World Bank are better placed to learn than USAID and MOFERT. These organizations, however, do not necessarily learn the same things, and/or interpret what they learn in the same way. Thus, the second hypothesis is that what is learned is shaped by the organization's value orientation. Learning in the World Bank and USAID focuses on cost-benefit and other such economic issues, while Sida and MOFERT learn with a view to preserving good political relations with the recipient countries. In short, they give only second consideration to the economic aspects of foreign aid.

The Modernization Phase

The almost boundless optimism that existed during the first phase produced confidence that development policy was a relatively simple matter. The agencies had a sense of direction, provided by the modernization paradigm, which implied that developing countries only had to follow the example of the already industrialized world to succeed. The World Bank, like USAID and Sida, translated this premise into policies that involved moving large chunks of capital and a focus on technical assistance, i.e. reliance on outside experts and capacity-building. Even the Chinese, although they largely confined their aid in these early days to other communist allies, acted on an optimistic premise that countries in Africa were ripe for revolution. What the Chinese themselves had experienced was the model to follow.

The project focus was another common factor. The Chinese had their own version, the so-called "turn-key" project, which implied that the external investors would start the project but hand it over in due course to their local counterparts once they had been trained to run it effectively. Projects were treated as convenient mechanisms for both donor budgets and recipient country development plans, because they had clear organizational and temporal boundaries. Another common assumption was that the larger the project, the greater the impact. In short, the motto was to invest financial and human capital in feasible projects, and results in terms of economic development would follow.

It didn't take too long for agencies to realize that projects were rather artificial creations in their local developing country environment. Not only did they typically lack forward and backward linkages, as already suggested. Projects also lacked connections to the "bigger" development picture. That they were actually carried out and managed over the heads of local beneficiaries only added to their estranged character. The four agencies shared much of this experiential learning, but there were also differences. The Chinese were the least affected by the experiences drawn from this phase. Their conclusion was essentially that Chinese foreign aid works in other Communist countries and the time has come to extend it to other countries, especially in Africa. Their votes would be important in the United Nations and other settings where the Chinese had to compete with the Soviet Union and the US for global influence.

Like the Chinese, Sida also drew a political lesson. Sweden took the lead in OECD circles to redefine the agenda. The Sida lesson entailed two principal points. The first was that countries that emphasize equality and social justice are more deserving than other countries. It even argued that development was impossible without emphasis on social equality. The other and related point was that more emphasis should be placed on sectoral programs rather than projects. The "feedback distance" was simply too long and complicated during this first phase. In addition, the specific lessons learned from micro-level projects did not easily translate into macroeconomic or political lessons. That is why there was a shared sense of frustration in the OECD-affiliated member agencies and a willingness to try something else. Sida alone, although it was at its peak of influence in the international development community at the time, could not alter the paradigm. The aid agencies needed the assistance of a couple of high-powered "blue ribbon" United Nations (UN)-led commissions to shift the focus from modernization to basic needs and, by implication, from economic entrepreneurs to poor peasants.

The Basic Needs Phase

Government was still viewed as the sole agent of development, but its role was no longer about promoting growth as much as it was about reducing poverty. It is no coincidence that the 1970s were the years in which "universal" primary education and health care were proclaimed as the relevant policy goals. Sectoral programs that integrate a range of interventions aimed at helping the poor became the preferred implementation mechanism, an example being the integrated rural development program. Sida funded the first such program in Ethiopia in the late 1960s and it was adopted as model by other agencies, not the least the World Bank. During the twelve years that Robert McNamara served as President (1968-1980), the World Bank became a major advocate and sponsor of basic human needs programs. USAID was the last of the Western agencies to adjust to this new paradigm, but it eventually did so, as confirmed by the 1973 reform of the Foreign Assistance Act called "New Directions."[14] Although China was never part of the process that led OECD-affiliated agencies to change their paradigmatic thinking, its aid not only expanded in the 1970s, but also came to include a greater emphasis on support of small-scale agriculture and primary health care.[15] One well-known contribution was their reliance on "barefoot" doctors, i.e. medical personnel that would move around local communities to help sick people rather than waiting for them to come to the clinic.

The choice of program over project was not only justified on the premise of greater effectiveness. It was also seen as a more convenient approach for managing development. It allowed agencies to channel larger sums of money into single units. Furthermore, the feedback was now aggregated in the field by program managers who were generally closer to the agencies than project managers had ever been. The task of program management, however, soon turned out to be the "Achilles Heel" of the new approach to development management. Coordinating and integrating multiple tasks within specified territorial jurisdictions, e.g. districts or regions, consumed a lot of time and money. The administration of sectoral programs simply became too top-heavy. In the end, the World Bank, but also USAID, started to question the extent to which governments in developing countries, especially Africa, had the capacity to allocate and manage resources in a cost-effective manner. This time, Sida was much slower in accepting the possibility of a shift in paradigm. It had a strong commitment to support countries articulating a socialist approach to development, which, by definition, entailed a strong reliance on government. The Chinese, largely independently, began to move in the direction of a new paradigm driven by changes in domestic economic policies at the end of the 1970s.

---

14 Stephen Snook, "An Agency under Siege: USAID and its Mission in Tanzania" in Hyden and Mukandala, *Agencies in Foreign Aid*, pp. 86-94.

15 Ai Ping, "From Proletarian Internationalism to Mutual Development: China's Cooperation with Tanzania 1965-95" in Hyden and Mukandala, *Agencies in Foreign Aid*, pp. 175-176.

Compared to what happened in the late 1960s when political considerations helped shift the paradigm, economic considerations were the strongest reason for change in the late 1970s. Lessons learned on the ground in many developing countries as well as general trends in the global economy in the latter part of the decade pointed to the need for new ideas. Keynesian thought about "demand management" that had dominated development economics was not helpful when it came to dealing with inflationary trends caused by higher energy prices. Drawing on lessons of the sectoral management phase and responding to new challenges in the world economy, the World Bank became the catalyst for a new paradigm. The Berg Commission, appointed specifically to propose new ways forward for African countries, decisively influenced what the Bank, and eventually the other agencies decided to do.

The learning in the form of paradigmatic change that occurred during the late 1970s can be summarized as follows. The World Bank took advantage of its relative autonomy to spearhead the transformation, while Sida, despite its relative autonomy, fell behind because it was too closely wedded to a politically-inspired paradigm. Sida did not really come to terms with the new paradigm until the mid-1980s after some rather painful transition within the agency and in its relations with countries such as Tanzania, which it had long favored.[16] The USAID found it much easier to adjust because its own thinking ran parallel to that of the emerging World Bank approach. The Chinese move in the same direction had little to do with the thinking going on in the OECD-affiliated agencies and, as suggested above, was determined more by idiosyncratic factors within the Chinese economy and politics.

The Economic Reform Phase

The paradigmatic shift that took place in the late 1970s and early 1980s was more marked and radical than had occurred a decade earlier. It called for a change not only in the way development was administered, but also in terms of the role of the state. The change between the first and second phase was important in its reorientation from support for growth and innovation toward resource redistribution and poverty reduction. Yet, the dominant role of the state was not called into question. The change between the second and the third phase was transformative in two important respects. The first is that it shifted the focus from state to market. The second is that it turned attention away from downstream aspects of the policy process (project management and program administration), in favor of upstream interventions at the policy level. It is important to point out that while the Chinese were increasingly moving toward a market economy at home and "mutual development" through support of, e.g. joint enterprises, in their relations with other developing countries, they never joined the OECD countries in demanding economic policy reform in recipient countries. In this respect, China was on its own track, although in paradigmatic terms it operated at parallel rather than at cross-purposes with Western agencies.

---

16 Ole Elgstrom, "Giving Aid on the Recipient's Terms: The Swedish Experience in Tanzania," in Hyden and Mukandala, *Agencies in Foreign Aid*, pp. 144-146.

There are three important things to say about learning during this phase. The first is that it was essentially focused on economic variables: stabilization of public finance and structural reform of the economy at large. This reform packages became known as "Structural Adjustment." It reflected the dominance of the World Bank, but USAID during the Ronald Reagan years very much emphasized the same priorities. While the Chinese never ventured into calling developing country policies into question, Sida eventually gave up some, if not all, of its political justifications for aid and adopted the new narrow focus on economic issues.

The second learning issue is that aid agencies placed greater emphasis on coordination. Establishing a common position on key issues became necessary to demonstrate the agencies' firm commitment to economic reform. This gradually led to the emergence of the "Washington Consensus," so called after the geographic location of the World Bank and its sister organization, the International Monetary Fund. Under the auspices of this consensus among the donors, consultative meetings were arranged on a regular basis with countries that received policy advice and support. At these meetings recipient governments were asked to report back to a panel of donors on progress with economic reform issues. Leaders from developing countries who participated in this kind of hearing compare it to a graduate school examination with professors testing a student candidate.

The third issue is that learning as a consequence of policy feedback was becoming increasingly more difficult. During the first and second phases, feedback was quite specific. It entailed data on projects or programs that were designed as autonomous managerial or administrative activities. Although such data were not always accurate or reliable, it provided "hard" data that could be processed rather easily in the context of specific evaluation activities. The challenge was to aggregate data in meaningful ways. The problem in the third phase proved to be the opposite. Data at the macro policy level are already aggregated, but typically more diffuse. This is particularly true since much of the statistics in developing countries are incomplete and often inaccurate. The absence of precise and reliable data made the discourse more contested. Recipient-country governments often raised questions about the quality of data to avoid the most demanding calls for reform.

With Structural Adjustment donors accepted a role on the sideline, albeit as actors setting specific conditionalities. By focusing on policy reform, their ability to have a direct influence on development was reduced. Conditionalities typically served as a disincentive for developing countries to adopt reforms. The opportunity for learning from what was going on in these countries was similarly curtailed, not because the feedback distance was long, but because it was too generalized and "doctored" by sovereign governments with an interest in "putting their best foot forward." In this situation, the World Bank became the main depository of economic development data. More than ever before, the agencies turned their eyes away from recipient country realities and relied on information they generated themselves about these countries.

The Chinese escaped some of these problems, because they remained focused in their market-reform approach on the micro level. Thus, their interest in mutual development articulated itself in increasing support for joint enterprises, a way of making their engagement in enterprises that previously had been handed over to local managers more permanent. The problem that the Chinese encountered was that the political and administrative hierarchy was not very receptive to lessons learned. Field personnel at the enterprise level reported their experience but staff in the diplomatic missions and back in Beijing were unwilling or uninterested in taking these reports into account. Learning from the experience with joint enterprises was very limited indeed. Chinese aid continued being driven more by diplomatic or political considerations.

The lesson that USAID, Sida, and the World Bank eventually drew during the 1980s was that the "miracle of the market" was not enough to improve the prospects for development in many countries. They instead began to turn their attention to the importance of reforming the state. More institutional diversity and choice in the political realm emerged as the core of a new paradigm.

The Governance Phase

This most recent phase, which was brought on less by the agencies themselves than by the collapse of Communism and ensuing political trends, is in some respects a continuation of the third. The emphasis continues to be on interventions at upstream level. The difference between the two most recent paradigms is that one can be summarized as "getting prices right" versus "getting politics right." The latter is more demanding and implies a deeper intervention into the sovereignty of recipient countries. But reforming politics is also a more difficult and contested issue. Learning, therefore, has become, if anything, more generalized and as such, less helpful in terms of assessing degree of policy effectiveness.

The relative consensus among the OECD agencies and the international finance institutions has continued, though each agency has adopted a fresh position within this consensus. The Chinese have retained a different position from these organizations. Sida, because of its emphasis on political considerations, has moved its position forward more than any of the agencies covered here. It now insists on growing respect for human rights, conflict resolution, and the role of civil society in development. The World Bank and USAID have continued to stress economic considerations. The latter, while using the same rhetoric as Sida, interprets "governance and democracy" issues, not as ends-in-themselves, but as means to improve economic development. In this respect, it stands closer to the World Bank, which has adopted its own language in order to deal with the challenges of the most recent phase. The World Bank, for instance, is by charter prevented from using language that suggests it is involved in challenging the political sovereignty of a country. It continues to operate on the old assumption that development and politics are two separate things and that one can pursue the former without violating the latter. Thus, words like "institution" and "governance" have become synonyms for phenomena that bilateral and other multilateral agencies can speak more frankly about.

The limits to learning have become especially evident in this most recent phase. The problem with the new emphasis on promoting "good governance" is that it is difficult to agree on indicators that can be meaningfully used to measure performance. While economic policy reform at least offers a few measurable macro indicators, however lopsided that they may be from the perspective of a recipient-country consumer or citizen, finding corresponding performance indicators for political process phenomena is much more controversial. Efforts continue, however, to identify such indicators. Analysts both in the World Bank, OECD and other donor-related institutions continue to argue for quantitative indicators of phenomena that are qualitative in nature.[17] They are no closer today, however, in terms of knowing, for instance, what the relationship is between good governance, on the one hand, and economic and/or social development, on the other.

The Chinese have learned one important lesson since the 1990s and that is that they were right in not extending their interventions to the political level. Their own conclusion is that, from a political point-of-view, the costs far outweigh the benefits. They have expanded their economic cooperation, both in terms of trade and investment, but do not insist on political reform. Given that China remains a Communist one-party state, this is not surprising and it reflects the influence ideology and Beijing continue to exert in determining what the Chinese do in individual recipient countries. Even so, it is clear that the distance between the Chinese, on the one hand, and the OECD-affiliated agencies, on the other, is much shorter today than it was in the first and second phases. The former now have a much more pragmatic approach to development and the prospects for learning should, if anything, grow in the Chinese aid administration. In fact, MOFERT, with its emphasis on economic cooperation and trade, is the only agency today that tries to incorporate lessons learned at the micro level, however difficult this task is.

Conclusion

Several interesting conclusions can be drawn from this review of how aid agencies operate and learn from experience. The most salient may be that the mainstream donor agencies have become increasingly dependent on each other, not only for paradigmatic direction, but also because they, especially the World Bank, possess the most exhaustive and systematic data to back up their decisions. Their real problem is that the macro data that they apply have their own shortcomings, because of faults in national statistics in developing countries from which this database is derived. The "reality" that the World Bank and the other mainstream donors construct in developing countries tends to be artificial and quite significantly removed from the reality that local citizens experience.

This discrepancy between empirical and socially constructed reality has emerged in spite of efforts by the donors to learn the hard lessons of their operations in

---

17 See especially the work done by Danny Kaufmann and his colleagues at the World Bank Institute.

developing countries. As this chapter has tried to show, however, the long cultural distance between the "donor world" and developing country realities as well as the problems of aggregating a myriad of project or program specific data have left the aid agencies increasingly out of touch with the empirical realities of developing countries. The accumulative lessons that these agencies have drawn amount to an admission that they are better off relying on their own paradigms and macro data about developing countries than spending resources trying to make sense of the idiosyncrasies that crop up in project and program evaluations. These more specific assessments – and they are being carried out on an ongoing basis within these agencies – are even less significant for policy today than they were in the 1960s and 1970s when the assumption still prevailed that it was possible to learn meaningful lessons by aggregating project or program data. This largely self-inflicted alienation from the empirical realities of poverty and development has been reinforced by the growing emphasis on macro data that question the strategies and behavior of recipient country governments. Positive rhetoric about "partnership" notwithstanding, aid agencies have limited access to sovereign state institutions and are at least one step removed from being able to internalize lessons about policy or politics.

Some thirty years ago, Pressman and Wildavsky wrote their seminal study on implementation problems of federal programs demonstrating that these programs work not because of the rules adopted but rather in spite of them.[18] Theirs was a cautiously optimistic saga. It is more difficult to find hope in the story about the mainstream aid agencies, at least as far as productive learning from field experience goes. What they have learned and how they have done it is increasingly derived from sharing experiences with each other. The learning is lateral rather than vertical. The fact that they have engaged in "double-loop" or paradigmatic learning (changing not only strategy and tactics but also objectives on a regular basis about every ten years), does not mean that they have become more policy effective.[19] This sophisticated level of learning has been possible because it has been confined to a discourse among like-minded agencies sharing the same "safe" epistemic walls. It is no surprise, therefore, that alternative institutional mechanisms to those of the mainstream donor community are emerging. The World Social Forum as a challenge to the mainstream World Economic Forum is a case in point.

The final observation concerns our "control" case, the Chinese. They have been on their own track and have had little, if any, contact with the mainstream agencies. They have increasingly come to policy conclusions similar to the latter, but because of being alone and driven exclusively by foreign policy considerations in Beijing, the Chinese agency (MOFERT) has been more dependent on drawing lessons from their own field experiences. Such lessons were ignored by Beijing for a long time because of the autocratic nature of the government and culture, but with

---

18 See the discussion in Tom Burns and G. M. Stalker, *Management of Innovation* (London: Tavistock Publications, 1962).

19 Chris Argyris and Donald A. Schon, *Organizational Learning II: Theory, Method, and Practice* (Reading, MA: Addison-Wesley, 1994).

gradual liberalization, the opportunities for learning productively from the field have increased. Feedback may continue to be timid but what MOFERT learns and how it learns offers more promise of being able to enhance policy effectiveness than what the mainstream agencies attempt today.

PART 5
What Have We Learned about Organizational Learning?

Chapter 14

What Have We Learned about Organizational Learning?

M. Leann Brown

In Chapter 1, we identified several theoretical concerns that continue to bedevil organizational learning theorists. In this chapter, we will summarize the light shed on these concerns by the empirical cases of this volume. Is organizational learning best conceptualized as changes in routines, policies, goals and paradigms as a consequence of information, ideas and experience; as ideational interaction among organizational entities; or as changes in organizational leaders' ideas, beliefs, and paradigms? This answer, of course, is that organizational learning may occur in all of these ways. Maintaining the customary distinctions among social, organizational and individual-level analysis is not empirically valid or theoretically helpful – the social learning literature investigates learning among organizational personnel and clusters of organizations (in ecologies of learning) and "leaders" are not just individuals, but instead are personnel who occupy organizational *roles*. What has this volume contributed to our understanding of learning as a process and/or outcome? What have we learned about the different levels of learning sophistication or complexity within organizations?

Most contributors to this volume focus analytical attention on learning dynamics or processes, for example, acquiring new information, ideas, beliefs and understanding via policy feedback (failure or success), research, epistemic communities, discourse, or learning by doing. However, isolating these organizational processes for analysis is a formidable task, and, thus, indicators of learning must be identified. Changes in organizational routines, procedures, policies, norms, goals and paradigms represent the most easily identified indicators of learning. Given that many factors aside from learning affect ultimate organizational outcomes, most concur that these processes and changes may or may not result in more effective policies or goal achievement.

Contributors to this volume concur with existing organizational learning literature that several levels of learning sophistication may be identified. The most simple and common forms of learning are relatively small and incremental changes in organizational routines, procedures and policies deriving from experience, particularly policy failure. In Chapter 13, Goran Hyden describes how aid policy feedback gathered on the project and/or program levels is difficult to aggregate precluding policymakers' making sense of and benefiting from information from the field. Without benefit of high quality and accurate feedback, simple learning did not occur. Instead shared beliefs (ideology) among elites serve as the basis for paradigmatic and policy changes that do not yield more effective policies. In Chapter 2, Brown provides evidence that, due to policy issues' novelty, scientific uncertainty and political volatility, the organization (in this case the European Union) failed to achieve simple (first order) learning from scientific experts and organizational paralysis and dysfunctional behavior ensued. However, second and fourth order learning (changes in goals and "learning how to learn") did occur as a consequence of these food crises. In Chapters 5 and 6, Michael Oliver and Michael Zarkin explain how policy failures and technological change over time spurred governmental actors to embrace paradigmatic change. These cases provide strong evidence that simple forms of organizational learning do not necessary translate into more sophisticated levels of learning, i.e. paradigmatic learning or "learning how to learn." Indeed, simple learning may reduce the likelihood and/or preclude the organization's needing to engage in more sophisticated forms of learning. Alternatively, failure to adapt incrementally may generate crises, and induce more profound levels of change. Most analysts agree that complex forms of organizational learning involving paradigmatic change are difficult and unusual phenomena, and likely to occur only as a consequence of crisis and/or significant personnel change.[1]

Several chapters point out the importance of organizational research, policy imitation or transfer, and experts and/or epistemic communities. In Chapter 5, Zarkin discusses the contribution of epistemic communities to affecting paradigmatic change in the telecommunications sector. However, Eric Morgan's Chapter 4 study of the interaction of the Russian and global epistemic communities in the energy sector is the volume's most explicit example of policy learning via epistemic communities. Morgan finds that consensus is tenuous within the Russian epistemic community, and that Russia's undeveloped political and economic institutional context deters productive learning in its energy sector. Further, the global and Russian epistemic communities hold competing paradigms and ideas, deterring efficient sharing of information. As a matter of fact, while some transfer of information is occurring between the global and Russian energy epistemic communities, they may also be engaging in competitive learning along parallel tracks.

Endogenous Factors that Facilitate or Deter Organizational Learning

Several chapters in this volume provide evidence that relatively small organizations with horizontal patterns of authority and communication are generally more likely to experience effective learning than larger, multilevel and hierarchical ones. Such factors as leadership, the quality of information processing and storage systems, and

---

1   See Philip E. Tetlock, "Learning in U.S. and Soviet Foreign Policy: In Search of an Elusive Concept," in George W. Breslauer and Philip E. Tetlock, eds. *Learning in U.S. and Soviet Foreign Policy* (Boulder, CO: Westview Press, 1991,) p. 28 and Jack S. Levy, "Learning and Foreign Policy: Sweeping a Conceptual Minefield," *International Organization* vol. 48 (1994), p. 286.

social capital including open communication, fairness and trust also figure largely in an organization's capacity to learn. In Chapters 8 and 9, Mike Kenney and Brian Jackson assert that drug trafficking and terrorist organizations' small, network-like ("flat") organizational structures provide them decided learning advantages relative to the states that wish to destroy them. In Chapter 12, Karen Guttieri describes compartmentalization in the mammoth, multi-service, organization that is the US military that deters effect integration of learning. The military has elaborate learning systems but has failed to utilize them effectively. Specifically, it may store away "lessons noted" with the consequence that new understandings remain unintegrated and underutilized in other aspects of military practice such as doctrine, officer training, and field operations. The recent report on prisoner abuses in Abu Greib prison in Iraq failing for months to come to the attention of top Pentagon officials provides striking confirmation of this phenomenon. In Chapter 10, Bill Campbell documents the learning challenges faced by a large, multilevel, dogmatic organization with relatively rigid top-down authority structures. Campbell also opines that Vatican efforts to reestablish centralized control over Church doctrine despite Vatican II's putative liberalizing tendencies communicated a lack of trust in the Latin American bishops.

In contrast to a somewhat linear conceptualization of incoming information serving as the basis for organizational learning, several of our contributors writing within social learning and constructivist orientations are interested in how various actors' interaction and discourse affect organizational learning. In Chapters 5 and 6, Oliver and Zarkin portray governmental actors interacting over time to create new policy paradigms. And, Ellis's constructivist analysis in Chapter 7 portrays US decisionmaking entities' discourse creating and reflecting, in some cases, competitive identities and norms to yield the policy decision to intervene in Somalia.

Exogenous Sources of Organizational Learning

Several of our cases reiterated that the quality of incoming information (e.g. policy feedback, expert and scientific information, and "lesson drawing" or policy transfer from other organizational contexts) influences ability of organization to achieve productive learning. In general, learning is enhanced to the degree that incoming information is accurate, relevant, comprehensive and clear. Ambiguity and uncertainty may be two-edged sword. Faced with uncertainty and ambiguity, organizational personnel may be more willing to engage in research and solicit information from epistemic communities. On the other hand, policymakers may resort to various heuristic devices (including ideology and other cognitive schema) to guide policy decisions that may bias interpretation. In Chapter 2, Brown illustrates the deleterious effect of scientific uncertainty on decision making about bovine hormones and BSE, and, again, in Chapter 14, Hyden describes how in response to poor quality data from the field, elites' ideological constructs serve as the basis for aid policy decisions.

We have noted several times that our contributors make clear the competitive as well as cooperative nature of learning. Learning processes may be competitive in the sense that actors compete to frame policy issues and act as advocates, persuaders and teachers for their preferred ideas and policy recommendations. In Chapter 4, Morgan describes Russian and global energy communities as interacting cooperatively and competitively simultaneously. Kenney and Brian Jackson (in Chapters 8 and 9) present respectively illicit learners competing overtly with states who seek to destroy them. The ecology of learners concept may connote that entities are interdependently and competitively linked. However, several analysts move beyond depicting competitive learning to describing organizations in crisis, with their primary goals and/or existence at risk.

The Interaction of Ideas, Knowledge and Learning with Political and Economic Factors

All chapters of this volume identified and confirmed the existence of interactive relationships among ideational, knowledge, learning factors with more overtly political and economic factors. We have rather studiously avoided using the language of "power" because it lacks specificity. However, if one adopts the frequently-used definition of power as the ability of one actor to get another to undertake some behavior the latter would not otherwise undertake, than providing new information, knowledge, and ideas and such activities as framing, teaching, advocating and persuading via those means constitute a form of power.

Several chapters provide empirical evidence of the importance of leadership in facilitating or deterring effective learning. Most learning literature notes that lower-level personnel usually lack the ability to implement lessons learning without the support or acquiescence of organizational leaders. In Chapter 3, Paolo Spadoni assigns importance to Congressmen's learning, among other factors, in fostering change in US foreign policy toward Cuba. In Chapter 7, Ellis describes the first US President Bush's leadership role as both "learner" and "teacher" within the ecology of learners that yielded the 1992 decision to provide humanitarian assistance in Somalia. And, in Chapter 10, Campbell reminds us that leaders are found on multiple levels in larger organizations, and they may assume different roles in learning processes. The Latin American bishops facilitated communication, selected and reframed broad goals articulated by the executive leadership within the Church, and synthesized these doctrines with practical knowledge and demands from lower-level Church members.

However, Campbell and others' studies also highlight how difficult it is for leaders to learn and how they may represent important barriers to organizational learning. Leaders are often too busy to engage in prolonged periods of research, information gathering or reflection. Guittieri points out that leaders may be invested in status quo practices and prone to exploit existing competences rather than develop or embrace new ones. In the case of the Catholic Church, when the Latin American bishops serving as middle managers attempted to facilitate productive learning, upper-level churchmen acted aggressively to reestablish control over doctrine and participation and actually engaged in anti-learning strategies including sending mixed messages and restricting the participation of bishops with alternative points of view. In Chapter 4, Morgan explains that state control over information and the lack of input from wider societal actors from the legal profession and the press, a legacy of the communist past, deprives the Russian epistemic community of important sources of information.

Thus, we do not naïvely assume that learning provides exclusive explanations for policy change, but concur instead with Robert Keohane's critique of purely power-oriented, rationalistic theories of international organizations:

> [R]ationalistic theories seem only to deal with one dimension of a multidimensional reality: they are incomplete, since they ignore changes taking place in consciousness. They do not enable us to understand how interests change as a result of changes in belief systems. They obscure rather than illuminate the sources of states' preferences.[2]

Of course, states represent only one example of learning organizations.

Learning by Illicit Actors

An important contribution of this volume that illicit actors are included among the organizations studied. Idealist scholars who implicitly associate learning with positive outcomes generate most organizational learning literature. Chapters 8 and 9 depart from this trend by investigating how drug trafficking and terrorist organizations learn. Obviously the previously discussed generalizations apply to illicit organizations, however, the conditions within which they operate are extreme. Illicit organizations operate in very competitive rather than cooperative environments, as a matter of fact, they exist in a constant state of crisis because they must learn in a timely fashion or be destroyed. Moreover, the factors generally regarded as conducive to effective learning are missing: including an open exchange of information, cooperation and trust, and institutionalized systems of information storage. Kenney and Jackson provide convincing evidence, however, that the high negative and positive incentives for learning and the virtually flat network structures of these organizations make surviving illicit organizations important examples of learning organizations.

Conclusion

A final word on why, despite the epistemological and methodological challenges associated with the concept of "organizational learning," it is important to develop

---

2   Robert Keohane, "International Institutions: Two Approaches," *International Studies Quarterly* 1988, p. 391.

this body of thought. Organizations in the 21st century have moved beyond industrial age structures and management models to those shaped by information, knowledge, and technology. Most concur that a knowledge-based age requires new forms of organizations and new approaches to management and goal achievement.[3] At a recent conference, a former United States ambassador reported that his personal experience suggested that organizations do not learn. All theorists of organizational learning concur that that simple forms of learning are more common than paradigmatic learning and "learning how to learn." However, we contend that all organizations are constantly learning[4] – the concerns are whether they learning the "right" lessons and whether the lessons learned can be translated into productive learning, i.e. effective policies that enhance goal achievement. The policy-relevant conclusions deriving from these cases are simple – productive organizational learning is more likely to occur when:

- the organization is open to information from the external environment including feedback from their and other organizations' policy experience, research and epistemic communities.
- organizational structures are nonhierarchical and flexible, i.e. modeled on networks in which authority, responsibility, information and decision-making are decentralized. All personnel should be empowered to participate fully in governance and policy decision-making to unleash the organization's creativity.
- the organizational culture values information- and knowledge-generating activities; frequent, open and honest communication; trust; and fairness.
- organizational leadership (at all levels) is a source of and is adept at conveying new information, ideas, and beliefs, and creates and sustains institutional structures, processes and cultures that facilitate productive learning.
- organizational size (including the number of hierarchical levels, subunits and personnel) is relatively small.
- when "lessons learned" and new understandings are integrated throughout the organization.
- the organization is challenged in some way. Congruent with an oft-quoted Chinese proverb, crises may represent opportunities for learning sometimes at profound levels. However, crises deriving from and/or accompanied by profound disagreements in norms and paradigms among policy actors or pathologies in communication and trust may result in organizational paralysis

---

3   Ralph D. Stacey, *Complex Responsive Processes in Organizations: Learning and Knowledge Creation* (New York: Routledge, 2001), p. 1.

4   To reiterate – all organizations discussed in the volume have in place multiple mechanisms to facilitate learning: research capacity; access to experts, consultants and epistemic communities; systematic training and simulation procedures; discourse mechanisms such as conferences, hearings and papers; innovative and entrepreneurial leaders; and, probably most important, policy assessment and feedback mechanisms.

and unproductive learning.
• decisionmakers remain cognizant of organizational cognitive, structural and process as well as political deterrents to effective learning.

References

Aall, Pamela, Lt. Col. Daniel T. Miltenberger, and Thomas G. Weiss, eds., *Guide to IGOs, NGOs, and the Military in Peace and Relief Operations* (Washington, DC: United States Institute of Peace Press, 2000).

Adibe, Clemant, *Managing Arms in Peace Processes: Somalia* (New York: United Nations Institute for Disarmament Research, 1995).

Adler, Emanuel, "The Emergence of Cooperation: National Epistemic Communities and the International Evolution of the Idea of Nuclear Arms Control," in Peter M. Haas, ed., *Knowledge, Power, and International Policy Coordination* (Columbia, SC: University of South Carolina Press, 1997).

Akers, Ronald L., *Social Learning and Social Structure* (Boston: Northeastern University Press, 1998).

_____ and Gary F. Jensen, eds., *Social Learning Theory and the Explanation of Crime: A Guide for the New Century* (Somerset, NJ: Transaction Publishers, 2002).

Allard, C. Kenneth, "Lessons Unlearned: Somalia and Joint Doctrine," *Joint Forces Quarterly* (Autumn 1995).

Allison, Graham and Philip Zelikow, *Essence of Decision: Explaining the Cuban Missile Crisis* (New York: Longman, 1999).

al-Zawahiri, Ayman. "Knights under the Prophet's Banner," *Al-Sharq al-Awsat* (December 4-7, 2001).

Argyris, Chris, *On Organizational Learning*, 2nd ed. (Oxford: Blackwell Publishers, Ltd., 1999).

_____ and Donald A. Schon, *Organizational Learning II: Theory, Method, and Practice* (Reading, MA: Addison-Wesley, 1996).

_____, *Organizational Learning: A Theory of Action Perspective* (Reading, MA: Addison-Wesley, 1978).

_____, "Double Loop Learning in Organizations: Continuity and Change," *Harvard Business Review* vol. 55 (1977).

Arreola, Antroy A., "Who's Isolating Whom? Title III of the Helms-Burton Act and Compliance with International Law," *Houston Journal of International Law* vol. 20 (1998), pp. 353-378.

Arrow, Kenneth J., *The Limits of Organization* (New York: W.W. Norton, 1974).

Aspinwall, Mark D. and Gerald Schneider, "Same Menu, Separate Tables: The Institutionalist Turn in Political Science and the Study of European Integration," *European Journal of Political Research* vol. 38 (2000), pp. 1-36.

Astaneh-Asl, Abolhassan, interviewed by Terry Gross, *Fresh Air*, National Public Radio (October 16, 2001), <www.npr.org>.

Averch, Harvey and Leland Johnson, "The Behavior of the Firm under Regulatory Constraint," *American Economics Review* vol. 52 (1962), pp. 1052-1069.

Axelrod, Robert and Michael D. Cohen, *Harnessing Complexity* (New York: Free Press, 2000).

Bachelet, Pablo, "Embargo Foes in Disarray as U.S. Mulls Cuba Options," *Reuters* (April 25, 2003).

Baldwin, Andrew L. and Ilka Lewington, "Russia," *Utility Regulation, 1997: Economic Regulation of Utilities and Network Industries Worldwide* (London: Centre for the Study of Regulated Industries, 1997).

Balmaceda, Margarita Mercedes, "Gas, Oil and the Linkages between Domestic and Foreign Policies: The Case of Ukraine," *Europe-Asia Studies* vol. 50 (1998).

Bandura, A., *Social Learning Theory* (Englewood Cliffs, NJ: Prentice-Hall, 1977).

Barlow, Dennis C., "A Planner's Guide for the Employment of Civil Affairs in Latin America," in John W. DePauw and George A. Luz, eds., *Winning the Peace: The Strategic Implications of Military Civic Action* (New York: Praeger, 1992), pp. 117-139.

Bates, Stephen, "Belgium Removes Pork from Sale as New Dioxin Scare Hits Country," *The Guardian* (July 24, 1999).

Bateson, G., *Steps to an Ecology of Mind* (New York: Ballantine, 1972).

Baum, Dan, "Battle Lessons: What the Generals Don't Know," *The New Yorker* (January 17, 2005), pp. 42-48.

Benkard, C. Lanier, "Learning and Forgetting: The Dynamics of Aircraft Production," *Research Paper No. 1560* (Stanford, CA: Graduate School of Business, Stanford University, 1999).

Bennett, Colin J., "Review Article: What is Policy Convergence and What Causes It?," *British Journal of Political Science* vol. 21 (1992), pp. 215-233.

_____ and Michael Howlett, "The Lessons of Learning: Reconciling Theories of Policy Learning and Policy Change," *Policy Science* vol. 25 (1992), pp. 275-294.

Bergen, Peter L., *Holy War, Inc.: Inside the Secret World of Osama bin Laden* (New York: The Free Press, 2001).

_____and Thomas Luckmann, *The Social Construction of Reality: A Treatise on the Sociology of Knowledge* (New York: Anchor Books, 1966).

Berman, Larry and Emily O. Goldman, "Clinton's Foreign Policy at Midterm," in Colin Campbell and Bert A. Rockman, eds., *The Clinton Presidency: First Appraisals* (Chatham, NJ: Chatham House Publishers, 1996).

Bertram, Eva, Morris Blachman, Kenneth Sharpe, and Peter Andreas, *Drug War Politics: The Price of Denial* (Berkeley, CA: University of California Press, 1996).

Betancourt, Darío and Martha L. García, *Contrabandistas, marimberos y mafiosos: Historia social de la mafia colombiana (1965-1992)* (Bogotá, Colombia: *Tercer Mundo Editores*, 1994).

Bickel, Keith B., *Mars Learning: The Marine Corps Development of Small Wars Doctrine, 1915-1940* (Boulder, CO: Westview, 2001).

Bijker, Wiebe, *Of Bicycles, Bakelites, and Bulbs: Toward a Theory of Sociotechnical Change* (Cambridge, MA: MIT Press, 1995).

Bijman, Jos, "Recombinant Bovine Somatotropin in Europe and the USA," *Biotechnology and Development Monitor* vol. 27 (1996), pp. 2-5.

Blyth, M., "'Any More Bright Ideas?': The Ideational Turn of Comparative Political Economy," *Comparative Politics* vol. 29 (1997), pp. 229-250.

_____, "From Ideas and Institutions to Ideas and Interests: Beyond the Usual Suspects?," Paper presented at the Eleventh Conference of Europeanists, Baltimore, MD (February 26-28, 1998).

Boadle, Anthony, "Little cheer in Cuba over Bush's U.S. election win," *Reuters* (November 3, 2004).

Booth, A., "Britain in the 1950s: a 'Keynesian' Managed Economy?," *History of Political Economy* vol. 33 (2001), pp. 283-313.

_____, "New Revisionists and the Keynesian era in British Economic Policy," *Economic History Review* vol. 54 (2001), pp. 346-366.

Britton, A., *Macroeconomic Policy In Britain 1974–1987* (Cambridge: Cambridge University Press, 1991).

Brock, Gerald, *Telecommunications Policy for the Information Age: From Monopoly to Competition* (Cambridge, MA: Harvard University Press, 1994).

Bureau for International Narcotics and Law Enforcement Affairs, US Department of State, *International Narcotics Control Strategy Report 2005*, Volume 1, "Drug and Chemical Control" (March 2005), <http://www.state.gov/documents/organization/42867.pdf>.

Burns, Tom and G. M. Stalker, *Management of Innovation* (London: Tavistock Publications, 1962).

Caiden, Gerald, *Administrative Reform Comes of Age* (New York and Berlin: Walter de Gruyter, 1991).

Cairncross, A. K., *The British Economy since 1945: Economic Policy and Performance, 1945-1990* (London: Routledge, 1992).

James Cameron's "Titanic" Explorer (Fox Interactive CD-ROM, 1997).

Carvey, Dan, "Congress Fires its First Shot in Information Revolution." *Congressional Quarterly Weekly Report* vol. 54 (1996), pp. 289-94.

Center for International Policy, "U.S. Senate Announces Cuba Working Group." (March 23, 2003).

Chapman, Anne W., *The Origins and Development of the National Training Center 1976-1984* (Fort Monroe, VA: Office of the Command Historian, US Training and Doctrine Command, 1992).

Chandrasekaran, Rajiiv, "Inexperienced Hands Guide Iraq Rebuilding," *Washington Post Foreign Service* (June 25, 2003), p. A01.

Chemers, Martin M., *An Integrative Theory of Leadership* (Mahwah, NJ: Lawrence Erlbaum Associates, Publishers, 1997).

Chivers, C. J. and David Rohde, "Turning Out Guerrillas and Terrorists to Wage a Holy War," *New York Times* (March 18, 2002).

Clarke, P., ed., *The Keynesian Revolution and its Economic Consequences* (Northampton, MA: Edward Elgar, 1998).

Cleary, Edward, *Crisis and Change* (Maryknoll, NY: Orbis Books, 1985).

_____, "Journey to Santo Doming," in Alfred T. Hennelly, ed., *Santo Domingo and Beyond* (Maryknoll, NY: Orbis Books 1993).

Cohen, Jeffrey E., "The Telephone Problem and the Road to Telephone Regulation, 1876-1917," *Journal of Policy History* vol. 3 (1991), pp. 42-69.

Cohen, Michael D. and Paul Bacdayan, "Organizational Routines Are Stored as Procedural Memory," *Organization Science*, vol. 5 (1994), reprinted in Michael D. Cohen and Lee S. Sproull, *Organizational Learning* (Thousand Oaks, CA: Sage, 1996), pp. 403-429.

Coleman, Jonathan R, "The Economic Impact of U.S. Sanctions with Respect to Cuba," *Cuba in Transition* (Washington, DC: Association for the Study of the Cuban Economy, 2001).

Coleman, W., "Policy Convergence in Banking: a Comparative Study," *Political Studies* vol. 42 (1994), pp. 274-92.

Coleman, William, D., Grace D. Skogstad, and Michael M. Atkinson, "Paradigm Shifts and Policy Networks: Cumulative Change in Agriculture," *Journal of Public Policy* vol. 16 (1996), pp. 273-301.

Coles, Harry L. and Albert K. Weinberg, *Civil Affairs: Soldiers Become Governors* (Washington, DC: Office of the Chief of Military History, 1964).

Commission of the European Communities (hereafter Commission), *Food Safety: from the Farm to the Fork*, <http://europa.eu.int/comm/food/fs/sc/scf/background_en.html>.

_____, *Commission Decision of 16 April 1974 Relating to the Institution of a Scientific Committee for Food*, *OJ* L 136 (Luxembourg: EU Publications Office, 1974).

_____, *Final Scientific Report of the Committee for Veterinary Medicinal Products* Documents No. III/3006-7/93 FINAL (January 23, 1993).

_____, *Commission Decision 95/273/EC of 6 July 1995 Relating to the Institution of a Scientific Committee for Food* (OJ L 167, July 18, 1995).

_____, *Product Safety, Consumer Health and Food Safety* (1997), <http://europa.eu.int/scadplus/leg/en/lvb/l32013.htm>.

_____, *Foodstuffs. Green Paper: The General Principles of Food Law in the European Union* (1997), < http://europa.eu.int/scadplus/leg/en/lvb/l21220.htm>.

_____, *Communication from the Commission to the Council and the European Parliament, WTO Decisions Regarding the EC Hormones Ban.* COM(1999) 31 final (Brussels, February 10, 1999).

_____, *Opinion of the Scientific Committee on Veterinary Measures relating to Public Health, Assessment of Potential Risks to Human Health from Hormone Residues in Bovine Meat and Meat Products.* XXIV/B3/SC4 (April 30, 1999)

_____, *White Paper on Food Safety*, COM (1999) 719 final (Brussels, January 12, 2000).

_____, *Communication from the Commission on the precautionary principle*, Brussels, February 2, 2000 (COM 2000) 1, <http://europa.eu.int/comm/dgs/health_consumer/library/pub/pub07_en.pdf>.

Congress Daily, "Twelve Members Seek Easing of Cuba Embargo," (June 18, 1997).

Congress Daily, "Helms, in Dramatic Departure, Backs Easing of Cuban Embargo," (March 24, 2000).

Congress Daily, "Nethercutt Cutting a Cuba Deal," (June 27, 2000).

Congress Daily, "Cuba Trade Backers Blast GOP Compromise," (June 29, 2000).

Cubanet, "A letter to the president," (August 12, 2003), <http://www.cubanet.org/CNews/y03/ago03/12e7.htm>.

Daft, Richard L. and Karl E. Weick, "Towards a Model of Organizations as Interpretation Systems," *Academy of Management Review* vol. 9 (1984), pp. 284-295.

Darling, Marilyn and Charles Perry, *From Post-Mortem to Living Practice: An In-depth Study of the Evolution of the After Action Review* (Boston: Signet, 2001).

Deeg, R., "Institutional Transfers, Social Learning and Economic Policy in Eastern Germany," *West European Politics* vol. 18 (1995), pp. 38-63.

Derthick, Martha and Paul J. Quirk, *The Politics of Deregulation* (Washington, DC: Brookings Institution, 1985).

Deutsch, Karl W., *The Nerves of Government: Models of Political Communication and Control* (New York: The Free Press, 1966).

Directorate General for Health and Consumer Protection (DGXXIV) of the European Commission, *Midterm Review of the Commission's Scientific Advisory System.* (Brussels: May 21, 1999).

Dodd, Lawrence C., "Learning to Learn: the Political Mastery of US Senators," *Legislative Studies Section Newsletter* no. 16 (November 1992).

_____, "Political Learning and Political Change: Understanding Development across Time," in Lawrence C. Dodd and Calvin Jillson, eds. *The Dynamics of American Politics: Approaches and Interpretations*. Boulder, CO: Westview Press, 1994), pp. 331-364.

_____ and Calvin Jillson, eds., *The Dynamics of American Politics: Approaches and Interpretations*. Boulder, CO: Westview Press, 1994).

Dodgson, Mark, "Organizational Learning: A Review of the Literatures," *Organizational Studies* vol. 14 (1993), pp. 375-394.

Dolowitz, D. P., "British Employment Policy in the 1980s: Learning from the American Experience," *Governance* vol. 10 (1997), pp. 23-42.

_____, *Learning from America: Policy Transfer and the Development of the British Workfare State* (Brighton, UK: Sussex Academic Press, 1998).

_____, "Learning from Abroad: The Role of Policy Transfer in Contemporary Policy Making," *Governance* vol. 13 (2000), pp. 5-24.

_____, S. Greenwold, and D. Marsh, "Policy Transfer: Something Old, Something New, Something Borrowed, but Why Red, White and Blue?," *Parliamentary Affairs*, vol. 52 (1999) pp. 719-730.

_____, R. Hulme, M. Nellis, and F. O'Neal, *Policy Transfer and British Social Policy: Learning from the USA?* (Philadelphia PA: Open University Press, 1999).

_____, "A Policy–maker's Guide to Policy Transfer," *Political Quarterly* vol. 74 (2003), pp. 101-108.

Dominguez, Jorge I., "U.S.-Cuban Relations: From the Cold War to the Colder War," *Journal of Interamerican Studies and World Affairs* vol. 39 (1997), pp. 49-75.

Doty, Roxanne Lynn, "Foreign Policy as Social Construction: A Post-Positivist Analysis of U.S. Counterinsurgency Policy in the Philippines," *International Studies Quarterly* vol. 37 (1993), pp. 297-320.

Drake, Richard. *The Revolutionary Mystique and Terrorism in Contemporary Italy* (Bloomington, IN: Indiana University Press, 1989).

Drew, Elizabeth, *On the Edge: The Clinton Presidency* (New York: Simon and Schuster, 1994).

Drozdiak, William, "Bush Plan Worries Europeans; Removing U.S. Troops From Balkans Is Seen as Divisive," *Washington Post* (October 24 2000), p. A07.

Drug Enforcement Administration (DEA), US Department of Justice, *The Illicit Drug Situation in Colombia* (Washington, DC: Publications Unit, Intelligence Division, November 1993).

_____, *Colombian Opiate Assessment* (Publications Unit, Intelligence Division, DEA Headquarters, 1994).

Dye, Roy Thomas, *A Social History of Drug Smuggling in Florida*, unpublished PhD dissertation (Tallahassee, FL: Florida State University, 1998).

Eden, Lynn, *Whole World on Fire: Organizations, Knowledge, and Nuclear Weapons Devastation* (Ithaca, NY: Cornell University Press, 2004).

Eisner, Marc Allen, *Regulatory Politics in Transition* (Baltimore, MD: Johns Hopkins Press, 1993).

Elgstrom, Ole, "Giving Aid on the Recipient's Terms: The Swedish Experience in Tanzania," in Goran Hyden and Rwekaza Mukandala, eds., *Agencies in Foreign Aid* (London: Macmillan, 1997).

Ellsberg, Daniel, *Secrets: A Memoir of Vietnam and the Pentagon Papers* (New York: Viking, 2002).

Ely, Richard, *Monopolies and Trusts* (New York: The Macmillan Company, 1912).

Embargo Update, "Senators Offer President Support on Sales to Cuba," (December 7, 2001), <www.giraldilla.com>.

Engelberg, Stephen and Adam Bryant, "Warnings Unheeded—A Special Report: F.A.A.'s Fatal Fumbles on Commuter Plane's Safety," *New York Times* (February 26, 1995).

Etheredge, Lloyd S., *Government Learning* (Cambridge, MA: Center for International Studies, Massachusetts Institute of Technology, 1979).

_____, *Can Governments Learn?* (New York: Pergamon, 1981/1985).

Etzioni, Amitai, "Dual Leadership in Complex Organizations," *American Sociological Review* vol. 30 (1965).

"Euro 8m Budget 'Insufficient' Warns Food Authority Chief," *European Voice* vol. 8 (December 18, 2002).

European Information Service, "Food Safety: European Authority Up and Running," *European Report* (June 4, 2003).

_____, "Food Safety: Rules on Requests for Opinions from Food Safety Authority Changed," *European Report* (June 25, 2003).

European Parliament (EP), Committee on the Environment, Public Health and Consumer Protection and Committee on Agriculture and Rural Development of the European Parliament. *Bovine Spongiform Encephalopathy (BSE) - (Creutzfeldt-Jakob Disease) CJD: Our Health at Risk?* Info Memo: Hearing No. 17 (Brussels, June 24-25, 1996).

_____, *EP BSE Inquiry Report*A4-0020/97/A (February 7, 1997), <http://www.mad-cow.org/final_EU.html>.

_____, *Opinion of the Committee on Industry, External Trade, Research and Energy for the Committee on the Environment, Public Health and Consumer Policy on Public Health: Effects of Endocrine Disrupters on Human and Animal Health (Communication)* (COM(1999) 706- C5-0107/2000-2000/2071 (COS), 1999.

_____, Committee on the Environment, Public Health and Consumer Policy, *Report on the Commission Communication to the Council and the European Parliament on a Community Strategy for Endocrine Disrupters – a Range of Substances Suspected of Interfering with the Hormone Systems of Humans and Wildlife* COM(1999) 706-C5-0107/2000 – 2000/2071(COS), Final A5-1097/2000, 2000.

Evans, M. and J. Davies, "Understanding Policy Transfer: A Multi-Level, Multi-Disciplinary Perspective," *Public Administration* vol. 77 (1999), pp. 361-385.

Fallows, James, "Blind Into Baghdad," *The Atlantic* (January/February 2004).

Farah, Douglas, "New Threat From Colombia: Heroin Traffickers Aggressively Marketing Nearly Pure Drug in U.S.," *Washington Post* (March 27, 1997).

Farkas, Andrew, *State Learning and International Change* (Ann Arbor, MI: University of Michigan Press, 1998).

Feldman, Martha S., "Resources in Emerging Structures and Processes of Change," *Organization Science* vol. 15 (2004), pp. 295-309.

_____ and Brian T. Pentland, "Reconceptualizing Organizational Routines as a Source of Flexibility and Change," *Administrative Science Quarterly* vol. 48 (2003), pp. 94-118.

Felkins, Katherine, H. P. Leighly, Jr., and A. Jankovic, "The Royal Mail Ship Titanic: Did a Metallurgical Failure Cause a Night to Remember?" *JOM* [formerly *Journal of Metals*], vol. 50 (1998), pp. 12-18.

Fiedler, Fred E., *A Theory of Leadership Effectiveness* (New York: McGraw-Hill Book Company, 1967).

Fiol, C. Marlene and Marjorie A. Lyles, "Organizational Learning," *Academy of Management Review* vol. 10 (1985), pp. 803-813.

Fishel, John T., *Civil Military Operations in the New World* (Westport, CT: Praeger,1997).

Fisk, Daniel W., "Cuba: The End of an Era," *The Washington Quarterly* vol. 24 (2001), pp. 93-106.

Forest, James J. F., ed., *Teaching Terror: Strategic and Tactical Learning in the Terrorist World* (Lanham, MD: Rowman & Littlefield, 2006).

Fritz, Jan-Stefan, "Knowledge and Policymaking for the Environment: A Critique of the Epistemic Communities Approach," Paper presented at the Annual Convention of the International Studies Association, Washington, DC, (February 16-21, 1999).

Gamble, A., "Economic Policy," in Z. Layton-Henry, ed., *Conservative Party Politics* (London: Macmillan, 1980).

Garnett, M. and M. J. Oliver, "The Art of Learning and Forgetting: the Conservative Party, 1974-9," *Twentieth Century British History*, forthcoming 2006.

Garvin, David, *Learning in Action: A Guide to Putting the Learning Organization to Work* (Boston: Harvard Business School Press, 2000).

Ghent, Bill and David Hess, "Seeking an End to Sanctions," *National Journal* (June 24, 2000).

Ghio, Jose Maria, *The Latin American Church in the Wojtyla Era: New Evangelization or 'Neo-integralism'?* (Notre Dame, IN: Kellogg Institute, 1990).

Glaeser, Martin G., *Outlines of Public Utility Regulation* (New York: Macmillan, 1927).

Glanz, James, "Clues of Asthma Study Risks May Have Been Overlooked," *New York Times* (July 27, 2001).

Granfield, Patrick, *The Limits of the Papacy: Authority and Autonomy in the Church* (New York, NY: Crossroads Publishing, 1987).

Gray, Colin, *Nuclear Strategy and National Style* (Lanham, MD: Hamilton Press, 1986).

Gray, Paul, "The Scientific Committee for Food," in M.P.C.M. Van Schendelen, ed., *EU Committees as Influential Policymakers* (Aldershot, UK: Ashgate, 1998), pp. 68-88.

Greenway, J., "Policy Learning and the Drink Question in Britain, 1850-1950," *Political Studies* vol. 56 (1998), pp. 903-918.

Greener, I., "Social Learning and Macroeconomic Policy in Britain," *Journal of Public Policy* vol. 21 (2001), pp. 133-152.

Groombridge, Mark A., *Missing the Target. The Failure of the Helms-Burton Act* (Washington, DC: The Cato Institute, June 5, 2001).

Guggenheim, Ken, "Lawmakers temper bid to ease Cuba embargo," *Associated Press* (April 22, 2003).

Gunaratna, Rohan, *Inside Al Qaeda: Global Network of Terror* (New York: Columbia University Press, 2002).

Gusterson, Hugh, *Nuclear Rites: A Weapons Laboratory at the End of the Cold War* (Berkeley, CA: University of California Press, 1996).

Guttieri, Karen. "Professional Military Education in Democracies," in Thomas Bruneau and Scott Tollefson, eds., *Soldiers and Statesmen: Institutional Bases of Democratic Civilian Control* (Austin, TX: University of Texas Press, forthcoming).

_____, "Symptom of the Moment: A Juridical Gap for US Occupation Forces," *International Insights* vol. 13 (1997), pp. 131-156.

_____, *Toward a Usable Peace: United States Civil Affairs in Post-Conflict Environments*, PhD Dissertation, University of British Columbia, 1999.

Haas, Ernst B., *When Knowledge Is Power: Three Models of Change in International Organizations* (Berkeley, CA: University of California Press, 1990).

Haas, Peter M., ed., "Introduction: Epistemic Communities and International Policy Coordination," *International Organization* vol. 46 (1992), pp. 1-36.

_____, ed., *Knowledge, Power, and International Policy Coordination* (Cambridge, MA: Massachusetts Institute of Technology, 1992).

_____, ed., *Knowledge, Power, and International Policy Coordination* (Columbia, SC: University of South Carolina Press, 1997).

_____, "International Institutions and Social Learning in the Management of Global Environmental Risks," *Policy Studies Journal* vol. 28 (2000), pp. 558-575.

Hall, Peter A., *The Political Dimensions of Economic Management* (Ann Arbor, MI: University Microfilms International, 1982).

_____, *The Political Power of Economic Ideas: Keynesianism Across Nations* (Princeton, NJ: Princeton University Press, 1989).

_____, "Policy Paradigms, Experts and the State: the Case of Macro-economic Policy Making in Britain," in Stephen Brooks and Alain G. Gagnon, eds., *Social Scientists, Policy and the State* (New York: Praeger, 1990).

_____, "Policy Paradigms, Social Learning, and the State: The Case of Economic Policymaking in Britain," *Comparative Politics* vol. 25 (1993), pp. 275-296.

_____ and Rosemary Taylor, "Political Science and the Three New Institutionalisms," *Political Studies* vol. 4 (1996), pp. 936-957.

Hannan, Michael T. and John Freeman., "The Population Ecology of Organization," *American Journal of Sociology* vol. 82 (1977), pp. 929-964.

Hanson, Brooks, "Learning from Natural Disasters," *Science* vol. 308 (May 20, 2005), p. 1125.

Harris, Gardiner, "F.D.A. Seizes Millions of Pills From Pharmaceutical Plants," *New York Times* (March 5, 2005).

Harston, Julian J.R.C., "Opening Speech by Deputy Special Representative of the Secretary-General of the United Nations, Bosnia and Herzegovina," in Peter Viggo Jakobsen, ed., *Civil-Military Co-operation Lessons Learned and Models for the Future*. Report from the DUPI Conference in Copenhagen, September 1-2, 2000 (Copenhagen: Danish Institute of International Affairs, 2000).

Healy, Jon, "New Telecommunications Age Hits a Snag in the Senate," *Congressional Quarterly Weekly Report* vol. 52 (1994), p. 1776.

Heclo, Hugh, *Modern Social Politics in Britain and Sweden: From Relief to Income Maintenance* (New Haven, CT: Yale University Press, 1974).

Hedberg, Bo, "How Organizations Learn and Unlearn," in P. Nystrom and W. Starbuck, *Handbook of Organizational Design* vol. 1 (Oxford: Oxford University Press, 1981).

Hennelly, Alfred T., *Theology: Documentary History* (Maryknoll, NY: Orbis Books, 1990).

_____, *Santo Domingo and Beyond* (Maryknoll, NY: Orbis Books, 1993).

Henry, Nicholas, *Public Administration and Public Affairs* (Englewood Cliffs, NJ: Prentice Hall, 1989).

Hermann, Charles F., "Changing Course: When Governments Choose to Redirect Foreign Policy," *International Studies Quarterly* vol. 34 (1990), pp. 3-31.

Hernández-Cata', Ernesto, "The Fall and Recovery of the Cuban Economy in the 1990s: Mirage or Reality?" *International Monetary Fund Working Paper* (April 2001).

Hess, David, "Farmers Win Cuba Vote as Panel OKs Spending Bill," *National Journal* (May 10, 2000).

Hill, Barry T., General Accounting Office, Testimony before the Subcommittee on Forest and Forest Health, Committee on Resources, House of Representatives, "Fire Management: Lessons Learned from the Cerro Grande (Los Alamos) Fire and Actions Needed to Reduce Fire Risks," released August 14, 2000, GAO/T-RCED-00-273, <http://www.nps.gov/cerrogrande>.

Hoffman, Bruce, *Inside Terrorism* (New York: Columbia University Press, 1998).

_____, "Terrorism Trends and Prospects," in Ian O. Lesser, Bruce Hoffman, John Arquilla, David Ronfeldt, and Michele Zanini, eds., *Countering the New Terrorism* (Santa Monica, CA: RAND Corporation, 1999), pp. 7-38.

Holmes, M., *Political Pressure and Economic Policy, British Government 1970-74* (London: Butterworth, 1982).

Hood, C. C., *Explaining Economic Policy Reversals* (Buckingham, UK: Open University Press, 1994).

Hook, Stephen, *National Interest and Foreign Aid* (Boulder, CO: Lynne Rienner Publishers 1995).

Horwitz, Robert B., *The Irony of Regulatory Reform: The Deregulation of American Telecommunications* (New York: Oxford University Press, 1989).

House Record, "Stenholm Votes for Increased Exports, Democracy," House of Representatives (July 21, 2000).

House Record, HR 2138, "Bridges to the Cuban People Act of 2001," (June 12, 2001), <http://thomas.loc.gov/cgi-bin/query/D?c107:16:./temp/~c107TbkTyv::>.

House Record, HR 5022, "Freedom to Travel to Cuba Act of 2002," (June 26, 2002), <http://thomas.loc.gov/cgi-bin/query/D?c107:17:./temp/~c107YNbO9p::>.

House Record, HR 179, "Expressing the sense of the House of Representatives regarding the systematic human rights violations in Cuba," (April 7-8, 2003), <http://thomas.loc.gov/cgi-bin/query/D?c108:11:./temp/~c108JqqVxE::>.

House Record, HR 2071, "Export Freedom to Cuba Act of 2003," (May 13, 2003), <http://thomas.loc.gov/cgi-bin/query/D?c108:12:./temp/~c108hDpDfn::>.

Howe, G., *Conflict of Loyalty* (London: Macmillan, 1994).

Huber, George P., "Organizational Learning: The Contributing Processes and the Literatures," *Organizational Science: A Journal of the Institute of Management*

Sciences vol. 2 (1991), pp. 88-115, reprinted in Michael D. Cohen and Lee Sproull, eds., *Organizational Learning* (Thousand Oaks, CA: Sage, 1996), pp. 1-20.

Hudson, Heather E., *Global Connections: International Telecommunications Infrastructure and Policy* (New York: Van Nostrand Reinhold, 1997).

Hufbauer, Gary Clyde, Jeffrey J. Schott, and Kimberly Ann Elliot, *Economic Sanctions Reconsidered: History and Current Policy* (Washington, DC: Institute for International Economics, 1990).

Hutchins, Edwin, "Organizing Work by Adaptation," *Organizational Science*, vol. 2 (1991), reprinted in Michael D. Cohen and Lee S. Sproull, *Organizational Learning* (Thousand Oaks, CA: Sage, 1996), pp. 20-57.

Hyden, Goran and Rwekaza Mukandala, eds., Agencies in Foreign Aid (London: Macmillan, 1997).

Hyland, William G., *Clinton's World: Remaking American Foreign Policy* (Westport, CT: Praeger, 1999).

Ikenberry, J. G., "The International Spread of Privatization Policies; Inducements, Learning and Policy Bandwaggoning" in E. Suleiman and J. Waterbury, eds., *The Political Economy of Public Sector Reform* (Boulder, CO: Westview Press, 1990).

Independent Commission on Kosovo, *Kosovo Report* (London: Oxford University Press, 2001).

Institute for National Strategic Studies, National Defense University, *Strategic Assessment 1998*, (Washington, DC: NDU Press, 1998).

"Interview with Byron Dorgan," *Newsweek* (September 7, 2001), <http://www.ibike. org/cuba/ofac/010817-dorgan.htm>.

Jachtenfuchs, Markus, *International Policy-Making as a Learning Process? The European Union and the Greenhouse Effect* (Aldershot, UK: Ashgate, 1996).

Jackall, Robert, *Moral Mazes: The World of Corporate Managers* (New York: Oxford University Press, 1988).

Jackson, Brian A. "Technology Acquisition by Terrorist Groups: Threat Assessment Informed by Lessons from Private Sector Technology Adoption" *Studies in Conflict and Terrorism* vol. 24 (2001), pp. 183-213.

_____ with John C. Baker, Kim Cragin, John Parachini, Horacio R. Trujillo, and Peter Chalk, *Aptitude for Destruction, Volume 1: Organizational Learning in Terrorist Groups and its Implications for Combating Terrorism* (Santa Monica, CA: RAND Corporation, 2005).

Jain, R.B., *Bureaucratic Politics in the Third World* (New Delhi: Gritanjali Publishing House, 1989).

Jakobsen, Peter Viggo, ed., *Civil-Military Co-operation Lessons Learned and Models for the Future* (Copenhagen: Danish Institute of International Affairs, 2000).

James, O. and M. Lodge, "The Limitations of 'Policy Transfer' and 'Lesson Drawing' for Public Policy Research," *Political Studies Review* vol. 1 (2003).

Jarosz, William W. and Joseph S. Nye, "The Shadow of the Past: Learning from History in National Security Decision Making," in Philip Tetlock, Jo L. Husbands,

Robert Jervis, Paul C. Stern and Charles Tilly, *Behavior, Society, and International Conflict* (New York: Oxford University Press, 1993).

Jenkins-Smith, Hank C., and Paul A. Sabatier, "The Dynamics of Policy-Oriented Learning," in Paul A. Sabatier and Hank C. Jenkins-Smith, eds., *Policy Change and Learning: An Advocacy Coalition Approach* (Boulder, CO: Westview Press, 1993), pp. 41-56.

"Jersey Police Arrest 4 in Alleged Plot to Sell 555,000 Pills," *New York Times* (August 3, 1980).

John Paul II, "Opening Address at the Puebla Conference" in John Eagleson and Phillip Scharper, eds., *Puebla and Beyond* (Maryknoll, NY: Orbis Books 1979).

Johnson, David and James Risen, "Traces of Terrorism: The Intelligence Reports; Series of Warnings," *New York Times* (May 17, 2002).

Johnson, David E., *Preparing Potential Senior Army Leaders for the Future: An Assessment of Leader Development Efforts in the Post-Cold War Era* (Santa Monica, CA: RAND, 2002).

Johnston, Alistair Iaian, "Thinking About Strategic Culture," *International Security* vol. 19 (1995).

Jordan, A., "'Private Affluence and Public Squalor?'" The Europeanisation of British Coastal Bathing Water Policy," *Policy and Politics* vol. 26 (1998), pp. 33-54.

Josephson, Paul R., "Atomic-Powered Communism: Nuclear Culture in the Postwar USSR," *Slavic Review* vol. 55 (1996).

Joulwan, George A. and Christopher C. Shoemaker. *Civilian-Military Cooperation in the Prevention of Deadly Conflict: Implementing Agreements in Bosnia and Beyond* (New York: Carnegie Corporation, 1998).

Kacerosky, Edward J., "Search Warrant Affidavit of Special Agent Edward Kacerosky," Case No. 93-470-CR-WMH (September 1 and 5, 1994).

Kaplan, Fred. "Err War," *Slate* (October 3, 2003).

Kenney, Michael C., "Outsmarting the State: A Comparative Case Study of the Learning Capacity of Colombian Drug Trafficking Organizations and Government Counter-Narcotics Agencies," unpublished PhD dissertation (Gainesville, FL: University of Florida, 2002).

_____, "From Pablo to Osama: Counter-Terrorism Lessons from the War on Drugs," *Survival* vol. 45, no. 3 (2003), pp. 187-206.

_____, "How Terrorists Learn," in James J. F. Forest, ed., *Teaching Terror: Strategic and Tactical Learning in the Terrorist World* (Lanham, MD: Rowman & Littlefield, 2006).

_____, *From Pablo to Osama: Trafficking and Terrorist Networks, Government Bureaucracies, and Competitive Adaptation* (University Park, PA: The Pennsylvania State University Press, forthcoming 2007).

Keohane, Robert, "International Institutions: Two Approaches," *International Studies Quarterly* (1988).

Kilborn, Peter T. "Ambitious Effort to Cut Mistakes in U.S. Hospitals," *New York Times* (December 26, 1999).

Kim, Daniel H., "The Link between Individual and Organizational Learning," *Sloan Management* vol. 35 (1993), pp. 37-50.

Kingdon, John W., *Agendas, Alternatives, and Public Policies* (Boston: Little, Brown and Company, 1984).

Kitfield, James, "Zero Defects, Zero Initiative," *National Journal* vol. 28 (April 5, 1996), p. 793.

Klijn, E. H., J. Koppenjan and K. Termeer, "Managing Networks in the Public Sector: A Theoretical Study of Management Strategies in Policy Networks," *Public Administration* vol. 73 (1995), pp. 437-54.

Korten, David, and R. Klauss, eds., *People-Centered Development: Contributions Toward Theory and Planning Frameworks* (West Hartford, CT: Kumarian Press, 1985).

Kratochwil, Friedrich and John Gerard Ruggie, "International Organization: A State of the Art on an Art of the State," *International Organization* vol. 40 (1986), pp. 753-775.

Kuhnert, Caroline, "More Power for the Soviets: Perestroika and Energy," *Soviet Studies* vol. 43 (1991).

Kull, Steven, "What the Public Knows that Washington Doesn't," *Foreign Policy* vol. 101 (1995-96), pp. 102-115.

Kuhn, Thomas S., *The Structure of Scientific Revolutions* (Chicago: University of Chicago Press, 1962/1996).

Kuznets, Simon, "Economic Growth and Income Equality," *American Economic Review* vol. 45 (1955), pp. 17-26.

Kyre, Martin and Joan Kyre, *Military Government and National Security* (Washington, DC: Public Affairs Press, 1968).

"La flor maldita," *Semana* (September 10, 1999).

Lawson, Nigel, *The New Conservatism* (London: Centre for Policy Studies, 1980).
_____, *The View From No. 11* (London: Bantum Press, 1992).

Lernoux, Penny, "The Long Path to Puebla" in John Eagleston and Philip Scharper, eds., *Puebla and Beyond* (Maryknoll, NY: Orbis Books, 1979).

Levitt, Barbara and James G. March, "Organizational Learning," *Annual Review of Sociology* vol. 14 (1988), pp. 313-340.

Levy, Jack S., "Learning and Foreign Policy: Sweeping a Conceptual Minefield," *International Organization* vol. 48 (1994), pp. 279-312.

Levy, Matthys and Mario Salvadori, *Why Buildings Fall Down: How Structures Fail* (New York: Norton, 1992).

Leyva De Varona, Adolfo, *Propaganda and Reality: A Look at the U.S. Embargo against Castro's Cuba* (Miami: The Endowment for Cuban American Studies, 1994).

Lighthall, Frederick, "Launching the Space Shuttle *Challenger*: Disciplinary Deficiencies in the Analysis of Engineering Data," *IEEE Transactions on Engineering Management*, vol. 39 (1991), pp. 63-74.

Litonjua, M. D., *Liberation Theology: A Paradigm Shift* (Lanham, MD: University Press of America, Inc., 1989).

Littlechild, Stephen C., *Regulation of British Telecommunication Profitability* (London: Department of Trade and Industry, 1983).

Livingston, Steven and Todd Eachus, "Humanitarian Crises and US Foreign Policy: Somalia and the CNN Effect Reconsidered." *Political Communication* vol. 12 (1995), pp. 413-429.

Lodge, M., "Institutional Choice and Policy Transfer: Reforming British and German Railway Regulation, *Governance* vol. 16 (2003), pp. 159-178.

Loudon, Irvine, *The Tragedy of Childbed Fever* (Oxford: Oxford University Press, 2000).

Lowi, Theodore, J., "American Business, Public Policy, Case Studies, and Political Theory," *World Politics* vol. 16 (1964), pp. 687-91.

Lupsha, Peter A., "Transnational Organized Crime versus the Nation-State," *Transnational Organized Crime* vol. 2, no. 1 (1996), pp. 21-48.

MacKenzie, Donald, *Inventing Accuracy* (Cambridge, MA: MIT Press, 1990).

"'Made in' Colombia," *Cambio* (July 24, 2000), pp. 36-37.

Majone, G., "Cross-national Sources of Regulatory Policymaking in Europe and the United States," *Journal of Public Policy* vol. 11 (1991), pp. 79-106.

Manwaring, Max, Karen Guttieri and Michael Dziedzic, *The Civil Dimensions of Military Operations Conference Report*. Co-sponsored by the US Army War College and Institute for National Strategic Studies, Washington DC, September 23-24, 1998.

March, James G., *The Pursuit of Organizational Intelligence* (Malden, MA: Blackwell Publishers Ltd, 1999).

_____, "Adaptive Coordination of a Learning Team," in James G. March, ed., *The Pursuit of Organizational Intelligence* (Malden, MA: Blackwell Publishers Inc., 1999), pp. 156-178.

_____, "Exploration and Exploitation in Organizational Learning," *Organization Science* vol. 2, no. 1 (1991), pp. 71-87.

_____, "The Uncertainty of the Past: Organizational Learning under Ambiguity," in James G. March, ed., *Decisions and Organizations* (New York: Basil Blackwell, 1988), pp. 335-358.

_____, "Introduction: A Chronicle of Speculations About Decision-Making in Organizations," in James G. March, ed., *Decisions and Organizations* (New York: Basil Blackwell, 1988), pp. 1-21.

_____, "The Uncertainty of the Past: Organizational Learning under Ambiguity," *European Journal of Political Research* vol. 3 (1975), pp. 147-171.

_____and Johan P. Olsen, *Rediscovering Institutions: The Organizational Basis of Politics* (New York: Free Press, 1989).

_____, with Lee S. Sproull and Michal Tamuz, "Learning from Samples of One or Fewer," in James G. March, ed., *The Pursuit of Organizational Intelligence* (Malden, MA: Blackwell Publishers Inc., 1999), pp. 137-155 and in Michael D. Cohen and Lee Sproull, *Organizational Learning* (Thousand Oaks, CA: Sage, 1996), pp. 1-20, reprinted from *Organization Science* vol. 2 (1991), pp. 1-13.

_____, Martin Schulz, and Xueguang Zhou, *The Dynamics of Rules: Change in Written Organizational Codes* (Stanford, CA: Stanford University Press, 2000).

Marquis, Christopher, "Bush's Allies Plan to Block Effort to Ease Ban on Cuban Travel," *The New York Times* (November 13, 2003).

McCarthy, John D. and Mayer N. Zald, "Resource Mobilization and Social Movements," *American Journal of Sociology* vol. 82 (1977), pp. 1212-1241.

McCoy, Jennifer L., *Political Learning and Redemocratization in Latin America: Do Politicians Learn from Political Crises?* (Miami: North-South Center Press, 2000).

McCraw, Thomas K., *Prophets of Regulation* (Cambridge, MA: Belknap Press, 1984).

McGrath, Alister E., *The Blackwell Encyclopedia of Modern Christian Thought* (Malden, MA: Blackwell Publishers, 1995).

McGee, Jim and Brian Duffy, *Main Justice: The Men and Women who Enforce the Nation's Criminal Laws and Guard its Liberties* (New York: Touchstone, 1997).

Mermelstein, Max as told to Robin Moore and Richard Smitten, *The Man Who Made it Snow* (New York: Simon and Schuster, 1990).

Mermin, Jonathan, "Television News and American Intervention in Somalia: The Myth of a Media-Driven Foreign Policy," *Political Science Quarterly* vol. 112 (1997), pp. 385-403.

Meyer, M. et al., *Limits to Bureaucratic Growth* (New York and Berlin: Walter de Gruyter, 1985).

Miller, Danny. "A Preliminary Typology of Organizational Learning: Synthesizing the Literature," *Journal of Management* vol. 22 (1996), pp. 485-505.

Mills, Mike, "A Digital Breakthrough," *Congressional Quarterly Weekly Report* vol. 52 (1994), p. 66.

_____, "Spirit of Cooperation Breaks Media Industry Gridlock," *Congressional Quarterly Weekly Report* vol. 52 (1994), p. 426.

Miltenberger, Daniel T., "Part III: The Military," in Pamela Aall, Lt. Col. Daniel T. Miltenberger, and Thomas G. Weiss, eds., *Guide to IGOs, NGOs, and the Military in Peace and Relief Operations* (Washington, DC: United States Institute of Peace Press, 2000), pp. 181-252.

Morgenstern, Joe, "The Fifty-Nine-Story Crisis," *New Yorker* (May 29, 1995), pp. 45-53.

Morrison, John E. and Larry L. Meliza, *Foundations of the After Action Review Process* (US Army Research Institute for the Behavioral and Social Sciences, 1999).

Moskos, Charles C., John Allen Williams, and David R. Segal, *The Postmodern Military: Armed Forces After the Cold War* (New York: Oxford University Press, 2000).

Nagl, John A., "Learning to Eat Soup with a Knife: British and American Army Counterinsurgency Learning During the Malayan Emergency and the Vietnam War," *World Affairs* vol. 161 (1999).

National Academy of Public Administration, *Study of the Implementation of the Federal Wildland Fire Policy*, Phase I Report: *Perspectives on Cerro Grande and Recommended Issues for Further Study* (December 2000).

National Defense University, Institute for National Strategic Studies, *Strategic Assessment 1998* (Washington, DC: NDU Press, 1998).

National Defense University Symposium, "Beyond Jointness: The Civil-Military Dimensions of Peace Operations and Humanitarian Assistance," June 2-3, 1999 (Washington, DC: Institute for National Strategic Studies, 2000).

National Defense University Workshop Proceedings: "Planning for Post-Conflict Reconstruction: Learning from Iraq," July 29, 2004 (Washington, DC: Institute for National Strategic Studies, 2004).

National Park Service, Board of Inquiry, Final Report, *Cerro Grande Prescribed Fire* (National Park Service, 2001).

Neufeld, Mark, "Reflexivity and International Relations Theory," in Claire Tureene Sjolander and Wayne S. Cox, eds., *Beyond Positivism, Critical Reflections on International Relations* (Boulder, CO: Lynne Rienner Publishers, 1994), pp. 11-35.

Neustadt, R. E. and E. R. May, *Thinking in Time: The Uses of History for Decision Makers* (New York: Free Press, 1986).

Neyer, Jurgen, "The Standing Committee for Foodstuffs: Arguing and Bargaining in Comitology," in M.P.C.M Van Schendelen, ed., *EU Committees as Influential Policymakers* (Aldershot, UK: Ashgate, 1998), pp. 148-163.

Nonaka, Ikujiro and Hirotaka Takeuchi, *The Knowledge-Creating Company: How Japanese Companies Create the Dynamics of Innovation* (Oxford: Oxford University Press, 1995).

Oakley, Robin, "Analysis: Hope and Blame in Britain," (October 26, 2000), at <http://europe.cnn.com/2000/WORLD/europe/10/26/bse.oakley/index.html>.

Office of Human Research Protections, U.S. Department of Health and Human Services, letter to Johns Hopkins University School of Medicine suspending all of the school's human subjects research (July 19, 2001).

Official Journal of the European Communities (OJ), various issues.

Oliker, Olga, et. al., *Aid During Conflict: Interaction Between Military and Civilian Assistance Providers in Afghanistan, September 2001–June 2002* (Santa Monica, CA: RAND, 2004).

Oliver, Michael J., "Social Learning: A Necessary Precondition to Policy Transfer?," Paper presented to the *Policy Transfer Conference*, University of Birmingham, UK, October 26-27, 1996.

_____, "Social Learning and Macroeconomic Policymaking in the United Kingdom since 1979," *Essays in Economic and Business History* vol. 14 (1996), pp. 117-131.

_____, *Whatever Happened to Monetarism? Social Learning and Macroeconomic Policymaking in the United Kingdom since 1979* (Aldershot, UK: Ashgate, 1997).

_____, "British Economic Policy and Performance since 1945: an Early 21st Century Assessment," in Michael J. Oliver, ed., *Studies in Economic and Social History* (Aldershot, UK: Ashgate, 2002).

_____ and Hugh Pemberton, "Learning and Change in Twentieth Century British Economic Policy," *Governance* vol. 17 (2004), pp. 415-441.

Olsen, Howard and John Davis, *Training US Army Officers for Peace Operations: Lessons From Bosnia,* Special Report, United States Institute of Peace (October 29, 1999).

"Operation OUTREACH: Tactics, Techniques and Procedures," Center for Army Lesson Learned *Newsletter* No. 03-27 (October 2003).

Organization for Economic Co-operation and Development/International Energy Agency, *Russia Energy Survey, 2002* (March 2002).

Ortiz, Román D. "Insurgent Strategies in the Post-Cold War: The Case of the Revolutionary Armed Forces of Colombia," *Studies in Conflict and Terrorism* vol. 25 (2002), pp. 127-143.

Palamarchuk, Sergey I., Sergei V. and Nikolai I., "Getting the Electricity Sector on Track in Russia," *The Electricity Journal* (October, 2001).

Pallomari, Guillermo, "Direct Testimony of Guillermo Pallomari," *Trial Transcript in the United States of America vs. Michael Abbell, William Moran, Luis Grajales, Eddy Martinez, Ramon Martinez, J.L. Pereira-Salas, et al, Defendant*s, Case No. 93-470-CR-WMH, vol. 39 (US District Court, Southern District of Florida, Miami Division, July 23, 1997).

Pape, Robert A., "Why Economic Sanctions Do Not Work." *International Security* vol. 22 (1997), pp. 90-136.

Parmet, Herbert S., *George Bush: The Life of a Lone Star Yankee* (New York: Scribner, 1997).

Pemberton, Hugh, "Policy Networks and Policy Learning: UK Economic Policy in the 1960s and 1970s," *Public Administration* vol. 78 (2002), pp. 771-792.

Pepper, G. T. and Michael J. Oliver, *Monetarism Under Thatcher – Lessons For The Future* (Northampton, MA: Edward Elgar, 2001).

Perito, Robert M., *Where Is the Lone Ranger When We Need Him? America's Search for a Postconflict Stability Force* (U.S. Institute of Peace Press, 2004).

Perkins, Jerry, "Embargo hurts U.S., Cuban tells Iowa," *The Des Moines Register* (December 11, 2002).

Perrow, Charles, *Normal Accidents: Living with High-Risk Technologies* (Princeton, NJ: Princeton University Press, 1999).

Peters, Philip, *A Policy toward Cuba that Serves U.S. Interests* (Washington DC: The Cato Institute, 2000).

Peterson, Scott. "Fatigued, US Troops Yearn for Home," *Christian Science Monitor* (July 7, 2003), p. 1.

Petroski, Henry, *Design Paradigms: Case Histories of Error and Judgment in Engineering* (Cambridge, MA: Cambridge University Press, 1994).

_____, *Engineers of Dreams: Great Bridge Builders and the Spanning of America* (New York: Vintage, 1995).

Phillips, Charles, *The Regulation of Public Utilities: Theory and Practice* (Arlington, VA: Public Utilities Reports, Inc., 1985).

Piczak, Todd, "The Helms-Burton Act: U.S. Foreign Policy toward Cuba, the National Security Exception to the GATT and the Political Question Doctrine," *University of Pittsburgh Law Review* vol. 61 (1999), pp. 287-327.

Pierson, Paul, "When Effect Becomes Cause: Policy Feedback and Political Change," *World Politics* vol. 45 (1993), pp. 595-628.

_____, "The Path to European Integration: A Historical Institutionalist Analysis," *Comparative Political Studies* vol. 29 (1996), pp. 123-163.

Pincus, Walter, "Seized Materials May Help Thwart Future Attacks," *Washington Post* (April 3, 2002), p. A14, <http://www.cnn.com/SPECIALS/2002/terror.tapes>.

Ping, Ai, "From Proletarian Internationalism to Mutual Development: China's Cooperation with Tanzania 1965-95," in Goran Hyden and Rwekaza Mukandala, eds., *Agencies in Foreign Aid* (London: Macmillan, 1997).

Popper, Micha and Raanan Lipshitz, "Organizational Learning Mechanisms: A Structural and Cultural Approach to Organizational Learning," *Journal of Applied Behavioral Science* vol. 34 (1998), pp. 161-179.

Przeworksi, A. and H. Teune, *The Logic of Comparative Social Inquiry* (New York: Wiley-Interscience, 1970).

Public Utility Research Center Brochure, Warrington College of Business Administration, University of Florida, Gainesville, FL, 1999, <*www.purc.org*>.

Rapley, John, *Understanding Development: Theory and Practice in the Third World* (Boulder, CO: Lynne Rienner Publishers, 1996).

Reese, Thomas, *The Politics and Organization of The Catholic Church* (Cambridge, MA: Harvard University Press, 1996).

Reilly, John E., "The Public Mood at Mid-Decade," *Foreign Policy* vol. 98 (1995), pp. 76-93.

Reiter, Dan, *Crucibles of Beliefs: Learning, Alliances, and World Wars* (Ithaca, NY: Cornell University Press, 1996).

Rejai, Mostafa and Kay Phillips, *Leaders and Leadership: An Appraisal of Theory and Research* (Westport, CT: Praeger, 1997).

Reuter, Peter, "After the Borders are Sealed: Can Domestic Sources Substitute for Imported Drugs?," in *Drug Policy in the Americas*, edited by Peter H. Smith (Boulder, CO: Westview Press, 1992), pp. 163-177.

Revkin, Andrew C., "Gauging Disaster: How Scientists and Victims Watched Helplessly," *New York Times* (December 31, 2004).

Rhodes, R.A.W. and David Marsh, "New Directions in the Study of Policy Networks," *European Journal of Political Research* vol. 21 (1992), pp.181-205.

Rice, Berkeley, *Trafficking: The Boom and Bust of the Air America Cocaine Ring* (New York: Charles Scribner's Sons, 1989).

Richardson, Jeremy, "EU Water Policy," in Hans Bressers, Laurence O'Toole, Jr. and Jeremy Richardson, eds., *Networks for Water Policy, A Comparative Perspective* (London: Frank Cass, 1995).

Richter, Paul, "Armey Urges End to Cuba Sanctions," *Los Angeles Times* (August 9, 2002).

Ricks, Thomas E., "Intelligence Problems in Iraq are Detailed," *Washington Post* (October 25, 2003), p. A01.

Riddell, Roger, *Aid Dependency* (Stockholm: Swedish International Development Cooperation Agency, 1995)

Roberts, Adam. "What is a Military Occupation?" *British Yearbook of International Law 1984* (Oxford: Clarendon Press, 1985), pp. 249-305.

Rose, Richard, "What is Lesson-Drawing?" *Journal of Public Policy* vol. 11 (1991), pp. 3-30.

_____, *Lesson-Drawing in Public Policy: A Guide to Learning across Time and Space* (Chatham, NJ: Chatham House Publishers, Inc., 1993).

Rosenau, James N., *Turbulence in World Politics, A Theory of Change and Continuity* (Princeton: Princeton University Press, 1990).

Rothstein, Bo, "Political Institutions: An Overview." in Robert E. Goodman and Hans-Dieter Klingemann, eds., *A New Handbook of Political Science* (New York: Oxford University Press, 1998).

Roy, Joaquin, *Cuba, the United States, and the Helms-Burton Doctrine. International Reactions* (Gainesville, FL: University Press of Florida, 2000).

Ruggie, John G., "International Responses to Technology," *International Organization* vol. 29 (1975), pp. 557-583.

Runciman, W. G., "Has British Capitalism Changed since the First World War?," *British Journal of Sociology* vol. 44 (1993), pp. 53-67.

Sabatier, Paul A., "Knowledge, Policy-Oriented Learning, and Policy Change," *Knowledge: Creation, Diffusion, Utilization* vol. 8 (1987), pp. 649-692.

Sacks, P. M., "State Structure and the Asymmetrical Society: An Approach to Public Policy in Britain," *Comparative Politics* vol. 12 (1980), pp. 349-376.

Sagan, Scott D., *The Limits of Safety: Organizations, Accidents, and Nuclear Weapons.* (Princeton, NJ: Princeton University Press, 1993).

Sandoval, Moises, "Report from the Conference" in John Eagleson and Phillip Scharper, eds., *Puebla and Beyond* (Maryknoll, NY: Orbis Books, 1979).

Sarkesian Sam C. and Robert E. Connor, Jr., *The US Military Profession into the Twenty-First Century* (London: Frank Cass, 1999).

Saward, Michael, "Advice, Legitimacy and Nuclear Safety in Britain," in Anthony Barker and B. Guy Peters, eds., *The Politics of Expert Advice* (Pittsburgh, PA: University of Pittsburgh Press, 1993).

Scarborough, Rowan, "U.S. Rushed Post-Saddam Planning," *Washington Times* (September 3, 2003), <http://www.washtimes.com/national/20030903-120317-9393r.htm>.

Schneider, A. and H. Ingram, "Systematically Pinching Ideas: a Comparative Approach to Policy Design," *Journal of Public Policy* vol. 8 (1988), pp. 61-80.

Schumacher, Eric, *Small is Beautiful* (New York: Harper and Row, 1973).

Schwartz, John with Matthew L. Wald, "Echoes of *Challenger*: Shuttle Panel Considers Longstanding Flaws in NASA's System," *New York Times* (April 13, 2003).

Scientific Committee on Animal Health and Animal Welfare, *Report on Animal Welfare Aspects of the Use of Bovine Somatotrophin* (March 10, 1999), <http://europa.eu.int_comm._food/fs/sc/scah/out21_en.pdf>.

Scott, Richard W., *Organizations: Rational, Natural and Open Systems,* 4th ed. (Upper Saddle River, NJ: Prentice Hall, 1998).

Seabrook, John, "The Tower Builder," *New Yorker* (November 19, 2001), <http://www.newyorker.com/fact/content/articles/011119fa_FACT>.

Seale, Patrick, *Abu Nidal: A Gun for Hire* (New York, NY: Random House, 1992).

Senate Press Release, "Senator Roberts: Administration's Cuba Policy Undermines Trade Promotion Authority Bill," (April 11, 2002), <http://www.lawg.org/roberts.htm>.

Senate Press Release, "Dorgan Says Cuba Interested in Buying Additional Peas from North Dakota," (August 7, 2002), <http://dorgan.senate.gov/newsroom/record.cfm?id=186307>.

Senate Press Release, "Baucus Introduces Legislation to Eliminate Cuba Travel Ban on Senate Floor, Senator Urges Opening Doors, Bringing Democracy to Region," (April 30, 2003), <http://216.239.33.104/search?q=cache:7of5ytx5AD4J:www.senate.gov/~finance/press/Bpress/2003press/prb043003.pdf+cuba+baucus&hl=en&ie=UTF-8>.

Senate Record, S. HRG. 104-212, "Cuban Liberty and Democratic Solidarity Act," (June 14, 1995).

Senate Record, S14998-15000, "Cuban Liberty and Democratic Solidarity [*Libertad*] Act of 1995," (October 11, 1995).

Senate Record, "Statement of First District Rep. Jim Leach Regarding the Cuban Food and Medicine Security Act of 1999," (April 29, 1999).

Senate Record, Vote No. 251, "Agriculture Appropriations," (August 3, 1999).

Senate Record, S7537, "Flexible Trade Policy Toward Cuba," (July 25, 2000), <http://thomas.loc.gov/cgi-bin/query/D?r106:16:./temp/~r1061bX9ky>.

Senate Record, S7629, "Embargo on Cuba," (July 26, 2000), <http://thomas.loc.gov/cgi-bin/query/D?r106:7:./temp/~r106RmLQ1G>.

Senate Record, S1241, "Trip to Latin America," (February 27, 2002), <http://thomas.loc.gov/cgi-bin/query/D?r107:1:./temp/~r107wSQAZm>.

Senate Record, S 950, "Freedom to Travel to Cuba Act of 2003," (April 30, 2003), <http://thomas.loc.gov/cgi-bin/query/D?c108:6:./temp/~c108hDpDfn::>.

Senate Record, S 9368, "Travel to Cuba," (July 15, 2003), <http://thomas.loc.gov/cgi-bin/query/D?r108:2:./temp/~r108ayxQ7O::>.

Senge, Peter M., *The Fifth Discipline: The Art and Practice of the Learning Organization* (New York: Doubleday, 1990).

_____, "Introduction" in Marilyn Darling and Charles Perry, eds., *From Post-Mortem to Living Practice: An In-depth Study of the Evolution of the After Action Review* (Boston: Signet, 2001).

Serrano Cadena, Rosso José, *Jaque mate: De cómo la policía le ganó la partida a "el ajedrecista" y a los carteles del narcotráfico* (Bogotá, Colombia: *Editorial Norma*, 1999).

Simon, Herbert A., *Administrative Behavior: A Study of Decision-Making Processes in Administrative Organizations* (New York: Macmillan, 1947).

_____, "A Behavioral Model of Rational Choice," *Quarterly Journal of Economics* vol. 69 (1955), pp. 99-118.

_____, *Administrative Behavior: A Study of Decision-Making Processes in Administrative Organizations*, 4 ed. (New York: The Free Press, 1997).

Simon, Jeffrey D. *The Terrorist Trap: America's Experience with Terrorism* (Bloomington, IN: Indiana University Press, 1994).

Smith, Wayne, "Our Dysfunctional Cuban Embargo," *Orbis* vol. 42 (1998), pp. 533-544.

Snook, Stephen, "An Agency under Siege: USAID and its Mission in Tanzania," in Goran Hyden and Rwekaza Mukandala, eds., *Agencies in Foreign Aid* (London: Macmillan, 1997), pp. 86-94.

Sobrino, Jon, *The Church and The Poor* (Maryknoll, NY: Orbis Books, 1984).

Spadoni, Paolo, "Don't Change Export Rules on Cuba," *Orlando Sentinel* (December 27, 2004).

_____, "The Impact of the Helms-Burton Legislation on Foreign Investment in Cuba," *Cuba in Transition* vol. 11 (Washington, DC: Association for the Study of the Cuban Economy, 2001).

Stacey, Ralph D., *Complex Responsive Processes in Organizations, Learning and Knowledge Creation* (London: Routledge, 2001).

Steinbruner, John D., *The Cybernetic Theory of Decision* (Princeton, NJ: Princeton University Press, 1974).

Stern, Jessica, *The Ultimate Terrorists* (Cambridge, MA: Harvard University Press, 1999).

Stevenson, Charles A., "The Evolving Clinton Doctrine on the Use of Force," *Armed Forces and Society* vol. 22 (1996), pp. 511-535.

Stone, Alan, *Wrong Number: The Breakup of AT&T* (New York: Basic Books, 1989).

_____, *Public Service Liberalism* (Princeton, NJ: Princeton Press, 1991).

Stone, D., "Learning Lessons and Transferring Policy across Time, Space and Disciplines," *Politics* vol. 19 (1999), pp. 51-59.

Substance Abuse and Mental Health Services Administration, *Overview of Findings from the 2003 National Survey on Drug Use and Health*, NSDUH Series H-24, DHHS Publication No. SMA 04-3963 (Rockville, MD: Office of Applied Studies, 2004), <http://oas.samhsa.gov/NHSDA/2k3NSDUH/2k3OverviewW.pdf>.

Sullivan, Mark P., "Cuba: U.S. Restrictions on Travel and Legislative Initiatives in the 106th Congress," *U.S. Congressional Research Service* (October 13, 2000).

Temin, Peter, *The Fall of the Bell System: A Study in Prices and Politics* (Cambridge: Cambridge Press, 1987).

Tetlock, Philip E., "Learning in U.S. and Soviet Foreign Policy: In Search of an Elusive Concept," in George W. Breslauer and Philip E. Tetlock, eds., *Learning in U.S. and Soviet Foreign Policy* (Boulder, CO: Westview Press, 1991), pp. 20-61.

Thatcher, Margaret H., *The Downing Street Years* (London: HarperCollins, 1993). _____, *The Path To Power* (London: HarperCollins, 1995).

Third Superceding Indictment, *United States of America vs. Michael Abbell, William Moran, Luis Grajales, Eddy Martinez, Ramon Martinez, J.L. Pereira-Salas, et al, Defendants*, Case No. 93 470-CR-WMH (no date).

Thomas, James B., Stephanie Watts Sussman and John C. Henderson., "Understanding 'Strategic Learning': Linking Organizational Learning, Knowledge Management, and Sensemaking," *Organization Science* vol. 12 (2001), pp. 331-345.

"The 2000 Campaign: 2nd Presidential Debate Between Governor Bush and Vice President Gore," *The New York Times* (October 12, 2000), p. A22.

Thompson, H., *The British Conservative Government and the European Exchange Rate Mechanism, 1979-1994* (London: Pinter, 1996).

Thoumi, Francisco E., *Political Economy and Illegal Drugs in Colombia* (Boulder, CO: Lynne Rienner Publishers, 1995).

Topf, Richard, "Conclusion, Advice to Governments--Some Theoretical and Practical Issues, in Peters, B. Guy and Anthony Barker, eds., *Advising West European Governments; Inquiries, Expertise and Public Policy* (Pittsburgh, PA: University of Pittsburgh Press, 1993).

Tufte, Edward R., *Visual Explanations: Images and Quantities, Evidence and Narrative* (Cheshire, CT: Graphics Press, 1997).

Turner, Stansfield, *Caging the Nuclear Genie: An American Challenge for Global Security* (Boulder, CO: Westview Press, 1997).

United States Army, *Stability and Support Operations* Field Manual FM 3-07, 2003.

United States European Command, *Operation Support Hope 1994 After Action Report*.

US Department of Defense, "DOD Dictionary of Military Terms," as amended through June 5, 2003, <http://www.dtic.mil/doctrine/jel/doddict/index.html>.

US Joint Center for Lessons Learned Quarterly *Bulletin* vol.6 (December 2003).

U.S. Chairman of the Joint Chiefs of Staff Instruction 1800.01A (December 1, 2000), <http://dtic.mil/doctrine>.

"U.S. Senator Urges Cuban Ties," Associated Press (June 3, 1999).

Vaughan, Diane, *The Challenger Launch Decision: Risky Technology, Culture, and Deviance at NASA* (Chicago: University of Chicago Press, 1996).

_____, "The Dark Side of Organizations: Mistake, Misconduct, and Disaster," *Annual Review of Sociology*, vol. 25 (1999), pp. 271-305.

Webbink, Douglas, "The Recent Deregulatory Movement at the FCC," in Leonard Lewin, ed., *Telecommunications in the US: Trends and Policies* (Dedham, MA: Artech, 1981).

Weick, Karl E., *The Social Psychology of Organizing*, 2nd ed. (New York: Random House, 1979).

_____, *Sensemaking in Organizations* (Thousand Oaks, CA: Sage Publications, 1995).

Weir, M. and Theta Skocpol, "State Structures and the Possibilities for 'Keynesian' Responses to the Great Depression in Sweden, Britain and the United States," in Peter Evans, D. Ruescheneyer, and Theta Skocpol, eds., *Bringing the State Back In* (Cambridge: Cambridge University Press, 1985).

Weldes, Jutta, Mark Laffey, Hugh Gusterson, and Raymond Duvall, "Introduction: Constructing Insecurity," in Jutta Weldes, Mark Laffey, Hugh Gusterson, and Raymond Duvall, eds., *Cultures of Insecurity* (Minneapolis, MN: University of Minnesota Press, 1999).

Wendt, Alexander, *Social Theory of International Politics* (Cambridge: Cambridge University Press, 1999).

Westwick, Peter J., "Secret Science: A Classified Community in the National Laboratories," *Minerva* vol. 38 (2000), pp. 363-391.

_____, *The National Labs: Science in an American System, 1947-1974* (Cambridge: Harvard University Press, 2003).

Wigginton, Peter, *The Popes of Vatican Council II* (Chicago: Franciscan Press, 1982).

Wilkinson, Paul, "Editor's Introduction: Technology and Terrorism" in Paul Wilkinson, ed., *Technology and Terrorism* (London: Frank Cass, 1993), pp. 1-11.

Wilson, James Q., *Political Organizations* (New York: Basic Books, 1973).

Winch, D., *Economics and Policy: A Historical Study* (London: Hodder and Stoughton, 1969).

Wong, Leonard. "Stifled Innovation?," (Carlisle Barracks, PA: United States Army War College Strategic Studies Institute, 2002).

Wood, David, "Training for The New Warfare," (November 19, 2003) <Newhouse. com>.

Workshop Proceedings, "Planning for Post-Conflict Reconstruction: Learning from Iraq," Institute for National Strategic Studies, National Defense University (July 29, 2004).

World Bank, *Accelerated Development in Sub-Saharan Africa* (Washington, DC: World Bank, 1981).

Zabludoff, Sidney Jay, "Colombian Narcotics Organizations as Business Enterprises," *Transnational Organized Crime* vol. 3, no. 2 (1997), pp. 20-49.

Zarkin, Michael, *Social Learning and the History of US Telecommunications Policy, 1900-1996* (Lewiston, NY: The Edwin Mellen Press, 2003).

Index

For Product Safety Concerns and Information please contact our EU
representative GPSR@taylorandfrancis.com
Taylor & Francis Verlag GmbH, Kaufingerstraße 24, 80331 München, Germany

www.ingramcontent.com/pod-product-compliance
Lightning Source LLC
Chambersburg PA
CBHW050701280326
41926CB00088B/2417